TALBOT COUNTY: A HISTORY

TALBOT COUNTY

A HISTORY

by DICKSON J. PRESTON

NORMAN HARRINGTON
Picture Editor

TIDEWATER PUBLISHERS
Centreville, Maryland

Copyright © 1983 by Tidewater Publishers

All rights reserved. No part of this book may be used or reproduced in any manner whatsoever without written permission except in the case of brief quotations embodied in critical articles and reviews. For information, address Tidewater Publishers, Centreville, Maryland 21617.

Library of Congress Cataloging in Publication Data

Preston, Dickson J., 1914-
    Talbot County: a history.

    Bibliography: p.
    Includes index.
    1. Talbot County (Md.)—History. 2. Talbot County (Md.)—Description and travel. I. Harrington, Norman. II. Title.
F187.T2P73   1983   975.2′32   83-40048
ISBN 0-87033-305-4

Manufactured in the United States of America
First edition

To

Mary Elizabeth Starin

Curator of the Maryland Room
Talbot County Free Library,
1957-1981.
Her enthusiasm, helpfulness,
and knowledge
made this book possible.

Contents

	Preface	ix
CHAPTER 1.	A Shore Dimly Seen	3
2.	First Settlers	22
3.	Building a County	39
4.	King Tobacco	59
5.	Golden Years	77
6.	The Revolution	109
7.	The Rise of Easton	138
8.	The Long Depression	171
9.	The Civil War Era	199
10.	The Age of Steam	229
11.	The Gasoline Revolution	269
12.	After the Bridge	304
	Notes on Sources	348
	Illustration Credits	362
	Index	363

Preface

FOR THE STUDENT of local history, Talbot County is a wonderland of opportunities. Source material abounds; from Captain John Smith's *The Generall Historie of Virginia, New England, and the Summer Isles* (1624) to James A. Michener's fictional *Chesapeake* (1978), more has been written about Talbot than about any other Maryland county, or indeed than about almost any similar region in America. Countless family histories, collections of letters, memoirs, diaries, biographical sketches, journals, and other items are available for study. The county's land records, wills, inventories, and other official documents are almost entirely intact since the 1660s; and Talbot has been fortunate in having one or more local newspapers, most issues of which have been preserved, since 1790.

Of all these, by far the most voluminous and rewarding is the vast collection of essays, annals, and notes put together over a period of thirty years by Dr. Samuel A. Harrison (1822-1890), physician, educator, scholar, and the finest historian the Eastern Shore has produced. Unfortunately, his great work is known to the modern public only indirectly, if at all. Many of his essays on people and events, first published in Talbot newspapers in the 1870s and 1880s, were republished with little or no editing in 1915 in the two-volume work entitled *History of Talbot County Maryland 1661-1861*. This carried the byline, not of Dr. Harrison, but of his son-in-law, Oswald Tilghman who had compiled it largely from what he described as Dr. Harrison's "relics." The rest of Dr. Harrison's papers, including much unpublished material, were deposited with the Maryland Historical Society in Baltimore, where they are still available for study.

Somehow the public got the idea that Tilghman rather than his father-in-law had done the research and writing represented in the 1915 work; and to this day it is usually referred to as "Tilghman's History of Talbot County." This is both an error and an injustice. Dr. Harrison rather than Oswald Tilghman was the principal author, and in the preparation of the present history we have indicated this. We have also relied heavily on the additional material, published and unpublished, contained in his papers.

Other major sources are discussed in the Notes on Sources.

One further note: some readers may be puzzled by our spelling of place names, which varies in a number of cases from that found on modern maps. The problem arises because many spellings have changed over the centuries. As a general rule we have spelled the name as it was spelled at the time being written about. Hillsborough, for example, was spelled out in full until very recent times, when it was shortened to Hillsboro. We feel it would be incorrect to refer to the nineteenth century village as Hillsboro when all contemporary references used the longer spelling. Readers will note other examples.

On the nagging little question of whether to spell the town and parish St. Michaels or St. Michael's, however, we have simply made an arbitrary decision. In these pages, St. Michael's (with an apostrophe) refers to the parish, to equate it with St. Paul's and St. Peter's parishes. St. Michaels without an apostrophe refers to the town and election district, even though an apostrophe was often used as late as the nineteenth century. This may not satisfy purists, but at least it is consistent.

In general, we hope readers will recognize this book for what it is: an outline of the main events in Talbot County's history rather than a comprehensive treatment. No work which seeks to cover four hundred years in fewer than four hundred pages could be otherwise. Our aim, both in text and pictures, has been to provide a brief guide for the reader to major milestones in Talbot's past, and perhaps to stimulate interest in further study.

TALBOT COUNTY: A HISTORY

ONE

A Shore Dimly Seen

IT WAS a weary and bedraggled band of fifteen men who came sailing up Hooper's Strait on an early June morning in 1608. Their vessel was an open barge, its hull weather-beaten, its square sail tattered and patched with their own shirts. Six of their number were "gentlemen," useless for any kind of practical work, and of the rest only two or three had had any practical sailing experience. Only their leader, a bearded twenty-eight-year-old English-born adventurer who styled himself Captain John Smith, had a vague idea of where they were headed or what they were looking for; and even he was bemused by the current notion that the great South Seas, gateway to Cathay and the fabled riches of the Orient, lay only a few miles westward.

They had undergone a rough week since setting forth June 2 from the raw new colony of Jamestown on an exploratory voyage up the great bay then beginning to be called the "Chisapeack." The "salvages" they had encountered had alternately attacked them with wave on wave of arrows and greeted them with songs, dances, and other gestures of friendship. They had been beset by a fierce spring storm which washed their mast and sail overboard and almost swamped the barge, and stranded for two days by wind and rain on marshy, mosquito-infested isles.

By now they were heartily sick of this "Eastern Shore," as Smith had already named the lowland on the eastern side of the bay. Much of its coastline seemed to consist of broken islands and marshy promontories good for nothing but "to cut for hay in summer, and to catch fish and foule in winter." Its rivers were really tidal inlets, brackish as far up as they could explore them; as a result they had run so short of fresh water that, as one of the voyagers reported, they would gladly have exchanged a hundredweight of gold for a cask of drinkable water. Worse, it was obvious that none of the rivers was going to lead them to a passage into the South Seas, since they came from the east and not the west where the Pacific Ocean lay.

Captain John Smith

So they turned northwestward with glad hearts that spring morning and headed for a line of cliffs they could perceive faintly across the bay. That night they anchored in the shelter of what Smith called "Riccards Cliftes" (now known as Calvert Cliffs) for his mother's family. Henceforth, on this first exploratory trip, they stuck strictly to the bay's western shore.

But Smith had noticed something lying behind the line of islands he later labeled the "Winstone Iles" on his celebrated map. It was a shore dimly seen in the distance through the loblolly pines and hardwoods that covered the isles. He devoted only a few words to it in the report he wrote of his voyage, saying that the islands were "ouergrowne with woods, as all the coast beyond them so farre as we could see...."

Meager though they were, those words were recorded history's first mention of the mainland which today we know as Talbot County.

As the summer wore on, Smith's voyagers learned much more about the bay—though nothing about the long stretch of Eastern Shore coastline between the Sassafras River and the Little Choptank. On this first trip, which lasted forty-nine days, they journeyed as far north as the Patapsco before turning back, and spent weeks exploring the Potomac all the way to its Great Falls. They had numerous adventures and mishaps, being forced at times to subsist on spoiled bread, handfuls of Indian corn, and whatever other food they could trade trinkets for with the natives. In one cove they found fish so plentiful that, having foolishly set forth without fishing gear, they tried unsuccessfully to catch them in frying pans; on another occasion, while they were spearing fish with their swords near the mouth of the Rappahannock, Smith was so badly stung by a fish with "a long tail like a riding rodde," (a stingray) that he almost died. The crew actually went ashore on a little island and dug his grave; but thanks to the ministrations of Walter Russell, the "doctor of physicke" who had come along, the sturdy captain recovered rapidly and even ate the offending fish for supper. The spot where the grave was dug is still called Stingray Point.

On a second voyage, launched July 24 after only three days rest in Jamestown, Smith and a partly-new crew went all the way up the bay and explored its northern reaches. They found the four rivers which flow into it—the Susquehanna, North East, Elk, and Sassafras—and encountered a tribe of giant people called the Susquehannoughs or Susquehannocks, who spoke a language different from the Delawares of Virginia, used birchbark rather than log canoes, and smoked three-feet-long ceremonial tobacco pipes. Another people—Smith never used the word "Indian," which had not yet come into vogue—were the Tockwhoghes (from whom came the name Tuckahoe), living in villages along the Sassafras. Altogether Smith spent almost twelve weeks between June and September on the Chesapeake and its tributaries; he never did get a good look at the Eastern Shore mainland from Swan Point in Kent County south to Hooper's Strait off Dorchester. The map that he later drew shows that he was not aware of the existence of the Chester, Wye, Miles, Tred Avon, or Choptank rivers, nor even of the peninsulas which reach out to Kent and Tilghman islands.

Much later—about 1626, in a second edition of his map—Smith put a label on the land that is now Queen Anne's and Talbot. He called it Brookes Forest. This designation puzzled historians for centuries, but modern scholarship makes its origin clear. Smith named the region not for anyone connected with his explorations but for John Brooke, a member of the Virginia Company in England who supported him in a 1624 controversy. It didn't really matter; no one after Smith's time ever called the area Brookes Forest.

As for the three large islands which Smith named (also long after his voyages) the Winstone Iles, speculation is that they were the imperfectly seen land masses later called Sharp's Island, Poplar Island, and the western shore of Kent Island. From a distance of several miles, Smith

Detail from Captain John Smith's map of Chesapeake Bay, 1626 edition, identifying area that is now Talbot County as "Brookes Forest."

might well have envisioned Sharp's Island, then a hefty seven hundred acres, and the southern end of Tilghman Island as a single piece of land. In fact, legend says they were once linked by a land bridge, and certainly there was less water between them in 1608 than later, when Sharp's began to be devoured by erosion. Their dense woods would have concealed the mouth of the Choptank and Tred Avon, just as Poplar and Kent islands blocked Smith's view of Eastern Bay, which led into the Miles and Wye.

Captain John Smith was by no means the first European to explore Chesapeake Bay, nor even the first to reach the latitude of present Talbot County. Long before him, Italian and Spanish sea captains had entered the mouth of what the Spaniards variously called "Bahia de Santa Maria" (St. Mary's Bay) or "Bahia de Madre Dios" (Bay of the Mother of God). One source suggests that John Cabot, the Venetian who sailed for England's King Henry VII, was the bay's discoverer during his voyage in 1498. Another possibility is Amerigo Vespucci, the Italian for whom America was named.

At any rate, first to set foot on the Eastern Shore was almost certainly Giovanni da Verrazano, a Florentine in the service of the king of France. In 1524 he anchored his ship, the *Dauphine*, in what is now Chincoteague

Bay, and went ashore with a landing party. The Europeans were startled at the sight of naked men and nearly naked women; they tried to capture a young Indian girl "of much beauty and tall of stature," but she fought them off with her fists and screams. Exploring inland, Verrazano and his crew penetrated for eight miles, until they were stopped by the cypress swamps of the Pocomoke River. There they turned back, and thus missed by a few miles the honor of being first to gaze upon the middle waters of the great bay.

Probably the first European to see what is today Talbot County was a Spaniard, Juan Menéndez de Marques. On an exploratory voyage in 1573, he went up the "Bahia de Santa Maria" almost to its head. Like Smith after him, Menéndez coasted along the Western Shore, but he could hardly have avoided seeing at least the islands which later became a part of Talbot, and probably caught glimpses of the mainland also.

Other Spaniards followed, sailing from bases in Florida, recording the bay's splendid possibilities for settlement, its "admirable ports and important fresh water streams and well-seeded valleys." But it was their hated rivals, the English, who got there first, by establishing a successful colony at Jamestown in Virginia in 1607.

The Indians, of course, had been there all the time. But they were only "salvages," to be feared in the beginning, then patronized, lied to and exploited, and finally to be destroyed by whiskey and disease or driven far away from their beloved Chesapeake.

Also arriving in advance of the English had been French fur traders, nameless and illiterate men who pushed ahead of the known explorers everywhere on the North American continent. Captain Smith in 1608 encountered a "lusty Salvage named Mosco" near the Potomac who had a full black beard, almost unknown among the Indians. The English decided he must be the son of a Frenchman by an Indian mother. Mosco evidently also thought he was half-white; he immediately attached himself to Smith's party, became their friend, guide, and counselor, and even changed his name to Uttasantasough, an Indian word for Englishman. Clearly he felt a closer kinship to these strange white men from across the sea, who had beards like his, than to the beardless natives with whom he had been reared.

But these French traders left no other monuments than their half-breed children and an almost mythical role in Indian folk memory. Being illiterate, they kept no records of their explorations, drew no maps, established no place names. They were soon forgotten, and the bay with its wondrous possibilities became an English inland sea.

Smith's 1608 voyages, for all their place in history, were regarded as failures at the time. The captain had three chief assignments from his

A "Sasquesahanoug" Indian. Detail from Captain Smith's earliest map of Chesapeake Bay.

masters in the Virginia Company: to search for gold mines; to find a passage to the South Seas; and to seek survivors of Sir Walter Raleigh's lost colony at Roanoke Island, which had vanished without a trace after its 1585 founding. He failed in all three. No survivors turned up, and no South Seas passage was discovered; every river he explored to the west was blocked a few miles upstream by falls or rapids. As for gold, there is evidence he actually did find some, but didn't recognize it. Near the falls of the Potomac his men came upon an area of "tinctured spangled scurf that made many places seem as gilded." Digging there, they turned up loam sprinkled with pin-dust of yellow spangles. But Smith knew better than to fall for the notion that this was really gold; already the Jamestown colonists had made idiots of themselves by shipping quantities of iron pyrite (fool's gold) back to England. He merely made a note of the phenomenon and moved on. Ironically, says Philip L. Barbour in his excellent modern biography of Smith, a profitable working gold mine was established in the nineteenth century at almost the exact spot where Smith's "spangled scurf" was located.

It remained for another Englishman by way of Jamestown, William Claiborne, to recognize the possibilities of the upper bay, and especially

Captain William Claiborne

the Eastern Shore, that had been overlooked by Smith. Claiborne came out to Virginia in 1621, a brash, impetuous youth of twenty-one with great ambitions and the talent to achieve them. Appointed the colony's surveyor, he laid off choice lands for himself, established a reputation as an Indian fighter, and soon was made a member of the governor's council and secretary of the colony.

On exploring trips in 1626 and 1627 to the northern reaches of the Chesapeake, he conceived a bold dream. Here, on unclaimed land inhabited only by Indians, he would establish a great fur trading empire. Its base would be the large island which jutted out like a land bridge into the heart of the bay, and which he named the Isle of Kent for his native Kent County in England. Along the way he noted and named other strategic islands—Palmer's, a rocky isle in the mouth of the Susquehanna; Claiborne's, to which the permanent name of Sharp's would be given; and Popeley's (later Poplar), one thousand acres of fertile land which he named for an associate, Lieutenant Richard Popeley. These last two islands were the first parts of Talbot County to be definitely located and given names.

In August, 1631—three years before Lord Baltimore's first colonists arrived—Claiborne established a settlement on Kent Island. This was far more than just a trading post, as some historians have scornfully asserted; it was a permanent community, with a stockaded fort, store, church, and other structures. It was surrounded by plantations, and to one of these, called Crayford for the Claiborne family estate in Kent, he brought his English bride, the former Elizabeth Butler, in 1635.

The story of Claiborne's long and complex struggle with the Calverts over control of Kent Island and Chesapeake Bay is not in the province of this history. But the story of Popeley's or Poplar Island definitely is. It was the first place in Talbot County to be planted, the first to be settled, the first to see the tragedy of an Indian massacre, the first for which we have detailed information about living conditions. In many ways Talbot history properly begins on Poplar Island, for more than three centuries an integral part of the county but now almost entirely vanished as a result of relentless erosion.

Records of Claiborne's colony indicate that the island was inhabited, at least part of the time, as early as 1632. It wasn't a very glamorous beginning—a herd of pigs had been turned loose on the island, and one Daniel Cugley was their keeper. On September 3 of that year Claiborne noted a payment to Cugley of two hundred pounds of tobacco "for a boare of Popeleys Island." But at least it gives Talbot County pride of origin by almost two years over Lord Baltimore's Maryland founders, who didn't arrive until March 25, 1634.

In 1634 a number of men from Kent Island spent the spring and summer on Popeley's, clearing and planting fields, undoubtedly in corn and tobacco. The next year Claiborne granted the entire island to his favorite cousin, Richard Thompson, who had come out from England with Kent Island's founders in 1631 and had lived at Claiborne's house on Kent while looking for a suitable place to build his own plantation.

Thompson soon afterward transported from England his wife and child, along with a maid servant named Dousbell Gladdus and six men servants, noted in the record as "able workers." They constructed houses, barns, and outbuildings, cleared more land, and planted additional corn and tobacco. By the spring of 1637 the future Talbot's first plantation was a going concern, with buildings, fields, and at least ten residents.

Then tragedy struck. In the summer of 1637 Thompson went off on a fur trading expedition. He returned to find his wife, child, maid servant, and six workers all murdered, his livestock slaughtered, and his house and farm buildings burned to the ground. The outrage was blamed on a band of marauding Nanticoke Indians.

So ended in disaster the first settlement in what became Talbot County. With nine victims, it was the worst massacre by Indians in the county's history, although there would be others—and murders of Indians by whites as well.

As for Richard Thompson, he remained in the Kent Island colony and became one of Claiborne's stoutest supporters. He represented Kent in the Maryland General Assembly at St. Mary's, and was chosen as one of the first commissioners when Kent County was created in 1642. Whether he married again is not known, but he never returned to Popeley's Island; although he kept ownership of the land there, he built a new plantation on Kent, and lived on it until he died. Undoubtedly the memory of what he had seen on that summer's day in 1637 was too terrible ever to be forgotten.

Through the remainder of the seventeenth century the island's name had many variants. In the free and easy spelling of the time, it appeared as Popeleys, Popelese, Popleys, Poples, Poplies, Popplers, and Poplers. Popeley himself went back to Virginia, and eventually Marylanders forgot there had ever been such a person. They settled on calling the place Poplar Island under the impression that it was named for a kind of tree that grew there.

It also acquired new owners. In 1654 it was possessed by Thomas Hawkins, who sold half of it that year to Seath (Seth) Foster, later noted as the owner of what is now Tilghman Island and one of Talbot County's founding commissioners.

Hawkins was a full-time resident of the island, probably the first since the 1637 massacre. And his was the first household of which we have detailed knowledge on what became Talbot soil. As such the inventory of his estate, filed after his death in 1656, reveals much about how the settlers would live who soon thereafter began to clear fields and establish homes on the Talbot mainland.

His plantation was a substantial one, surprisingly so considering all the circumstances. He had a sizable house, several outbuildings, farm equipment, servants, a boat, and horses, hogs, and cattle. He even possessed five paintings and a small library, consisting of two Bibles, a book of sermons, a concordance (biblical index), and a volume entitled *The Practice of Piety*. These in themselves were marks of culture; in the seventeenth century many men of substance, and most women, were illiterate. On his floor was a "Turke" carpet, and for use over his fireplace an embroidered mantel cloth. There were also linen and coarse cotton cupboard cloths, tablecloths, and napkins; three feather beds with bolsters, pillows, and coverings; a leather couch; six leather "chayers"; a chest of drawers, and one old table.

No forks appear in the inventory, although they were in use by that time among well-to-do English families. But Hawkins—or his wife, Elizabeth—had a looking glass, a prized possession in colonial America.

Other household implements included a chamber pot, warming pan (for bed use), a pair of scales with brass weights, a gridiron and tongs for the fireplace, a flagon, a saltcellar, a smoothing iron and two flatirons, a chafing dish, a cheese press, a pie plate, twelve trenchers (wooden plates), three porringers (small bowls), one wine cup, an assortment of pewter and brass dishes and candlesticks, a brass frying pan, a great brass kettle, a butter churn, two milk trays, two milk tubs, a mortar and pestle, two sifting trays, and a corn barrel. From these it can be imagined how Mrs. Hawkins and her woman servant, Mary Bally, managed the household: all cooking was done in the fireplace, or outdoors in summer, and all foodstuffs were produced on the premises. Hawkins owned thirty-one hogs and thirty head of cattle, including a two-year-old bull, although if he had chickens, they were not considered worth listing. Bread was made from corn pounded into flour by hand with the mortar and pestle, in the Indian fashion.

There was no mention of silver plate or cash money, not even copper pence; few Marylanders of that early period possessed such things. Hawkins's most valuable possessions were his black horse with saddle and bridle, which he bequeathed to his friend Seth Foster; his livestock; his 1656 tobacco crop of 1,362 pounds; and his servants, who were valued in accordance with the time they still had to serve. There were three of these, all white; a fourth had "runn away" and therefore was valued at nothing. All told Hawkins's estate, not counting his land, was valued at 27,864 pounds of tobacco, a considerable amount for the period.

Such was an Eastern Shore household at a time when Talbot's virgin mainland territory was just beginning to catch the eyes of English emigrants hungry for land and a place to build their own independent establishments. Within the next ten years much of the choice tidewater acreage on a rich crescent stretching from the Wye to the Choptank, and reaching northward to Chester River, would be claimed by survey or patent, and houses much like Hawkins's would be springing up on coves and creeks through the area.

What was it like, this land the transplanted English, Welshmen, and Scots of Maryland and Virginia were so eager to possess? Why did this particular region attract so much interest, when unclaimed land by the millions of acres was going begging in the two colonies' western reaches, when a whole virgin continent lay open to be won? To understand the eastward land rush, which preceded the westward rush by more than a century, it is necessary to understand the basic economics of seventeenth century Maryland.

The planter of that period had only one market: England. Therefore he had no use whatever for acreage in the hinterland, no matter how fertile or cheap; there was simply no way he could get his money crop—which consisted entirely of tobacco—from an inland plantation to the British market. He had to have access to easy and inexpensive water transportation all the way to England. While it was not as absolute a requirement, he much preferred level land, easy to clear and cultivate, to provide the new fields which tobacco constantly demanded as it exhausted the soil of the older ones.

The Eastern Shore filled both these needs admirably. It was flat, monotonously so to some tastes; no place within the present confines of Talbot County rises more than sixty-five feet above sea level. Its basically sandy soil was well drained, with few stones to dull the blade of the planter's hoe. Its low shoreline provided countless creeks, coves, and tidal rivers which offered haven to the shallow draft oceangoing ships of the seventeenth century. The ebb and flow of tides was very moderate by English standards, making the loading and unloading of ships a simple process. In many places English vessels could sail to within a few hundred feet of plantation wharves, and so there was no need to build seaports, or indeed towns of any sort, in order to conduct commerce.

In some ways the region was one of excesses, at least when compared with the English countryside. Winters were colder, summers hotter and more humid. Periodically the bay was swept by great storms, thunder squalls that seemed to rise from nowhere and suddenly build up tornado force winds that could swamp a boat in seconds. The record made of the one which beset Captain Smith and his crew in June, 1608, will be familiar to every weekend sailor who has ever cruised the bay. Off Bloodsworth Island, "we discovered the wind and waters so much increased with thunder, lightning, and raine, that our masts and sayle blew overboard, and such mighty waves overracked us in that small barge, that with great labour we kept her from sinking, by freeing (bailing) out the water. Two days we were inforced to inhabit these uninhabited isles, which for the extremitie of gusts, thunder, raine, stormes, and ill wether we called Limbo." (Limbo was then believed to be the place on the very border of Hades where souls waited anxiously to see if they would be consigned to hell or heaven.)

The other type of powerful storm which early explorers encountered—the hurricane—is also familiar to modern Talbot Countians. No one realized then that they were moving storms; that fact would remain unknown until Benjamin Franklin discovered it in the late eighteenth century. But their effects were recorded on a local basis as they swept northward on the Atlantic seaboard from tropical waters to rake Chesapeake Bay and roar on into New England. The worst of these during the exploratory period were a series of four in a row between August 10 and September 6, 1591, when five hundred Spanish sailors drowned and much gold from the Spanish treasure fleet went to the bottom of the ocean, and in 1635, when hundreds of pine trees were snapped in two in New England and eight Indians drowned while fleeing from their wigwams before fourteen-foot tides at Narragansett.

Nor were others of nature's bounties in this new land always beneficial. Henry Callister of Oxford, writing in 1743, complained that the first Europeans on the Eastern Shore had found "an immense forest, full of vermin of various sorts and sizes. . . . We are swarming with Bugs, Musketoes, worms of every sort both Land and Water, Spiders, Snakes, Hornets, Wasps, Sea Nettles, Ticks, Gnats, Thunder and Lightning, excessive heat, excessive cold—irregularities in abundance."

However, he was favorably impressed by the "great variety of strange Birds, Beasts and fishes, trees and plants" which existed in myriad display. "Nothing less than a whole volume," he continued, "could give a catalogue of the rarities of this new world."

These rarities were indeed strange and wondrous to British eyes. Every early traveler wrote in superlatives of the animal and bird life he observed. Of particular interest were the bluebirds, redbirds (cardinals), tiny hummingbirds, "not much larger than a humble bee," and the marvelous mockingbirds, which could imitate any sound on earth after hearing it a few times. They were so prized in England that in 1698 the high sheriffs of every Maryland county, including Talbot, were ordered to take part in a drive to capture a hundred of them for the entertainment of the court of King William III.

Wild turkeys—native to America but introduced in England from the Middle East, which explains their name—roamed in flocks of four to five hundred. Big old toms might weigh as much as fifty pounds. "Pa'-tridges" (bobwhites) were so tame the Indians trapped them by laying trails of corn to huts, then closing the door once they entered. Great flocks of wild pigeons, later hunted to extinction, darkened the sky overhead. So did the blackbirds both redwings and grackles; Captain Smith's men enjoyed a feast of them, finding them every bit as tasty as the singing blackbirds which were baked into pies in England.

As for waterfowl, they were everywhere in winter. Robert Evelyn, writing in the 1640s, told of seeing a flock of ducks which covered a square mile in flight. Two Dutch missionaries who traversed the Eastern Shore in the winter of 1679-80 were astonished at the ducks they saw:

> The water was so black with them that it seemed when you looked from the land upon the water, as if it were a mass of filth or turf, and when they flew up there was a rushing and vibration of the air like a great storm coming through the trees.

They wrote of the wild geese:

> They rose not in flocks of 10 or 12 or 20 or 30, but continuously, wherever we pushed our way, and ... there was such an incessant clattering made with their wings upon the water when they rose, and such a noise of those flying higher up, that it was all the time as if we were surrounded by a whirlwind or a storm.

The Indians hunted ducks and geese much as gunners would do for centuries afterward. Lurking in the reeds or lying flat in their canoes, they deployed primitive decoys made of reeds to entice the birds to come in close, then slew them with showers of arrows. They also relished the great white whistling swans which wintered in large rafts throughout the Eastern Shore, serving them up boiled or roasted on open fires. Turkeys provided not only food but feathers for decoration, as did the eagles, ospreys, hawks, and vultures, called "buzzards" by the English.

The bay's waters were another prime source of food. The Indians built their villages along shores where oysters were plentiful, piling up huge mounds of shells which today mark their permanent locations. They enjoyed crabs so much that later, when they were restricted by treaty to reservations, they demanded written guarantees of "crabbing rights" to the end of time. Turtles, especially the big snappers and the smaller but delicious diamondback terrapins, provided both food and shells for tools.

Wolves traveled in packs of forty to fifty, and were such a menace that the early Talbot County government paid bounties of one to two hundred pounds of tobacco each for their heads. Other common animals in the Talbot forests and streams were foxes, beavers, otters, mink, muskrats, raccoons, ground hogs, or woodchucks, rabbits, squirrels of various types and sizes, rattlesnakes and other reptiles, and bobcats or lynx. Early Marylanders called these medium-sized cats "lyons" and "tygers," giving rise to much confusion back home in England, especially when they reported the "lyons" could be frightened off merely by setting up an "effigy of a man"—a scarecrow—at the edge of the forest.

White-tailed deer were so plentiful that, according to one early account, "venison nauseated our appetites. . . . Plain bread was rather courted and desired than it." An Indian hunter would trade the carcasses of seven deer for a single "match-coat," a winter garment made from a cheap dyed blanket. (By the eighteenth century, however, the native deer had been hunted almost to extinction, and closed seasons had to be instituted, with heavy fines for violators; today's deer population is a reintroduced species.) Some elk were found, though they were more frequent to the north and west; and bison, the so-called buffalo of the interior, seldom ventured onto the Eastern Shore. However, one report describing a "camel-mare" which was brownish black in color, had a hump, and was seven feet high could hardly have fit anything else.

Black bears still roamed the woods long after the white settlers arrived. An English visitor who was in Talbot County about 1705 told of a bear hunt he had witnessed on the Wye River estate of William Coursey:

> Wee took Guns and gott three Mastie (mastiff) dogs, . . . and when wee came wee saw the Beare at the top of a great Oake upon one of the uper most limbs. Wee all charged our guns with a Brace of Balls, and the first that fired shott him thro the Body which made him Roare and groan sadly.

A second shot wounded the bear again and a third brought him tumbling to the ground, "where he had liked to have spoyled all our dogs" if one of the hunters had not shot him through the head. Afterward there was a feast of bear meat. "Some was Roasted some Boyled some Broyled. . . . I thought itt as good as Roast Beefe it being verry juicey and harty food full of Gravey."

This same traveler, whose name unfortunately has been lost, also dined on the "great ffox squirrel" (Delmarva fox squirrel) and found it "rare good meat" when boiled with a bit of bacon. He liked it much better than American rabbits, which were "verry small" compared with the English hare. But he was delighted to see, if not to eat, tiny creatures he called ground squirrels. These were "not much biger than a Mouse, of the Redish collour striped with black all along the sides and back with a pretty tayle that covers itt all over when it sitts upon itts hinder parts." He was, of course, describing a chipmunk.

Fish he mentioned in his 1705 account included white and yellow perch, rockfish (even then the local name for striped bass), catfish, drum, sheepshead, eels, herring, shad, and sturgeon. Big sea turtles were caught from time to time; one taken in the Chester River weighed ninety pounds. Some of the oysters were "as big as a horse's hoof." Sharks evidently frequented the bay. In the 1640 annual report of the Jesuit fathers for Maryland, an account was given of a "huge fish" which had been seen to seize a man and bite off a "large portion of his thigh." The pious father who reported this had no pity for the victim; he thought the bite was a "most merited" example of God's retribution because the man had previously boasted of swallowing his Ave Maria beads.

The Wye Oak at Wye Mills, often called Maryland's state tree, nearly five hundred years old.

One striking feature of early Talbot County was the dense forest which covered nearly all of it. There were great loblolly pines, four feet or more in diameter, from which the Indians fashioned their canoes by burning out the inner wood; giant white oaks, hundreds of years old, superb raw material for the houses and shipbuilding of a later day; red oak, sweet gum, spruce pine, red and white cedar, cypress, tulip poplar, sycamore, locust, soft maple, hickory, walnut, chestnut, beech, and a host of wild fruit trees, including persimmon, plum, and cherry. Sassafras was especially prized; tea made from its roots was supposed to have almost magical powers, and the early settlers dug roots up by the ton and dispatched whole shiploads back to England. The undergrowth was a tangle of vines, among them blackberries, creepers, trumpet vines, and poison ivy (but not honeysuckle—that was a nineteenth century import from Japan). Through all this wound Indian trails worn a foot deep in places by thousands of moccasined feet over many centuries. These generally ran from the tidal head of one river or creek to the next, and provided the routes along which the English would build their first roads.

Even more significant from the standpoint of future Talbot history was the tidal water which virtually surrounded it. From the very beginning—as it still is today—this was the controlling factor in the county's development, the feature that set it apart from other regions. Nowhere else in America did earth and salt water meet in so small an area over so many miles of tidal shoreline. The Wye River and its branches on the north, the Miles and Tred Avon bisecting the center, and the Choptank and Tuckahoe on the south and east came near to making Talbot an island, so that no place within its permanent borders would be more than about three miles from tidewater. The statistic often quoted is that the present Talbot County has 602 miles of tidal shoreline, more than any other county in America. Whether or not this is precisely accurate is beside the point. What was important is that in the seventeenth as in the twentieth century land met water in a unique and valuable way.

The shoreline contours viewed by the first English arrivals were only roughly what they are today. More than three centuries of erosion and silting have sunk thousands of acres beneath the bay, and converted other acreage which once was marsh or creek bed into dry land. It is noteworthy that many places prominent in early Talbot records—Poplar and Sharp's islands, for instance, as well as the outer reaches of the peninsula known as Bayside and even the sites of Doncaster and York, early towns—have vanished, while others easily reached by boat in the seventeenth century are now high and dry. The Third Haven Meeting House (1682-84) and the Court House at Easton (first built in 1711-12) are examples; both were originally placed conveniently near water which is now far away. If there is one geographical fact that is constant about the Eastern Shore, it is that its contours are subject to constant change.

The entire bay has been subject to this same process over millions of years. At least four times, geologists say, melting ice from receding glaciers has created a great river which came rushing down from the Appalachians to meet the ocean and form a bay. The most recent of the great ice ages ended less than twenty thousand years ago, so that the bay Captain Smith beheld—and the one we know—is by any standard practically brand new. It is in fact not a proper bay at all, but a drowned riverbed formed when rising salt water from the ocean backed up into the valley of the Susquehanna some fifteen thousand years ago. Scientists believe the same process of freezing and melting will be repeated in the future—although hopefully not too soon.

Even that is not the start of the story. Beneath Talbot's flat surface lie layer upon layer of strata which bespeak changes going back millions, even billions of years. Buried hundreds of feet down are formations from what is known as the cretaceous period, perhaps a billion to five hundred million years ago. Above them are clay, sand, and marl layers from the Eocene and Miocene eras, and on top of all is the Pleistocene layer, laid down in the last two to three million years, when man was learning to walk, talk, use tools, cook food, and make love, war, and trouble for the world.

The sand layers of those early strata are of crucial importance to modern Talbot County. Through them flow underground rivers which cross deep beneath Chesapeake Bay from the Appalachian plateau to provide sweet, clean, cold water for the county's hundreds of deep wells. Without them the county as we know it could hardly exist. The few small and unimportant fresh water streams could not possibly provide a sufficient water supply. When the first settlers arrived these underground rivers bubbled to the surface in the form of natural springs and artesian wells. Increased use for new homesites, indoor plumbing, pools, dishwashers, and all the demands of modern living have dropped their level sharply, an ominous portent of problems to come.

During that last ice age, and no doubt long before it, strange creatures roamed the region. Evidence of some of them has been found; on a farm in Oxford Neck a workman in 1866 dug up tusks and bones of what was identified as a woolly mammoth, a smallish elephant which long ago became extinct. Professor Edward Cope of Philadelphia, who identified it, also found remains of a southern mammoth, a related species, and a giant prehistoric snapping turtle.

Somewhat later than the mammoths came human beings, primitive people of Asiatic origin who crossed into Alaska and gradually spread throughout the two American continents. When these Asiatic peoples first reached the Delmarva peninsula is obscure, but they had been here for many centuries when the first explorers arrived. They were neither very numerous nor as highly organized as others of their race—for instance, the Delaware confederacy of Virginia, the Iroquois nation of New York, or the western Sioux. That was another advantage for the Eastern Shore; its native population, while troublesome at times, was relatively easy to subdue or if necessary to eradicate. These natives gave the English who stole their land far less trouble over it than did the fierce and proudly independent tribesmen of the north and west. Beginning about 1618 they were called Indians, a word first applied to the Caribbean peoples when the islands they inhabited were thought to be part of the East Indies.

Talbot was singularly fortunate from the settlers' point of view. In the midseventeenth century there were no settled Indian towns within its modern borders, and few if any Indians appear to have been living there. Mounds of oyster shells and concentrations of arrowheads, stone axes, and other artifacts which mark the locations of villages date from an earlier time. The Indians used Talbot as a hunting ground, and

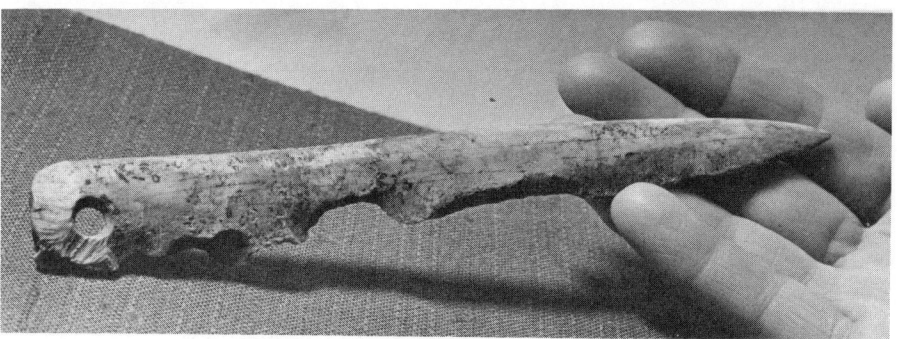

Top, Indian arrowheads, or "projectile points," dating, left to right, from 7000 B.C. to 1000-1600 A.D. *Middle,* an awl made of a deer's antler, and, *left,* stone net sinkers used for catching fish.

roamed through it at will, but their permanent home sites were south of the Choptank and north of the Wye.

At least five tribes or nations, however, lived near enough to Talbot to play a role in its early history. Taken from south to north, these were the Nanticokes from the river by that name; the Choptanks, closely related to the Nanticokes, with villages on the south bank of the river from which they took their name; the Matapeakes and/or Monoponsons (perhaps two names for the same small tribe) of Kent Island; the Wicomesses, no relation to the Wicomicos, with a fortified town south of Chester River; and the Susquehannocks or Susquehannoughs, who lived on the Susquehanna but claimed sovereignty over the Eastern Shore tribes by virtue of occasional murderous raids.

The tragic story of what happened to these tribes will be discussed in detail in Chapter 3. At this point it is enough to picture them as they were when the first English arrived: shy people, rather primitive, almost childlike, who lived along the rivers, hunted and fished, and raised maize, beans, squash, and tobacco in forest clearings which they made by girdling trees. Their villages were governed loosely by tribal chiefs and medicine men called werowances. Women and children performed the menial tasks; the men were hunters, fishers, and—on occasion—warriors. They had no intoxicating liquors, and no concept of the idea of land ownership, which the English held so dear; to them the land and the rivers belonged to everyone.

Every contact Captain John Smith and his men had with them served to point up their basic friendliness and curiosity. The Accomacks of the Virginia shore, after two well-armed "grim and stout salvages" had checked out the strange white men, entertained them in grand style at their village. The Nanticokes, whom Smith called the Kuskarawaocks, at first tried to kill the intruders with showers of arrows but later showered them instead with presents, food, and precious fresh water. Even the mighty Susquehannocks invited them to their villages thirty miles up the river, presented them with venison, wicker baskets, war shields, and bows and arrows, and shared with them their ceremonial tobacco pipes. The Tockwhoghes along the Sassafras actually fell down in worship before Smith, thinking him a god.

While capable of treachery and even vicious cruelty, the Indians Smith met showed little emotion toward the English except curiosity and a lurking desire to test their strength in combat. It was the white men who turned them into drunken murderers.

TWO

First Settlers

TALBOT County's first recorded landowner, unfortunately for history, was not exactly one of nature's noblemen. He was in fact a scoundrel, one of early Maryland's least admirable characters—a lecher, a blasphemer, and quite possibly a murderer whose crimes were the talk of St. Mary's in his day.

He called himself Captain William Mitchell, although exactly what he was a captain of is far from clear. In the winter of 1648 he met Caecilius Calvert, the second Lord Baltimore, in England, and soon talked his way into his lordship's confidence. The Calverts badly needed settlers to build up their raw new Maryland colony, and Mitchell promised to provide a goodly number of them.

In the next three years, he grandly pledged, he would transport to Maryland himself, his wife and children, and sufficient "artificers, workmen, and other very useful persons" to make up a total of thirty new settlers in the colony by 1651. He didn't say just how this was to be achieved; but Lord Baltimore was so impressed that he appointed Mitchell to the governor's privy council, executive body of the colony, even though he'd never been there, and made him a justice of the peace, to take office as soon as he arrived. On July 2, 1649, Baltimore put his seal on a special warrant instructing his agents at St. Mary's to issue a grant of three thousand acres of land to Mitchell provided he made good on his promise. If he failed to transport the full thirty persons, the grant was to be reduced by one hundred acres for every one he fell short.

Mitchell did come to Maryland, and took his seat on the governor's council. He also brought over his children and an unspecified number of servants—but not his wife, or at least not all the way to the new world. She died on the voyage, and it was later charged in court that he had poisoned her to clear the way for someone else.

Meanwhile a tract of land, supposed to be one thousand acres, was surveyed for Mitchell as the first installment on his three thousand-acre allotment. Called Rich Neck, it was the first tract ever claimed on the

Talbot County mainland. It was located just north of the present Claiborne, and included the estate still called Rich Neck Manor, where Tilghman Point juts out into Eastern Bay.

At St. Mary's, however, Mitchell was soon in trouble. Thomas Hatton sued him—and collected 2,570 pounds of tobacco—for "boarding and entertainment" of Mitchell's servants for almost a year before the captain himself arrived. One of those transported, William Smith, sued for 10,000 pounds of tobacco, charging that after he had been persuaded to leave his home in Bedfordshire and "adventure" to Maryland, Mitchell had not only refused to pay his expenses but had seized his household goods. The provincial court ruled that Smith had been "seduced from his Countrey, wife and Children by the fair and false promises of this Mitchell," and ordered the captain to pay Smith's board bills and the cost of his passage back to England, Smith being "an Old aged man of 61 years." Smith's daughter, Susan Warren, told the court she was with child by Mitchell, and he was ordered to pay for her maintenance until the child was born.

Then came a succession of far more serious accusations. In June, 1652, Mitchell was arrested and jailed on charges that he had committed "Murther Atheisme and Blasphemy," along with sundry other crimes. At his trial witnesses testified that he had made fun of Christian beliefs, that he was strongly suspected of having "brought his late wife to an untimely end in her late Voyage hitherward by Sea," that he had lived in adultery both with Susan Warren and his "now pretended wife," Joan Toast, and that he had given Mrs. Warren "physicke" in a poached egg to try to make her lose her baby, which had been born dead.

The court found Mitchell guilty on four major counts; but in what appears to have been a shocking miscarriage of justice, the judges sentenced him only to pay a fine of five thousand pounds of tobacco, give bond for his future good behavior, and live apart from Joan Toast until they could be married. Later the governor remitted two thousand pounds of the fine. Susan Warren was given a crueler sentence than her seducer; convicted of fornication as a result of her testimony, she was ordered to receive thirty-nine lashes on her bare back.

Mitchell's light treatment was doubtless due to his friendship with Lord Baltimore, but nevertheless his credit and his reputation in the colony were ruined. He was soon removed from the council, and spent much of his remaining years in Maryland defending himself against damage suits filed by angry plaintiffs whose bills he had not paid.

Even before his trial he had had to dispose of his Eastern Shore estate to raise money for lawyers' fees and damages. He sold his rights to Rich Neck to two attorneys, Phillip Land and Henry Fox. On October 20,

1651, they were issued a formal grant for the tract which Mitchell had earlier claimed.

It seems unlikely that Mitchell ever saw the Talbot County land he had so briefly owned. His memory as Talbot's first landholder was preserved only in the fact that for many years Rich Neck carried the alternate name of Mitchell's Point. Few if any Talbot residents knew just who the Mitchell so honored had been, which is probably just as well.

Talbot's second group of landowners, luckily, were of a better breed. They began having surveys made of tracts along the St. Michaels (Miles) River in 1658, and what was at first a trickle eventually became a flood. Some were land speculators, but others were genuine settlers who cut clearings in the forest at the edge of creeks and coves, brought in their families, and set out to seek their fortunes as tobacco planters.

At this point two widely believed myths about Talbot's early settlement need to be laid to rest. One has it that the way was opened by a treaty with the Susquehannock Indians negotiated on the future site of St. John's College in Annapolis July 5, 1652. Actually this treaty had little to do with settlement of the Eastern Shore; while the Susquehannocks relinquished their rights to the area, the land was not really theirs to give away since they had never lived there. The other myth is that as soon as surveying began in 1658, there was a great rush of settlers into the newly opened lands. That isn't quite the way it was.

Only ten tracts, covering a total of about three thousand acres, were surveyed in 1658, and it appears that none of these was actually patented until a year or two later. Those early surveys were casual affairs, based on a quick scanning by a surveyor of likely pieces of land, often a dozen or more in a day. Then a claim was filed in St. Mary's in the name of the prospective owner, and only after that did the complicated business of applying for and receiving an official grant in the name of the Lord Proprietary begin. Still later would come the process of settling on the chosen estate, clearing fields, and building a house.

While there undoubtedly were squatters who came over from Kent Island to the mainland in the 1650s, little real settlement was accomplished until after Talbot County was created in the late winter of 1661-62.

Among the 1658 surveys were a few landmark estates: Linton on the Wye, surveyed for Edward Lloyd; Wade's Point on Bayside, for Zachary Wade; Groce (or Gross) Coat, near Linton, for Roger Gross; and Morgan St. Michael, the future site of Doncaster, for Henry Morgan.

In 1659 the pace stepped up and attention turned to the Tred Avon. Of 48 surveys that year, totaling about twenty-two thousand acres, fifteen were identified as being on Tred Avon Creek or a variation of that name. By far the largest, however, was an estate claimed by Edward Lloyd called Hir Dir Lloyd, three thousand and fifty acres of the region's finest waterfront property running all the way from Oxford Neck down to what became Dickinson Bay. Later sold piecemeal by the Lloyds, this formed the basis of a number of Talbot's outstanding home sites in the years to come. At the same time Lloyd claimed a four hundred-acre parcel which he, or the clerk, spelled Cross Dower; as Crosiadore, meaning "cross of gold," this became the seat of the Dickinson family, which held it for nearly three hundred years.

Many other well-known properties were surveyed during 1659: Choptank Island (Tilghman Island), 1,200 acres, for Seth Foster; Bullen, 300 acres, for Thomas Bullen; Plinhimmon (now spelled Plimhimmon), 600 acres, for Henry Morgan; Anderton, 600 acres, for John Anderton; Ottwell, 500 acres, for William Taylor; Ratcliffe Mannour, 800 acres, for Captain Robert Morris; Chancellor's Point, first called Woolsey, for Philip Calvert, chancellor of the province; Kirkham, 350 acres, for Thomas Kirk; Grafton Mannour, 1,000 acres, for John Harris, who gave his name to Harris Creek; Canterbury Mannour, 1,000 acres, for Richard Tilghman; Tilghman's Fortune, 1,000 acres, for Richard's cousin, Captain Samuel Tilghman; and Martingham, 200 acres, for William Hambleton, first of a long line of distinguished Talbot Countians by that surname.

At the same time properties were being claimed in the region to the north which would be part of Talbot County until Queen Anne's County was formed in 1706. Notable among them were My Lord's Gift and Cheston-on-Wye, surveyed for the Coursey brothers, Henry, John, and William; Readbourne, later the home of one branch of the Hollyday family, for George Reed or Read; and Meersgate, later called Cloverfield, for William Hemsley, whose descendants would play a leading role in the history of Wye Mills.

By 1661 the time was ripe for real growth on the Eastern Shore. Maryland was finally at peace after nearly ten years of intense struggle for control of the colony between Puritan forces acting in the name of Oliver Cromwell and predominantly Catholic officials representing Lord Baltimore. All that was needed to spur an influx of settlers was an organized government for the sprawling area which covered half the Eastern Shore; and that came with the creation of Talbot County sometime during the late winter of 1661-62.

Exactly when Talbot County was established, or by what agency, remains a mystery. No document of any kind, no record of legislative action, governor's proclamation, nor judicial decree has ever been found.

The problem of dating Talbot County's birth is further complicated by the fact that in the seventeenth century, and well into the eighteenth, England and her colonies still operated under the old Julian calendar, in which the New Year began on March 25. All of January and February, plus most of March, were considered part of the old year. The modern Gregorian calendar, with January 1 designated as New Year's Day, did not become official until 1752.

Thus a date listed in early records as occurring in February, 1661, actually occurred in February, 1662, as the modern world reckons time. And that was the case with Talbot County; the first official reference to it by name came in a document dated February 18, 1661, but which under the modern calendar we would consider as February 18, 1662. Hence the confusion over even the year in which Talbot County was born.

At any rate, by February 18, 1661 (or 1662 if you prefer) Talbot was already in existence, although how it had come about no one knows. On that day the governor's council issued commissions to six men to serve as a court of justice "for the peace in Talbott County," and named Moses Stagwell, a Kent Island resident, to be temporary clerk. Next day Stagwell also was appointed temporary sheriff.

The six men entrusted with Talbot's first government were Richard Woolman, who served as presiding justice, William Coursey, Seth Foster, James Ringgold, Thomas South, and Thomas Hynson, Jr. In addition two members of the governor's council who lived in the new county, Edward Lloyd and Henry Coursey, were *ex officio* members of the court. All except Lloyd and Foster were identified with the area north of the modern Talbot border, where settlement had begun somewhat earlier than in Talbot County proper.

Sometime in March (again the record is missing) these justices or commissioners—the words were used interchangeably—met and chose John Morgan to be their nominee for both sheriff and clerk. The nomination was forwarded to St. Mary's for Governor Calvert's approval, and returned to Talbot "with all speede," reaching there April 10.

First meeting of the county court of which there is a record was held April 25, 1662, at the home of William Coursey on the Wye River in what is now Queen Anne's County. The meeting's minutes reflect the casual pace with which Talbot County government began: only four members were present—Woolman, Foster, and William and Henry Coursey—and no business of importance was transacted. All that was done was to record "ear marks"—the symbols settlers cut into the ears of hogs and cattle to distinguish ownership in the days before fences.

According to tradition, the county was named for Lady Grace Talbot, sister of Lord Baltimore and wife of Sir Robert Talbot, an Irish

COUNTY COUNCIL OF TALBOT COUNTY, MARYLAND
EASTON, MARYLAND 21601-3178

HERBERT L. ANDREW III, President
CLINTON S. BRADLEY III, Vice President
NANCY J. CLEM

SYLVIA J. GANNON
HERMAN F. MIELKE
MARY FOSTER, Secretary

PROCLAMATION

BIRTH OF TALBOT COUNTY

WHEREAS, no document has ever been found to establish the official birthday of Talbot County; and

WHEREAS, records do reveal that the first Court of Justice, as the County Commissioners Office was called, did meet and record business on April 25, 1662; and

WHEREAS, by historic circumstance, Talbot County now has a choice of selecting its official birthday; and

WHEREAS, the Talbot County Committee For Observance of Maryland's 350th Anniversary recommends the declaration of an official birthday for Talbot County;

NOW, THEREFORE, BE IT RESOLVED that We, the County Council of Talbot County, hereby proclaim April 25 to be the official birthday of Talbot County; and we urge all citizens to recognize and commemorate this day in an appropriate manner.

Given Under Our Hands and the Great Seal of Talbot County, Maryland this 19th day of April, in the Year of Our Lord One Thousand Nine Hundred and Eighty Three.

Herbert L. Andrew, III, President
Clinton S. Bradley, III, Vice President
Nancy J. Clem
Sylvia J. Gannon
Herman F. Mielke

Proclamation by County Council of Talbot County, April 19, 1983, designating April 25 as the county's official birthday.

patriot and statesman. There is no recorded confirmation of this belief. It rests merely on the assumption that because she was Lord Baltimore's sister, she must have been the person honored by the name.

The first justices were not without executive experience; most had previously been members either of the Kent County court or the governor's council. But the area they were to serve was so vast, and their legal powers so ill defined, that they understandably moved very slowly in asserting their authority.

Even the borders of the new county were maddeningly vague. Its territory ran from somewhere north of the Chester to somewhere south of the Choptank, and on the east faded off into the uninhabited territory along Delaware Bay, where the Dutch, Swedes, and English all had claims. On the west the county's jurisdiction ended at Chesapeake Bay—except that Sharp's and Poplar islands were included in Talbot, while Kent Island constituted a county of its own.

In this vast area, nearly five times the size of the present county, lived an estimated six to twelve hundred whites and an unknown number of Indians. The whites clung like barnacles to the tidal shoreline, leaving the interior to the Indians, bears, timber wolves, wildcats, deer, and rattlesnakes. Clearly it was not going to be an easy county to govern—but it was a job that had to be done.

Maryland law didn't help much. Their commissions gave the justices too much power in some respects, and not enough in others. There were conflicting functions—sometimes they acted as the county's executives, sometimes as lawmakers, sometimes as prosecutors and judges. As executives, they set the tax rate, paid bounties on wolves' heads, arranged for care of the elderly and orphans, distributed county funds, appointed ferry keepers, highway supervisors, and local constables, and in general administered county affairs. As judges they were instructed to "Chastise and Punnish all persons Offendinge against the forme of Any the Laws and Orders of this Our Province," and as prosecutors to "inquire into any offenses with which Justices of the Peace in England might lawfully be concerned." But they were admonished to be fair; their commissions required that they "doe equal right to the poor as to the Rich to the best of your Cunning witt and Power."

They were also the county's official witch-hunters, a duty taken seriously in seventeenth and eighteenth century Maryland. But they did not have the power to execute witches; that was reserved to the provincial court in St. Mary's, and later Annapolis. When Virtue Violl was charged with having "wasted" the body of a certain Ellianor Moore while "seduced by the devil" in 1712, she was indicted by a Talbot grand jury but transported for trial to Annapolis, where she was found not guilty.

In practice many cases which came before the county court involved moral offenses; Maryland in the 1660s had puritanical legal standards almost as strict as those in New England. The newly arrived settlers, like frontiersmen everywhere, were a rough-and-ready lot, free with their fists and with slanderous accusations, as bawdy, rude, and contentious as the society they had left behind in bawdy, rude, contentious Britain.

FIRST SETTLERS

Detailed records of the first twelve years of Talbot court sessions, published in *The Archives of Maryland*, reveal how different these early settlers were from the courtly cavaliers and gracious ladies some romantic writers have portrayed them as being. They got drunk, beat up their servants, gambled, stole each others' hogs, sang lewd songs about their neighbors, committed adultery, ran out on their bills, and haled each other into court on the slightest pretext. Considering the small number of people in the county, the justices had to deal with an exceedingly high percentage of the early population.

Servant girls were got with child with monotonous regularity. Among them were Sarah Sprudance, Ann Mungummery, Elizabeth Crookshanks, Martha Cheshill, Ann Hylliard, Elizabeth Stuckey, Mary Barnett, and Frances Smith, to name but a few. Most of these young women paid the standard penalty for their sins with thirty lashes on the bare back, but in some cases the court showed its humane feelings by postponing the whipping until after the child was delivered. The fathers, if known, usually got off with a fine.

But sin was not confined to the lower classes. High county officials, including some of the justices themselves, were accused of crimes ranging from hog stealing to adultery. Dr. Richard Tilghman, founder of the distinguished family, was convicted of extortion of taxes and trying to collect fees from patients which he had already collected from the county, and dismissed from his position of high sheriff. George Robbins, another ancestral patriarch who established the plantation called Peach Blossom, was bound over to the provincial court for allegedly stealing and butchering hogs belonging to a neighbor.

Two of the court's first justices, Richard Woolman and Seth Foster, also were accused of hog stealing. Both sat in on their own hearings, and used their powers as public officials to punish their accusers. Woolman forced Thomas Wilkinson to apologize "in open court and upon his knees" for having made the charge; but Foster was not satisfied with a court apology when Robert Knapp, for whom Knapp's Narrows is named, called him "a hogg stealing fellow from his Cradle." Even after the apology, Knapp later testified, Foster and his wife "most violently sett upon your Petitioner & beate him soe much that your Petitioner was forced to keepe his bed." The court ruled in favor of the Fosters, and refused to grant Knapp damages.

Another of the six original justices, Thomas Hynson, Jr., was charged with committing fornication with Ann Gaine "Contrary to the Laws of this Province." He confessed, but said he was "very sorrowfull" and had since made Ann his lawful wife. Nevertheless he was suspended for a year and a day from his post as justice. Ann appeared in court "acknowledging her faulte with extreme sorrow," and her scheduled punishment of thirty lashes was suspended.

Brutal treatment of servants was common and accepted. Justice Thomas South was charged with chasing his servant, John Shorte, into the water with a tobacco stick, intending to beat him, and then standing idly by while Shorte drowned. A jury called to consider the case held South guiltless, ruling that Shorte had in effect committed suicide since he had gone into the water of his own volition. Francis Carpender was indicted for the murder of servant Samuel Yeoungman not because he "broke his head" while beating Yeoungman with a stick, but because he had neglected to have the injury properly treated.

Servant suicides were frequent enough to indicate that many who had bound themselves for a term of years to pay for their passage from England bitterly regretted the bargain. In such cases a jury had to decide whether the victim had taken his own life, and if so to deny him Christian burial—in effect consigning him to hell for eternity. The decision was not always easy. When Robert Haukings was found dying with a string around his neck, the jury ruled that he had committed suicide. But when David Anderson was found dead after a night of heavy drinking, the ruling was that his death was accidental, since he had not intended to kill himself when he got drunk.

Charges of malicious gossip and scandal mongering were frequent. Bridgett Johnson faced such a charge for saying she had found her common-law husband, John Clymer, and Elizabeth Madbury in bed together. "Once I did love the said Clymer much but now I doe hate him as bad as a toade," Bridgett was quoted. Clymer insisted that he was only resting, being unable to do so at home because of Bridgett's nagging; and Elizabeth said she was asleep and thought it was her husband who was in bed with her. The court ruled that Bridgett's complaint was "only in Mallice" and ordered her to have "twenty lashes well laid on her Bare Backe by the Sheriff." John Wickes was fined one thousand pounds of tobacco and ordered to make a public apology after the court listened to a "Scandallous song" about the wife of John Wedge which Wickes allegedly had sung at a party.

Two civil suits which were heard involving horse race betting are said to have been the first in horse-loving Maryland's history. In one, Thomas Hallings sued Petter Whaples for two hundred pounds of tobacco, but Whaples said it "was a wagger at a Horse Rasse" and therefore not collectible. The court agreed with Whaples and dismissed the suit. However, when Jonathan Browne testified a year later that William Hemsley owed him one thousand pounds of tobacco for a race bet, the judges reversed themselves and ordered the loser to pay up. The issue of whether gambling debts are legal obligations has been debated ever since.

In marked contrast to the general moral laxity was the strict self-discipline of members of the Society of Friends or Quakers, who were prominent among the earliest Talbot County settlers. These deeply religious people had been persecuted both in England and America for their beliefs. They were accused of disrupting civil authority by refusing to do military duty, give testimony in court, take oaths, serve on juries, or accept public office. Some had been hanged in Boston, and others jailed and then whipped until they left the province. In Maryland two Quakers, Thomas Thurston and Josias Cole, had been brought to trial in 1658 for refusing to take the oath of fidelity to Lord Baltimore, and when they appeared in court had refused to take off their hats. Partly as a result of this the governor's council in 1659 ordered all Quakers who did not leave Maryland voluntarily "to be apprehended & whipped from Constable to Constable untill they be sent out of the Province." Virginia also ordered the expulsion of Quakers living in Lancaster County and neighboring areas in 1660.

Many of those expelled came to Talbot County, where they were effectively out of the reach of either the Maryland or Virginia authorities. Here they quickly formed a strong and close-knit organization which amounted virtually to a separate governing body within the loose structure of the county government. Quaker meetings disciplined errant members, arranged help for needy widows and orphans, decided disputes over business affairs and land ownership, and enforced a stern moral code. Followers of the evangelical English preacher, George Fox, they combined a belief in the "inner light," by which every person communed directly with God, with a hard practicality which stood them in good stead in conquering the Talbot wilderness.

Members of the Society of Friends in Talbot were forbidden to "follow Drunkenness, Pleasure, or Gameing;" to be other than honest or just in their dealings; to be "evil speakers, backbiters, slanderers, foolish jesters or talkers;" to serve dissension; or to be married "contrary to ye order of ye Truth"—in other words outside the Friends meeting, by a priest or magistrate. Quaker marriage ceremonies were—and still are—simple affirmations by the couple that each took the other as man and wife "solemnly in the fear of God," with all Friends who were present bearing witness. But before the couple could marry, their intentions must be declared at three successive meetings, and their backgrounds were thoroughly investigated to make certain they were not involved in any other love affairs. Members who deviated from these strict rules

Third Haven Meeting House built in 1682-84. Photograph taken about 1910.

were subject to disciplinary action or even "disowning"—expulsion from the society.

Among the earliest Quakers to reach Talbot County were Richard Gorsuch, Howell and Thomas Powell, and Walter Dickinson, all of whom had been driven out of Virginia; John Edmondson, who built the first house at Cedar Point on the Tred Avon; and John Pitt or Pitte, whose name is perpetuated in the fact that it was near "Pitte his bridge" that the Court House later was built in what became Easton. The first birth on record in Talbot was that of Sarah, daughter of John and Sarah Edmondson, on January 24, 1664/65, although tradition says Hannah Martin, daughter of Thomas Martin, was born at Hampden on Island Creek even earlier.

Both Pitt and Edmondson acquired much land in the new county. Edmondson, at least temporarily, outdid even the Lloyds, with 9,900 acres of land credited to his name in parcels scattered throughout Talbot, Dorchester, and the future Caroline County. He gave the Quakers the land on which Third Haven Meeting House was built, and his name survives in Edmondson (or Edmundson) Neck southwest of Easton. The two were partners as merchants, probably the first in the lower part of Talbot. They also were fur traders; on September 7, 1666, they were granted a license to deal with the Indians to the extent of "two thowsand Armes Length of Roanoke," the shell beads which along with "peake" were the Chesapeake Indians' version of what farther north was called wampum.

Other early Quaker families included those of William Stevens, Jr.; William Sharp or Sharpe, son of Dr. Peter Sharpe, for whom Sharp's Island was named; Thomas Taylor, a power in Maryland politics who before he became a Quaker had been speaker of the House of Delegates;

Bryon O'Mealy or O'Mealia; William Southbee; Ralph Fishbourne; William Berry; Henry and John Parrott; Robert Kemp, and others. The Bartlett and Dixon families, who came a little later, would write large chapters in Talbot history.

Most noted of the county's Quakers, though not among the earliest to arrive, was Wenlock Christison, who came to Talbot about 1670 and acquired a plantation near the head of what is now Glebe Creek called Ending of Controversie. The story of his wanderings and sufferings before he reached sanctuary in Talbot County is one of the most dramatic in the annals of American Quakers.

A native of England, Christison became "convinced of the Truth" soon after George Fox began his ministry. By the 1650s he was in New England. At Plymouth, Massachusetts, he was jailed, stripped, whipped, and robbed of his clothes and money for his defiance of the Puritan regime. In Boston he was again imprisoned in 1660, banished from the Massachusetts Bay Colony, and warned he would face the death penalty if he ever returned. But he did return, openly attending the trial of his friend and fellow Quaker, William Leddra, who was subsequently condemned to death and hanged March 14, 1661/62. Christison was seized by authorities and, according to Quaker historian George Bishope, told: "Unless you renounce your religion you shall surely die."

When Christison refused to recant, he was put on trial for his life with Governor Endicott, one of the most vindictive of all the Massachusetts Puritans, presiding as judge. Christison received a death sentence; but by then public reaction had set in against the Puritan excesses. Instead of being executed, he was once more banished.

He turned up again in Boston in 1664, this time to meet two Quaker women, Mary Thompson and Alice Garey, who were returning from Virginia, where they had been whipped so savagely that blood "had run down in abundance from their Breasts." The three were arrested, stripped to the waist, lashed to a cart, and, says Bishope, "whipp'd through Boston, Roxbury and Denham. Wenlock received ten cruel stripes, in each town, and the two women, his companions, six apiece." The three were then "driven into the wilderness."

Christison's later wanderings took him to Rhode Island and the West Indies. By the time he moved to Talbot County, he had a wife and children.

He soon became a leader of the Quaker community in the county. Dr. Peter Sharpe, a wealthy Quaker who lived at Calvert Cliffs, made him a gift of 150 acres of land and the house called Ending of Controversie as a symbol of his "true affection and brotherly love," and in recompense for the sufferings Christison had undergone for his faith.

Christison prospered and added more land, and, far from being persecuted, was elected a Talbot County delegate to the Maryland General Assembly. He died about 1678.

Another Quaker victim of Puritan savagery who had Talbot connections was Mary Dyer, an early associate of Christison in Boston. She was condemned to death for witchcraft and hanged from an elm tree in Boston Common June 1, 1660. Her granddaughter's grandson was Nicholas Hammond III, one of the most prominent Talbot Countians of the early nineteenth century and first president of what became the Easton National Bank.

In Talbot County, far from the scenes of hatred and brutality, the Quakers lived in at least outward harmony with their Puritan neighbors, who formed a second major element among the county's early immigrants. Many of the Puritans had come to Maryland from Virginia in 1649 in response to Lord Baltimore's famous Toleration Act and had supported the Puritan revolt which took control of the colony for a time in the 1650s. After that conflict was settled in Lord Baltimore's favor, they migrated in sizable numbers to the Eastern Shore from their first Maryland community, Providence on the Severn River, on the site where the United States Naval Academy is today.

Of all the Talbot Puritans, by far the most influential—and most interesting—was Edward Lloyd, first of a long line of men by that name who would dominate the county's economic and social life for more than two centuries. Lloyd was an intriguing figure, a man of many talents: skilled politician, expert surveyor, fur trader, planter, merchant, land speculator, transatlantic shipper, tobacco buyer, and agent for immigrants. Despite his Puritanism, he was no fanatic in the mold of his New England compatriots; he had a knack for landing on the winning side of any dispute, whether religious or economic. His influence undoubtedly helped smooth the way for the good relations between Quakers and Puritans which distinguished the formative years in Talbot.

From his name, a common one in Wales, he would seem to have been of Welsh descent. But he himself was probably born in Virginia, where an Edward Lloyd who may have been his father was active as early as 1623. By the 1640s, the younger Lloyd was a leader of the Puritan group which lived along the Nansemond and Elizabeth rivers in lower Norfolk County. His name appears on a list of men arrested there early in 1649 for refusing to attend the established Anglican church or hear the Book of Common Prayer.

When these Puritans moved to Maryland, established Providence, and brought about the formation of Anne Arundel County, Lloyd became the new county's first chief executive, with the title of commander. He figured prominently in the turbulent events of the 1650s, helping to overthrow Lord Baltimore's regime in the name of Oliver Cromwell, and serving on the Puritan Board of Commissioners which ruled the province for several years and which in 1656 tried Josias Fendall, Lord Baltimore's appointed governor, on a charge of "actions dangerous to the public peace." Yet when the Puritans were ousted in a settlement favorable to Baltimore, Lloyd emerged without a scratch. He was named to the new governor's council, probably as a gesture to the Puritans, and soon gained possession of at least four valuable land grants, totaling nearly 5,000 acres, in what became Talbot County.

Lloyd moved from Providence to Talbot about 1661, apparently just before the county's formation. Soon afterward he built the first Wye House (the present one dates from the 1780s), a good-sized structure with a central hall and two dependent wings, of which one survives in greatly remodeled form in the building now called the Captain's House.

He did not remain long in Talbot. About 1668 he put his Maryland affairs in the hands of his son, Philemon, and moved permanently to England. There he pursued a successful career as an overseas merchant, dealing principally in the Maryland tobacco trade, until his death about 1695. Married three times—each time to a widow—he had only one known son, Philemon, born in Virginia in 1646, although family tradition suggests there may have been an Edward who died young. He made his eldest grandson, Edward Lloyd II, his legal heir, and thus founded a dynasty which was one of the longest in America. Almost until the twentieth century a succession of men named Edward Lloyd would make Wye House their base as they won prominence in the affairs of the county and state.

Others among the settlers who came in rapidly once the county was established were a varied lot. Included were adventurers looking for quick riches in a new land; younger sons of titled or established British and Irish families; Scotsmen such as William Hambleton and Patrick Mullikin, both of whom founded dynasties of their own in a modest way; yeomen, traditional tenant farmers, who were being driven off the land in increasing numbers in England, Wales, and Ireland; workers from the slums of London and other cities who came as indentured servants; even black slaves, although there were very few of these at first. What bound all except the blacks together was a common desire for elbow room, for independence, for a chance to work out their own lives away from the entanglements of the old world, to seek their fortunes on land of their own choosing. And there was plenty of that in seventeenth century Talbot.

One most unusual early Talbot County resident was Alexander D'Hinojosa, the exiled former governor of the Dutch colony near New Castle, Delaware. After his colony was seized by the English, D'Hinojosa was granted sanctuary by Maryland Governor Charles Calvert. In 1669 he bought Poplar Island from Seth and Elizabeth Foster for three hundred pounds sterling, and lived there with his large family for many years. In 1671 he, his wife, and their seven children were granted naturalization as citizens of Maryland. What eventually happened to D'Hinojosa is not clear; one account has him dying in Prince George's County in extreme poverty, but another says he returned to the Netherlands and lived to a "ripe old age."

By the 1670s Talbot County had perhaps three thousand residents. Membership on the county court had been increased from the original six to eleven, and the county divided for administrative purposes into hundreds, each with its own constable. These districts were survivors from medieval times in Britain, when shires were marked off into segments that could produce a hundred fighting men apiece. In Talbot they were merely geographical subdivisions, but the term continued in use until the modern election districts replaced them—and in the case of "Bay Hundred," the old name for the Tilghman Peninsula, it lasted even longer than that.

The highlight of Talbot's first dozen years as a county undoubtedly came in 1672 and 1673 when George Fox, founder of the Society of Friends, visited the county four times in the course of a missionary journey through colonial America. He found the county bustling with activity and the Quakers at the peak of their prestige. They had established meetings in several areas, and by 1669 had built at least one wooden meeting house, at Betty's Cove near the Miles River on what later became the North Bend estate. Not long afterward meeting houses were erected near the Kemp plantation in Bay Hundred, in Trappe District on the site of the present Scott's United Methodist Church, in Tuckahoe, and on Transquakin Creek in Dorchester County. The largest of them all was the Great Meeting House on Tred Avon (or Tread Haven) Creek, built in 1682-84. Later called Third Haven Meeting House, it is still in use, and is believed to be the oldest active wooden house of worship in the United States.

Fox's published journal provides a vivid contemporary picture of living conditions in Talbot at the time of his visits. He first arrived in May, 1672. After a series of meetings on the Western Shore, he crossed

George Fox

the bay and attended "a very great heavenly meeting, near Great Choptank River," apparently in Dorchester County. The Indian "emperor" attended and afterward, with two "kings" and four "nobles," stayed the night with Fox at a Quaker home. The Indians were "very loving." On May 6, with a large party of Quakers and two Indian guides, Fox set out by land for New England, traveling the length of Talbot County through the woods on horseback and camping out at night.

In September he came back, traveling through "many bad bogs" and heavy rain to the house of Robert Harwood on Miles River. Next day he attended a nearby Friends' gathering, and then went to lodge with John Edmondson on Tred Avon Creek. After a "First-day" (Sunday) meeting at which a judge's wife said "she had rather hear this man (Fox) once than the priests a thousand times," he went off to Kent Island and some other stops.

In a few days he was back at Edmondson's, where he lodged during the general meeting of all Maryland Friends, the second ever held in the province and the first of many in Talbot. This began October 3, and lasted five days, of which the first three were open to the public. Presumably the sessions were held at Betty's Cove, although Fox never said so and there is no independent record of it. What he did write in his journal, however, makes clear that wherever it took place it was the greatest public gathering held in the young county up to that point:

Many of the world were at the public meetings, some Papists, clerks of their courts, and there were eight justices of the peace, and one of the judges and his wife, and another judge's wife, and many considerable persons of quality. And they judged that there was a thousand people; and one of the justices said, that he never saw so many people together in the country, though it was rainy weather. And Friends and people were generally satisfied and convinced, and the blessed power of the Lord was over all.

Fox traveled by boat each day from Edmondson's house at Cedar Point to the meeting place, a distance he reckoned at four to five miles. Presumably this was along the Tred Avon and up Dixon's Creek, which reaches to within a short distance of the supposed Betty's Cove site. He reported there were so many boats on the water that "it was almost like the Thames in London." Even though the meeting house had recently been doubled in size, it would not hold all the people who attended.

His final visit to Talbot came in March, 1673. After another stop at "Great Choptank" he journeyed again to Tred Avon Creek for a "glorious meeting," and on up to the Wye, where on April 1 "we had a very precious meeting. . . . And the judge of that country and his wife were there and they were very tender. And many other people. Thereaways the Truth is of a good savour."

Fox left Talbot County fully satisfied that the great turnouts and strong interest he had witnessed meant that the entire populace soon would be "convinced of the Truth" and become Quakers. But he was mistaken; perhaps Quaker discipline was too strict and its moral standards too high for the general public. At any rate, while the Society of Friends retained a strong influence in the county, its numbers never increased much beyond what they had been at the time of his visits. It would be another century before a similar but less restrictive religious movement, led by "the people called Methodists," captured the minds and hearts of the Talbot public.

THREE

Building a County

ONCE the settlement of Talbot County was permanent, county and provincial leaders were faced with a troublesome problem: what to do about the Indians who still roamed the region, clinging as they did to their old ways in the face of an overwhelmingly superior civilization.

Though relatively few in number, there were enough Indians to be a serious nuisance. They were an alien force, and occasionally murderous, especially when inflamed by drink. From time to time ugly incidents occurred. In 1666 John Jenkins, believed to have been the builder who constructed the first Wye House, and his wife were found slain in their home. The grand jury which investigated reported that "by the Goods that have bin Carried away wee doe Conceive, the Indians have Committed the Massacray."

In 1667 Captain John Odber, military commander of the district, and his servant were murdered, allegedly by Wicomesses Indians. That produced demands for vengeance from white settlers throughout the Eastern Shore. The settlers enlisted the help of the other tribes and sent out an expedition which wiped out the entire nation, to the last man, woman, and child, in what may have been America's first genocidal war.

From the beginning of the Maryland colony, the Wicomesses had been the most obstinate of the Eastern Shore tribes in their resistance to white encroachment into their traditional lands. Believed to have been the people Captain John Smith designated on his map as the "Ozinies," they had a fortified village south of Chester River in present Queen Anne's County at the time the first English arrived. From this base they let it be known at once that they would have nothing to do with English customs or English law. When the governor's council of the new colony demanded in 1634 that certain Wicomesses be executed for killing whites on Kent Island, a Wicomesses spokesman replied:

> It is the manner amongst us Indians, that if any such like accident happen, we do redeem the life of a man that is so slain, with a 100 arms' length of

Roanoke, and since that you are here strangers, and come into our country, you should rather conform yourselves to the customs of our country, than impose yours on us.

As years passed they persisted in their insistence that the whites were interlopers, and that white settlers were fair game. St. Mary's replied with equal savagery. In 1641 Governor Calvert issued orders to shoot any Wicomesses on sight if they set foot on Kent Island, then the only settled part of the Eastern Shore. By the time Talbot County was formed, the Wicomesses had been forced out of their ancestral home and were turned into woodland skulkers, implacable enemies of the settlers, killing and robbing where they could, and wintering in the unwanted marshes along the Nanticoke River. Many of them lived at "Sicacone Towne" on what later became part of the Nanticoke reservation.

Their final agonies as a nation began after the murder of Captain Odber and his servant. White authorities demanded that the killer or killers be turned in for trial and execution. The Indians argued that the slaying was justifiable because previously "the English had kill'd them a woman" at the Talbot County home of William Hemsley. The whites ignored this claim; the death of an Indian woman was of little interest to them. Instead an armed group headed by William Coursey seized four Wicomesses as hostages and took them to St. Mary's for trial before the Council of Maryland. Although no evidence was produced linking the four to Odber's murder, all four were sentenced to death and one was actually executed. The other three were made slaves for the personal benefit of Governor Calvert and his brother Philip.

Two years later a Wicomesses named Anatchcom, who said it was his wife who had been killed at Hemsley's house, was turned in by the Choptanks as the man who had actually committed the Odber murders. He denied it, but admitted being in the party. That was enough for the trial judges; they found him guilty and ordered him "to be shot to death here at St. Mary's sometime before three of the Clock this afternoon." The Choptank chiefs who had turned him in were suitably rewarded for their "fidelity" to the English and their treachery toward their fellow Indians.

No investigation was ever conducted into the death of the Indian woman. It was a classic example of "white men's justice" in which the death penalty was habitually demanded for Indians who killed whites, but nothing was done about whites who killed Indians.

Worse was to follow. Not content with executing two Wicomesses— one possibly guilty but the other certainly innocent—provincial authorities decided to punish the entire tribe. The help of the Nanticokes was enlisted; in return for their promise to deliver up "the whole nacon of Wicomesses," the Nanticokes received a written guarantee, soon broken, that "the Priviledge of Hunting crabbing and fowling and fishing shall be preserved to the Indians . . . to the worlds end."

A colonial expedition with Major Thomas Ingram of Talbot County as field commander was quickly organized. He was authorized to raise an army of 410 men, including 60 from Talbot, by drafting every tenth able-bodied man in the province. Each man was to supply his own clothing, gun, sword, powder, shot, and flints, and every sixth man was to bring along an axe. Details of the war that followed have been lost, but it was certainly a great success from the whites' point of view. Philemon Lloyd, colonel of the Talbot militia who took part, later reported with grim satisfaction that it had been "brought to an end by the defeat and total destruction of a nation of savages called the Wicomesses." As nearly as can be determined, not a single man, woman, or child was left alive.

The other tribes who played roles in early Talbot history were dealt with in less brutal but just as effective ways. The story of their degradation and eventual fate has been called "the darkest chapter in Maryland history"—perhaps even worse than the story of Maryland's treatment of its black slaves. It was in general a preview of the tragic destiny which awaited the Indians throughout America.

The Nanticokes, whom Captain Smith had called the Kuskarawaocks, were considered by the settlers to be almost as bad as the Wicomesses. They were reputed to be expert poisoners, a skill which made them feared and hated by the other tribes. But they were too numerous to be exterminated, although expeditions were occasionally sent against them with that purpose in mind. Captain John Price, who led a force to the Eastern Shore in 1647, had orders to use any method he saw fit in "destroying the sd. Nations (Nanticoke and Wicomesses) . . . eyther by killing them, taking them prisoners, burning their howses destroying their Corne, or by any other meanes as he shall judge convenient." He got nowhere; but eventually rum and disease succeeded where armed might had failed. A report in 1697 said the Nanticokes had ten towns, but that some of these, though called towns, "have not twenty families in them." It added:

> The Eastern Shore Indians . . . decrease very much by reason of the Small Pox a distemper they had not before the Europeans came amongst them, and by their old way of poisoning, which they are very expert in; but the greatest cause of all is their being so devilishly given to drinking, especially of Rum, for procuring which they will even sell or pawne all they have.

A five thousand-acre reservation east of Vienna was laid out for the Nanticokes in 1684, with the usual guarantees of "perpetual" protection against white encroachment, and a second reservation centering on Broad Creek in present Delaware was granted them in 1711. However, by the 1740s they had had enough of the white man's promises. At the invitation of the Six Nations of the Iroquois Confederacy, they received permission from Governor Ogle to leave Maryland and emigrate to an area around Otsiningo (now Binghamton), New York. Gathering up the bones of their ancestors, they began a long, slow trek northward which was one of the most pathetic episodes in Maryland history. Although they had passes signed personally by the governor, many were arrested and jailed by the sheriffs of the counties through which they passed. Others died along the way. Those who reached the north formed a small league known as the Three Nations with fragments of the Shawnees and Mohicans.

In 1767 ambassadors from the Nanticokes came back to Maryland and negotiated a settlement with Governor Sharpe for their lands in Dorchester, Somerset, and Worcester counties. But in 1776 there came a curious epilogue. Chiefs of the Iroquois Confederacy with whom General Philip Schuyler was attempting to negotiate a treaty for aid against the British suddenly raised the issue of the Nanticokes, saying many who had not joined the exodus were being held in Maryland against their will, and demanding something be done about it. Schuyler passed the word on to the war office in Philadelphia, from where Secretary Richard Peters wrote to the Council of Safety in Maryland: "This idea, tho' not founded in Truth creates much uneasiness and is constantly held up by the Indians in their conferences with the General." The question was also raised in the Continental Congress, which called on Maryland to give it "immediate attention." The puzzled Marylanders reported back that they had investigated but could find no Nanticokes who were being held against their will. From subsequent developments it appears the Iroquois chiefs had simply raised the issue as a bluff to win better concessions from the Americans. At any rate, they didn't bring it up again. That disposed of the Nanticokes, although a small settlement of people still living near Seaford, Delaware, claim to be of Nanticoke descent.

The Choptanks, who were the most closely associated of any tribe with early Talbot history, were easily brought under control. Although related to the Nanticokes, they were far less warlike; they lived in fear of the other Indians and were always anxious to win favor from the whites for protection against their enemies. Their villages were on the south bank of the Choptank, and they hunted and fished on the Talbot side.

When these areas began to draw white settlers, they complained in 1669 that "the English do daily encroach on them." The Lord Proprietary, with the approval of the assembly, made them an outright grant of territory stretching from the present site of Cambridge to Secretary Creek, and running three miles southward into the woods. The ground rent was to be six beaver skins annually.

On May 7, 1699, this was spelled out more precisely in a "perpetual" treaty granting the Indians a fifteen thousand-acre reservation. The site of Cambridge was taken over by the English at this time. Whites were forbidden forever from settling on the Indian land. But of course they did anyway, buying choice plantation sites for next to nothing, or simply moving in. The Indians were gradually squeezed eastward along the river. In 1719 Tom Bishop, a Choptank who had taken an English name, complained that his people "are now driven into a small narrow neck called Locust Neck." An investigation in 1724 showed that only a small part of the original grant remained in possession of the Indians. Their chief lamented that they had been "made drunk" by unscrupulous whites and then induced to sell.

Many of the Choptanks joined the Nanticokes in the migration of the 1740s, but a pitiful remnant stayed on in what little was left of their reservation. In answer to a query from Thomas Jefferson, Dr. William Vans Murray of Cambridge visited the Locust Neck area in the 1780s and found only nine members of the tribe. One of them, Mrs. Molley Mulberry, was said to be a widowed queen, but remembered only a few Indian words. In an ancient house, Dr. Murray found the bones of a Choptank chief who had been dead for seventy years.

Dr. Murray, who thought these Choptanks were the remnants of the Nanticokes, reported to Jefferson:

> Taken at Locust-Neck Town—The remains of an ancient Indian Town on Goose Creek, Choptank River in Dorset, Maryland—Five wigwams and a board house with a glass window now form the whole that is left of the Nanticoke tribe which was an hundred years ago numerous and powerful.

By 1799 only five of the nine remained. Mrs. Mulberry and her son Henry Mulberry were still alive, but did not long survive. In 1801 the Maryland General Assembly authorized appointment of a trustee to dispose of the twenty acres of land "belonging to a certain Choptank Indian, Molley Mulberry, lately deceased and leaving no descendants." With that act the Indians of the Choptank River disappeared from the annals of American history.

The Matapeakes, a small tribe which lived on or near Kent Island, and perhaps roamed into northern Talbot County, remained in that vicinity until the 1760s. They had sold the island, which they called Monoponson, outright to William Claiborne in 1634 for trading goods he valued at twelve pounds sterling (about sixty dollars). But they remained there anyhow, causing little or no trouble, for more than a hundred years. Finally they simply picked up their possessions and departed; no one knows where they went. James Bryan, a Queen Anne's County resident born in 1755, wrote of them:

> I remember the Indians; their last dwelling place was upon the northwest side of the island near the (mouth) of Broad Creek; and they lived in their cabins of bark, upon a small tract of woodland.... I was then a well-grown boy. They always seemed friendly.... I also remember the very time of their departure. They left the Island near the mouth of the Creek, and turned their faces westward.

All the Matapeakes left behind was their name, familiar to generations as a terminus of the Chesapeake Bay ferry which preceded the Bay Bridge, and more recently as the site of a state park and the Chesapeake Bay model.

The Susquehannocks, mightiest of all the warrior tribes around the bay, had lost most of their military strength to war, liquor, and smallpox before Talbot County was created. They retreated into the "Indian country" of western Maryland and Virginia, and eventually wound up in western Pennsylvania where, to their shame, they were "treated like women" by the still virile Iroquois. There they were known as the Conestogas. That name gave rise to two familiar Americanisms—the famous covered Conestoga wagon, in which (at least according to Hollywood) the pioneers conquered the West; and the "stogie," a foul-smelling cigar originally called that because the Conestoga wagon drivers smoked them.

So passed in blood, squalor, disease, and rum the Indian presence in Talbot County and its environs. But the Indians left a legacy which should not be forgotten. They gave the settlers corn and tobacco, the staple crops on which Talbot's first prosperity was built; log canoes, standard transportation in early times and today familiar ornaments on Talbot waters; beans, pumpkins, squash, and herbs; the gourds which served as kitchen implements for many a poor family; duck decoys, and other methods of hunting and fishing unknown to the English. From Indian women their white sisters learned how to pound corn kernels into meal, and how to make corn pone and hominy. The Indians were also responsible for that Eastern Shore delight, corn on the cob; late August was known as the time "when roasting ears were in season" and the Indians were apt to be on the march. They taught the planters how to clear fields by girdling trees, thus saving the labor of clearing brush and rooting out stumps, and how to plant, tend, and harvest tobacco and other crops.

The Indians also left their stamp on the county's borders, in the names of the waters which nearly surround it. Choptank, from an Algonquian word indicating a village or place, eventually came to be applied both to the river and the tribe which lived along its banks. Tuckahoe, applied to a creek and district in Talbot, comes from the Tockwhoghs, whose villages were on the Sassafras; in the seventeenth century certain edible roots favored by the Indians were called "tuckahoe truffles." Chesapeake itself was an Indian word, although its original meaning is in dispute. Some scholars say it signified "Mother of Waters," others that it meant "Great Salt Sea," and still others "Country on a Great River." Captain John Smith, one of the first to popularize it, thought it had come simply from the Chesapeake Indians who lived on the Elizabeth River, near the great bay's mouth.

Not the least in importance was the Indians' role as the county's first road builders. The trails they marked and packed down through the forests were followed faithfully by white settlers in constructing their first crude highways. Some county roads still in use follow almost exactly those prehistoric Indian tracks.

Once the Indians were under control, or largely so, Talbot's settlers turned their attention to more immediate matters: intracounty transportation and establishing a permanent seat of government. St. Mary's was clamoring for roads and ferries, and Lord Baltimore himself was anxious to set up a system of ports and market towns on the English model. From his vantage point in London, these appeared much more practical than they proved to be in the Talbot wilderness.

Ferries came first. On June 16, 1668, the county court awarded Jonathan Hopkinson a contract "for to keepe Ferry for horse and footte at all times and Accassions," for which he was to be paid two thousand pounds of tobacco a year. This first ferry was probably between points on the Wye River's various branches; Hopkinson lived near the mouth of Skipton Creek, then considered an extension of the Wye East. In 1671 a ferry was established across the "wading place" (now Kent Narrows), linking Kent Island to the mainland. Next came the Miles River Ferry (1677), the Oxford Ferry (1683), and ferries across the Choptank at Dover and Chancellor's Point. All these were subsidized from county funds, as the Oxford Ferry still is.

Building roads proved more difficult. St. Mary's insisted every county should have a highway system, but there was little demand for one in

Talbot, where everyone traveled by water. In any case the task was far beyond the young county's feeble finances. Building a true road system would take fifty years; before that roads were simply horse paths following the Indian trails through the bogs and forests, marked by blazes on trees and dotted with "Indian bridges," which were nothing more than logs thrown across streams.

Responding to St. Mary's demands, the Talbot justices named William Coursey and John Edmondson "Overseeares and Repairers of the High Wayes" in November, 1669, but little road work was actually done as a result. By 1672, however, some construction was underway; that year 4,000 pounds of tobacco were paid out of county funds for "makeing high Waies," and four new men named "overseeares" with power to draft men and supplies as needed. In 1673 they charged bills against the county for 203 man-days of work.

The 1672 assignments, if nothing else, provide valuable clues in dating the establishment of various places and institutions in early Talbot. Mentioned were "the Church by the highwaie between Chester River and Wye River" (old Chester Church, later St. Paul's Parish Church, which was located at Hibernia, about a mile south of the present Centreville); "the Mill" south of the church (Old Wye Mill, still operating three centuries later); "the Highwaies in these Neck" (undoubtedly Miles River Neck, one of the first areas to be settled); and "the Towne at the Mouth of Wye River" (the little port later called Doncaster, long since vanished). So we know these places existed as early as 1672. Another highway assignment, dated 1687, provides the earliest known reference to Old Whitemarsh, the St. Peter's Parish Church of which picturesque ruins south of Easton still exist. That year William Dickinson of Crosiadore was named "to keep the highway from George Cowley's (on Dividing Creek, now Trappe Creek) to the Church at Whitemarsh."

Next the justices took up the question of establishing a permanent seat for the county government. At first they had met at the homes of members of the court, including Seth Foster's house on Tilghman Island, William Taylor's at Ottwell, and Edward Lloyd's at Wye House. By 1670 they had fixed on the plantation of Jonathan Hopkinson on Skipton Creek as a convenient central point. Hopkinson had a tavern as well as being ferry keeper, which made things handy for the justices. The election of January 17, 1669/70, was held there, with every qualified voter in the county being required to travel from his home to Hopkinson's plantation if he wanted to cast his ballot.

On August 27, 1674, the justices voted to buy ten acres of land from Hopkinson "for ye building of a Court House and a Prison." Nothing came of this, and on March 4, 1675/76 a new contract was signed, this

Old Wye Mill, founded about 1670, still operates three centuries later under the aegis of students of nearby Chesapeake College.

time for twenty acres. Still no court house was built, although Hopkinson did construct a jail, described as fifteen by twenty feet, made of timbers a foot square with an underpinning of stone, and divided into two rooms, each containing a window fitted with "firm substantiall Iron Bars." Perhaps prophetically, a jail was thus the first building ever constructed for the use of the Talbot County government.

Until Hopkinson died in 1677, the justices met in an existing house on his plantation. Then they went back temporarily to meeting at the homes of members. Soon they made an arrangement with Elizabeth Winkles, a widow, to act as their innkeeper and hostess; but she proved unsatisfactory. Finally, on August 19, 1679, they signed an agreement with Richard Sweatnam, an experienced carpenter as well as an innkeeper, to build what became the first permanent Talbot County Court House on their twenty-acre site near Skipton Creek.

On March 16, 1679/80, Sweatnam submitted detailed plans for the new building. It was to be fifty by twenty-three feet in extent, three stories high, constructed of wood, with a court hall eighteen feet square. That would make it by far the largest building on the Eastern Shore, and the fee Sweatnam was to receive for building it, 130,000 pounds of tobacco, was much the largest sum the young county had ever been required to raise in taxes.

In addition to his fee, Sweatnam was to live in the structure rent free for seven years and to maintain it as an ordinary, or house of entertainment. (This was standard practice; even the Maryland State House at St. Mary's doubled as an inn.) Meanwhile Sweatnam, in addition to his construction work, was to make sure that the justices and lawyers who had business with the court had ample supplies of food and drink. For this he had exclusive rights; when the widow Winkles tried to set up a rival tavern, the court issued an order that "noe ordinary be Keep upon the plantation of Elizabeth Winkles by herself or any other person during the time that Mr. Richard Swetnam is a building the Court House."

Just when the fine new Court House was completed is uncertain, but it was probably in use by November, 1682, when Sweatnam was alloted an extra two thousand pounds of tobacco for adding a porch. In 1686 the General Assembly gave it a name, passing legislation which among other things called for a town and port to be established "at or near the Court House . . . and the lands adjacent, to be called York."

So the infant county seat village had a Court House, a jail, a tavern, and a name, if nothing else. Very soon it also acquired a half-mile race track built, according to tradition, directly in front of the Court House. This was in existence as early as 1689, and appears to have been a

Talbot County Court House at York, 1681-82, as sketched by Dr. H. Chandlee Forman, on the basis of specifications in the county records.

straight run rather than an oval, since a deed mentioning it referred to "a bounded red oak standing at the end of the half-mile race near the Court House."

More was to come: on November 18, 1690, the court ordered Thomas Bruff to "fix and sett up before the Court House doore the stock, pillory and whipping post, by act of assembly appointed." Up to then these cruel devices for punishing criminals had been lacking in Talbot, although as noted earlier court-ordered whippings were common. Additional stocks, pillories, and whipping posts were ordered in 1700 for Doncaster and Williamstadt (Oxford).

In March, 1693, John Salter, who had succeeded Sweatnam as innkeeper, was instructed to "erect and build up at the towne of York a stable of forty foote long and twenty foote wide, with a convenient place at one end to secure bridles and saddles thereby." That indicates York on occasion had a good many visitors, although such a large stable may have been intended for racers as well as riding horses.

Three incidents which have come down to us confirm the impression that York in its heyday was a lively little place. Two of the incidents occurred while Sweatnam was innkeeper, the third while Salter was presiding as host.

Sweatnam, it appears, enjoyed practical jokes. One day, having killed a small rattlesnake, he had it skinned, boiled, and set up on a plate with butter and parsley. When an overnight guest asked what there was for supper, Sweatnam told him: "I have a rare cold eele if you like that." The visitor devoured the "eele" with gusto, and afterward declared "he never supped better in his life."

Next morning Sweatnam couldn't resist; he told his guest he had eaten rattlesnake, not eel, and called in the maid who had skinned and boiled it to prove his story. Thereupon, according to the chronicler, the shocked victim jumped on his horse and went home "and had a verry severe fitt of sickness so that he lost all his haire." Afterward he sued Sweatnam for damages and—at least as the tale was told later—collected twenty thousand pounds of tobacco.

York's court house tavern was also the scene in 1692 of one of Talbot County's most celebrated drinking bouts. This was a two-day affair involving a number of prominent men, including Richard Bennett III, later described as "the richest man in North America," and the Reverend John Lillingston, Anglican rector of St. Paul's Parish.

These two were among a dozen jovial fellows who took a room on an upper floor of the building during a session of the county court. Apparently their purpose was to show their scorn for the current Maryland government; at any rate, after several drinks, they marched downstairs and interrupted court proceedings with loud cries and rude gestures. They were thrown out bodily.

Many drinks later, Bennett, Lillingston, and their accomplices returned to the court chamber, but found the justices gone. According to witnesses this drunken group rode their horses into the courtroom and tied them to the rail of the judges' bench. They then went outside and played at placing each other in the stocks and pillory. Fistfighting broke out; some later said the Reverend Lillingston was one of those who threw punches, others that he merely watched.

Next day they ordered food and drink brought to a point on the creek bank. According to evidence given by William Finney, later Talbot County sheriff, "there they drank that day at the point till they were so drunk that they fell together by the Ears and Michael Earl flung Joseph Greene into the water."

On a complaint by innkeeper Salter, all were arrested and taken to St. Mary's for trial. Lillingston and perhaps others were found guilty of "prolonged and aggravated drunken carousing," but received a pardon from the governor "on account of His Majesty's happy success and late victory against the French" in what was known as King William's War.

The third incident, while grimmer on the surface, was in its own way just as much a farce. This was the trial of an Indian, Poh Poh Caquis, in 1683 on a charge of having attacked William Troth, a Talbot Quaker, at the house called Troth's Fortune on the Choptank. The prosecutors

Troth's Fortune, as it looked in a 1930s photo for a U. S. Department of Interior survey of historic houses.

obviously wanted to make an example of the case; for what amounted to nothing more than a charge of drunken assault, they assembled the full majesty of the English law, and summoned the Indian leaders of the area to witness what happened when one of their race dared attack a white man.

The facts, brought out through witnesses, were simple enough. Poh Poh Caquis had entered Troth's house and sat down by the fire, claiming he was cold. Mrs. Troth, who was about to have a baby, went looking for her husband. There were some harsh words. While Troth was at the door greeting an arriving visitor, Thomas Bussey, the Indian loaded his gun and pointed it at Troth. Troth turned, saw the gun, and grappled for it. In the melee it went off, but no one was hurt. Poh Poh Caquis then "tooke to his tomahawke" and chased Troth outside the house. Troth yelled for someone to bring him his own gun, and the Indian fled. When he was about thirty yards away, Troth shot at him and believed he had wounded him. The Indian got away, but was later captured.

Poh Poh Caquis said in his defense that "he was drunk and knew not what he did. . . . Otherwise, he would not have shot at Wm. Troth, or have done any mischief." The special two-judge panel of Colonel Philemon Lloyd and Henry Coursey which was hearing the case sternly replied that drunkenness was no excuse. If it were, they said, "then the English might make themselves drunk & kill the Indians." They informed the assembled chiefs, who included kings Ababco and Tequassino of the Choptanks, that under English law the prisoner "deserves death, but the English (are) not desirous to exercise the rigor of the law." They therefore ordered him to "be carried to the whipping post, and have twenty lashes laid on his bare back," and then to be returned to the bar for further sentencing. The Indians agreed that one of their own "greate men," Wewohquap, would administer the whipping in order to demonstrate that they did not condone the crime.

Afterward Lloyd, who appears to have been the harsher of the two judges, single-handedly ordered that Poh Poh Caquis "be banished to some remote part beyond the sea." The Indians were shocked by this cruel judgment, and old King Ababco, who had always tried very hard to get along with the whites, took the case to a hearing before the governor and council at St. Mary's. There he argued through an interpreter that many Indians, including himself, had been shot at by whites without anything being done about it. In any case, he said, the banishment was invalid because Judge Coursey had not concurred in it. The high tribunal agreed, and released Poh Poh Caquis into Ababco's custody with a stern lecture about the Indian leaders' responsibility for seeing that none of their tribesmen got drunk.

The irons were struck off the prisoner, and the old chief embraced him with joy and "greate Testimonys . . . of thankes and acknowledgement to his Lordship" for being so generous as not to send poor Poh Poh Caquis overseas or have him executed. Governor Calvert issued yet another of his futile proclamations forbidding the sale of "Brandy Rumm or other strong liquors" to the Indians. Like other such orders, it was widely ignored.

Such was the nature of crime and punishment in the days of Talbot's first Court House.

Meanwhile, other villages were growing up at strategic points around the county. Most prominent of these was Oxford, at a place near the mouth of what was then called Tread Haven Creek (with many variations in spelling), where there was a fine natural harbor deep enough for the shallow-draft oceangoing ships of the time.

Oxford was mentioned by name in Talbot records as early as 1669, and in 1671 was grandiosely described as "the city of Oxford" in a transaction involving the sale of two small houses. In 1670 it appeared on Augustine Hermann's celebrated map of Virginia and Maryland, the first Talbot town to be designated as such. By then it had at least one

Seal of the Port of Oxford

store, probably operated by John Edmondson and John Pitt, along with one or two taverns and some residences.

In the next several years it was a principal beneficiary, along with Doncaster or Wye-town and some points on the Chester which were then in Talbot County, of St. Mary's persistent efforts to pump life into Lord Baltimore's dream of creating on the English model a system of market towns and ports in Maryland.

The first of these came June 5, 1668, when Governor Charles Calvert ordered the erection of a number of ports around the colony for "unlading of goods and merchandizes out of shipps & boats & other vessells." Those in Talbot were to be at Chester Point in the Chester River and at Captain Robert Morris's land on Tred Avon Creek, possibly at the site of Ratcliffe Manor, for which Morris had secured a patent. However, when a second attempt was made in 1669, the place designated as a port for lower Talbot was almost certainly Oxford. It was described as "afore the Town Land in Truduven." William Stephens, Jr., who owned the land on which Oxford grew, had claimed in 1668 to have donated thirty acres to the Lord Proprietary "for the settling and building of a Towne...."

No discernible results came of this directive, nor of another in 1671 under which ports were to be located "at the land of Jonathan Sybery at the Mouth of Wye River (the site of Doncaster), at Corsica Creek, and at "Tredaven Creek in Choptank River." His Lordship's grand design was running into the facts of life in colonial Maryland: planters had no need for either ports nor market towns, since they could trade directly from their wharves with English ships.

Nevertheless, St. Mary's persisted. In November, 1683, came the fourth attempt in fifteen years to put the plan into effect. Under legislation voted by the assembly, "towns, ports and places of trade" were to be established in Talbot at four locations—near Tred Avon Creek (Oxford), in King's Creek (the site of Kingston), in Wye River (Doncaster), and at the fork in Chester River (upstream from the site of Chestertown). For the first time specific instructions were given for the appointment of comissioners, purchase of town sites, laying out of streets, lanes, alleys, provision for churches, chapels, market houses and other public buildings, and division into lots to be offered for sale.

It was under this law—although Oxford was not named and it applied equally to scores of other places in Maryland—that the town came officially into existence. On August 2, 1684, the appointed comissioners met, staked out the designated area into a hundred one-acre lots, formally named it Oxford, and assigned a number of the lots to purchasers.

But Oxford did not immediately spring into prosperity. Only thirty of the hundred lots were taken up in 1684, and many of them were forfeited when their buyers failed to build houses on them. For one reason or another, the whole business of surveying the town and laying out streets and lots had to be repeated in 1694 and again in 1707.

By that time the provincial government was in the midst of its twenty-year persistent effort to build Oxford into a true city, the Eastern Shore equivalent of Annapolis. In action after action, the General Assembly and the governor made it clear they expected—wrongly as it turned out—that Oxford would become not only the Eastern Shore's major port but also its business and political center. In fact it was Easton, not Oxford, which eventually became the Eastern Shore's "little capital," but that was to come about nearly a century later.

In 1694 came the first attempt to make Oxford the capital of the Eastern Shore. Then temporarily called Williamstadt in honor of the Dutch King William III of England, Oxford was designated along with the newly created capital of Annapolis as one of two official ports of entry for the entire province. Each was to have a collector and naval officer, who were required to live within the town limits. The captain of every ship entering Maryland waters was to report to one of these officials and show a certificate proving that all goods on board, with certain exceptions, had been manufactured in England, Scotland, Ireland, or Wales. Also, before departing, the captain was to pay the Lord Proprietary's duty on tobacco. First appointee as collector for Oxford was Thomas Collier, with William Aldern as deputy.

At the assembly session of May, 1695, instructions were issued to set aside "the Island at William Stadt" (an area at the eastern end of the Strand, then an island but now joined to the mainland) for "Publicke buildings as a Church, a Schoole, a Court House &c." Parish lines were to be redrawn to take the parish church away from St. Michael's and put it in Oxford. From that time on, the high sheriff of Talbot County was required to live in Oxford; evidently the legislators already had visions of making Oxford the county seat, as they tried unsuccessfully to do later. There was even a proposal that county commissioners, jurors, and

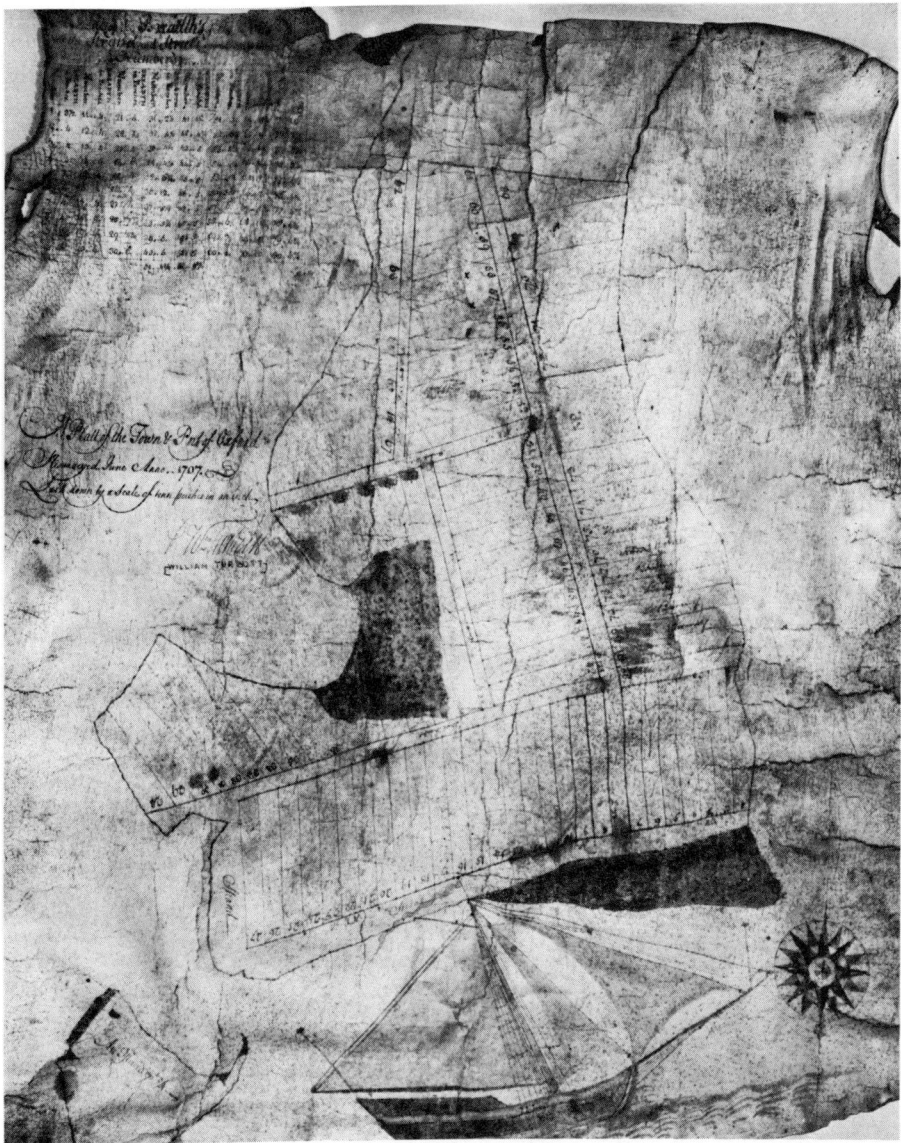

A plat of the Town of Oxford by William Turbutt, 1707.

other officials be chosen only from Oxford residents, but this was rejected because the town didn't have enough people. To boost population, merchants who brought their families to live in Oxford were granted special trading concessions in 1696 over merchants who lived outside the town limits.

Another indication of the town's special status in the eyes of the legislators came in acts of 1695 and 1704 regarding road markings, the primitive version of highway signs. In the 1695 act all roads leading to Annapolis and Oxford were to be cleared to a width of twenty feet and marked with four notches blazed on convenient trees; in the 1704 act the notches were to be replaced by the letters "A" for Annapolis and "W" for Williamstadt.

Almost none of this bold planning was ever accomplished. A school envisioned for Oxford in the 1695 act was never built; nor did the town become the seat of a parish until the nineteenth century. Throughout the colonial era it remained a part of St. Peter's Parish, with the church four miles away at Whitemarsh. In 1706 the waters over which Oxford's collectors had jurisdiction were sharply reduced when four new ports of entry were created. From then on the town had to vie with Chestertown, then called Newtown, as a center of Eastern Shore commerce. Oxford remained a busy little port almost until the Revolution, but it never did become a city. Its peak population, even in its most prosperous years, was never as much as the 749 persons who were residents in 1980. More likely it was nearer to Dr. Harrison's estimate of "two to three hundred."

Doncaster or Wye-town had a far briefer existence. A hamlet of sorts existed there as early as 1672, and in 1684 it was laid out into streets and lots in response to the same legislative act under which Oxford got started. Its site was at the point where the Wye East River meets Eastern Bay, on the mainland just south of what was then called Crouch's Island but is now Bruff's Island. The Lloyds, who owned most of the land in the area, were its principal promoters.

A town plat dated 1695, described by Dr. Henry Chandlee Forman in *Tidewater Maryland Architecture and Gardens*, shows a Roman Catholic chapel believed to have been sponsored by Henrietta Maria Lloyd, the Catholic wife of Philemon Lloyd. This apparently had been built at least two years earlier. The will of Mrs. Peter Sayer, who died in 1698, ordered a chapel to be built over the grave of her Roman Catholic husband; but whether this was to replace the earlier chapel or to be a second one is not clear.

By 1700 the little town had a tavernkeeper, Richard Bruff, and stocks and whipping post for the punishment of wrongdoers. In 1707 its backers sent a plat of "Donkester"—or at least the northern half of it—to Annapolis in support of their bid to make it the new county seat. This plat shows only four improved lots out of fifty, and Dr. Forman has estimated that "there were probably never more than a dozen buildings" in the town.

In later years Doncaster slowly faded into oblivion and was forgotten, except for a Lloyd-owned farm called Wyetown. However, relics recalling it have since been found—notably the gravestone of Francis Butler, high sheriff of Talbot, who drowned in 1689, and the foundation of a large structure, discovered in 1912, which contained a number of human bones.

As for York, its doom was sounded in 1706 when the assembly passed legislation creating Queen Anne's County from the northern half of Talbot. For York the change meant rapid decline; from being near the center of a large county, it was suddenly at the northern edge of a smaller one.

Obviously a new county seat would be needed, and a bitter debate arose over where it should be located. Edward Lloyd II, who by that time was president of the governor's council in Annapolis, favored Doncaster, very near his home at Wye House. He succeeded in getting the Council, which constituted the upper house of the Maryland General Assembly, to approve Doncaster as "the most proper and Convenient Place for the said Court House to be fixt." But the lower house did not agree; its delegates, especially those from the Western Shore, still hoped to make Oxford the Eastern Shore's dominant city. After considerable debate the House of Delegates voted April 1, 1707, "that the County Court House be erected and settled at Oxford." A conference committee, of which a majority was not from Talbot, voted for Oxford, and a bill making Oxford the new county seat became law April 15. Beginning August 19, 1707, sessions of the county court were held at Oxford, and plans were started for building a permanent court house there.

But the matter was far from settled. Residents of other sections of the county protested that Oxford was almost as hard to get to by land as York had been. They wanted a court house nearer the center of the county. Betty's Cove, the one-time site of the first Talbot Quaker meeting house, was proposed and even approved by the Lloyd-dominated governor's council. Then, apparently out of nowhere, support appeared for an entirely new site—an abandoned piece of worn-out tobacco land called Armstrong's Old Field in the middle of the county, where a road from the little port of Dover crossed the north fork of Tred Avon Creek by Pitt's Bridge in its wanderings northwestward through the county.

At this point the General Assembly decided to leave the question up to the voters of Talbot County. It ordered a primitive popularity poll to be conducted by the sheriff on the first Monday in April, 1709. Those who favored Oxford were to go there and be counted by a special three-judge panel. Those who preferred Pitt's Bridge were to appear there at the same time and be counted by a different panel of judges.

The result of this peculiar poll appears nowhere in the records, but apparently Oxford won out by a narrow margin. On October 29, 1709, the assembly voted one more time to establish the Court House at Oxford. In November agreement was reached with Daniel Sherwood and Nicholas Lowe to construct there a court house building, modeled on the newly completed one at Queenstown, at a cost of 120,000 pounds of tobacco.

However, dissension continued, and eventually Oxford's opponents won out. Under pressures of unknown origin, the House of Delegates reversed itself a year later, voting on October 31, 1710, in favor of Armstrong's Old Field. Shortly afterward, the governor's council assented. An act ordering the new Court House to be built "at or near a bridge called Pitt his Bridge at the head of Treadhaven Creek on Philemon Armstrong's land" was signed into law November 4, 1710, by Edward Lloyd, who was acting governor.

The two-acre tract finally selected was exactly where the present Court House stands. The justices first assembled there, in a house belonging to Philemon Hemsley, June 19, 1711. Hemsley received the contract to build the new structure. It was to be of brick, but considerably smaller than the York Court House—thirty feet by twenty, and only one-story high, with a back wing eighteen feet by twelve for the main courtroom. It also was a good deal cheaper, costing only 115,000 pounds of tobacco against York's 130,000. And the practice of renting the Court House to an innkeeper was abandoned; instead Henry Frith, who already had a tavern nearby for those who needed refreshment, was hired as caretaker at 800 pounds of tobacco per year.

The new court building was first occupied for a session of the county justices June 17, 1712, and the new gaol, which cost an extra fifty thousand pounds of tobacco, was completed late in 1713. So was born the place which became known as Talbot Court House, then the town of Talbot, and finally Easton.

As for York, it died swiftly and quietly once it was shorn of its status as county seat. The justices met there for the last time June 17, 1707. The Court House was ordered demolished in 1708 and the lead from the roof was sold to John Sherwood. The race track grew up in weeds; the stable tumbled down; the wharf at the water's edge rotted away. Today nothing but an occasional bit of ancient brick dug up by a farmer's plow remains to mark the spot where once stood Talbot County's first permanent court house.

FOUR

King Tobacco

"SMOKING is a custom loathsome to the eye, hateful to the nose, harmful to the brain, dangerous to the lungs."

So wrote King James I of England, anticipating by more than three centuries the Surgeon General of the United States. But His Majesty's subjects paid even less attention to the royal warning than many Americans do today to the strictures of the nation's chief health officer. Englishmen went mad over the "sot-weed" which Sir Walter Raleigh had first introduced from far-off Virginia. For every person who sided with King James, a dozen agreed with Robert Burton, who rhapsodized in his *Anatomy of Melancholy* (1621): "Tobacco, divine, rare, superexcellent tobacco which goes far beyond all the panaceas, ... a sovereign remedy for all diseases." Frenchmen, too, became tobacco smokers; they even liked the ranker, less fragrant variety called orinoco which was the best the Eastern Shore of Maryland could produce in competition with the sweet-smelling Virginia leaf. Most Talbot County tobacco was of this low-quality type and the English merchants who bought it promptly transshipped it to France.

To the early settlers tobacco was literally money—the common currency in which they traded as well as the only thing they could produce and sell for cash. They were utterly dependent on their annual tobacco crop for all the goods they had to buy from Britain—tools, cloth, furniture, kitchen utensils, spices, salt, gunpowder, nails, scissors, needles, thread, saddles and bridles, guns, knives, gloves, even shoes and stockings. None of these were produced in Maryland, nor could they be under the mercantile laws by which Britain fattened her own economy at the colonists' expense.

That was why the fate of early Talbot, like that of all Maryland, became tied to this single, nonconstructive, land-consuming crop. Tobacco could not be eaten, fed to hogs, burned for fuel, nor fashioned into anything of use; but it paid the bills and kept the family going. So tobacco was king, and every man its subject. For Talbot's first eight decades it was King Tobacco that held reign. It dictated the settler's life style, put his women and children to work, absorbed all his energies, and as often as not sent him to bankruptcy at best or to an early grave at worst.

Talbot's rise, in fact, was linked directly to fluctuations on the London tobacco market. Its fertile lands became available at a time when prices were high, seeming to foreshadow endless prosperity for those who dared uproot their lives in Britain and make the long leap over the Atlantic. Even the subsequent drop in tobacco prices which brought depression to most of Maryland in the late seventeenth century helped Talbot County at the expense of the Western Shore. New land, easy to clear and plant, promised better crops at lower cost than that in the older counties. By the hundreds, planters who had first settled in St. Mary's, Calvert, Anne Arundel, or Isle of Kent poured over to the Eastern Shore mainland to try their luck.

But tobacco was a cruel taskmaster. It required long and arduous hand labor, particularly in the hot and humid summer months. It gave an uncertain return; no planter knew when he shipped off his crop whether it would sell for enough to get him out of debt. Worst of all, it quickly exhausted the soil, so that new fields had constantly to be cleared and the old ones abandoned to grow up in weeds and brambles. Early county records are sprinkled with references to these exhausted tracts, called "So-and-So's Old Field." In colonial parlance that meant that the fields had once produced tobacco but now were good for nothing. "Armstrong's Old Field," where the first Court House on the the site of Easton was built, was one example; but there were many others.

The system of tobacco culture used in early Talbot was primitive and inefficient. Yet for many years no efforts were made to improve it. George Alsop, writing in 1666, described it:

> Between the months of March and April they sow the seed (which is much smaller than mustard-seed) in small patches, . . . and about May the plants commonly appear in those beds: In June they are transplanted from their beds and set in little hillocks in distant rowes, dug up for the same purpose; some twice or thrice they are weeded, and succored from their illegitimate Leaves that would be peeping out of the body of the Stalk. They top the several plants as they find occasion. . . . About the middle of September they cut the Tobacco down, and carry it into houses (made for that purpose) to bring it to its purity [cure it]. And after it has attained, by a convenient attendance upon time, to its perfection it is then tyed up in bundles, and packt into Hogsheads, and then laid (before) the Trade.

For the planter who had no servants or slaves—which included a majority of seventeenth century Talbot Countians—this meant constant

Tobacco barn at Clay's Hope, near Bellevue, on National Register of Historic Places.

attention and unremitting work. Everything else had to be neglected; the early planters worked at growing tobacco with such single-mindedness that laws were passed requiring them to plant at least two acres of corn along with their tobacco. Otherwise they might have starved to death while seeking to get rich; and even so in some years bread, flour, and other foodstuffs had to be imported from Pennsylvania, where grain and not tobacco was the major crop.

From June to September, every member of the family was put to work. While the men chopped at weeds with clumsy hoes—mere slabs of iron attached to sticks thick as a man's wrist—the women and children were kept busy nipping off the tops of the plants to ensure better middle-leaf growth, and plucking out the sucker shoots which appeared at the juncture of leaf and stalk. The bright green tobacco worms that feasted on the leaves also had to be removed by hand.

Proper curing was all important. The method followed in Talbot County had been devised in Virginia by John Rolfe, better known to history as the husband of Pocahontas. The cut tobacco was strung upon lines in open-sided barns, which were usually much bigger than the planters' houses, so that the early autumn air could dry it. When ready for market the great hogsheads, each containing four hundred or more pounds, were rolled to the planter's wharf or to the nearest port. For many years rolling the hogsheads was a task assigned to sailors from the English ships, who complained bitterly that it was work "unfit for Men" and that it had brought "many an able Sailor" to his death. Maryland had the reputation "of being one of the worst countries in the Universe for Sailors," they charged in a 1729 petition to the legislature for relief. The seamen were finally freed from this onerous duty by law in 1747, but that didn't end the rolling of tobacco; planters merely shifted it to their black slaves, who had no way to seek relief.

From earliest times those Talbot planters who could afford it began buying indentured servants to help with the heavy work and make it possible to produce larger tobacco crops. A few of the wealthiest men imported black slaves from Barbados or elsewhere in the West Indies; but in Talbot's first half century almost all the field hands and kitchen maids were white—English, Irish, or Scottish immigrants who hoped to "work out their time" and become independent planters in their own right. These were bought and sold in the same way as blacks, except that their value depended on how long they had yet to serve, whereas the blacks were slaves for life.

The extent to which white servants predominated over blacks in early Talbot can be seen from a study of estate inventories in the county between 1676 and 1707. Out of 141 heads of households tabulated, only 28 owned black slaves, and 13 of these had only one. By contrast, 61 had white servants. More than half, however, listed neither type. As late as 1704 Talbot County had only 460 black slaves in a total population of 4,230—little more than ten percent. Slavery in Talbot eventually became a major problem; but it was largely an eighteenth century development.

Until 1663 servants—including some blacks as well as whites—received fifty acres of free land when their time expired. At least five acres of this had to be "plantable" to make sure the freedmen weren't paid off entirely with land in the middle of a swamp. Their masters also were required to provide them with clothes, a hoe, axe, and a supply of corn to tide them over until they got started on their own. After 1663 the allotment of land was canceled, but the master's other obligations remained. By 1715 the award on termination of service, as spelled out in the law, was:

For men—one new hat, one new suit of kersey or broadcloth, a white linen shift, a pair of "French fall shoes," stockings, two hoes, a gun of twenty shillings value, a supply of ammunition, and three barrels of Indian corn.

For women—a waistcoat and petticoat of "new half-thick or Pennistone" (coarse woollen cloth), a new shift of white linen, shoes and stockings, a blue apron, two white linen caps, and three barrels of Indian corn.

Mingled with the servants who had come voluntarily were many convicts, the dregs of British prisons, who were hated and feared by the general populace. But there were also Scottish and Irish rebels whose only crime had been to oppose the English, and who were rounded up and deported from their homes after the uprisings of 1689, 1715, and 1745. These people were quickly assimilated into the pattern of Talbot County life.

The universal dependence on tobacco gave rise to a stock character—the "Maryland planter"—usually pictured in English writings as loud-mouthed, leathery-faced, ignorant, profane, and greedy. The type was certainly not unknown in Talbot. Such men were immortalized in 1708 in a satiric narrative poem by Ebenezer Cooke, and lampooned even more incisively in John Barth's modern novel, *The Sot-Weed Factor*, which embroiders on Cooke's verses. The poem and novel tell the story of an English "factor" (tobacco merchant), supposedly Cooke himself, who comes to Maryland in search of riches and winds up getting fleeced by an unscrupulous Quaker, hoodwinked by sharp lawyers, and generally taken in by the colonists he had hoped to outwit. Both are rewarding reading, especially as an antidote to the "romantic" view of colonial Talbot life. Barth's work has been called "the finest American novel," and Cooke's ribald portraits of Maryland characters still have bite after nearly three hundred years. The Eastern Shore Quaker he met was

> A Pious Conscientious Rogue
> As e'er woar Bonnet or a Brogue,
> Who neither Swore nor kept his Word
> But cheated in the Fear of God.

His planters might well have been Talbot Countians of the day:

> In Shirts and Drawers of Scotch-cloth blue.
> With neither Stockings, Hat, Nor Shooe.
> These Sot-weed Planters Crowd the Shoar,
> In Hue as tawny as a Moor;
> Figures so strange, no God design'd,
> To be a part of Humane Kind.

Cooke's lampoon was not far off the mark. Marylanders—and Talbot Countians were no better than the rest—were criticized by numerous other observers for their hard drinking, laziness, and crudity. Patrick Falconer, writing home to England in 1684, described them as "a Debauched, Idle Lasy People, all that they Labour for is only as much Bread as serves them for one Season, and as much Tobacco as may furnish them with Cloaths.... The Indian wheat (corn) is what they trust to, and if that fail them they may expect to starve."

Even the Calverts, who prospered from the ground rents and tobacco duties they collected from their Maryland colonists, had nothing but contempt for many of the planters. "If there be any that live in a poor manner, it is not from the low price of tobacco, but from their own sloth, ill husbandry, and profusely spending their crops in Brandewine, and other liquors," Caecilius Calvert wrote in the 1660s. Sixty-five years later his descendant, Governor Benedict Leonard Calvert, complained that the planters were "generally proud, petulant and Ignorant," and that their insistence on controlling their own affairs was "unnaturall" and "repugnant to the very End for which Government was Instituted."

Nor were these early Marylanders, except for minority sects such as the Quakers and Roman Catholics, much concerned with religion. The savage passions of the sixteenth and early seventeenth centuries had burned out, leaving them apathetic or even antichurch. Report after report sent back to England complained of godlessness and low moral standards. "The Lord's Day is profained; religion is despised, and all notorious vices are committed; so that it is become a Sodom of uncleanness, and a pest house of iniquity," the Reverend John Yeo wrote to the Anglican bishop of London in 1676. "No very good character can be given either of the Religion or Moralls of the people in generall, ... many of them having never been christened nor careing that their children should be, and very few of the rest ever coming to the sacrament," Governor Francis Nicholson wrote in 1698.

Before the Anglican Church was established as the tax-supported official religion in the 1690s, it did not have wide support in Talbot County. The Quakers had at least four meeting houses and the Roman Catholics, few in number but strong in wealth and prestige, had a chapel at Doncaster and perhaps others elsewhere. The Anglicans had only three small wooden churches: one at Hibernia near the future Centreville, one at St. Michaels, and one at Whitemarsh. There may have been a fourth, the chapel at Wye Mills, but its founding date is uncertain. The others all have claims to date from the 1670s or earlier.

Qualified Church of England clergymen were even fewer. James Clayland was acting as a minister at St. Michaels as early as 1673, when Andrew Skinner made a gift of fifty acres of land to be used for his support "during the tyme of his ministry"; but Clayland's credentials as well as his morals were later challenged by Governor Nicholson, who called him "scandalous and not qualified" in 1698 and asked the bishop of London to remove him. Nicholson also questioned the credentials of Joseph Leech, mentioned as a preacher at both St. Paul's and Whitemarsh.

Best known early Anglican rector in Talbot was the Reverend John Lillingston, who was active at least as early as 1681 and was rector at St. Paul's as well as the Wye chapel until his death in 1709. Though remembered for his participation in a wild spree at York Court House (see Chapter 3), Lillingston in the main was considered one of Maryland's most able clergymen. In 1704 he was recommended for the proposed (but never created) post of suffragan bishop, to supervise Anglican rectors throughout Maryland as the representative of the bishop of London. After his death the Maryland General Assembly voted his family his full salary for the year 1709 on a plea that they were left in need because of his "extensive and conspicuous" charities.

No other Protestant sect took root in early Talbot, although elsewhere in Maryland there were strong colonies of Presbyterians, Independents, and Anabaptists.

The Establishment Acts of the 1690s, growing out of the Glorious Revolution of 1689 which had put the Protestant William of Orange on the throne of England, brought drastic change to Talbot's religious makeup. The Church of England became the state church, and every Marylander, no matter what his private beliefs, henceforth was required by law to pay forty pounds of tobacco per year in support of the church and its ministers. This was the famous "40 per poll" which continued to cause bitter dissension throughout the eighteenth century even though it was reduced to thirty pounds in 1747.

Under an "Act for the Service of Almighty God and the Establishment of the Protestant Religion within this Province," passed May 10, 1692, Talbot County was to be laid out into three parishes: St. Paul's, largely in what is now Queen Anne's County; St. Michael's, in the center of present Talbot; and St. Peter's, in the southern half of the county but including Oxford.

These were in being by October, 1696. Each parish had a governing body of six vestrymen, who were to keep lists of all taxable persons and provide them to the sheriff. He was allowed five per cent for collecting the "40 per poll." The funds were in addition to all other taxes; they were to be used first for building and maintaining a church and chapel, and second for support of a minister, if the parish had one. The vestry were empowered to make additional levies if needed for construction or maintenance. As time passed the fees for the minister's support became known as his "living"; the number of taxables in a parish determined whether it was considered a "good" living or a poor one. Curiously, "taxables" included female slaves but not free women and children. By definition they were all free or servant males sixteen and over and both male and female slaves sixteen and over.

Left, Old Whitemarsh Church and, *right,* Rectory, photographed about 1890.

These early parishes were far more than mere church territories, as parishes are today. Each was a geographical and political entity, carefully bounded by law, and the vestry were civil officers with power to police the morals of persons in the parish. The 1692 act which created them reaffirmed the old Puritan moral standards first voted in the 1650s. Sunday work was forbidden, and strong punishment prescribed for Sunday drunkenness, swearing, gaming, and "other unlawful pastimes and debaucheries" which the law said were indulged in by "many wicked Lewd and disorderly people."

At the same time, the Act of Toleration was repealed. Harsh laws were soon passed restricting the activites of Roman Catholics, whom Governor Nicholson for one considered "professed enemyes" of the province. For most of the eighteenth century Catholics could not vote or hold office, build public churches or chapels, wear swords in public, or enjoy many other privileges open to those who were willing to take the "test oath" denying the supremacy of the Pope in Rome. At one point the death penalty was prescribed for Jesuit priests who attempted to convert non-Catholics. There were also some restrictions against Quakers; John Edmondson, for instance, was denied his seat as a Talbot delegate to the legislature in 1692 because he refused on religious grounds to take the oath of allegiance to Lord Baltimore. Five Talbot Quakers—William Berry, Howell Powell, John Pitt, Loveless Gorsuch, and Obedia Judkin—were fined five hundred pounds of tobacco each in 1673 for "Refusseing to Sarve in a Grand Jury." After 1702, however, Quakers were permitted to substitute simple affirmations for oaths in legal matters, and in general they fared much better than Roman Catholics. As for

Jews and other non-Christians, they could not vote in Maryland until the 1820s.

Using tobacco for money was not a very satisfactory system. Tobacco was bulky, and its value went up and down with every rise and fall in the London market. Quality varied greatly. Various obligations were paid with what was described as "good sound merchantable tobacco in cask" but actually was trash containing weeds, stems, and broken leaves. Talbot planters, especially the less devout and the non-Anglicans, became adept at paying off their church taxes in their worst tobacco and selling the good stuff overseas. The clergy complained bitterly that the junk they received could only be turned to a profit by trading it for rum, thus forcing them to help corrupt the morals of the very parishioners whose welfare they were supposed to oversee. They didn't get a lot of sympathy. Not until after 1747 was an official inspection system set up, with public warehouses at such ports as Oxford, Kingston, and Lloyd's Landing on the Choptank, Emerson's Landing (now Wye Landing), Doncaster, and the Broad Creek approach to St. Michaels, where tobacco could be examined to determine if its quality was as good as its producers said it was. By then King Tobacco's long reign in Talbot County was almost over.

Despite these drawbacks, tobacco remained the universal currency for almost a hundred years. Taxes and wages were paid in it; property was bought and sold in it; estates were evaluated in it; merchants dealt in it; even the bounties for wolves' and crows' heads which were a major item of expense to the early county government were paid in it. What it was worth in modern terms is difficult to define; a pound of tobacco in Maryland might be valued at anywhere from one to six English pence, depending on its quality and the price in England. Sometimes it was even less. When Richard Macklin bequeathed twenty thousand pounds of tobacco to St. Paul's Church in 1705, the vestry sold it to Richard Tilghman for fifty pounds sterling. That works out to only a little more than half a penny a pound. But as a general rule, translating tobacco into modern dollars and cents at the rate of two cents a pound is as good as any other. Thus a workman who received twenty pounds of tobacco a day, a common early wage, was earning about forty cents in modern terms. Of course, forty cents bought a lot more then than it does now.

Here and there, an occasional Talbot Countian made a fortune out of tobacco—but not by growing it. Those who became wealthy were almost invariably merchants trading in tobacco rather than planters producing it. They took in their neighbors' crops on consignment, shipped them to England, and from their well-stocked storehouses supplied the planters' needs on credit until payment for the tobacco was received. This might be called an early version of the company store: the planter was always in debt to the merchant, often for his crops of two or three years ahead. And the merchant "held always the whip hand," as Richard Bennett III, one of the greatest traders of his time, admitted, because of the planter's need for clothes, tools, and other items which had to be imported from England.

There were laws against excessive interest rates on loans and mortgages, but no controls over the prices charged by merchants or how much they allowed in credit for the tobacco they took in. Many deplored the system. Governor Benedict Leonard Calvert complained in 1729 that "tobacco Merchants, who deal in Consignments, get great Estates, run no risque, and Labour only with the pen; the Planter can scarcely get a living, runs all the risques, . . . and must work a Variety of Labour." But it remained in effect, at first under local merchants and later under "factors" employed as agents for the great British shipping firms, until the eve of the Revolution.

Prime examples of merchant-planters in Talbot County were the Lloyds. Although they became known for their vast holdings in land and slaves, they got their start primarily as traders dealing in the tobacco crops of others as well as their own. After his return to England about 1668, Edward Lloyd I handled the British end of the family business, while his son Philemon had charge of affairs in Maryland. The inventory of Philemon's estate at the time of his death in 1685 reveals that he was a merchant-trader on a very large scale. It also demonstrates the kind of goods Talbot Countians were importing at the time.

Included were almost no luxury items except some cloth of silk and other fine fabrics, and various spices such as cloves, pepper, mace, cinnamon, and nutmegs. Even the most affluent Talbot Countians had not yet risen to the luxury level. But Lloyd had for sale thousands of ells of cloth of all types: ozenbrig, Holland dock, Ficklenbergs, Portreys, canvas, linen, Scotch cloth, calico, fustian, red cotton, plain cotton, hair cloth, narrow and broad "blew" cloth, Dowlas, Lockram, dimity, fine serge, broadcloth, crepe, flannel, sheeting, and woolens, along with needles, thread, thimbles, buttons, silk laces, and plain and fancy ribbons.

Ready-made items included more than one hundred pairs of shoes; men's, women's and boys' wool and worsted stockings; Irish hose; children's bodices; girls' petticoats and other garments; frocks of diaper cloth (the word had a different meaning in the seventeenth century); a few crepe and silk gowns, and one Romole neck cloth with handkerchiefs to match. This last was a sign that English fashions were beginning to appear in Talbot; it was a scarf of thin silk, originally from Persia, which was highly prized by London ladies.

On hand in wholesale quantities was a vast array of household goods and tools: pewter bowls and dishes, brass candlesticks, iron pots, pot racks, trays, chests, beds complete with bolsters and rugs, blankets, frying pans, smoothing irons, candlewicks, combs of horn and ivory, paper in reams, soap in casks, and sealing wax; nails, dowels, padlocks, staples, hooks, hinges, latches, and swivels; adzes, augers, axes, knives, chisels, hammers, files, saws, and scissors; tobacco hilling hoes, fishing lines, spades, horse collars, bridles, bitts, girth webbs, and snaffles; imported salt, gunpowder, guns, and shot; grindstones and millstones, and two pairs of iron fetters, presumably for locking up malingerers. Almost the only locally produced items in which Lloyd dealt were fifty-five deer skins and a loft full of lumber of assorted sizes and types.

It added up to an impressive display, housed in various Wye House rooms and what was undoubtedly a large separate outside warehouse. The appraisers valued it at more than £400 sterling, an enormous sum for those days. The extent to which Lloyd dealt in credit is shown by the fact that of his total personal estate, appraised at £3,444 sterling, £333 was in bills of exchange on British firms and £1,197 in debts due him by his customers.

The average planter had no such advantages as Philemon Lloyd, who had started with ample capital and control of thousands of acres of land. Most Talbot planters were at the mercy not only of the tobacco buyer and the London market, but of the weather and their own human weaknesses. A planter who ordered too much from England, or whose crop failed, was in danger of losing his family's only means of support, the land on which his tobacco grew. Some great Talbot estates were built at least in part on mortgage foreclosures.

Bad weather was a constant threat. The hurricane of 1667 destroyed three-quarters of the tobacco crop with heavy rain, wind, and hail "as big as turkey eggs." In the bitter winter of 1694-95, cattle, hogs, and horses died by the thousands of starvation and exposure all over Maryland; the toll in Talbot County alone was 5,019 cattle and 7,151 swine.

The planters complained loudly and often, as farmers always have, that their livelihoods were being ruined by the weather, crop failures, insects, foreign affairs, high-priced help, and almost anything else that occurred to them. Consider the lament of a 1700 commentator at a time when the British and French were engaged in one of their innumerable wars:

> The planters have suffered extremely (during) this present war in the markets being shutt up, so that after the numerous hazards of unseasonable

weather, lack of plants, the ffly, the grounde worm, the horne wormes, (the tobacco) having been house burnt, frost bitten, the dangers of sea and our enemys, . . . (they) have had not near the value of their labour or expense . . . so that for many years last past, servants and slaves have proved burthensome to many masters, and helpt by hard labour to impoverish them.

But if plantation existence was crude and sometimes cruel, it had its compensations. The early settlers had planted great orchards of apple, pear, cherry, quince, and peach trees. The first peaches, tradition says, were set out by George Robins on the bank of the creek later called Peachblossom, and when they bloomed for the first time crowds of visitors came up the creek by log canoe to gaze at them in awe. By 1705 peaches were so plentiful that a traveler reported they were knocked down by the bushel to feed the hogs. He also said large amounts of liquor "not much inferior to Brandy" and "a great quantity of Brandy from sider" were distilled by the hard drinking Talbot planters.

Cattle, hogs, and horses for the most part roamed wild. The horses were small but wiry and strong; every Talbot Countian learned to ride as soon as he or she was big enough to climb aboard a horse. Racing long remained a favorite sport. Fox hunts, also popular, were rugged affairs over fields and woods, often extending for many miles and lasting several days. One was reported to have started near Queenstown and to have finished a week later near Lewes, Delaware, with the hunters stopping at a different plantation each night for an evening of drinking and gambling. Bearbaiting (while the bears lasted), bullbaiting, cock fighting, and other savage sports imported from England were other favorites.

Not all enjoyed the horse races, nor the moral laxity which often accompanied them. The Quakers in 1715 complained to the governor and council about the "drunkenness, fighting, whooping, hallowing, swearing, cursing, wrestling, horse racing, and abundance of wickedness and immoralities" that took place outside their yearly meetings on Tred Avon Creek and West River. An executive order was issued barring wrestling, horse racing, and the sale of liquor (except in licensed taverns) within two miles of a Quaker meeting; but in 1725 they were back again with the same complaint. This time penalties which included jail or fines were imposed.

Travel by log canoe, fitted up with a keel, two leg-of-mutton sails, and a jib, or by the small open sailing vessels called shallops, was universal. Sometimes the well-to-do traveled through sheltered waters in barges rowed by servants or slaves. Road travel was strictly on foot or by horseback; carts, wagons, carriages, and other horse-drawn vehicles were almost nonexistent before 1740. The first four-horse carriage ever seen in Talbot is said to have been imported from England by Nicholas Lowe, who lived at Anderton but did business in Oxford. The story goes that when it first appeared hooting boys and barking dogs chased it down the road, and that Lowe spent much of his own money improving the highway so that his wife, the widow of a wealthy Oxford merchant, could enjoy the ride.

Every man and boy was a hunter, more for the table than for sport. The native deer became almost extinct from overhunting, but there was plenty of small game, and myriads of ducks, geese, and swans to be gunned in winter. Once the planters put their minds to it, there was plenty of other food; vegetables of all sorts, meat, milk, butter, and cheese from cows, salt pork and smoked hams, fruit both cultivated and wild, nuts and berries, and, of course, corn cooked up in a variety of ways. Money might be scarce and debts piled high, but no one need starve.

Windmills for grinding corn into meal were scattered widely over Talbot County, and water-powered grist and saw mills soon appeared wherever there was a stream of sufficient size. Among those known to have been in existence by about 1700 were the Wye Mill, a mill on what is now called Mill Creek in northern Talbot, another on "the Freshes of St. Michaels River" (later Potts Mill), and Abbott's Mill, on a creek in Trappe District known like its larger sister as the St. Michaels or Miles. Most of these continued in operation down to recent times. Like Talbot's ghost towns, they are now forgotten; but as the county's first and most enduring industry, milling played a key role in the county's history.

Among Maryland counties, Talbot was at its zenith as the eighteenth century began. On the Western Shore the economy was faltering; answering questions from the British Lords of Trade in 1697, Governor Nicholson reported the colony's population was decreasing due to continued low tobacco prices, and that many planters "have been obliged to try their fortunes else where." He said "the most & best land" for tobacco culture had already been "cleared & worne out" so that the crops were shrinking year by year, and that the only other exports were "an inconsiderable quantity of ffurs and Sassafrax roots."

But this gloomy picture scarcely applied to the Eastern Shore, of which Talbot County was central. There, population had increased fivefold in forty years. Talbot in 1701 was the second most populous county in the province, behind only vast Somerset, which included all the region now divided into Somerset, Wicomico, and Worcester. Even after it was shorn of half its territory by the creation of Queen Anne's County in 1706-7, Talbot remained third in total population and second in the number of whites. The 1712 census gave it 4,178 people, of which 492 were blacks, compared with 4,999, of which more than 1,500 were blacks, in Anne Arundel. Somerset still led the province in total population with 5,662.

The entire Eastern Shore, although starting later, had developed much more rapidly than the older Western Shore. The two halves into which Maryland was divided by the bay were just about equal in wealth, population, and influence: in 1712, the six existing Eastern Shore counties had 22,108 persons to 22,709 for the same number of counties on the Western Shore.

It is not easy to envision today what Maryland looked like then—a string of settlements clinging closely to tidewater, stretched out like a pair of parentheses on either shore of the bay. Inland there were almost no white inhabitants; central and western Maryland were still Indian country. Baltimore city was an uninhabited cow pasture, and all of Baltimore County contained fewer than 3,000 people. The most thickly settled area in the province was Talbot County, even though it had no towns worthy of the name except Oxford.

Talbot also led the province in shipbuilding. A 1697 report listed at least eleven active yards in the county, and thirty-nine vessels which had been or were being built there. They ranged in size from a sloop of only four hogshead capacity to a full-sized ship of 450 tons under construction for English owners at Thomas Skillington's Tred Avon Creek shipyard.

Skillington's was probably the largest shipyard in the province, both in original construction and in refitting and repair. Its location at the mouth of Trippe Creek made it a convenient place for British vessels arriving at Oxford to put in for an overhaul. Legend says it also served as a repair yard for pirate ships, although in reality there were few if any of these on the Chesapeake at any time. The pirates were more active in Delaware Bay, then under jurisdiction of Pennsylvania; most notorious among them was the famous Captain Kidd, later hanged in England, who aroused great alarm when he appeared in Delaware Bay, reportedly with forty armed men and "a vast treasure," in the summer of 1699. Armed patrols had to be posted at the head of the Choptank and elsewhere to prevent British seamen from jumping ship at Oxford and running off to join the pirates, who paid much better than the English did. For defense against the pirates and the French privateers, who were considered just as bad, merchant ships traveled in convoys with heavily armed escorts. One of these, the *Elizabeth*, built at Skillington's shipyard for Gilbert Livesley of London, carried twenty-four guns and ninety-six fighting men.

Other Talbot shipbuilders around 1700 included Robert Graison, credited with constructing a 300-hogshead "pink" at Kingston and a 120-ton vessel on Miles River; Solomon Summers of Island Creek, who had built ships of 300 and 400 tons; Quakers William Dickinson, William Sharpe, and Ralph Fishbourne; Andrew Tonnard, active both on Island Creek and Porridge Creek; George Ferguson on Dividing (Trappe) Creek; William Whitaker on Tred Avon Creek, and Jeremiah Hookes.

In provincial affairs, Talbot men at the turn of the century played prominent roles. The second Edward Lloyd was speaker of the house, president of the senate, and major general of militia over a period of years. He served as de facto governor of Maryland from 1709 to 1714 in the absence of a royal appointee from England. His brother, the second Philemon, was secretary of the province. A Lloyd kinsman, Richard Bennett III, built Maryland's first great financial and shipping empire from his seat on Bennett's Point, just across the river from Wye House. Matthew Tilghman Ward, who lived at Rich Neck, was launched on a career which would make him president of the council, major general of militia, and the most influential native Marylander in provincial politics. Other families which would play dominant roles in colonial Maryland through the American Revolution—among them the Tilghmans, Goldsboroughs, and Hollydays—were well established on estates in Talbot County.

But perhaps the most influential Talbot Countian of them all was a woman—Henrietta Maria Lloyd, wife of Philemon Lloyd I, whom she survived by a dozen years. She was not only the wealthiest woman on the Eastern Shore but its acknowledged social leader and a capable business operator who managed the complex affairs of Wye House with skill and profit from the time of her husband's death in 1685 to her own death in 1697.

In many ways "Madam" Lloyd—the title was considered an honor then, the Maryland equivalent of "Lady" in England—was one of the most remarkable women Talbot County has ever known. She had wealth, beauty, charm, and power, but also pride and fierce independence of mind; and she founded such a prolific dynasty of descendants that she has with justice been called "the great ancestress of the Eastern Shore."

She bore twelve children by two husbands—two by Richard Bennett II, who was drowned while duck hunting in Wye River when she was barely twenty, and ten by Philemon Lloyd. Both Edward Lloyd II and Richard Bennett III were her sons; as mentioned earlier, one became governor of Maryland and the other its wealthiest business tycoon. Nearly all the others grew up to marry well and produce long and distinguished lines, which usually included a girl child named Henrietta Maria in her memory.

Nor was she noteworthy only as a mother. She was a staunch and outspoken Roman Catholic at a time when Papists were a despised minority in Maryland. She was so strong-minded about this that her husband found it necessary to write into his will that *his* ten children must be raised as Protestants, no matter what she did about the other two. How she managed a household with such a double religious standard is difficult to imagine. But she did it; Richard Bennett and his sister Susannah remained devout Roman Catholics all their lives, while their ten half brothers and sisters were loyal Anglicans. In her own will, she contributed land for the support of the Catholic chapel at Doncaster, and she aided the Romanist cause in other ways. As one historian put it, "she threw over the Roman Catholic priests the protection of her long social standing in Maryland. . . . No Archbishop . . . could have been more of a stay and prop to American Catholicism than this estimable woman."

Even under the threat of armed force, she was as cool as any man. In 1689 a ragtag army led by Richard Sweatnam, innkeeper at the York Court House, invaded Wye House in the name of the Protestant Reformation, claiming Madam Lloyd was storing arms and ammunition there which might be used by the Catholics and Indians in a counterrevolution. Henrietta Maria stood them off with calm courage, and later took Sweatnam to court and made him issue a public apology.

She dazzled Talbot's budding social circle with her imported wardrobe and her impeccable family background. Among the nouveau riche ladies who were just then beginning to think of themselves as aristocrats even though their husbands might have started as dirt farmers, she had no challengers.

Her personal "wearing clothes," checked over piece by piece after her death by a team of male appraisers, were amazing for a woman of her time and place. They included eleven gowns and petticoats, some of them of silk and satin; one mantle, three coats; three sets of stays; ten pairs of shoes; five pairs of silk stockings and numerous pairs of cotton and wool stockings; four headdresses, and numerous smaller items. For jewelry she owned a pearl necklace, a diamond ring, a gold ring, a mourning ring (about which more later), five other rings, several sets of earrings, and a cross on a pendant to signify her status as a Roman Catholic. She also possessed 322 ounces of silver plate, the colonial equivalent of money in the bank, valued at five shillings per ounce for a total of eighty pounds, ten shillings, but only two pounds, twelve shillings, and sixpence in cash. Her accoutrements included a riding gown

The graveyard at Wye House where ten generations of the Lloyd family are buried, including Henrietta Maria Lloyd.

and sidesaddle; for all her wealth, Henrietta Maria Lloyd had to ride to the chapel at Doncaster or to a neighbor's party on horseback if the weather was too rough for boating or Lloyd's Cove was frozen over.

Her family credentials were as impressive as her silks and jewels. Born Henrietta Maria Neale in Spain, she was the daughter of James Neale, a favorite of Caecilius Calvert and for more than twenty years his representative at various courts in Europe. Her mother, Ann Gill Neale, was said to have been a lady-in-waiting to Queen Henrietta Maria, wife of the luckless (and eventually headless) King Charles I of England; and according to tradition the Queen served as Henrietta's godmother. Whether this was fact or legend, she was undeniably named for the queen (as also, incidentally, was the province of Maryland). She proudly exhibited a ring bearing a death's head, a tiny portrait of King Charles, and the date of his execution by Cromwell's forces, which she said had been given her mother by the queen after the king's death as a token of gratitude for her loyalty. The ring still exists; handed down as an

Old Martingham, ancestral home of the Hambleton family. Earliest timbers in the house are said to date from the 1660s.

heirloom through numerous generations of her descendants, it is now a possession of the Maryland Historical Society in Baltimore.

Her gravestone also still exists, second only to her husband's as the most ancient in the time-honored Lloyd family graveyard at Wye House. Carved on it, still faintly visible, is her epitaph:

> HENRIETTA
> MARIA LLOYD
> Shee who now takes her rest within this tomb,
> Had Rachells face and Leas fruitful womb,
> Abigails wisdom, Lydeas faithful heart,
> With Marthas care and Marys better part.
> Who died the 21st day of May [Anno]
>   Dom. 1697 50 years —
>   months 23 days.
> to whose memory Richard Bennett dedicates this tomb.

FIVE

Golden Years

THE middle years of the eighteenth century have been called Talbot County's golden era, even its time of greatness. Romanticists later would look back on those years with warm nostalgia, picturing them as peopled with gentlemen of brilliance and ladies of charm and beauty who played at bowles, attended the races at Oxford and Talbot Court House, and danced and gambled at night in their handsome Georgian waterfront mansions, their every want filled by smiling, liveried servants.

This, of course, was not the reality; nothing could be. But in general it was a good period, perhaps the best, for Talbot. Life moved slowly in familiar patterns; class lines were firmly fixed; landed families prospered as never before nor since; Oxford reached and passed its colorful peak; and the county was awhirl with social activities of every sort.

Nevertheless, there was an underside to this society, and it was characterized by poverty and want, ignorance and disease, real suffering, especially for the landless poor and the helpless blacks. These conditions were accepted as a part of eighteenth century life; nowhere else in the colonies—or for that matter in England and Europe—was it different. It was the age of the aristocrat, whether titled or not, when those at the top closed in among themselves, and ruled by what they considered almost divine right. In Talbot County this was especially marked. Its aristocracy, built on land, slaves, and pride of birth, has been called "the purest in America." Its elite class controlled politics as they did everything else, and their social inferiors made no protest. Lloyds, Tilghmans, Hollydays, Goldsboroughs, and their kin were consistently chosen for public office, just as their ladies consistently decided who was "acceptable" in society and who was not. Wealth was not the key factor in this, although it helped; family was what counted most. This was the social pattern which would remain in Talbot—some say to its sorrow—long after the days of prosperity for the landed classes had passed.

With the establishment of Queen Anne's County, which became effective May 1, 1707, Talbot County's wandering borders took final shape. Before that there had been frequent changes. Creation of Dorchester County in 1668 had fixed Talbot's southern and southeastern boundaries permanently at the Choptank. In 1671 its area was further trimmed as Kent County was extended from the island to the mainland and given jurisdiction north of the Chester. Included in this reshuffle was Poplar Island, which was a part of Kent County from 1671 to 1696. Then Kent Island itself, along with Poplar, was given to Talbot County, and all of the present Queen Anne's County north of Corsica Creek and eastward from the head of its main eastern branch was made a part of Kent. The action of 1707 placed Kent Island in the new Queen Anne's County, to which it was naturally linked, and fixed the Talbot-Queen Anne's border at its present line. After that there would be no further changes; creation of Caroline County in 1774 from parts of Queen Anne's and Dorchester counties did not affect Talbot.

Near the center of this territory stood, in not very splendid isolation, the little brick Court House, completed in 1712, and a tiny cluster of taverns and houses which grew up around it. When court was in session this could be a fairly bustling place, but in other times it didn't amount to much. On maps it was marked with the name of Talbot Court House, which fit it neatly because almost nothing was there for many years except the Court House.

First order of business for the county commissioners who met there periodically was to take care of their own needs by granting Henry Frith a license to keep a tavern and fixing the prices he could charge. Next came orders for some roads and bridges so that people from remote parts of the county could get to the Court House. One was to run to Miles River Ferry (where Miles River Bridge is now located), crossing Tred Avon Creek's north fork by a bridge a few hundred yards south of the present Route 33 stoplight. Another, granted on petition of residents in northeastern Talbot November 17, 1713, was to run from Robert Grundy's mill on Tuckahoe Creek to Talbot Court House, roughly along the future route of Old Cordova Road. An already existing road wandered northwest across the county from the little port village of Dover on the Choptank and crossed the Tred Avon by Pitt's Bridge near the Court House. It acquired the name of Dover Road, not for Dover, Delaware, but for the village on the Choptank where it started.

Other tavern keepers soon joined Frith. Their customers on occasion created a ruckus by bowling in the street. In 1722 the county court found it necessary to issue an order "that the Publick Houses in this county are hindered (prohibited) from keeping their nine pins in the street during

Bowling balls from Wye House, circa 1778, are photographed on grass in front of an enlargement of an early nineteenth century woodcut showing a game of skittles (bowling) being played on a town street. Such games were forbidden in Easton in 1722 while court was in session.

the sitting of this Court, and that no persons whatsoever, are suffered to play at them during the Term aforesaid."

Like York before it, Talbot Court House soon acquired a race course. A clue to its location is found in a deed dated June 20, 1733, which described a lot as being "on the east side of the race ground" and "near the Court House." That would place it in the heart of today's downtown Easton.

On race days, this track drew thousands of spectators from all parts of the Eastern Shore. Racing, as mentioned earlier, had always been a favorite sport in Talbot, but it rose to fever pitch after Governor Samuel Ogle introduced blooded racing stock from England into Maryland in the 1740s. The *Maryland Gazette* reported in 1754 that on the day of a race for a prize of twenty pounds sterling at Talbot Court House, "upwards of a thousand" riding horses besides many carts and carriages were on the grounds and "a great many people" were present. Among them was Governor Horatio Sharpe, who had donated the twenty pounds sterling purse. In his honor a stage nearly sixty feet long and twenty feet across had been erected in the middle of the grounds, and from this primitive grandstand, said the *Gazette*, his excellency and favored guests could "view the horses quite around the track." Winner of the big race on the day's program was a horse owned by Hugh Rice, who lived at Fairview on Miles River Neck.

Except during race meetings and sessions of the courts, however, Talbot Court House had not much to boast about. Jeremiah Banning, born in 1733, later wrote that in his first boyhood memory of it, the county seat was "a trivial place, and only contained three tippling houses (taverns) and a taylor's shop." It remained a "trivial place," with only a few houses, artisans' shops, and taverns, until the 1780s.

More important to Talbot's economy in the eighteenth century was the port of Dover at the mouth of Barker Creek (originally called Robin Hood Creek) on the upper Choptank. First mentioned by name in the records in 1663, Dover soon afterward became the site of a ferry and boat landing established by John Barker. Through much of the following century it was Oxford's chief rival as a port of call for English vessels, and for an odd reason: the teredo or shipworm, a saltwater pest which devoured the hulls of wooden-bottomed oceangoing ships. After a long Atlantic crossing, vessels would put in at Oxford to report and unload cargo, then sail around the southern tip of Talbot and up the Choptank to Dover, where the water was sufficiently fresh to kill the worm. There they would stay for three or four months while a cargo of tobacco for the homeward voyage was being assembled.

From this circumstance, Dover developed into a trading center in its own right. At midcentury it had at least two large merchandizing establishments. In 1748 Anthony Bacon, brother of the Reverend Thomas Bacon of St. Peter's Parish and himself a major London merchant, established a partnership with James Dickinson to operate a "great store at Dover on Choptank." About the same time Robert Morris and J. Hamner, cofactors at Oxford for the Liverpool trading firm of Foster Cunliffe & Sons, set up a store at Dover which they operated apparently for their own profit. Eventually (see Chapter 7) Dover even challenged Talbot Court House for the right to be the Eastern Shore's "little capital" and the seat of its principal courts. When this bid failed and the tobacco trade died, Dover's demise was swift. Today nothing remains to mark it but the name of Dover Street in Easton, a few ancient gravestones, and a crumbling steamboat wharf.

One of the important county roads of the eighteenth century led from Oxford across to the parish church at Whitemarsh, and then on to Dover by a route not now easy to trace. This became a favorite thoroughfare for sailors traveling between the two ports. At the halfway point, a

An eerie tombstone at the site of the town of Dover, photographed in 1917 by the late James Clayland Mullikin, the author of the pamphlet, *Ghost Towns of Talbot County*.

few hundred yards west of the church, a tavern and village sprang up with the colorful name of Hole-in-the-Wall. Fanciful stories have been told about this name—that the tavern was so called because it had a hole in the wall through which smuggled goods could be passed in emergencies, and alternatively that common sailors peeked through the hole to watch ships' officers enjoying their food and drink. But the prosaic truth probably is that it was named for a famous London tavern of the eighteenth century which was a hangout for thieves and highway robbers. At any rate Talbot's Hole-in-the-Wall retained its name until the midnineteenth century, when postal officials unimaginatively retitled it Hambleton for a local politician.

By the middle of the eighteenth century Talbot's planters, many of whom were shifting from tobacco to wheat as their main cash crop, had greatly improved their financial status. As they acquired capital, they built bigger and better houses to replace the simple structures of half a century earlier.

Top, Ottwell, *bottom,* Compton.

Sometimes this was done by incorporating parts of the old house into a new and larger one. Compton, Ottwell, Fairview, Hampden, and Martingham are among many existing examples of this; although all claim seventeenth century origin, their main parts date from the eighteenth.

Sometimes more space for the family was achieved by keeping the old house and adding new and larger units at one end as needs dictated and finances permitted. These are called "telescope" or "spyglass" houses because their sections appear as if they could be folded into each other like the segments of a telescope. An example is the lovely house at Wye Landing, first occupied by the Emersons who had an eighteenth century store and warehouse there. Its oldest—and smallest—segment may date from as early as 1710; its middle section was probably built

Fairview, photographed about 1930.

around 1740; and its largest wing, on the right, was added in the 1780s. Other examples in Talbot are Plimhimmon, home of Tench Tilghman's family after his death, and Myrtle Grove, the Goldsborough family seat.

Occasionally an entirely new house was built, either on a new site or on the foundations of an old one, modeled on the handsome English Georgian country houses of the period. One such is Ratcliffe Manor, built between 1756 and 1762 by Henry Hollyday I from bricks and other materials fashioned on the premises. Tradition says many of the colonial Talbot houses were made of English bricks brought by ships as ballast, but all the evidence indicates this was not the case. The planters were capable of making their own bricks, if very little else.

As highways improved, land travel became more frequent. In the 1740s carts, wagons, gigs, and even heavy four-horse carriages appeared. Milady of fashion no longer had to ride sidesaddle, or mount a pillion behind a man, as the beautiful Quakeress from Somerset, Sarah Covington, had been doing at the turn of the century when both Edward and Philemon Lloyd fell in love with her at once. (Edward won out, and she succeeded Henrietta Maria Lloyd as mistress of Wye House.) Two-wheeled contraptions called "chairs" were in vogue for long trips; Dockery's livery stable at Chester Mill (Centreville) advertised in 1747 that for a modest fee "gentlemen may be furnished with a chair and horse and a man to attend on them for convenient travel between Chester Town and . . . Talbot Court House."

All of these new devices were imported. Talbot Countians still made almost no finished articles for their own use, a condition which would endure until the Revolution. As Banning recorded, in his youth "scarce a pair of shoes were made in Talbot County, or even in America.... Those for both whites and Negroes were imported.... Boots were very seldom seen except when imported, and used only by the rich and fashionable. There were no saddles made in the country, and very few imported, so that it was considered a great and expensive luxury to own one." Joseph Bruff, who set up shop as a gold and silversmith at Talbot Court House sometime before 1767, was one of only a very few skilled artisans in the county.

Nor were Talbot Countians noted for their bookishness, although there were a few fine private libraries. St. Michael's Church maintained a lending library for laymen, which included such meaty titles as Ashton's *Death Bed Repentance, Kind Cautions to Prophane Swearers,* and *Rebukes to the Sin of Uncleanness.* The Quakers had their own library at what by the middle of the eighteenth century was being called Third Haven Meeting House as general usage changed the name of Tred Avon (or Tread Haven) Creek to Third Haven Creek. The Quaker library was the county's oldest, having been founded in 1676 and augmented by a gift of books from George Fox himself in 1691. Robert Morris, Henry Callister, and the Reverend Thomas Bacon, all associated with Oxford but all educated in England, possessed large libraries for their own use, and Cunliffe's store at Oxford, managed by Morris and later by Callister, sold books on religious and maritime subjects.

But there were few if any other book dealers in colonial Talbot. Most residents who wanted reading matter had to send off to Philadelphia for it, and not many bothered. Of 1,283 Talbot estates examined in a survey of reading habits before the Revolution, nearly half did not have any books, and another fourteen percent had only a Bible. Only seventeen of the 1,283 had more than twenty books, according to the survey.

For that matter, many Talbot County men and even more women could not read or write. The county had no schools before 1728 except those maintained in private homes, usually by well educated but penniless indentured servants. A public school projected for Oxford in 1696 was never built.

The first organized institution for learning was the Talbot County Free School, launched in 1728 in a building on land near Betty's Cove, halfway between Talbot Court House and St. Michaels. This school had a long and distinguished career under the general direction of the rectors of St. Michael's and St. Peter's parishes. Eventually it reached the status of an academy, offering courses in Latin, Greek, and mathematics as well as simple reading, writing, and arithmetic. Only boys were accepted, of course; the idea of girls learning Latin and Greek or doing sums would have seemed not only a waste of time but ridiculous.

The names of only two of its many masters have come down to us. One was George Ewing, an Irishman and an indentured servant, who absconded in 1745 taking with him a Negro man named Nero and two geldings. The board of visitors offered a reward of five pounds sterling for his recapture, but there is no record that he was ever found. The other, more distinguished, was George Rule, master for a quarter of a century. When a lottery was proposed in 1764 to bail the school out of financial difficulties, the announcement said that thanks to its current master (Rule), it had "for many years, even under great disadvantages, been looked upon as perhaps the best and most frequented in the Province."

The Talbot County Free School lasted until revolutionary times. Eventually its building burned down, the property on which it stood was sold, and the proceeds of four hundred pounds sterling used to help found Washington College in Chestertown. Henceforth for many years Talbot again had no schools except private ones and a small school established by the Quakers for their own families.

Nevertheless, as early as the 1740s there were signs of cultural progress. Oxford even had a group of amateur musicians who met regularly to play the violin. Henry Callister, who had just arrived from the Isle of Man, joined them but had a low opinion of their talents. He wrote of Oxford in 1745 that "we abound in fiddlers, but most wretched ones they are.... They are content if they exceed the vulgar." As for the English tunes performed by his fellow Manxmen back home, he said, "they murther them here ten times worse than the county fiddlers in the Island."

John Adams, the acid-penned New Englander who became the second U. S. president, had an even lower opinion of Maryland's level of culture, especially as it applied to the colony's self-appointed aristocracy. During a 1777 stay in Baltimore, he wrote in his journal:

> The lands are cultivated, and all sorts of Trades are exercised, by Negroes, or by transported Convicts, which has occasioned the Planters and Farmers to assume the Title of Gentlemen.... They hold their Negroes and Convicts, that is all labouring People and Tradesmen, in such Contempt, that they think themselves a distinct order of Beings. Hence they never will suffer their Sons to labour, or learn any Trade, but they bring them up in Idleness or what is worse in Horse Racing, Cock fighting, and Card Playing.

Edward Lloyd V

But if Adam's sarcastic shoe fit, Talbot County's social dandies of the colonial era weren't aware of its pinch. Horse racing, cock fighting, card playing, and idleness were exactly what they enjoyed most.

Edward Lloyd V (1779-1834), who later became Maryland governor and U. S. senator, was so fond of cock fighting in his youth that he was nicknamed "Lord Cock-de-Doodle-Do" in a lampoon which appeared in an Easton newspaper. His father, Edward Lloyd IV (1744-1796), owned one of the greatest racing stables in America in pre-Revolutionary times. Lloyd's celebrated bay mare, Nancy Bywell, won the Annapolis Jockey Club's 100-guineas plate, richest race in Maryland, three times in a row, twice beating the famous Regulus, owned by William Fitzhugh of Virginia. Nancy Bywell's stamina was legendary; her 1773 victory over Regulus, when she was twelve years old, came in two straight four-mile heats.

Rivaling the race track at Talbot Court House was one at Oxford. Race days there were important social events. Matthew Tilghman wrote to his daughter, Mrs. Charles Carroll of Mount Clare in Baltimore, in 1771 that he had attended the Oxford races and that Governor and Mrs. Eden had been there. "Our ladies gazed, but except a very few did not approach," he reported. Three Talbot County men "had the pleasure of entertaining the grandees, and much bustle there was."

Persistent legend has it that the Reverend Dr. John Gordon, rector of St. Michael's Parish, enticed his wealthy parishioners to attend Sunday worship at the chapel-of-ease near his Miles River home by providing a race course to which they could repair as soon as the praying and preaching were finished. Unfortunately for legend, the story lacks proof.

Edward Lloyd IV and family, from the painting by Charles Willson Peale, 1771.

Many of Talbot's leading men of affairs were attorneys, judges, or legislators. They wore perukes (powdered wigs with pigtails) and knee breeches with wool, linen, or silk stockings. Those who could afford it acquired town houses in Annapolis, considered the "giddiest" capital in colonial America, and spent much of their time there, leaving plantation affairs in the hands of overseers. One such was Edward Lloyd IV, mentioned earlier. Almost as soon as he inherited his father's estate in 1770, he bought the unfinished three-story mansion in Annapolis which had been begun by Samuel Chase and completed it as his town residence. Now known as the Chase-Lloyd house, it is still an Annapolis showplace.

(Incidentally, it was in this house—though after the Revolution—that Lloyd's youngest daughter, Mary Tayloe Lloyd, was courted by a young law student named Francis Scott Key. According to family tradition, he wrote her love poems on scraps of paper, and she showed her scorn by using them as curl papers for her hair. But he persisted, and they were married January 19, 1802. Twelve years later he wrote a different kind of love poem—one to a flag in Baltimore harbor.)

Since most business was done on credit or in tobacco, "hard" money was scarce, although a bewildering variety of coinage floated around the county. British sterling was especially in demand. Most of it was squirrelled away in strong boxes and secret drawers, to be turned up only when a person died and an inventory was made of his estate. British coins included golden guineas worth twenty-one shillings, sovereigns or pounds worth twenty, and half sovereigns; silver crowns (five shillings), half crowns, florins (two shillings), shillings, and sixpence (half a shilling); and copper pence and half pennies.

By far the most common coins in use in Talbot County, however, were Spanish dollars, or pieces of eight, which came in assorted varieties: Seville dollars, Mexican dollars, Peruvian dollars, cross dollars, and pillar dollars, so called for the Pillars of Hercules depicted on the reverse. For the sake of making change these dollars could be divided into four pesetas or, more commonly, eight reals. The four peseta segments were pistaroons; the reals became known as "bits"—hence "two bits" was a quarter dollar. Another Spanish coin was the gold pistole, or doubloon, worth about sixteen shillings, nine pence.

Also in evidence was the old rix dollar, coined in several states of the Holy Roman Empire; the spread eagle dollar; and the "lion dollar" of Holland, which Marylanders called the dog dollar because the animal on it looked more like a dog than a lion. Most valuable coins in circulation in Talbot were Portuguese Johannas, called Jos for short, gold coins worth about £2 sterling. The moidore was another Portuguese goldpiece, valued at about 27 shillings. The French louis d'or, commonly called a livre, was equal to a British pound.

The problems such a multiplicity of coins engendered can be imagined. When a collection was taken up in St. Michael's Parish to aid sufferers from the great Boston fire of 1760, these contributions were received: seventy-two English guineas; 2 French double livres; 3½ Spanish pistoles; 2½ Portuguese Johannas; 119 Spanish pieces of eight; 4 Spanish pistareens; 18 English coppers; and unspecified amounts of English and Maryland paper money. Added up, all this came to £120 sterling—or so said the parish version of a certified public accountant. Parishioners probably took his word for it.

Although he lived in what after 1707 was Queen Anne's County, the death at midcentury of Richard Bennett III had profound effects on the future of Talbot County, and all of Maryland. He had spent a lifetime

Top, the orangerie at Wye House, considered a perfect example of eighteenth century design. *Bottom left*, the present Wye mansion, built about 1784. *Bottom right*, the Captain's House at Wye, circa 1661.

accumulating a vast fortune in land, slaves, shipping, and trade. His wealth at his death October 11, 1749, is impossible to estimate in modern terms, but it certainly would amount to many millions of dollars. The irrepressible Jeremiah Banning called him "poor Dick o' Wye, the richest man in North America," and the *Maryland Gazette* agreed. In his obituary the paper said "he was supposed to be the richest man on the continent." By the terms of his will, written just before his death, the childless Bennett bequeathed twenty-five thousand acres of land and numerous other valuable items to some 275 beneficiaries. More to the point, he named as his residual heir and chief beneficiary his nephew Edward Lloyd III of Talbot County. The will was challenged on grounds the eighty-two-year-old dying man had not known what he was doing, but upheld in court; and at one stroke Edward Lloyd, who was already wealthy, became himself the richest man in Maryland and possibly in North America.

From that time on the Lloyds of Talbot lived like English dukes on a baronial estate which covered almost fifty square miles in Cecil, Kent,

Top, Myrtle Grove has been in the Goldsborough family since it was built for Robert and Elizabeth Goldsborough in 1734 as a gift from his parents. It was partitioned from Ashby, the estate on which Robert Goldsborough settled in 1678 when he came to Maryland along with his brother, Nicholas, who located on property—Ottwell—near Oxford. The frame section at right is the original house. *Bottom,* entry hall at Myrtle Grove. The portrait at left by Charles Willson Peale is of Judge Robert Goldsborough, his wife, and two children when the brick section of the house was added in 1790.

The southeast parlor at Myrtle Grove

Queen Anne's, Talbot, and Dorchester counties. Their seat remained at Wye House, where they had a deer park in the English fashion and a handsome two-story heated greenhouse or *orangerie*, one of the few in colonial America, where exotic fruits such as oranges, lemons, and grapefruit—great rarities then outside the tropics—could be raised in winter. Edward Lloyd III, who died in 1770, paid taxes on 12,390 acres of land in Talbot County, 12,467 in Dorchester, 5,859 in Queen Anne's, 5,216 in Kent, and 360 in Cecil. Edward Lloyd IV, as we have seen, acquired a town house and a racing stable in Annapolis. Edward Lloyd V possessed more than five hundred slaves, and became one of the nation's greatest wheat farmers. Edward Lloyd VI (1798-1861) extended the family estates to large cotton plantations in Mississippi, Arkansas, and Louisiana. And Edward Lloyd VII (1825-1907) survived the disaster which Confederate defeat meant to the slaveholding classes and put the Lloyd lands back on a paying basis. Today the line if not the name lives on in Mrs. Morgan Schiller, born Elizabeth Key Lloyd, tenth of her family in succession to preside at Wye House.

By the time of Edward Lloyd III Talbot society as well as its political and economic life had become fixed in a pattern which would distinguish it for a century. At the top of the heap were the elite families—the

Tilghmans, Lloyds, Hollydays, Goldsboroughs, Chamberlaines, Haywards, and their relatives by blood or marriage. Most were descendants through one line or another of Henrietta Maria Lloyd, and cousins married cousins in an intricate pattern of relationships which served to bind them together every more closely.

As just one example, both Matthew Tilghman and his wife, Anna, nee Lloyd, were grandchildren of Henrietta Maria Lloyd, and hence first cousins. Their daughter Anna Maria Tilghman married *her* first cousin, Tench Tilghman, who on his father's side was Matthew Tilghman's nephew; and Tench's sister Henrietta or Hetty married Lloyd Tilghman, who was Matthew's son, her brother's brother-in-law, and her own cousin. If in Boston the Lowells spoke only to Cabots, and the Cabots only to God, in Talbot County it was the Lloyds and Tilghmans who spoke only to each other.

On the second level were the entrepreneurs, the movers-and-doers of Talbot society, men who had come from diverse backgrounds, drawn by a common interest in opportunity and profit. Few of these were Talbot natives: Robert Morris, Sr., the leading merchant of his time, was born in Liverpool; Henry Callister, who followed him at Oxford, and the Reverend Thomas Bacon, the leading intellectual among colonial Maryland clergymen, both came from the Isle of Man off England's west coast; Tench Francis, the attorney who was grandfather both to Tench Tilghman and Peggy Shippen, the Philadelphia belle who married Benedict Arnold, came to Talbot County as a boy from Dublin; Samuel and John Chamberlaine, leading Oxford merchants, were born at Sanghall on the River Dee in Cheshire.

Next below these were the mass of planters, men and women of small estate and lesser social position, who formed the bulk of colonial Talbot's landholders. The county may be noted for its great eighteenth century estates, but these—while conspicuous—were far fewer than the attention given them would indicate. Talbot plantations averaged only 329 acres in size in 1755, much smaller than the 472 acres of those in Anne Arundel. Many other white Talbot families possessed neither land nor slaves, but lived as tenants, servants, or overseers on the large plantations.

At the bottom of all others were the slaves, on whose labor the prosperity of everyone above them rested. Slavery had developed slowly in Talbot, but by the mid eighteenth century it was firmly established, and by the end of the revolutionary period nearly half of the county's population was black. The rise came more from natural increase than from direct imports from Africa; only a few large slave ships were ever recorded at the port of Oxford as unloading their cargoes in the county.

Most of the slaves who were imported came in small lots as deck cargo on vessels arriving from Barbados or other islands in the West Indies.

Although life for eighteenth century Talbot blacks was harsh, they undoubtedly were not as badly off as slaves on the sugar, rice, and indigo plantations in South Carolina and Georgia. Laws of the time were cruel and, unhappily, enforced with strict severity against slaves, convicts, and indentured servants but often winked at when the offenders belonged to the gentry. Under the Maryland code, any slave caught trying to escape could be shot with impunity. If a slave offered "any Violence to a Christian," no matter what the provocation, he was to be whipped for a first offense, branded for a second, and could be executed for a third. Arson, murder, robbery, and stealing of livestock all were punishable by death. Nor could blacks defend themselves against unfair accusations by whites by testifying to the circumstances; they had no legal rights whatever in court.

A classic example of the severity with which the "black code" was enforced in Talbot was reported in the *Maryland Gazette* June 14, 1745:

> Last week at Talbot County Court, a negro man was sentenced to have his right Hand cut off, to be hang'd, and then quarter'd, for the Murder of his Overseer, by stabbing him a few days before with a knife.

Under the law prescribing this sentence, which remained on the books until 1809, the man's mutilated remains were to be displayed on the Court House lawn as an example to other blacks. This was because, in the opinion of the legislature, "Negroes . . . have no Sense of Shame, or Apprehension of future Rewards or Punishments," and therefore mere hanging would not be a sufficient deterrent.

Ironically, if this was considered true, the fault lay not with the blacks but with their white masters. Few colonial Talbot Countians, or any other Marylanders, bothered to teach their slaves Christianity or to give them any other moral or religious training. It was widely believed that if slaves became Christians, they would demand their freedom under an ancient English dictum that only infidels, and never Christians, could be enslaved. When the Reverend Thomas Bacon pleaded with his St. Peter's parishioners to recognize that blacks were human beings with souls like whites, and to train them "in the knowledge and fear of Almighty God," he was regarded by many as a dangerous radical.

Outsiders looking at the Maryland slave system were as critical of its effects on whites as on blacks. The Duke de la Rochefoucault Liancourt, traveling on the Eastern Shore shortly before 1800, wrote that "in a country abounding in slaves, the whites do not apply much to labor.

Present-day remains of the slave quarters at The Wilderness, an early Talbot County estate on Island Creek.

Their ambition consists in buying Negroes; they buy them with the first sum of money they get, and when they have two of them they leave off working themselves . . . and their affairs are soon in a bad condition."

However, eighteenth century Talbot slave life did have certain compensations. Except on a few large estates such as that of the Lloyds, the pattern which developed was what is characterized as "domestic" rather than "plantation" slavery. Typically, a white family would own a black family, or at most two related ones. The whites would live in the large central house, the blacks in the kitchen or the "quarter," the universal term for a slave living area. Very seldom were slaves sold outside the family that owned them, and almost never outside of Maryland; they were regarded as too valuable both as workers and as status symbols. Most slaves were born, lived, and died on the same plantation. Thus Talbot County blacks, more than those farther south, developed loyalties to their own family groups, to the land which nurtured them, and often to the families of their white masters. If eighteenth century Talbot County slave life was hard and often cruel, it at least had the virtue of stability. A black knew where he lived, who his family was, and what he had to do to survive.

Throughout the late colonial period, a matter of deep concern to many Marylanders was the moral laxity of some members of the established Anglican clergy. While these were certainly not a majority, there were enough of them to rouse bitter resentment, especially among Roman Catholics, Quakers, "new light" dissenters, and the many nonbelievers, who had to pay taxes for their support no matter how debauched they were.

The problem stemmed from a fatal flaw in the Church of England's organization in Maryland. Under the system which remained in effect

The Reverend John Gordon, from a portrait by John Hesselius.

until the Revolution, only the Lords Baltimore could appoint ministers to Maryland parishes, and no one could remove or even discipline them once they were in office. The Lord Proprietary, the governor, the courts, the legislature, and even the bishop of London, who was titular head of churches in the colonies, all were powerless to act against a clergyman whose behavior was corrupt, immoral, drunken, or in any other way scandalous. And as years passed the later Lords Baltimore, dissolute men themselves, fell into the habit of sending to Maryland what has been described as "the refuse of the English clergy."

Luckily Talbot County suffered only briefly from this perennial problem. St. Michael's Parish in particular was fortunate: it had only two rectors during the entire period between 1708 and 1790, and both were men of high moral standards. The Reverend Henry Nichols (or Nicols), who served from 1708 to his death in 1749, was given high marks by his contemporaries. "(He) is very regular in his manner of life, and strict in the observation of the Rules of the Church," said one evaluation. Another, after his death, commented that "his life was exemplary, and Character unblameable, and well worthy of Imitation." The Reverend Dr. John Gordon, pastor from 1749 to 1790, was not only an ornament to the Anglican (and later Protestant Episcopal) church, but a patriot who

The Reverend Thomas Bacon, caricatured as "Signior Lardini" by Alexander Hamilton in his illustrated minutes as secretary of The Tuesday Club.

supported the American cause when few other Maryland clergymen were willing to do so.

A Scotsman with degrees from the University of Aberdeen and Oxford, Dr. Gordon arrived in Maryland in 1745 and served briefly as rector of St. Anne's Parish in Annapolis. There he became a founding member of the famous Tuesday Club, a society whose members met to sing, eat bacon and cheese, drink punch, smoke pipes, talk about contemporary politics, recite comic verses, and occasionally entertain their ladies with a ball at the State House. Dr. Gordon's nickname, bestowed by Dr. Alexander Hamilton, the club's leading spirit, was "Reverend Smoothum Sly." There he met the Reverend Thomas Bacon ("Signior Lardini") and Robert Morris ("Merry Makefun"), honorary members from Oxford. Later the three formed a club in Talbot which they called "The Eastern Shore Triumverate."

Although young Molly Tilghman, sister of Tench, complained in 1785 of his "slow croaking" as a preacher, Dr. Gordon played a strong role in community affairs. He headed the Board of Visitors of the Talbot County Free School, and in 1775 presided at meetings of the revolutionary Talbot Committee of Observation. In 1778 he took the controversial Oath of Fidelity to the State of Maryland. In 1783 he was one of the nine

Robert Morris, Sr.

Maryland clergymen who, under the leadership of the Reverend William Smith of Chestertown, signed a document which in effect established the Protestant Episcopal Church of America as a coequal partner with the older Church of England.

St. Peter's Parish, however, got a taste of one of the worst scoundrels in the history of the Maryland clergy. He was the Reverend Nathaniel Whittaker, who was sent to St. Peter's as curate (assistant pastor) when the Reverend Daniel Maynadier, who had been rector since 1713, became an invalid. The Reverend Maynadier, of French Huguenot background, had had his faults; he was described as "a Whig (antiroyalist) of the first rank, and reputedly a good liver, but a horrid preacher." But Whittaker was infinitely worse. Henry Callister called him "a brute of a parson." Governor Sharpe wrote to Lord Baltimore, who had sent Whittaker to Maryland, that "his sottishness and immoral Behavior had long since been considered as an intollerable Burthen" by his parishioners. In the vestry minutes of St. Peter's is a note that on April 4, 1743, the vestry adjourned to the house of the rector, (the Reverend Maynadier), in order to remonstrate against his continuing to employ the Reverend Whittaker, whom they characterized as "immoral and unworthy."

Eventually Whittaker was replaced as St. Peter's curate by the Reverend Thomas Bacon. But, far from being disciplined, he was actually promoted. Governor Bladen made him rector, not just curate, of Westminster Parish in Anne Arundel County. There he was soon in trouble again. The *Maryland Gazette* reported in 1749:

> We read that at a county court here the 9th of July of this year, a Mrs. S. C. of Patapsco, was fined the sum of one penny for whipping the Rev. Mr. N———l W———r with a hickory switch, it being imagined by the court that he well deserved it.

Still later, the Reverend Whittaker was given the rectorship of Coventry Parish in Somerset County despite the bitter protests of parishioners. He died there in disgrace—some say in jail—in 1766.

As for the Reverend Maynadier, he figures in a widely believed legend which holds that his wife, Hannah, died and was buried in the 1720s, then came to life when grave robbers tried to cut the rings off her fingers, and survived for many years afterward. No factual basis for this tale has been found; and it was never recorded until 1898, when it appeared in Prentiss Ingraham's *Land of Legendary Lore*.

The Reverend Thomas Bacon, who succeeded Whittaker as St. Peter's curate in 1745 and became rector in 1747 after Reverend Maynadier's death, was an entirely different sort of man than either of his predecessors. He was an intellectual, a scholar, a fine musician, and a sophisticate—too much so, in fact, for many of his parishioners. They resented his advanced ideas, especially on slavery, his closely reasoned sermons, which they couldn't always follow, and his free and easy style of living. Eventually he left the parish under a cloud after being haled into court and fined five thousand pounds of tobacco for marrying a young Talbot woman without observing the proper legal formalities of the Church of England. But he had a powerful impact on St. Peter's Parish and Talbot County.

For his part Bacon considered his parishioners sadly remiss in some respects—notably in their failure to teach Christianity to their slaves—and regarded many of his fellow Maryland clergymen with open scorn. "Infidelity (anti-Christian belief) has indeed arrived to an amazing and shocking growth in these parts," he wrote in 1750 to the secretary of the Society for Promoting the Gospel in Foreign Parts,

> and 'tis hard to say whether it is more owing to the ignorance of the common people, the fancied knowledge of such as have got a little smattering of learning, or the misconduct of too many of the clergy, especially in this province. Religion among us seems to wear the face of the country; partly moderately cultivated, the greater part wild and savage. . . . The misbehavior of some weak and (I wish I could not say) scandalous brethren lies open to the eyes and understanding of the meanest and most illiterate,

(and) furnishes the evil minded among them with a plausible objection to the truth of Christianity.

In his own life Bacon was no plaster saint. He drank, chewed tobacco, played cards, and enjoyed dancing parties. When it suited him, he was not above flouting the laws of both the church and the province. But he seems to have been motivated by a genuine desire to help his fellow men; his weaknesses were those of generosity and humanity, not of wickedness or evil.

Born about 1700 on the Isle of Man, Bacon was a mature man in his forties when he felt the call to enter the church. He had already published a scholarly volume entitled *A Complete System of Revenue in Ireland* while residing temporarily in Dublin. After much ecclesiastical study, he was ordained deacon September 23, 1744, and priest March 11, 1745, both times by his good friend Bishop Wilson of Sodor and Man, later bishop of Westminster. Soon after he came to Maryland as chaplain to Lord Baltimore, he became curate of St. Peter's and was inducted as rector in March, 1746-47.

As rector, Bacon delivered a series of controversial sermons on the duties of masters to their servants in which he reproached his hearers in strong terms for leaving their slaves in ignorance of Christianity. If they accepted as an article of faith that only Christians could be saved, he argued, then it was their duty as masters to see that "these poor people may receive their good things in heaven, since, it is plain, they cannot enjoy them upon earth." He also preached three sermons directly to blacks, telling them it was their duty to obey their masters and live Christian lives so that they could go to heaven. These sermons were published in England and sent to Anglican pastors throughout the colonies as a guide on how to deal with the question of slavery; but they aroused much resentment in Talbot County.

In 1750 Bacon took an even bolder step by announcing plans to start a charity working school in which poor children of both races would "be taught to read and write, and introduced to the knowledge and fear of the Lord." The instruction was to be free, but while whites would also receive free room and board, slaves were to be maintained at the expense of their masters. Whites were to be taught trades and sent out to apprenticeships, blacks to be trained as servants and plantation workers.

The idea attracted widespread support, including a substantial gift and an annual endowment from Lord and Lady Baltimore, and pledges of contributions from Virginia and the British Isles as well as from many prominent Marylanders.

There is evidence that the school may have opened in a small way as early as December, 1751. In October of that year the *Virginia Gazette* published a list of Virginia contributors and noted: "Said school is to be opened on the first day of December, next, in a small house, . . . and will be increased as soon as a proper building can be erected."

Whether this plan was carried out is not known, but a tract of 143 acres not far from Whitemarsh Church was purchased in February, 1753, and a two-story brick building constructed on it. According to Dr. Harrison, the school was formally opened in this building in May, 1755.

Unfortunately, it did not last long. Many of the subscribers failed to meet their pledges, and by the time the building was up, the sponsors had exhausted their funds, according to a letter from Governor Sharpe to Cecil Calvert dated May 23, 1760. "I think within two or three years after my Arrival in the Province (in 1753) there was no money left to maintain the Boys or pay the Master," Sharpe said. Sharpe also told Calvert in this letter that Lord Baltimore's agent in Maryland, Talbot's Edward Lloyd, had long since quit paying the twenty-five pounds a year pledged in the name of his Lordship and Lady.

Nor is it clear whether any blacks ever actually were trained at the school. Talbot slave owners were not enthusiastic about letting their blacks learn to read and write, especially if the masters had to pay their board bills. Early in 1754, therefore, Bishop Wilson wrote to Bacon suggesting that a fifty pound gift from an anonymous donor for the instruction of the blacks "be laid out in the purchasing a boy and a girl, who may be taught, and make useful servants for the school." But there is no inkling as to whether this was done.

In any case, by the time the school was opened in the new building, personal problems were absorbing much of Bacon's attention. His wife died in 1755, and his only son (he had three daughters) was drowned at sea in 1756. He was publicly charged with a morals offense by one Rachel Beck, and when found innocent, took her to court in a civil suit for slander. Miss Beck, described as a mulatto, was found guilty of spreading false rumors, fined one hundred pounds sterling, and jailed when she proved unable to pay. But the gossipers who had long plagued Bacon had a field day.

Meanwhile, Bacon had met Elizabeth Bozman, who eventually became his second wife, but at that time was a woman with personal problems of her own. As the sheltered daughter of Thomas and Mary Lowe Bozman, Miss Bozman was being courted by a handsome newcomer from England, the Reverend John Belchier. Belchier's smooth talk, polite manners, and "great good humor and modesty" made him welcome among the best families of Talbot; but in fact he was a fortune hunter who had left the parish of Barton in Norfolkshire hastily under scandalous circumstances. He soon won Miss Bozman's love, and she agreed to marry him; but for reasons he did not make clear, Belchier wanted the marriage kept secret. Bacon obligingly agreed, and performed the ceremony on December 10, 1755, apparently without the consent of Elizabeth's parents and certainly without legally publishing the banns or getting an official marriage license.

Disaster followed in short order. Belchier squandered Elizabeth's money and otherwise treated her shamefully; and in Philadelphia, where they had gone to obtain a ship for London, she learned to her horror that he already had a wife in England. She immediately left him and eventually reached home. There she was the object of pity and ridicule until the widowed Bacon, who was twice her age, married her himself, again without publishing the banns or obtaining a proper license.

Now the gossip mongers really had something to work on. On information supplied by Archibald McCallum, who was to receive half of any fine involved, Bacon was indicted, publicly tried, and convicted of "having privately contracted marriage with a certain Elizabeth Belchier, alias Bozman without having first made publication of his intent to marry at some church or chapel of ease, &c." He was ordered to pay a fine of 5,000 pounds of tobacco, but refused. McCallum then sued in civil court for his half of the fine, and won. Bacon had to pay not only the original 5,000 pounds but an additional 258 pounds of tobacco, and sixpence in cash, in damages. He was also indicted for the original "crime" of having married Belchier and Miss Bozman illegally, but the case was never tried.

In the gloomiest of moods, he lived on for a time in the house he had built at Dover in 1748 (although Oxford now proudly claims him, Bacon lived there only briefly; most of his thirteen years in Talbot were spent at Dover on the far side of the county). It was the lowest period of his life. Elizabeth had given birth to a daughter, increasing the family's needs; but, he wrote in a begging letter to Henry Callister, he had neither money nor credit to pay his bills, nor even a spade with which to dig a garden or seeds to sow in it if he did. He felt he had been deserted by almost all his friends. Even the music he had once enjoyed so much had "departed and gone into another world from me." He pleaded with Callister to send him a spade, some seeds, a cheese, and a bushel of salt so that his beef would not spoil. Also the latest news, if it was good, but "if bad keep it to your self for I have had no other for some time past and begin to be heartily tired of it."

Clearly it was time for him to leave Talbot County, and soon afterward he did. His last recorded appearance as preacher at Whitemarsh Church was on Easter Monday, March 27, 1758, and his last meeting with the St. Peter's vestry was May 27 of that year. Although he continued for some time to be rector of record at St. Peter's, his curate, the Reverend Thomas Thornton, actually performed the duties and collected the fees. Bacon was made rector of All Saints' Parish in Frederick County, and held this post until his death May 24, 1768. His monumental one-thousand-page work, *Laws of Maryland*, much of which he had compiled at Dover, was published in 1765.

As for the school for which he had held such high hopes, it apparently continued to operate for awhile, but as a pay rather than a charity school. And no more was heard about teaching blacks to read. At the request of its trustees, the Maryland General Assembly in 1789 transferred the then-unused land and buildings to the county for establishment of a poorhouse. Long used for this purpose, the main building survived until recent times, and its site is memorialized in what is now called Alms House Road.

One tangible monument to Bacon's memory remains in Talbot. The large brick addition to Whitemarsh Church, ruins of which are still visible off Route 50 south of Easton, was made necessary by the crowds Bacon drew with his brilliant and controversial sermons. It was completed in 1750, and served the parish—although sporadically in its later years—until it burned in 1897.

Aside from Thomas Bacon, by far the most interesting and impressive figure in pre-Revolutionary Talbot County was Robert Morris, Sr., father of the Robert Morris who gained fame—and lost a fortune—as "the financier of the Revolution." The younger Morris was in Oxford only briefly as a boy; but his father lived and prospered there for twelve eventful years, from 1738 until his tragic death by accident in 1750.

In his time Morris dominated the economic life not only of Oxford but of the entire Chesapeake Bay mercantile community. He was said to be "the most accomplished factor (without exception) of all Maryland." He was chiefly responsible for the 1747 tobacco inspection law which finally curbed long abuses in the sale and exchange of trash tobacco, and the switch from tobacco to real money as the means of keeping accounts and doing business.

Among other things, he was a superb natural salesman whose vibrant and domineering personality overwhelmed all who opposed him. Jeremiah Banning wrote of him:

> His great natural abilities o'erleaped every other deficiency. As a mercantile genius, twas thought he had not his equal in this land. As a companion and bon vivant, he was incomparable. If he had any public point to carry he defeated all opposition.... He was a steady sincere and warm friend ... and

The Charity Working School, founded by the Reverend Thomas Bacon, which later became the Talbot County Alms House.

had a hand ever open to relieve real distress. At repartee, he bore down all before him.

However, Banning also noted certain flaws in Morris's character: "a haughty and overbearing carriage, perhaps a too vindictive spirit, and ... an extreme severity to his servants." It was not uncommon in those days, Banning recalled, for people "of the first class" to get together and boast of new and ingenious ways of whipping Negroes. "And I am sorry to say," he added, "that the ladies would too often mingle in the like conversation, and seem to enjoy it."

Almost nothing is known of Morris's background except what he recorded in his will—that he was "the son of Andrew Morris, mariner, and Maudlin, his wife," of Liverpool. Banning noted that Morris had little schooling and was trained as a nail maker. If so, Morris certainly added to his education by reading, for at his death he had one of the better libraries in Maryland: 183 titles covering such diverse fields as philosophy, law, the classics, languages, history, biography, travel, the arts, science, medicine, literature, and religion.

Morris's years in Oxford coincided with the town's peak period as a port and trading center. He arrived about 1738 as chief factor for the great Liverpool trading firm of Messrs. Foster Cunliffe & Sons. It was a time when, again to quote Banning, "Oxford's streets and strand were ... covered by busy crowds, ushering in commerce from almost every quarter of the globe," and seven or eight large ships at once were often seen in the harbor.

Morris lived and had his warehouse at Oxford's principal corner. His home was in a building of which a small part survives in the inn bearing his name. From this headquarters he had general charge of all of Cunliffe's Eastern Shore operations, which included stores at Cambridge, Head of Wye (probably south of Queenstown), Newtown (Chestertown), and Townside (Crumpton on the Chester) as well as the main one at Oxford. He dealt in a great variety of products, buying not only tobacco but also wheat, corn, wood products, sassafras bark, meat, poultry and furs for shipment to Britain or the West Indies, and selling, in addition to manufactured goods and books, wine from Madeira and the Canary Islands, salt, molasses, fruit, and rum from the West Indies, black slaves from Barbados, and white indentured servants and convicts, principally from Scotland and Ireland.

The tragic accident which took his life came in July, 1750, when he was just thirty-nine years old and at the height of his career. Morris had been aboard the *Liverpool Merchant*, which had just reached harbor, welcoming Captain Samuel Matthews and, as was the custom, hoisting a few toasts to congratulate the captain on his successful voyage. With James Dickinson, he climbed into a small boat to go ashore, and the captain made preparations to salute Morris by firing the ship's guns. Something went wrong; the guns were fired when the boat was only about twenty yards away; and a piece of wadding struck Morris's right arm, breaking it above the elbow and inflicting a large and ugly wound. The wound became infected, and Morris died six days later, July 12, 1750. He was buried at Whitemarsh Church, where his reconstructed gravestone can be seen today.

Banning, who may have been an eyewitness as a youth of seventeen, maintained afterward that the premature firing was caused by a fly which lit on Captain Matthews's nose. When he reached up and brushed it off vigorously, his crewmen mistook the gesture as a signal to light the powder in the ship's guns. Banning also declared that Morris's faithful spaniel, Tray, refused to leave his master's bedside, and died there shortly after Morris did.

It was probably just as well for Morris's peace of mind that he did not live to see what happened to the little empire he had been building on Chesapeake Bay around the tobacco trade. Within a few years after his death the long reign of King Tobacco as Talbot's chief crop was over,

Henry Hollyday I, who built Ratcliffe Manor, and his wife, Anna Maria (Robins) Hollyday. From portraits circa 1760 by John Hesselius.

and Oxford was beginning its slow slide into oblivion. Many factors contributed to Oxford's decline—the rise of Baltimore as a port, the development of larger ships which could not moor in Oxford's shallow harbor, the shipworm, the disruptions in commerce caused by the French-English wars—but there is no doubt that decreased production of tobacco was a principal cause.

By the 1750s Talbot planters in large numbers were turning to wheat as their principal crop, along with greater quantities of rye, barley, oats, buckwheat, peas, and beans. Tobacco was still planted, but on fewer acres; low prices, poor quality, and soil depletion made it a losing proposition both for the planters and the merchants who traded with them. By the late 1750s it was no longer a major factor in the county's economy; an inventory taken in the fall of 1756 by Callister, who had succeeded Morris as the Cunliffe firm's chief Oxford agent, showed 3,436 bushels of wheat in the granary and only 7 hogsheads of tobacco in the warehouse. Soon afterward Cunliffe closed down its Oxford operation and went out of the Eastern Shore tobacco business altogether. Callister, who bought the company's store and plantation at Townside in Queen Anne's County, lost £2,000 sterling on the deal, and died in 1765 a broken and embittered man. By 1776 Talbot's agriculturists no longer even called themselves planters, a word associated with tobacco; they were now "farmers" and their plantations had become "farms."

The embargo on trade with Britain which launched the Revolution delivered the coup de grâce to Oxford; the last British ship ever to anchor in the town's harbor departed in the winter of 1775-76. But

Oxford's downfall had been signalled long before that. It had risen on the shoulders of King Tobacco, and it fell when King Tobacco died.

Although the climactic Anglo-French wars of the midcentury decided the course of empire in America, in Talbot County, far from the scenes of action, they produced more smoke than fire. There was a good deal of grumbling about taxes—including a special tax on bachelors administered by the Anglican vestry—and a hue and cry against the Roman Catholics, slaves, and Indians, who supposedly were plotting together to revolt and take over Maryland in the name of France. But Talbot Countians showed little enthusiasm for actually marching off to Canada to fight the French, or even for defending the settlers in western Maryland against French-inspired Indian raids.

When Governor Ogle called for Maryland volunteers in what was known as King George's War (1744-1748), few Talbot men responded. Callister, who helped with the recruiting, estimated that not more than twenty out of three hundred who signed up were "Natives or country born." Nearly all were sailors, drifters, or recent immigrants from Britain. Again, in what in this country was called the French and Indian War (1756-1763), Talbot's militia showed themselves less than eager to die on what seemed to them to be foreign (i.e., non-Eastern Shore) soil. Militiamen from the area ordered to the defense of Fort Frederick in western Maryland in 1758 flatly refused to obey their officers' commands.

One Talbot company of forty-five men did march as far as the present site of Claiborne on February 15, 1758, on their way to the Western Shore, but high winds and low tides kept them from embarking for two weeks. When they finally did sail, a gale blew them ashore at Chester on Kent Island. There they decided they'd had enough; complaining of frost-bitten toes, ears, and fingers, they disbanded and headed home.

The major incident of the war as far as Talbot County was concerned was the arrival at Oxford late in 1755 of a boatload of French Catholic refugees from the Nova Scotian province of Acadia. They had been systematically uprooted from their homes by the British army and, with thousands of others, were being distributed in the American colonies with no provision for their food or shelter. On the morning of December 8, 181 men, women, and children were dumped unceremoniously on the dock; the master of the sloop which had brought them announced he had no food to give them, and sailed away.

Many Talbot Countians greeted them with open hostility, or at the best cold indifference. Talbot County was not notable for its generosity toward its own poor. The Acadians were penniless and hungry; in a land of English-speaking Protestants, they were French-speaking Catholics, defiantly anti-British, as alien as if they had come from another planet.

Yet they couldn't be left to starve. Hasty relief efforts were organized with Callister and Bacon, themselves outsiders not long out of England, taking the lead. Callister advanced food and clothing out of the stocks of his Oxford store, expecting—vainly, as it turned out—to be repaid by the Maryland legislature. Bacon preached a sermon in their behalf at Whitemarsh Church the next Sunday, but it was a failure; his own contribution, he reported, was three times as large as that of the entire congregation combined. Colonel Edward Lloyd III argued that they should be jailed as enemy aliens, but reluctantly ordered his Oxford agent to contribute five pounds a week in subsistence money "in order to prevent their starving or being too heavy a burden on the town of Oxford." Under protest, he also took in a number of them at Wye House, and other Talbot and Queen Anne's countians opened their doors. Eventually shelter was found for every family.

The Acadians remained in Talbot County for several years. Local hostility did not subside. When some applied for poor relief because they could not find jobs and the Maryland legislature would not provide any funds for them, they were called "pests" and "beggars" and petitions were circulated demanding they be forcibly removed. Within a decade, however, most of them made their way to French Catholic Louisiana, where their descendants still live as the famous "Cajuns" (short for Acadians) of the bayou country.

One side effect was yet another burst of anti-Catholic feeling among the Protestants who predominated on the Eastern Shore. In September, 1756, Father James Beadnell, a Jesuit priest, was arrested on charges of "officiating mass" in the homes of David Jones at Easton Landing and Thomas Browning on Island Creek Neck, and trying to "seduce" Rachel McManus, a Talbot Quakeress, into the Church of Rome. He was not tried, but soon left for the Western Shore. For a number of years the only Roman Catholic priest in the area appears to have been Father John Lewis, who covered the entire Eastern Shore from Bohemia in Cecil County.

Then Father Joseph Mosley, another Jesuit, established a mission on a farm near the present Cordova in 1765, the first Roman Catholic structure in Talbot County since the chapel at Doncaster at the turn of the century. To get around the law which forbade public Catholic masses, he built a brick house and chapel under one roof so that his masses were given in what was ostensibly his private home. Such was the foundation of St. Joseph's Church, still flourishing, and now the oldest Roman Catholic Church on the Eastern Shore.

Hampden, on Island Creek. Most of the house dates from the eighteenth century, but tradition says the first white child in Talbot County, Hannah Martin, was born in the oldest portion, circa 1662.

By 1763 the French and Indian War was over; Britain had won control of eastern North America, and a young Virginia colonel named George Washington had emerged as a hero. Talbot settled back into its time-honored complacency.

But a far more important clash of historic forces was in the offing. Soon Talbot Countians would have to choose between their deep-rooted loyalty to Mother England and their economic interests as Americans. It would be a decision as difficult—and to many families as agonizing—as the more familiar one which split Talbot into warring camps in 1861.

SIX

The Revolution

FOR Talbot County, the American Revolution began November 25, 1765—almost ten full years before the "shot heard round the world" was fired at Lexington, Massachusetts.

On that day the county's freemen gathered at Talbot Court House, hanged a wooden effigy of a British tax informer from a gibbet twenty feet high, and pledged themselves, "at the risk of their lives and fortunes," to take whatever lawful action should prove necessary to preserve their ancient liberties against arbitrary taxation by the British Parliament.

Although they did not know it then, they had set their steps on a road that would lead inevitably to revolution, war, and independence.

Their target at the time was a limited one: the hated Stamp Act, voted the previous March by Parliament, which required that legal documents of all sorts must be inscribed on special stamped paper which could be bought only from agents of the British crown. Parliament said it was a routine revenue-producing measure; but the American colonists said it was a tax—and that taxes could not be imposed on them by Parliament because they had no representation there.

The money involved was unimportant. What was at stake was the fundamental issue out of which would grow the Revolution: whether Americans were freeborn citizens with all the rights of Englishmen, or whether they were mere puppets of Parliament and the crown.

As the Talbot Countians met, this question had the whole country in ferment. Already there had been a near lynching at Oxford, and everyone in the county was buzzing about it.

When the ship *Layton*, with Captain Jeremiah Banning in command, arrived at Oxford August 18, it had been besieged by a mob of aroused citizens. They demanded to know if it was true, as they had heard, that one of the ship's passengers was Zachariah Hood, who had been commissioned as stamp distributor for Maryland. Captain Banning admitted Hood was aboard, but said he had not known the man's identity when he sailed, or he never would have let him board the ship.

The Tavern of the Seven Stars was operated on this site as early as 1744 by Josiah Coleman. It was likely one of the places to which Talbot's freemen retired in 1765 to toast King George after protesting the Stamp Act. This building, at the corner of Washington and Glenwood in Easton, at one time housed the tavern. It was acquired in 1983 by the Talbot County Historical Society.

There were shouts of "Hang him! Hang him!" as the crowd surged forward. In Banning's succinct words, "Mr. Hood was threatened with immediate destruction." However, in the melee Hood escaped, and made his way to Annapolis.

There he received an equally angry reception. He was burned in effigy, his house torn down, and he was forced to flee once more. This time he went to New York, where a vigilante group which called itself "The Sons of Liberty" forced him to resign.

All this was in the background on that November day in 1765 when the Talbot citizenry gathered at the Court House. The question now was: how firmly would the general populace back up the hotheads? Would they support strong action, or meekly bow down to the power of Britain?

Talbot's freemen minced no words in making clear exactly where *they* stood. They first affirmed their "faith and true allegiance" to King George III, who they thought at that time was simply being misled by his advisors. But then, in resolutions adopted by roars of acclamation, they did "in the most solemn manner declare to the world"

> —That they were entitled to all the rights and liberties of British subjects, including trial by jury and the privilege of being taxed only with their consent, both of which in their opinion the Stamp Act violated.
> —That therefore they would, "at the risk of their lives and fortunes, endeavor, by all lawful ways and means, to transmit to their posterity, their rights and liberties."
> —That they would not "by any act of theirs, countenance or encourage the execution or effect of the said Stamp Act," and that they would hold in the utmost contempt any "Stamp-pimp, informer or favorer of the said Act."
> —That the effigy should hang on the gibbet before the Court House door until word came from England that the Stamp Act had been repealed.

Having thus so eloquently expressed themselves, the *Maryland Gazette* reported, "the gentlemen of the County adjourned to a tavern, where the King, the Royal family, and other loyal healths were drunk, everything concluding with the utmost decency and good order." There was only one casualty: according to Banning, the carpenter who fashioned the wooden effigy accidentally cut himself with his axe, and died of the wound.

It will be noted that these resolutions, strong as they were, fell far short of calling for outright independence. At that time Talbot Countians were by no means ready to cut their ties with Mother England, and many of them never would be. British Loyalists, so-called Tories, would be numerous in Talbot throughout the Revolution.

The Stamp act furore ended in anticlimax, as Parliament backed off and repealed the measure. But the issue stayed alive. The British would not yield on the principle that they had a right to tax the colonists, and they applied it again in 1773 by putting a tax on tea.

Once more there was an explosion. On October 14, 1773, the tea-carrying merchant ship *Peggy Stewart* was burned at the dock in Annapolis harbor. In Boston two months later men disguised as Indians boarded three vessels loaded with tea and dumped their cargoes overboard. Other tea ships were forced to turn back, and in Charleston, South Carolina, where some tea was unloaded, it was put into a warehouse and left there until it rotted.

The British government focused its reprisal on Boston. Early in 1774 Parliament voted to close the port of Boston, and four regiments of troops were dispatched to enforce the edict. Boston in turn called on the other colonies to join her in a general boycott of commerce with Britain. In Annapolis the Maryland Committee of Correspondence, with Talbot's Matthew Tilghman in the chair, received an urgent appeal for help from Samuel Adams May 23, 1774, and immediately dispatched it, along with an appeal of their own, to the county seat towns throughout the province.

That was the background for the so-called "Talbot Resolves," commemorated by a plaque on the Court House grounds, and recalled by occasional colorful reenactments. On May 24 "a number of gentlemen" met at the Court House and issued a statement affirming their support for Boston and their determination "to act as friends to liberty, and to the general interests of mankind," in the crisis. It was the first public expression in Maryland of willingness to back Boston against the British. Similar statements from other counties soon followed.

Whether or not any "resolves" were actually adopted remains an open question. The word was not used at the time, and in fact was never applied to the Talbot action until a Baltimore journalist made a speech about the "Talbot Resolves" (in the 1950s). And like their predecessors of 1765, the "gentlemen" who met in 1774 made haste to add that they wanted no part of American independence. Their only concern was "to promote that union and harmony between the mother country and her colonies, on which the preservation of both must finally depend." Nevertheless, they did take an early and eloquent stand favoring solidarity among the colonies, something that had been sadly lacking in the past.

Soon enough Talbot Countians were faced with the problem of backing up their fine words with action. Under Boston's urging, the Continental Congress which met in the fall of 1774 adopted a resolution

> *Talbot Court House, May 24, 1774.*
>
> ALARMED at the present situation of *America*, and impressed with the most tender feelings for the distresses of their brethren and fellow subjects in *Boston*, a number of gentlemen having met at this place, took into their serious consideration the part they ought to act, as friends to liberty, and to the general interests of mankind.
>
> To preserve the rights, and to secure the property of the subject, they apprehend, is the end of government. But when those rights are invaded—when the mode prescribed by the laws for the punishment of offences, and obtaining justice, is disregarded and spurned—when, without being heard in their defence, force is employed, and the severest penalties are inflicted; the people, they clearly conceive, have a right not only to complain, but likewise to exert their utmost endeavours to prevent the effect of such measures, as may be adopted by a weak or corrupt ministry to destroy their liberties, deprive them of their property, and rob them of their dearest birthright as Britons.
>
> Impressed with the warmest zeal for, and loyalty to their most gracious sovereign, and with the most sincere affection for their fellow subjects in *Great-Britain*, They are determined, calmly and steadily, to unite with their fellow subjects, in pursuing every legal and constitutional measure, to avert the evils threatened by the late act of parliament for shutting up the port and harbour of *Boston*; to support the common rights of *America*; and to promote that union and harmony between the mother country and her colonies, on which the preservation of both must finally depend.

An article reporting the Talbot Resolves of May 24, 1774 as published in *The Maryland Gazette*, Annapolis.

calling for an embargo on importation of British goods, but leaving enforcement up to local authorities. Annapolis passed the buck to committees of observation, composed of leading citizens, which were to be formed in each of the Maryland counties. And in March, 1775, the

Talbot committee met to consider what it should do when a British ship laden with forbidden goods actually entered Talbot waters.

The question was a sticky one. The committee was not a formal government body; it had no legal standing whatever except that derived from toothless resolutions passed in Philadelphia and Annapolis. And yet in the deteriorating situation it constituted the only government there was in Talbot County; the regular courts and the county commissioners were refusing even to meet except to handle routine matters. The committee members would have to make their own law, and to serve as prosecutors, judges, and jury in its enforcement.

The first case that came up was resolved easily enough. On March 21, 1775, Charles Crookshanks, a Talbot merchant, reported that the ship *Baltimore* had arrived from Glasgow with two bales of embargoed goods aboard, but he voluntarily promised that he would not accept them. Committee members thanked Crookshanks with sighs of relief, passed a resolution "that the said goods be sent back to Glasgow in the same ship without landing," and adjourned. There was no confrontation.

Next order of business was a case which, in the aura of high drama with which events of 1775 were surrounded, borders on the ridiculous. One of the resolutions adopted by Congress, in the interest of building up the colonial supply of wool, had barred the slaughter of lambs "yeaned" (born) after January 1 of the current year. On May 30 the committee was told Joseph Brascup's tavern at Talbot Court House, a favorite hangout of committee members, had served a leg of lamb so tasty and tender that it must have been a violation of the ban. Called in to explain, Brascup denied knowing whether the lamb had been yeaned before or after January 1, but promised not to buy any more lambs without getting what was in effect a birth certificate from the seller.

By then, however, a far more serious problem was in the offing. At the May 23 committee meeting, with the Reverend Dr. John Gordon in the chair, a letter was read from the Baltimore Committee of Observation reporting that the ship *Johnston*, laden with salt and dry goods, was headed for St. Michaels. She was owned by Gilbert & Gawith of London, and James Braddock, the firm's St. Michaels agent, was called in for questioning. Like Crookshanks, he promised that if the *Johnston* arrived, he would refused to handle its cargo.

Hailed by the schooner *Endeavor* as he sailed up the bay in June, Captain Jones of the *Johnston* was defiant. He had been told that twenty thousand British troops were being dispatched to America, and that by the time he arrived "all would be quiet." (What he apparently didn't know was that the troops had been sent to Boston, not Maryland.) At any rate, he refused to turn back, and on June 27 the *Johnston* anchored off

St. Michaels. Jones notified Braddock, who immediately passed the information to the committee. A delegation of four prominent Talbot Countians—Thomas Harrison, William Hambleton, Hugh Rice, and Richard Skinner—was dispatched to St. Michaels to board the ship and confront its captain.

On the morning of June 28, they examined Captain Jones's papers. These revealed an unexpected problem: in addition to salt and dry goods, the ship was carrying fourteen convicts and two indentured servants for sale on the local market. Braddock argued that Congress had passed no law forbidding the importation of convicts or servants, and the perplexed quartet finally agreed to let him accept them. But, they told Jones firmly, he could not land his salt and dry goods at St. Michaels or any other port in America; he must return at once to England without "breaking bulk" (landing any cargo), stopping only at Hampton Roads to take on bread and water. Still spluttering defiance, the captain sailed off.

The significance of this incident is quite clear in the light of history. It was in itself an act of revolution. The four men issued their order, not on the authority of the British crown nor of the proprietary government of Maryland, but solely as agents of the Committee of Observation of Talbot County and of the Continental Congress which had created it. Henceforth Americans, not Britons, would decide on affairs in America; and Talbot Countians, not Parliament, would control events within their jurisdiction.

Meanwhile, news of a much more sensational act of revolution had come down from beleaguered Massachusetts. On April 19 British troops had marched out of Boston and American militiamen had opposed them with armed resistance at the towns of Lexington and Concord. There had been heavy casualties on both sides. The war which everybody in Maryland had dreaded was a reality.

Dispatches reporting the battles traveled through the colonies at what then seemed a breakneck pace. An express rider galloped into New Haven on the morning of April 24. Relays of fresh horsemen carried the news on to New York, New Brunswick, Princeton, Trenton, Philadelphia. New Castle, Delaware, received word at 9:00 P.M. April 26, and Chestertown the next day. Although there is no record of it, it was undoubtedly on April 28—nine days after the event—that a notice was pinned to the court house door informing Talbot citizens of what had happened at Lexington and Concord.

Talbot did not receive the news with rejoicing or demonstrations. There were none of the wild outbursts of anger against Britain which

Jeremiah Banning's office on the shore of his home, The Isthmus, across the Tred Avon River from Oxford. The office became the Custom House when Banning was subsequently appointed the first United States Collector of Customs for Oxford by his friend, President George Washington.

occurred in New England. Nor was there any public outcry for independence. Most Talbot Countians still believed—and would continue to do so for another year—that somehow the British would back down if the colonies continued their united opposition.

One of the few who saw early and clearly where events were leading was Jeremiah Banning, who had recently retired to the life of a gentleman farmer after an adventurous twenty-two-year career as a mariner. Always an activist, he was too restless to sit back on his estate, the Isthmus on Plaindealing Creek, and watch the world he had known crumble around him. He soon got himself elected first lieutenant of a company of militia to be raised at Talbot Court House, and then captain of a company to be formed at Bartlett's Oak (Royal Oak). Both militias existed only on paper, and Banning realized that he knew all about the sea but nothing about military matters. Characteristically, he set out to learn for himself.

With an aide, Banning departed in June, 1775, on a two-months tour of the northern colonies. Their destination was Cambridge, Massachusetts, where the new Continental Army was being assembled with General Washington as its commander. There they met Washington, got a worrisome look at the raw recruits who formed his army, spent many hours listening to the instructions of experienced officers, and even had a long conversation between the lines with some British officers. Banning came home deeply imbued with the new spirit of American patriotism, and impressed by the "war-like preparation" he had observed in New York and New England, in contrast with the lackadaisical attitude he found in Talbot County. In New England, he reported, "nothing was seen but the disciplining of the militia—their marching and countermarching. Nothing was heard but the rattling of drums and the animating fife." At home there was much talk but little else.

Eventually Banning became a militia major. He did not serve outside Talbot County, but was in command at the nearest thing to a battle fought on Talbot soil during the Revolution. This was a brief skirmish in November, 1780, between his militia and a British landing party at Benoni's Point, said to have been named for his kinsman, Benoni Banning. There was some shooting, and the British departed. No one was reported injured.

Another Talbot County native who gained valuable experience in the summer of 1775 was Tench Tilghman. Born Christmas Day, 1745, at Fausley on what is now Glebe Creek, he had grown up in the socialite atmosphere of prewar Philadelphia, where he was regarded as something of a playboy. His only military experience was as lieutenant of a company so effete it was called "the Ladies' Light Infantry."

In August, 1775, he was still debating whether to cast his lot with the British or Americans in the coming conflict. His father, James Tilghman, was stubbornly pro-British, and two of his five younger brothers, Richard and Philemon, showed similar inclinations. Then came an assignment to travel into upper New York as secretary of a commission seeking to negotiate a treaty of alliance with the Indians of the Iroquois Confederacy.

For Tilghman, much of the month-long trip was devoted to frivolous matters; he flirted with the two pretty daughters of Major General Philip Schuyler, was adopted as a son by the chief of the Onandagos, and became betrothed to an Indian bride he had never met. But there was also time for deep reflection. A few weeks after his return he told his father he had reached a decision: he was going to fight on the side of the Americans.

His choice meant bitter division within the family. James, Sr., remained a British Loyalist, and eventually was arrested and interned for the duration of the war at his home in Kent County. Richard, also a Loyalist, left Maryland on the same ship that carried Robert Eden, the last British governor, back to England when the colony declared its independence. Philemon ran away and joined the British navy, in which he served throughout the war. James, Jr., and William were ardent patriots, and Thomas was too young to have to make a decision. As for Tench, his later career is a part of history: he became personal aide to General Washington, and served at his side with great distinction in nearly every major battle of the Revolution.

Lieutenant Colonel Tench Tilghman, from a miniature by Charles Willson Peale.

The split was typical of many Talbot families. A strong minority of the elite class never did fully support the Revolution. Some sat it out in silent disapproval, or gave it only lip service. Others, like Henry Hollyday of Ratcliffe Manor, refused on principle to take the oath of allegiance to the state of Maryland, and paid the penalty in harassment, triple taxation, seizure of their livestock, and open scorn on the part of their patriotic neighbors. Edward Lloyd IV was accounted a patriot but his younger brother, Richard Bennett Lloyd, was a Tory who married a London society belle, Joanna Leigh, and lived throughout the war in England. Out on Bayside old John Leeds, who had been clerk of Talbot County Court ever since 1738, was outspoken in his denunciation of independence. He was removed as clerk in 1777, but not silenced.

As for the poor and landless classes, they regarded the whole thing from the start as a "rich men's revolution" in which they were not involved except as possible cannon fodder. Anyhow, they had no voice in the great decisions of the war years. Under the suffrage laws of the time, carefully framed by Maryland's leaders to keep the "masses" from gaining control of the Revolution, only Protestant males who possessed at least fifty acres of land or a "visible estate" worth at least thirty pounds sterling could vote or run for office. That disenfranchised all but a thousand or so of Talbot's population of more than ten thousand.

THE REVOLUTION

Through the winter of 1775-76, Talbot County remained torn by indecision on the question of independence. No one much liked it, but some, like Matthew Tilghman, Tench's uncle and later his father-in-law, were beginning to accept it as inevitable.

Matthew Tilghman, who lived at Rich Neck, was Talbot's eyes and ears to the world and its foremost representative in affairs of the province and the emerging nation. In the formative years of Maryland statehood, he was "Mr. Everything" in the colony—chairman of every delegation to the Continental Congress, speaker of the House of Delegates, president of the convention which in 1775 established the Association of the Freemen of Maryland as the colony's de facto government, and as such literally Maryland's first citizen because his name led all the rest among those subscribing to the Articles of Association. He was chairman or a ranking member of every organizational body in Maryland from the Committee of Correspondence formed in 1774 to deal with the other colonies to the Constitutional Convention which late in 1776 wrote Maryland's first state constitution. So great was his influence and prestige that he has been called "the Father of Statehood" and "the Patriarch of Maryland."

Yet he was no flaming patriot of the Patrick Henry and Samuel Adams school. In some ways he was an enigma: an old-school aristocrat of the purest breeding who yielded to no one in his sturdy republicanism; a political archconservative who in Annapolis aligned himself with the colony's hot-headed young radicals; a leader who labored long and hard for Maryland statehood but never in his life said publicly how he felt about American independence. The one thing certain about him is that he spoke for Talbot County's established leadership; and in the winter of 1775-76 he was still engaged in secret last-ditch negotiations which he hoped would win British concessions and make independence unnecessary.

In the county, meanwhile, sputtering efforts were being made to organize an effective militia. Under an order issued by the Maryland Convention in January, 1776, all able-bodied men between sixteen and fifty except clergymen and physicians were called on to enroll in a militia company by March 1. Officers, almost entirely members of upper crust families, were named in Annapolis, strictly on a political basis. And the enlisted men who were accepted were also largely from the county's well-to-do families. The officers were instructed to be very careful about whom they let into the ranks. "Young, hearty robust men who are tied by birth, or family connections, or property, to this country, and are well-practised in the use of firearms, are by much to be preferred," said the orders from Annapolis.

The inefficiency of this system became apparent in March, 1776, when a British sloop-of-war, the *Otter*, was reported sailing up the Chesapeake. Wild rumors quickly transformed her into a full-scale man-of-war with at least forty-four guns, and the two tenders which accompanied her into a "British invasion fleet." There was instant panic throughout Maryland. The Council of Safety in Annapolis, which had charge of military operations for the province, sent messages flying in all directions on what to do if the British landed.

Talbot's Brigadier General James Lloyd Chamberlaine was told: "Immediately order your Battalion to hold themselves in readiness to March at a Moment's Warning," an order he could hardly obey since even the officers had just been appointed and there were almost no enlisted men. A company of regulars being organized by Captain James Hindman had no muskets nor uniforms, not even "hatts" and leather pants. When the Dorchester County militia were mustered in, it turned out that only one man out of eighty had a gun. The excitement died down when the little *Otter*, after her skipper had tried unsuccessfully to buy food in Annapolis, turned around and sailed back down the Chesapeake.

Talbot County redeemed herself for her earlier indecision in June, 1776, by beating both Maryland and the Continental Congress to the punch in adopting a resolution in favor of independence. At a meeting on or about June 25, while the Maryland Convention and the Congress in Philadelphia both were still debating independence, a group of freemen at Talbot Court House went on record as condemning the "lukewarm backwardness" of Maryland leaders on the issue and expressing "grief and astonishment" at the past record of the Convention in instructing Maryland delegates not to vote for a Declaration of Independence. They recited a long list of grievances much like those later written into the actual declaration by Thomas Jefferson.

Because of these, they said, "We cannot entertain the most distant expectations of a reconciliation on reasonable terms." Therefore they urged the Talbot delegates to the Convention to see to it that Maryland promptly adopted "such . . . measures as shall be judged necessary for promoting the liberty, safety and interest of America, and defeating the schemes and machinations of our enemies the King, Parliament and Ministry of Great Britain."

Significantly, the issue of the *Maryland Gazette* which reported this said the resolution was adopted only by "part of the freemen" of Talbot County, indicating the sentiments expressed were by no means universal. Nevertheless it was effective. Spurred on by this and similar statements from other counties, the Maryland Convention, which as recently as May 21 had unanimously forbidden its delegation in Congress from voting for independence, reversed itself on June 28 and instructed them to favor it. Maryland's decision was disclosed to the Congress in Philadelphia on July 1, and undoubtedly helped that body reach agreement the next day on the fateful statement:

> Resolved, That these United Colonies are, and of right ought to be, free and independent States; that they are absolved from all allegiance to the British Crown, and that all political connexion between them and the State of Great Britain, is, and ought to be, totally dissolved.

So Talbot County, even if not unanimously, played a small but significant part in the political process which brought about the creation of the United States.

Two men associated with Talbot County, for reasons of their own, failed to sign the formal Declaration of Independence which was adopted July 4.

Matthew Tilghman, who was chairman of the Maryland Delegation to the Continental Congress, was not in Philadelphia when the document was approved; he was in Annapolis presiding at the session of the Maryland Convention which put its own Declaration of Independence into final form on July 3. Nor did he bother to go up to Philadelphia on August 2 when other Maryland delegates—including Charles Carroll of Carrollton, who had not even been a member of the Congress when it voted for independence—assured themselves of a place in history by putting their names to the engrossed copy. For that matter, some delegates didn't get around to signing for as much as a year afterward—but Tilghman never did sign the Declaration.

Whatever his reasons were for not signing, Tilghman kept them to himself; and he worked as hard to make a viable body of the new state of Maryland as he had to bring it into being. But his failure to sign the Declaration of Independence has bothered admirers ever since. It has been said that he was too busy preparing for the forthcoming Maryland Constitutional Convention, at which he presided, to make the trip with other Marylanders on August 2; but that body did not convene until August 14, nearly two weeks later. Samuel Chase, who was a signer, managed to make it back to Annapolis in time for the opening session of the Convention. In any case that does not explain why Tilghman did not sign it at some later time, as a number of others did.

Two centuries later the question still remains unanswered: if, as his partisans insist, Matthew Tilghman was in favor of American independence, why didn't he say so by signing his name to the historic document declaring it?

Rich Neck Manor at Claiborne, from an early tintype view. The land grant dates from 1649. Matthew Tilghman lived here during the Revolution. The main house dates from the 1850s, but the kitchen wing at right may be a century older.

The other Talbot-connected nonsigner, John Dickinson, left no one in doubt about his reasons: he made an eloquent speech opposing independence in the Continental Congress June 20, 1776, and cast one of the few votes against it on July 2. Then he resigned from Congress and, being a loyal if not enthusiastic American, went off to join a regiment fighting for the very cause he had opposed.

Long before that, Dickinson had made important contributions to the emerging nation. His writings in the 1760s were credited with first giving Americans a sense of identity and unity, and he was author of a song which has been described as "America's first national anthem." So his stand on independence certainly did not stem from lack of patriotism, but from a deep conviction that Congress was making a fatally wrong decision.

Born in 1732 at Crosiadore, the Talbot home of the Quaker Dickinsons on the Choptank, young John moved with his parents as a boy of eight to another Dickinson estate near Dover in what is now Delaware but was then considered the "lower counties" of Pennsylvania. He studied law in London, and became a leader of both the Pennsylvania and Delaware legislatures. In the decade before the Revolution, his *Letters*

Matthew Tilghman, known as the father of statehood and patriarch of Maryland, from a pastel portrait by John Hesselius.

from a Farmer in Pennsylvania, published in pamphlet form, became the most widely quoted expressions of the American point of view in both England and the colonies.

Like Matthew Tilghman and many others, Dickinson was primarily concerned with the issue of taxation, not independence. But his letters gave voice to the popular idea that England's ancient liberties were an inalienable right of the American people, and his free use of such terms as "freedom" and "liberty" caught the public fancy. They became catchwords throughout the colonies. It seemed unimportant then that by freedom Dickinson did not mean freedom from British rule but freedom from British tyranny.

Early in 1768 Dickinson wrote a song to the music of an old English air, "Heart of Oak," and offered it to a Massachusetts publisher for the use of the Boston Sons of Liberty. Called "The Liberty Song," it swiftly swept the country, both for its catchy tune and its stirring words:

> In Freedom we're born and in Freedom we'll live. . . .
> Not as Slaves but as Freemen our money we'll give. . . .
> Then join hand in hand brave Americans all,
> By uniting we stand, by dividing we fall.

Soon everybody in America was singing "The Liberty Song," and John Dickinson's name was linked in the public mind with those of the

Crosiadore, traditional home of the Dickinson family, that was razed in 1976. The house was built in late Victorian times but was said to have incorporated the room in which John Dickinson, the Revolutionary War leader, was born in 1732.

most ardent patriots. That made it doubly painful—and doubly courageous—for him to stand up in the Continental Congress and tell the world that he was going to vote against the Declaration of Independence because he was convinced it would be a losing proposition for America.

On Wye Island, meanwhile, another man with strong Talbot connections had been giving a practical demonstration of what American life would be like if the colonies cut their ties with England. John Beale Bordley, whose wife was yet another descendant of Henrietta Maria Lloyd, began experimenting in the 1760s with self-sufficiency in agriculture in order to show how well Marylanders could get along without Britain once they set their minds to it. He shifted entirely from tobacco to wheat, set up his own brewery, and planted a vineyard on the island. In addition, says Maryland historian J. Thomas Scharf:

THE REVOLUTION

John Dickinson, from a miniature by John Beale Bordley.

He ground his own flour in his own hand-mills, fired his own brick in his own kilns, made his own kersey and linsey-woolsey for his servants on his own looms, from wool of his own raising, and hackled, spun and wove his own flax. He made his own casks to hold his beer and cider from cedar cut in his own woods, and even made his salt from Chesapeake water.

Bordley also pioneered in scientific agriculture, and wrote treatises on such novel notions as rotation of crops and use of manure and lime to improve fertility. Both during and after the Revolution his published reports were popular reading with Talbot farmers who were learning to do for themselves what had always been done for them by Mother England.

Once independence was a reality, Talbot men quickly got their first bitter taste of the war which came along with it. Captain James Hindman's company of regulars, after months of delay and frustration, were dispatched late in July to Philadelphia as reinforcements for Washington's Continental Army. There they found that Washington had gone to New York. They caught up with his forces in mid-August, just in time to take part in the terrible defeat known as the Battle of Long Island, when the British and Hessians routed the green Americans and slew them by the hundreds as they fled across the marshes of Gowanus Creek. Three Talbot Countians were killed, and several others wounded; but the hundred men of Hindman's company gave a good account of themselves. They were among the members of the "Maryland line" which

Captain Barnaby's house, Morris Street, Oxford, circa 1770.

stood firm in the face of terrible fire and were credited with saving the bulk of the American army from destruction.

For the next several months Hindman's company participated in battle after battle, nearly all of them disastrous. They learned to have the utmost contempt for their northern comrades, whom they accused of "base cowardice," selfishness, and theft of supplies and medicines. At Harlem Heights September 15 they looked on in horror as Connecticut troops fled so precipitously that even canings administered personally by Washington and other generals couldn't stop them. The Talbot Countians went without shoes or stockings and ate half-spoiled meat without salt or vegetables. Many of them sickened, and some died of camp fever because northern doctors would not distribute medicine to southerners.

By year's end many of the hundred who had set forth so bravely from Oxford in July were ready to desert. Home on leave for Christmas, Pollard Edmondson's two sons tried to explain to Talbot Countians what it was like, saying that many of the Maryland officers would quit the service as soon as their one-year enlistments were up, and many enlisted men might depart even before that. Captain Hindman himself resigned his commission and went back to civilian life early in 1777.

THE REVOLUTION

On the home front, too, war's grim reality was making itself felt. There were shortages of everything needed for the army: tents and tent cloth (old sails were much in demand), blanket cloth, knapsacks and haversacks, camp kettles, nails, saltpeter for making gunpowder, baggage wagons, lead for bullets. The colonists knew nothing about making glass, and a hasty call went out from Annapolis for three hundred "wooden bottles" to be used as canteens by the soldiers. As for weapons, it developed that only one man on the entire Eastern Shore, Elisha Winters of Chestertown, knew how to repair firelocks for muskets. In the emergency Joseph Bruff of Talbot Court House, who repaired clocks in his silversmith shop, was pressed into service.

But the worst shortage of all was in salt, vital to civilians and the military alike for preserving their beef and pork. Manufactured salt from England and the West Indies had always been plentiful and cheap. Now suddenly it vanished as the British ships ceased bringing it in as cargo. What little there was had been bought up in advance and hoarded away by wealthy planters and merchants in locked storerooms.

In the fall and winter of 1776, the Eastern Shore was swept by a wave of salt riots and salt raids. In Cambridge an angry band of more than one hundred armed men defied authorities who sought to punish persons who had broken into warehouses and helped themselves to salt. It was useless to call out the militia against the rioters; most of them were desperately short of salt themselves.

In Talbot the prime target, ironically, was Brigadier General James Lloyd Chamberlaine, commander of militia on the upper Eastern Shore. Chamberlaine had bought more than five hundred pounds of salt and stored it at Plaindealing, which he managed for his orphaned nephew.

On the night of December 27, 1776, a band of seventeen men led by Jeremiah Colston rode to Plaindealing, forced the caretaker's wife, Mrs. William Milward, to unlock the storeroom, and carried away seventeen and one half bushels of salt, only a tiny fraction of the general's hoard. They insisted on leaving thirty-five dollars in payment for it. The enraged general sent a posse after the raiders, but they caught no one except one young boy, whom they beat so savagely that he was laid up for days. But soon everybody knew who the raiders had been, and most Talbot Countians sympathized with them.

The case became a celebrated one. Chamberlaine put in a bill with the Maryland Council of Safety to repay his costs for chasing the "wicked mutineers" and insisted the salt was needed to protect the interests of the orphan, Thomas Chamberlaine, who owned Plaindealing. But John Gibson wrote the council that, far from being "wicked mutineers," the raiders were "men of reputation . . . sincere in their country's cause, . . .

which is more than can be said with truth of any ingrosser (hoarder) of salt here." Colston testified that he had 1,100 pounds of pork which was rapidly spoiling, and that he did not lead the raid until he had twice been rebuffed by Chamberlaine when he tried to buy salt.

The council shocked Chamberlaine by siding with the raiders. They refused to pay his expense claim, and instead sent him a stiff note saying it was the duty of anyone "having more salt than will answer his immediate needs, to spare some to those that are distressed." Chamberlaine angrily resigned his commission, and thereafter took no part in revolutionary affairs.

Salt continued to be a problem throughout the Revolution. Some did come through the British blockade, but it sold at extremely high prices on the Annapolis docks. Even so, Talbot farmers had no choice but to pay whatever was asked; without salt their meat would spoil and their families and slaves might starve. Some Talbot Countians, among them Henry Hollyday, took a lesson from John Beale Bordley's Wye Island experience and tried making salt themselves. Hollyday boiled down the brackish water of Tred Avon Creek, and dried the residue in the sun and wind. In August, 1777, he wrote his brother James that he could make a bushel of salt a week in good weather, and that while it had some straw and dirt in it, "every body who has tasted it, think it very good; and that it will cure provisions." The state also set up salt works at the mouth of the Potomac and on the ocean shore in Worcester County.

On top of everything else, a severe smallpox epidemic hit Talbot County in the spring of 1777. Hundreds were stricken and more than twenty died, among them such prominent men as Nicholas Goldsborough, William Trippe, and Henry Delahay. Dr. Nicholas Way of Wilmington was induced to come to Talbot County and try out his experimental program of inoculation, then the only known method of combating smallpox. Unlike the later vaccination process, in which a mild cowpox virus was injected to help the body build up immunity against the more deadly disease, Dr. Way injected patients with an actual case of smallpox, hoping it would be mild enough to spare their lives. So it was extremely hazardous; but so great was the dread of smallpox that more than two thousand persons in the county took the treatment. Some of them died, too; but a higher percentage survived than among those who contracted the disease naturally.

As the war dragged on, life in Talbot became a grim struggle for survival. Repeated rumors of a British invasion did not materialize, but that equally cruel scourge of wartime, galloping inflation, did. Prices spiraled up and up, and the value of the paper money issued by the state and by Congress plunged down and down. By the summer of 1780 the price of wheat, which had been 5 shillings a bushel at the start of the war, had shot up to £22, an increase of almost a hundred to one. Corn was selling for £12 a bushel, and pork by the barrel for £375. A pound of bacon cost 60 shillings, enough to feed a family for a month in 1775.

One ironic side effect was to give the vote to the very "rabble" whom Matthew Tilghman and his conservative cohorts had tried so hard to exclude from power. By 1780 anybody who owned three bushels of corn could qualify as a voter under the law limiting the franchise to those who had an estate valued at £30. Another side effect was to allow speculators to buy up property on credit and pay for it later in worthless currency. Some sizable Talbot fortunes were made—and lost—that way.

As in every war, patriotism was a costly virtue ignored by practical men. Much has been made of the fact that the Old Wye Mill, still in existence, provided flour to feed Washington's troops and thereby helped win the Revolutionary War. But it is seldom mentioned that the mill's owner, William Hemsley, charged the government for it at the astronomical rate of £144 (about $500) per barrel.

Nevertheless the Eastern Shore, with Talbot as its center, made an enormous contribution to victory in the war. Its farmers had switched from tobacco to wheat just in time. The Delmarva peninsula was America's principal grain-growing region, producing so much wheat and flour that it has been called "the breadbasket of the Revolution," without which the war could not have been won.

While speculators and black market operators were getting rich at home, some Talbot Countians were performing bravely on the battlefields. One notable example was young Perry Benson, the future hero of the Battle of St. Michaels in 1813. A born soldier, he joined the "Hearts of Oak" company of the Thirty-eighth Militia Battalion as an enlisted man in January, 1776, when he was barely eighteen. Later that year he was made an ensign (sublieutenant) in a "Flying Camp," a regular army force which provided the basis for the famous Maryland Line. He was a first lieutenant at nineteen, and a captain at twenty-one. In the Battle of Brandywine, although wounded himself, he is said to have assisted the seriously wounded General LaFayette from the battlefield.

By 1781 Benson was in the Carolinas, commanding Marylanders in such battles as Camden, Cowpens, and Hobkirk's Hill, where his firmness under fire was cited in dispatches by General Greene. At Fort Ninety-Six in South Carolina he was "fearfully wounded" while leading the First Maryland Regiment in a desperate assault against the British stronghold. A black soldier from Caroline County, Thomas Carney,

Talbot Court House, as it looked during the Revolutionary War. From an artist's conception by Harden Foote.

saved his life by picking him up, carrying him back to the American lines under heavy fire, and depositing him before the regimental surgeon.

Benson's chances of recovery were considered so slim that his commanding officer wrote a letter of condolence to his father; but the tough young Talbot Countian survived, although forever afterward his left arm was paralyzed. Forever afterward also, he made certain that whoever honored him honored Thomas Carney as well. When Benson as a peacetime brigadier general reviewed the militia, the man who had saved his life at Fort Ninety-Six rode by his side.

There were other heroes, black and white, who remained unsung—nameless Talbot Countians buried in unmarked graves at Brooklyn, Harlem Heights, Brandywine, Valley Forge, Cowpens, Guilford Court House, and elsewhere, or who died in the terrible epidemics which took a greater toll among American troops than did British bullets or Hessian bayonets. No roster of Talbot's dead in the Revolution has ever been attempted; even the names of those who served are only partially known.

It would be untruthful to pretend that the Revolution produced a great wave of popular patriotism in Talbot. It did not. Only after independence was won did men remember what "great patriots" they had been, and toast the flag and the new republic in drafts of ale, cider, or brandy.

Top, a craftsman's house of the late eighteenth century. The kitchen and dining area of cabinetmaker Joseph Neall's cottage, 1795, on Easton's West Street, as recreated by the Talbot County Historical Socity on the basis of Neall's inventory at his death in 1800. *Bottom*, the living/bedroom area of the Neall cottage. Apprentices and a servant girl slept in dormer rooms upstairs.

Things may have been otherwise in New England, but in Talbot County there was deep and sincere reluctance to make a final break with England. Almost nobody liked the war, and many openly opposed it.

The primitive draft in operation at the time was a constant source of resentment. While nearly every able-bodied man was required to sign up for the militia, the well-to-do could hire substitutes to take their places, and the poor had no recourse but to join up, run away, or simply refuse to serve. Many took the latter course. When Colonel Christopher Birckhead called a muster of the Thirty-ninth Militia Battalion May 19, 1777, nobody showed up but the battalion's officers. Captain Thomas Gordon and Ensign Thomas Jenkins were assigned to round up some enlisted men, but had little success; only a few appeared at another muster June 7. A year later Birckhead wrote Governor Thomas Johnson that of thirty-one new draftees in the Talbot area, "only three are willing to go on duty."

Interestingly, Talbot County's first convicted draft dodger was none other than Edward Lloyd, the richest man in the county and maybe in America. He was found guilty by the Talbot County Committee of Observation of failing to register for the draft, as required, by March 1, 1776, and sentenced to pay a fine of forty shillings. But Lloyd appealed to the Maryland Convention, of which he was a member. There, his friends conveniently "forgot" the matter.

Throughout the Eastern Shore, pro-British sentiment was strong enough to amount almost to counterrevolution. As early as June, 1776, the Caroline Committee of Observation reported that "sundry evil disposed persons" had been working to disunite the public and had prevailed upon several militia companies to lay down their arms. From Somerset came word that "internal enemies" were believed to have worked out a concerted plan for counterattack with the British. In Queen Anne's, Kent Island militia refused to serve under officers appointed by the Maryland Convention, and at an angry meeting demanded the right to elect their own officers. In eastern Queen Anne's, the sheriff reported, "near two-thirds of the people" were Tories. In Talbot there was no rioting except over salt, but a good many people did not wish the Revolution well, whether or not they had the nerve to say it out loud. St. Peter's Parish welcomed the Reverend Dr. John Bowie as its rector in 1780 even though he had recently been arrested in Worcester County for conspiring with the insurgents. In his defense, it should be added that Dr. Bowie served the county well, despite his early toryism, as pastor at both St. Peter's and St. Michael's and as master of a popular private school. The point is that his record was not held against him; too many local men were tarred with the same brush. Samuel Chamberlaine,

Jr., who was openly pro-British throughout the war, was elected to the General Assembly in 1788 despite his wartime dissidence and alleged "bigotry" in favor of the Church of England.

During the war, Tory resistance centered around a man named Cheney Clow, a resident of Delaware just across the Mason-Dixon line from Queen Anne's County. Many rumors circulated about Clow in 1777 and early 1778. He was supposed to have ten thousand followers in Delaware, and many in Queen Anne's, Caroline, and Talbot. Some said he was planning an attack on the Maryland Eastern Shore, and being reinforced by regular British troops. Whatever the truth about his strength, he was considered so dangerous that the militia was called out to raid his camp in the spring of 1778. Clow slipped away, but the raiders took several prisoners, who were locked up in jail near the Queen Anne's County Court House, then located in Queenstown.

Three days later, on April 20, about one hundred rebellious men marched on Queenstown with "colours displayed, drums beating, and with swords, clubs, guns, bayonets and other weapons." They launched a furious attack on the militiamen who were guarding the prisoners. There were many casualties on both sides.

One member of the mob, a Queen Anne's countian named John Tims, was later arrested and tried for treason at Talbot Court House. Found guilty, he was sentenced to die a horrible death. In a display of barbarity that is surely unsurpassed in Talbot legal annals, Judges Alexander Contee Hanson and Nicholas Thomas declared that the prisoner be:

> Drawn to the place of execution and be there hanged by the neck and cut down alive and that his entrails be taken out and burnt before his face and his head cut off and his body divided into four quarters and his head and quarters disposed of at the pleasure of the State.

However, Tims was pardoned by Governor Johnson. Clow himself was later captured and convicted of treason in Delaware. After spending years in jail during which his health was broken and his wife went insane, he was executed at his own request in 1787.

Even more pestiferous to Talbot's wealthy landowners than Cheney Clow's rebel gang were the "Tangier Island pirates" who raided Eastern Shore estates from their home bases on the lower islands of the Chesapeake. Though they acted in the name of Britain, these lawless marauders were more interested in robbery and plunder than in loyalty to King George. In their most notable foray, they raided Wye House on March 13, 1781, carried off much loot and some slaves, then crossed the Wye and plundered the Wye Island mansion of John Beale Bordley. (Legend says the British burned Wye House to the ground, but that appears to be pure fiction. Actually the original mansion, dating from the 1660s, was razed by Edward Lloyd IV after the Revolution to make room for the present Wye House.)

Outraged by such attacks, and unable to get any protection from Annapolis, Lloyd and other property owners in the area launched what might be called "the Eastern Shore Navy" in May, 1781. They agreed to pay expenses for twenty armed men aboard the barge *Experiment*, which was to cruise between Kent Point and Tilghman's Island watching out for marauders from the lower bay.

By midsummer the little Eastern Shore war fleet had been built up to at least three barges. Rendezvousing at Sharpe's Island July 28, they set out under command of Commodore Thomas Grason in search of the enemy. Two days later they found them: two barges and a whaleboat, all skippered by men notorious as bay raiders. One barge was captured, and the other two vessels put to flight.

On August 1 the victors put in at Miles River Ferry in triumph with their prize, and before admiring crowds told no-doubt exaggerated stories of their exploit. The captured skipper was identified as one McMullen, whose chief claim to fame was his kidnap of Harry Gale in Somerset County. On McMullen's orders his men had hanged Gale; but the victim had revived after being cut down and, said the official report, McMullen "could not prevail upon his crew to hang him a second time or drown him." So instead McMullen had made Gale take an oath not to bear arms against the King, and turned him loose.

The Eastern Shore Navy's small victory brought grim satisfaction to Matthew Tilghman, by then sixty-three and ailing, who had been having a tough war as head of the Council of Safety for the ill-equipped and often ignored Shore counties. "We will not attack the British fleet," he wrote his daughter Anna on August 3, "but as for any thing else we'll make nothing of 'em."

As events turned out the little flotilla didn't have to worry much longer about the British fleet. A great French armada had arrived off the Virginia capes, and General Washington and his board of strategy had decided on a desperate gamble to win or lose the war at one throw of the dice. Soon the Eastern Shore barges were engaged in helping transport an American army under General Lafayette from Head of Elk and Baltimore down the bay to confront General Cornwallis in Virginia.

The gamble paid off. Cornwallis surrendered at Yorktown October 19, 1781, and the war for all practical purposes was over. After six years of defeats, America had finally won.

Lieutenant Colonel Tench Tilghman appears at the right in this detail from the painting, "Washington and His Generals at Yorktown" by Charles Willson Peale. From left to right in the painting, done after the surrender of the British forces, are the Marquis de Lafayette, General Benjamin Lincoln, General George Washington, Comte de Rochambeau, General de Chastellux, and Colonel Tilghman.

One more Talbot County chapter remained to be written. Washington rewarded Talbot's Lieutenant Colonel Tench Tilghman for his years of devotion by giving him the honor of carrying the official news of Cornwallis's surrender from Yorktown to the Continental Congress in Philadelphia. Tilghman set off immediately on what has become known in Maryland as "Tilghman's Ride" although much of it was not on horseback but by boat.

The early stages of the trip were beset by delays and difficulties. Tilghman lost a whole night's sailing because of what he called "the stupidity of the skipper," who ran aground on the Tangier shoals. He was becalmed off Annapolis. When he got there, he found that the news had already arrived in a letter from Count de Grasse, commander of the French fleet, and had been forwarded to Philadelphia. Winds were light as he crossed the bay from Annapolis to Rock Hall, and another full day

Tench Tilghman's grave and a cenotaph honoring his memory, in Oxford Cemetery.

was lost. From there on he took no more chances with boats; he galloped the last hundred miles, pausing only to change horses and spread the glorious word of victory.

He reached Philadelphia shortly after midnight on the morning of Wednesday, October 28, found the house of Thomas McKean, president of the Congress, and began pounding furiously on the door. Watchmen thought he was drunk and almost arrested him before he convinced them who he was and why he was there. Finally McKean came to the door, accepted Washington's letter, and graciously thanked Tilghman for bringing the official word even though he had already received it unofficially.

For the rest of the night, as the watchmen made their rounds, they varied their usual time calls by the cry, "Two of the clock, and Cornwallis is taken" and so on. The Liberty Bell "tolled a joyous peal." At dawn cannon were fired. Congress met early in the morning, heard the dispatch from Washington, and listened to a round of speech making. Then they adjourned to church, and weary Tench Tilghman adjourned to bed.

Congress later voted him a horse with caparisons and a handsome sword in honor of his services, but Tilghman never saw them. He died

THE REVOLUTION

April 16, 1786, before the Paris-made sword was completed. Secretary of War Knox presented it to his widow, the former Anna Maria Tilghman, who kept it as a treasured memento for the next fifty years in the Talbot home her father, Matthew Tilghman, bought for her, Plimhimmon on Oxford Neck. Tench Tilghman's remains were first buried in Baltimore, but in 1971 were moved to the Oxford town cemetery.

The long war's final moments—and the agonizing slowness with which news traveled in those days—can be summed up in a few lines from Jeremiah Banning's day book:

> February 11, 1783—Received first hint via Baltimore via West Indies of peace between America and England. [This was a preliminary agreement which had been signed in Paris November 30, 1782.]
>
> March 28—Had information from Mr. Perry Benson that peace was confirmed. Hope it is so. Hearing much firing at Annapolis and some small arms at Oxford between 8 and 9 o'clock at night. My heart is happy with hope.
>
> March 28—Post brought news that on Monday 24th March the *Triumph*, from Cadiz in 36 days, brought the agreeable news to Philadelphia of a general peace having taken place. [This was the treaty recognizing America's independence, signed in Paris January 20.]
>
> May 13—Proclamation of cessation of hostilities published (posted) at Talbot Court House. [This had been issued by Governor Paca April 21, and dispatched to the sheriffs of the various counties April 25.]
>
> November 19—News of definitive treaty being signed 3d Sept. last between America and Great Britain came to hand.

The Revolution almost nobody had wanted was over, and the independence many people had dreaded was a reality at last. From now on what happened to America—and Talbot County—would be up to the Americans themselves.

SEVEN

The Rise of Easton

EMERGENCE of the bustling town of Easton from the sleepy village of Talbot Court House was the most startling development in Talbot County in the post revolutionary years. It introduced to power a new middle class—merchants, bankers, editors, doctors, lawyers, skilled artisans—who challenged, if they did not supplant, the old power structure based on pride of birth and ownership of land. Easton, with its brash optimism and its get ahead spirit, spoke for the new democracy which was taking over young America. If the eighteenth century had been the age of aristocracy, and the twentieth was to be the age of the common man, the nineteenth century fell somewhere in between: it was the age of the merchant, the go-getter, the opportunist—in a word, the businessman.

But before Easton as a town could even be born, it had to overcome a difficulty which threatened its existence. The Maryland General Assembly, seeking a suitable place for the "little capital" which statehood would require on the Eastern Shore, had decided in 1777 to build an entirely new town and state court building at Dover on the Choptank rather than try to pump life into dusty, decrepit Talbot Court House.

This made good sense, or so it seemed to the legislators at the time. Talbot Court House had only one asset, a sixty-five-year-old, one-story court building. That building would certainly have to be torn down and replaced by a new one if, as envisioned, the new General Court of Maryland were to hold alternate sessions on the Eastern Shore, and especially if, as some suggested, the legislature itself should convene on the shore every other year. The village was not on navigable water, an important consideration in those days of few and terrible roads; and while it was near the center of Talbot County, it was by no means near the center of the Eastern Shore as a whole.

Dover, by contrast, was on the broad Choptank, an easy reach by boat for those having business with the courts, coming either from the Eastern or Western Shore. It was very close to the geographical center of the

THE RISE OF EASTON

Eastern Shore; and the settlement of the Maryland-Delaware border dispute in 1768, the creation of Caroline County in 1774, and the opening of new wheat lands in the interior were all combining to shift population and wealth away from the old tidewater plantation areas and toward the southern and eastern portions of the shore. As it stood, Dover had not even as much going for it as Talbot Court House—a few scattered houses, some warehouses, and no-longer-prosperous stores. But what did that matter if a new town was going to have to be constructed anyway?

So the decision was made: as soon as time and money were available to build them, a new town would be laid out and a new state court building erected at the century-old port village of Dover. Talbot County could keep its county seat at "the Court House" if it liked, but the prestige and influence that went with state courts and state offices would go elsewhere.

Luckily for Easton's future, this was not to be. The plan had to be shelved for the duration of the war, and afterward powerful forces in Talbot used their political muscle to see that it was killed. They wanted the Eastern Shore's capital to be in the center of the county, not on its eastern edge, and they got their way.

However, the Dover proposal was still in Maryland's official future when, in 1786, its opponents moved in with a counterplan of their own. Talbot Court House was showing signs at last of shaking off its lethargy, or so its supporters claimed. In a petition to the legislature, a group of Talbot Countians asserted "that the village at the court-house of the said county hath considerably increased in number of houses and inhabitants, (and) that chief of the trade of the county is carried on there." They therefore prayed "that the said village may be erected into a town."

The General Assembly agreed, and on March 12, 1786, enacted legislation creating a town, to be called Talbot, and naming five commissioners to bring it into being. They were Jeremiah Banning, Hugh Sherwood of Huntington, John Stevens, Greensbury Goldsborough, and Alexander McCallum. Most of these men lived elsewhere in the county, but had real estate interests in the proposed town; Banning, for instance, had bought land there as early as 1776.

The commissioners were to meet before June 1, 1786, and have the town surveyed, the lots laid out and numbered, the streets, lanes, and alleys named and marked by "good sufficient cedar or locust posts or stones." (Some of the original stones can still be found.) According to Banning, he personally selected the major street names—Washington for the general, Goldsborough for the family which had adopted him as a boy, Harrison probably for the Talbot merchant, Samuel Harrison, Hanson for John Hanson, first "president" of the United States under the Articles of Confederation, and so on. One small alley, only a few feet wide, was designated on the first town plat as Magazine Alley because it led from the cobblestone powder magazine built during the war to the court house green where the militia trained. Today it is still there, a little-used footpath between buildings on Washington Street, a curious and almost forgotten relic of revolutionary times. Another recognizable landmark was at the proposed town's northern edge. Described in the metes and bounds as "the lot of major Joseph Bruff, whereon he lately lived," it was on the homesite of the veteran silversmith who had died in 1785. The site, occupied until his recent death by photographer H. Robins Hollyday, is next door to the present Safeway store, on Washington Street just south of Bay.

Other assignments of the commissioners were to oversee the sale of lots, on which a minimum price was set of seven pounds ten shillings (approximately twenty dollars), to hire a town clerk, and to remove "all nuisances that they shall find in any of the streets, lanes or alleys." They also were empowered to enforce, through a town bailiff, the law against letting geese or swine run at large through the streets.

It was two years after that before the new town's backers finally succeeded in winning repeal of the 1777 act ordering up a rival town and court house at Dover. This evidently required some strenuous political infighting; a letter dated July 14, 1788, reveals that Judge Robert Goldsborough, a state senator from Talbot, and John Henry of Dorchester, a future governor, were deeply involved. Goldsborough was to circulate a petition favoring the town of Talbot in Caroline, Queen Anne's, and Talbot counties, while Henry did the same in Dorchester, Somerset, and Worcester. Political pressure also was brought to bear on Gov. John Eager Howard and Western Shore members of the legislature.

The strategy worked, and the 1777 act was repealed December 22, 1788. Substitute legislation was passed the same day giving the town a new name—Easton—and decreeing that the courts and general business of the Eastern Shore should be conducted there "for ever hereafter."

That was the end for Dover; from then on it rapidly withered away. Its epitaph was sounded in the will of William Hughlett, probated December 30, 1845, leaving to his son Thomas, among other lands, "a field known by the name of Dover" which the elder Hughlett had purchased at a sheriff's sale.

Just who chose the name of Easton, or why it was selected, remain mysteries. It could have been for one of several English towns by that name, although no logical reason for honoring any of them has been found. In early days the spelling of "East-town" was sometimes used, and the town's founders may simply have had in mind pointing up the fact that Easton was the "east capital" of Maryland.

At any rate, Easton's growth was rapid once the new name was chosen. On December 25, 1789, it received an added boost: the General Assembly noted that the old 1712 Court House was "extremely inconvenient and incompetent" and ordered a new one built to house both the Maryland General Court and the county offices. The state put up more than eighty percent of the funds. Completed in 1794 by builder Cornelius West—who lost money on the deal—this structure survives in the oldest part of the vastly remodeled Court House which serves Talbot County today.

In 1790 provision was made for town commissioners, who didn't have to live in Easton but must reside within five miles. They were authorized to levy taxes on property, billiard tables, and dogs, and to regulate the price, quality, weight, and loaf size of bread offered for public sale. The billiard tax was £5 ($13.33) a year on any table within two miles of town, the dog tax fifty cents a year for males and a dollar for females. Strays were to be shot.

In 1794 town control was extended to the public road leading down to Cow Landing (Easton Point) and to the wharf which had been built at private expense there. The same act gave the town bailiff specific police powers "to prevent the tumultuous and irregular meetings of slaves, negroes and other dissolute and disorderly persons," and to punish "with moderate correction" any blacks found wandering the streets after midnight, when a curfew bell was sounded warning them to be in their homes.

Strict regulations were provided for operation of the market house, built with private funds at a site on Harrison Street between Goldsborough and Dover, where the Masonic Museum now stands. Fish and oysters, beef by the quarter or larger, whole hogs, butter by the firkin (about 20 pounds), cheese, grain, flour, bread, barreled beef and salt pork, and live cattle, sheep, and swine could be sold any day but Sunday; market days for other products were restricted to Tuesday and Saturday mornings. Butchering in or near the market was prohibited, and horses could not be brought inside the building. Slaves could not use the market to buy or sell anything.

At the same time the town was authorized to employ a regulator of scales, who doubled as clerk for the market; a firewood corder, who operated at a central location where all cordwood was to be sold; and an official hay weigher. The scale adjustor was paid forty dollars a year, the corder six cents a cord, and the hay weigher fifty-four cents a ton.

Top, earliest known photograph, circa 1860, of the Talbot County Court House in Easton, showing the market place on Washington Street. *Middle,* the Court House as it looked in 1876 at the time of the nation's centennial. Note the old armory at the far right. *Left,* Easton's second armory, built about 1810, became Easton's first firehouse but was demolished in the late nineteenth century when the "new" firehouse—now the Easton utilities office— was built on Harrison Street.

Top, Court House Square, circa 1935. *Bottom,* Court House gate, circa 1875.

Under these conditions Easton bloomed as no other Eastern Shore town had ever bloomed before. On May 11, 1790, James Cowan founded the shore's first newspaper, the *Maryland Herald and Eastern Shore Intelligencer*, and for many years afterward Easton had the shore's only newspapers except for a brief and disastrous experiment at Chestertown. Easton's importance was further enhanced when the federal court began holding semiannual sessions there in November, 1790, although these were discontinued after six years.

Business after business moved in, and stores went up all along Washington, Dover, Harrison, and Goldsborough streets. Banning, who could remember when Talbot Court House had been a "trivial place," recorded in 1793 that the town now "shines in spacious and elegant buildings, and with at least twenty stores, together with their bakers, butchers, brewers, market house, and tradesmen's shops of almost every description."

Banning was conservative in his estimate. At least forty businesses advertised in the *Herald* between 1790 and 1794. They included a printer-editor (Cowan), ten general merchants, two hatters, a silversmith, five tailors, a habit-maker (cloak maker), two tavernkeepers, a painting firm, two schoolmasters, a blacksmith, two physicians, a carpenter, a dancing master, an attorney, a firm of tanners, a "limner" (portrait artist), two watch-and-clock makers, a boot-and-shoe maker, a barber and bleeder, and a cabinetmaker. There undoubtedly were others who did not advertise.

Some of these artisans had unusual sidelines. Joseph Bruff, Jr., who had taken over his late father's silversmith shop, announced August 9, 1794, that he could offer militia officers "the newest and most approved patterns for sword mounting." Jacob Alborn, the town barber, offered his services as "hairdresser, bleeder, and tooth drawer" the same year. He also had a small supply of perfumery for sale. In combining these functions, Alborn was carrying on the tradition of English barbers, who since medieval times had not only cut hair but pulled teeth and done "leeching"—drawing blood by means of leeches, which was supposed to be a cure-all for nearly any ailment. The red-white-and-blue poles still found in front of barber shops originally signified this triple role.

Doctors—even reputable ones—also practiced the gruesome art of leeching, having no notion that its sole effect was to weaken their patients' resistance to disease. And by the late 1790s Easton was gaining the reputation it still retains, of being a "doctor's town." When Dr. Perry E. Noel announced in August, 1796, that he had opened an office opposite the court house and "settled permanently in Easton to practice physic," he made at least the sixth physician in the town. Others were Dr.

Sarah Glenn Douglas of Talbot County. An oil portrait by Rembrandt Peale, circa 1825.

John Coats, Dr. Ennals Martin, Dr. John Elbert, Dr. Charles Troup, and Dr. Tristram Thomas.

These early physicians, though trained in the best schools in Philadelphia, knew little or nothing about the true nature of disease. When an epidemic of yellow fever broke out in Philadelphia in 1793, they were as convinced as anyone else that it was transmitted by personal contact between human beings, rather than by mosquitoes as Dr. Walter Reed later proved. Town doctors helped organize a vigilante committee which was empowered to seize and hold all persons coming to Talbot from the Philadelphia area until they could be examined and pronounced "clean." One who was caught at the height of the panic was Francis Asbury, the apostle of Methodism. He recorded in his journal that when he arrived in Talbot County from the north in October, 1793, he was at first barred from houses and forbidden to preach at meetings because it was feared he might have brought the yellow fever with him.

Atmospheric conditions were also thought to be primary sources of disease. After a virus epidemic called "the head complaint" struck down hundreds of Talbot Countians in 1813-14, Dr. Ennals Martin wrote a learned scientific paper proving—to his own satisfaction, at least—that it had been caused by an earthquake in 1812 and the appearance of a comet in 1813.

But within the limits of the medical knowledge of their time, Easton's physicians were among the best in Maryland. When the Medical and Chirurgical Faculty of Maryland, the state's first medical society, was organized, Dr. Martin was one of the original petitioners and incorporators. At the society's first meeting, June 11, 1799, he was elected one of five members of the Board of Examiners for the Eastern Shore, charged with examining and granting licenses to candidates for medical practice. Dr. Noel and Dr. Stephen Theodore Johnson of Easton were also on the Board. In 1818 Dr. Martin served as president of the state society.

A brusque and forthright man who often quarreled on medical matters with his colleagues, Dr. Martin was not only for many years Talbot County's leading physician but also one of the true "characters" of his time. His brutal bedside manner was famous; he would literally seize a patient by the neck, hold his nose, and dump some nauseous medical dose down his throat when he opened his mouth to gasp for breath. Yet, despite his theories on the cosmic cause of viruses, he was in general an enlightened man, a vigorous proponent of cowpox vaccination to prevent smallpox when that was highly controversial, and one of the first to maintain that bleeding killed patients rather than curing them.

One of the earliest physicians in the Easton area was John Coats, who came down from Pennsylvania not long after the Revolution. Dr. Coats brought with him an intense love of the secret society of masonry, having served as deputy grand master of the grand lodge of Pennsylvania shortly before he left there. He organized a Masonic lodge in the future Easton in 1781, and in 1787 became the first grand master of the first grand lodge of Maryland, which met in a loft over the Harrison Street market until 1794. The present Coats Lodge of the Masonic Order in Easton commemorates his name.

The first limner known to have been in Easton was Andrew Boyer, who was active in December, 1793. No examples of his work are known to this writer, but a far more prominent artist, Rembrandt Peale, was in town a few years later. On September 3, 1799, Peale informed readers of the *Herald* that he was a "portrait painter in large and small"—meaning that he did miniatures as well as full-sized portraits—and that he intended to remain in Easton and vicinity a short while longer. He guaranteed that "no picture which is not a good likeness, and generally approved of, shall leave his hands."

Rembrandt's even more famous father, Charles Willson Peale, had visited Talbot County at length in 1790 on a mission which combined business with a search for romance. He painted portraits of a number of local people, but his main purpose was to find a wealthy woman who

> **MRS. REDHEAD,**
> BEGS leave thus publicly to return her most respectful thanks to her customers in general for the many past favors with which they have obliged her in her line of business, and flatters herself that she shall, by a due attention to her profession and to Fancy, merit a continuance of their encouragement.——In addition to MILLINERY, she informs the Ladies of Talbot and other Counties, that she now carries on MANTUA-MAKING, UPHOLSTERY, and PLAIN SEWING—In each of these three departments of business, they may be supplied upon the shortest notice, as she now has an assistant.
> Easton, Oct. 25, 1803.

> **Portrait Painting**
> IN CRAYONS AND MINIATURE,
> *Executed in the most fashionable style.*
> ——ALSO——
> PROFILES FROM THE PHYSIOGNOTRACE,
> BY *JOHN BRUFF.*
> At Mrs. Dawson's, opposite the Court-house.
> FOR SALE,
> A handsome assortment of LOOKING GLASSES, in elegant gilt frames. Old glasses taken in exchange.
> Easton, April 16, 1805.

would become his wife and stepmother to his seven children. A newly bereaved widower, he was portly and nearly fifty at the time.

While doing portraits of the Tilghmans of Gross Coate, Peale fell in love (or so he claimed) with the shy and lovely Mary (Molly) Tilghman. She seemed to reciprocate, but male members of the proud Tilghman family broke up the romance. Peale went back to Philadelphia, where his museum was featuring a live five-legged cow with two tails, and not long afterward married Betsey DePeyster, a fat, placid Dutch girl of twenty-five. Molly Tilghman married badly and had an unhappy life. Her restless ghost is said to haunt the old house at Gross Coate to this day.

In addition to itinerant painters, entertainers of all sorts were attracted to booming Easton in the 1790s. In May, 1792, a Mr. Bowen offered an exhibition of thirty large-as-life waxworks, including a "beautiful female figure" said to represent one of the belles of Baltimore whom Bowen didn't identify. On the side he had for sale likenesses of President Washington, a variety of "elegant prints," and a used guitar.

In October, 1792, Easton was host to Talbot's first recorded theatrical performance, staged in a room at Solomon Corner's Washington Street tavern. The "Maryland company of players," led by actors McGrath and Godwin, presented a comedy titled *A Bold Stroke for a Wife, or, The Guardians Outwitted*. Also on the bill were two shorter pieces, a pantomime called *The Drunken Peasant, or, Dwarf's Transformation*, and a farce, *The Mayor of Garrett*. The group came back in 1798, this time in a play called *Douglas*; and in 1799 two comic operas were presented by the troupe of Messrs. Rignal and Reinagle of Philadelphia. Another live performance in 1799, by the company of Mr. Ricketts, ended with a grand display of fireworks.

Two young buffalo directly from Kentucky were on display in Mrs. Bruff's alley in April, 1793. Those who wanted to "put their cows to the

Mary Tilghman of Gross Coate, from a portrait by Charles Willson Peale. It was while painting this portrait in 1790 that Peale fell in love with Mary. Her family broke up the romance.

male" in an effort to produce a cross-bred bovine could do so for thirty-five shillings (about six dollars). For those who just wanted a look, the charge was a quarter.

Dancing was another lively art popular in Easton, and assorted dancing masters advertised their schools. A Frenchman, Monsieur Curley, announced that at his school, to be opened June 1, 1792, pupils would be taught "dancing in its various parts, and in the most approved

> **CABINET WARE-ROOM.**
>
> The Subscriber has again commenced the manufacture of Cabinet Furniture, in the Store House of Thomas P. Bennett, on Washington street, near the corner of Dover street. He has just received from Baltimore a Stock of first rate Materials, selected by himself, and intends keeping a constant supply, which will enable him to furnish those who may please to favour him with their custom, with every variety of work in his line, he will endeavour by punctuality and attention to business, to merit a share of the public patronage.   JAMES NEALL.
>
> N. B. Also, Turning executed in its different varieties,   J. N.
>
> Easton, Nov. 23 3w

style, with elegance and grace in moving and attitudes." For advanced students there would be instruction in the High Steps, the Minuet de la Cour, and the Gavot. Citizen Robardet, who claimed to have instructed Martha Washington's grandchildren, held classes and a public ball in September, 1793. A town ballroom was built in 1796 by public subscriptions. The first of many Washington's Birthday balls was held there February 22, 1798. This drew a blast in the *Herald* from a correspondent who complained about how readily Easton's residents would give money for a dancing party, and how difficult it was to find funds with which to build a church. (The town's Episcopalians then were holding services in the Court House while they tried to raise enough money for Easton's first Episcopal Church, later built on Harrison Street.) This according to the *Herald* correspondent indicated Easton was becoming a den of "immorality and atheism," imported from godless, revolutionary France.

The holding of lotteries to raise money for almost every conceivable purpose was as prevalent as dancing. Even the churches didn't frown on these. In 1800 the vestry of St. Paul's Church staged a lottery, apparently unsuccessful, in hopes of raising enough money to pay off the indebtedness incurred in rebuilding Old Chester Church, south of Centreville, and repairing St. Luke's Chapel at Wye Mills. Some lotteries were strictly for private purposes. In 1790 Richard Chew announced a lottery to sell his lands and pay off his debts. W. W. Haddaway used a lottery to raise capital for his proposed ferry service from Haddaway's wharf (now

Lowe's) to Annapolis, which he opened April 1, 1796. Another lottery, for the dual purpose of buying a fire engine for the town of Easton and completing the public wharf at Easton Point, was announced May 1, 1792. Apparently it didn't do very well; at any rate, no fire engine was purchased and no fire company organized until after a disastrous blaze destroyed much of the Washington Street business section in 1808.

Fourth of July celebrations, unknown in the first post-Revolutionary years, caught on starting in 1794. That year there were two in Talbot, one in Easton and one at William Varnum's tavern in the hamlet known as "the Trap." Easton's was the more spectacular; the celebrating began at sunrise with the firing of fifteen guns, representing the fifteen states then in the Union. The guns were fired again at noon, and a large company assembled at the new court house, where they marched upstairs to enjoy a banquet laid out in the main courtroom. Fifteen toasts were drunk, in praise of subjects ranging from "the day of our glorious independence," to George Washington, the Rights of Man, and the Continental Congress of 1776. At the Trap there was also a good deal of gunfiring and toast drinking, after which (said the *Herald*) "the citizens dispersed in perfect harmony."

A more solemn show of patriotic fervor came February 22, 1800, in the memorial service for President Washington, who had died the previous December 14. According to the *Herald*, this was attended "by the greatest concourse of people that ever assembled here."

At noon the militia in uniform, all civil officers, and the public gathered on the Court House green. Captain William Goldsborough, called "Hessian Billy" because he had single-handedly killed three Hessian soldiers who attacked him at once, led his company of light infantry, with arms reversed and drums muffled, on a march to "the place of Divine Worship" on Harrison Street. This was the vacant lot, next door to the present town utilities building, where the Episcopalians planned to build their church as soon as they got enough money together to do so.

Following the infantry in solemn order were "an elegantly led horse, properly caparisoned"; Perry Benson; militia officers, two by two; militia members who didn't possess guns or uniforms; the civil officers; and the male citizens of Talbot, who also marched two by two and who wore black scarves on their left arms.

At the "place of Worship" the Reverend Joseph Jackson, rector of St. Peter's Parish, gave the opening prayer. A sermon "adapted to the occasion" was delivered by the Reverend John Bowie, who by then no doubt had forgotten his Tory sympathies during the war. After the ceremonies, the entire assemblage paraded back to the Court House and was dismissed.

Old Wye Church, Wye Mills, one of three chapels of ease of St. Paul's Parish, built in 1721. Repaired in 1800 with funds from a lottery held by the Vestry of St. Paul's. Restored in 1949 through the generosity of Arthur Amory Houghton, Jr., Wye Plantation, Queenstown.

It was an outpouring of veneration for one man such as Talbot would never witness again. Washington had been universally loved, but the same could not be said for his successors, John Adams and Thomas Jefferson, nor even for the policies he espoused as president. While he was still in office, partisan politics had begun to split Talbot's citizenry into warring camps, and when Washington retired, the process intensified. Those who favored Washington's plan for a strong federal government became known as Federalists, while those who backed Jefferson and his more liberal principles were called Republicans, later modified to Democratic-Republicans and still later to plain Democrats.

But those names were seldom used by the partisan of either side in Talbot political campaigns. It was an era of free-wheeling, no-holds-barred electioneering. Character assassination was the accepted order of the day, and published insults of the most slanderous kind filled the local newspapers. Editor Cowan of the *Herald* and Thomas Perrin Smith, who founded the rival *Republican Star* in 1799, fostered publication of vitriolic name-calling, accusations of theft and other crimes, and even lewd insinuations about the private lives of prominent citizens. The editors charged space rates for publishing letters to the editor, and thus made a tidy profit printing gutter insults.

A single sample will suffice to show the tone of this kind of material. It appeared on August 27, 1805, in the *Star*:

> For reasons satisfactory to my mind, I publish and declare William Barroll, Esq. of Chestertown, to be a SCOUNDREL.
>
> T. M. Forman

Two weeks later Barroll replied, calling Forman a "contemptible fellow" and challenging him to disclose his reasons for the insult, so that "the world shall see who is the scoundrel."

Many other examples could be given. The *Herald* carried such brief and to-the-point messages as: "John Turner of Easton is a coward," and "Richard Lyons (a Methodist preacher from Somerset County) perverts the truth." In the course of a lengthy controversy in 1805 Dr. Alexander Stuart of Kent County was described in the *Star* as a "lying varlet," a "driveler," and an "arch demon." He marched into the *Star*'s office demanding a retraction, and when editor Smith tried to argue that he had merely printed the insults, not endorsed them, Dr. Stuart threatened to use his considerable political influence to "crush" Smith. Later another irate reader horsewhipped Smith over a similar issue. Cowan also was beaten up in his office for remarks he had published about the Jeffersonians, whose policies he opposed.

In such a climate, loud street confrontations and even knockdown fights between political opponents were common. One infamous battle occurred at the polling booth in Easton during the 1798 congressional campaign between Federalist William Hindman and Democratic-Republican Joshua Seney. According to a witness, William Perry tried to bribe a voter with a one hundred dollar bill to vote for Hindman, but when the man was asked afterward how he'd cast his ballot, he shouted out: "Joshua Seney, by God!" "Whereupon," says the chronicler, "Will Perry knocked him down, and Jacob Gibson (the pro-Seney poll watcher) knocked William Perry down, and a pugilistic battle occurred immediately within the polls." Worst of all for Perry, Seney won.

Gibson, one of the participants in this slugfest, was for many years Talbot County's most noted street brawler, and beyond any doubt its all-time champion writer of vitriolic letters to the editor. For twenty-five years he kept Talbot Countians amused, entertained, enraged, and scandalized with a constant barrage of letters liberally larded with ridicule, satire, tirades, invective, and accusations.

A powerfully built man who kept in shape by doing most of his own farm work on his Miles River estate, Marengo, named in honor of a victory by his hero, Napoleon Bonaparte, he was willing at any time to back up his words with his fists. He hated the Federalists, scorned his aristocratic neighbors for considering themselves above menial work, and loved the Jeffersonians, all aspects of the French Revolution, and a good fight, although not necessarily in that order. It was he who knocked down editor Cowan, whom he despised for his Federalism. Later, in a letter which appeared in the *Star*, Gibson publicly castigated Cowan as a "noted drunkard" and said "poor lazy Cowan" had lost all his friends and was fast approaching bankruptcy. These insults had the sting of truth; Cowan did go bankrupt, and had to close down the *Herald* in November, 1805, leaving the *Republican Star* as the Eastern Shore's only newspaper.

Another of Gibson's famous battles was "a ferocious fight at the Court House door" with the Reverend John Bowie. History doesn't say who won, but it is doubtful it was the parson.

Despite his pugnacity, Gibson was a prime example of the democratic spirit pervading the country in the postwar years. Dr. Harrison, a great admirer, called him a "stout-hearted, large-brained, strong-armed man; . . . friend of the poor and lowly and enemy of the rich and lofty, . . . lifelong foe of aristocratic pretension (and) lover of democratic equality."

By the turn of the 19th century, Easton's status as a growing town was attracting attention throughout Maryland. It was even noticed by the *American Gazetteer*, published in Boston in 1798, which gave this description:

> Easton, the chief town of Talbot County, Maryland, formerly called Talbot Court House, is on the eastern side of Chesapeake Bay. It has a handsome court house, and market house, about 150 dwelling houses, and several stores for the supply of the adjacent country.

Elsewhere around the county, too, things were perking up, with Oxford the only notable exception. That once busy little port did not quite die, but it came close. It retained its ancient status as an official port of entry, but its first United States customs collector, Jeremiah Banning,

Oxford and Town Creek in a contemporary view, 1981.

had little to do in his tiny one-room office across the river at the Isthmus. It was there, in 1793, that he penned his magnificent lament for the lost glories of the town from which he had set forth on so many adventures:

> The poor, drooping, and forsaken Oxford, bereft of almost every comfort in life, hath nothing remaining to console it except its salubrious situation and fine navigation which may anticipate better times. Oxford, whose streets and strands were once covered with busy, noisy crowds, ushering in commerce from almost every quarter of the Globe, and whose rich, blooming lots echoed with fat, glowing kine—alas, now is shaded by wheat, corn and tobacco. The once well worn streets are now grown up with grass, save a few tracks made by the sheep and swine; and the strands have more the appearance of an uninhabited island than where human feet have ever trod.

By 1794 Oxford's total exports had dwindled to a value of just $6,956. Its ferry across the Tred Avon had long since ceased regular operation, not to be revived until 1836. Its population was down to about ninety—seventy whites and twenty blacks—who lived in the thirteen remaining houses and a few surrounding shacks. Not until the 1840s would it start a comeback.

For Banning as well, the glory days were over. So crippled with gout that he had to be carried to his office, he gave up his customs post to his adopted son Robert in 1795. Henceforth he devoted his time to polishing up his will and providing for the manumission of his twenty-nine slaves, many of whom (or their parents) he had personally brought from Africa. He died December 23, 1798, at the age of sixty-three, and was buried on his home plantation in an unmarked grave.

While Oxford sank into oblivion, other Talbot locations were growing into prominence. The crossroads hamlet called the Trap, later formalized as Trappe, acquired at least two general stores, a physician, an undertaker, a tailor, a retail liquor dealer, two taverns, a blacksmith, a pharmacist, and a "preaching house" maintained by "the people called Methodists." It already had a Quaker meeting house, on the site now occupied by Scott's United Methodist Church. By 1810 it was well on its way to becoming the prime trading center for southern Talbot's wheat and corn farmers.

St. Michaels had been little more than a cluster of houses surrounding the parish church before the Revolution, although some shipyards and two or three merchant-traders operated in the nearby waters. One of them, James Braddock, who was factor for Messrs. Gildart & Gawith of Liverpool, was first to recognize its potential. In 1778 he had a survey made and lots for a town laid out on land he owned in the area now known as St. Mary's Square. But Braddock died shortly afterward, and not until January 19, 1805, did the Maryland General Assembly enact legislation chartering a town to be established on the site favored by Braddock and his heir, John Thompson.

Commissioners were appointed, street names (most of them still in use) assigned, and the town was divided into four squares—St. Mary's, Braddock's, Thompson's, and Harrison's. The last was for Samuel Harrison, probably the same man for whom Harrison Street in Easton was named. He had a large store and warehouse at the place now called Canton, on Broad Creek back of the new town.

In the next few years shipbuilding in the vicinity reached its all-time peak. Well before the turn of the century St. Michaels-area craftsmen had developed the distinctive type of fast, lean-hulled, rakish vessel that later became famous as the "Baltimore clipper." Many of the master builders, in fact, shuttled between their Talbot homes and Fells Point, the shipbuilding center of Baltimore.

During the first decade of the nineteenth century, yards in or near St. Michaels were maintained by Harrison & Kemp, Perry Spencer of Spencer Hall, his brother Richard Spencer of Beverly, Thomas Wayman of Solitude, Thomas L. Haddaway, Impey Dawson, John Wrightson,

St. Michaels harbor with boat basin, foreground, and the Chesapeake Bay Maritime Museum on Navy Point, upper right. A contemporary view, 1981.

Skinner Harris, John Davis, and others. Farther afield, there were yards at Peck's Point, Ferry Neck, Church Neck, and Broad Creek Neck.

All this collective effort gave employment to a number of people, many of whom lived at what was called "Onion Hill," while others crowded into St. Michaels itself. It was not a "genteel" type of population; most of the inhabitants were mechanics, adzemen, carpenters, iron workers, and the like, many of them descendants of Irish or Scottish immigrants who had come as indentured servants or convicts. They lived with their large families in wooden houses which were not much more than shanties, and tended to celebrate on Saturday nights after they got their pay. Dr. Harrison said in his essay on St. Michaels that the town long had the reputation of having more court cases involving misdemeanors and other petty crimes than any other community in Talbot. But it was a population, unschooled and undisciplined, which was ripe for the mass appeal of the new and highly emotional "people's" religion called Methodism, just then sweeping through the Eastern Shore like a tidal wave.

Methodism had begun as a reform movement within the Church of England in the 1730s. John Wesley (1703-1791), its leading spirit, never did leave the Anglican church, although he was in large measure responsible for the eventual break between the two denominations. It was introduced on the Delmarva peninsula in 1739 by George Whitefield, but made little progress until young Francis Asbury came to America in 1770 as Wesley's missionary. When he arrived, Asbury found a small, weak movement of some four hundred members, mostly around New York and Philadelphia; at his death in Virginia March 31, 1816, the Methodist Episcopal Church in America, which he had founded under Wesley's direction, numbered 214,000 members and 2,000 preachers through the east and south. Much of the increase was due to Asbury's own prodigious labors; in forty-five years he traveled on horseback an estimated two hundred seventy thousand miles, ordained more than four thousand ministers, and, despite a stubborn throat ailment which made speaking difficult, delivered more than ten thousand sermons.

The first Methodist known to have preached in Talbot County was Joseph Cromwell, who addressed crowds at Wye Mills, St. Michaels, and Bay Hundred in 1777. Like many of his fellow circuit-riding preachers, he was illiterate but eloquent. Asbury wrote of him: "He is the only man in America with whose speaking I am never tired. . . . He never opens his mouth but some are cut to the heart."

In the summer of 1778 came Freeborn Garrettson, in contrast to Cromwell a man of considerable education and culture. He arrived in St. Michaels in July, and in his own words, "labored for two weeks, night and day with tears." In November he returned for a quarterly meeting of the local Methodist Society, which had been formed that same year. The formal session, held at the house of Richard Parrott on Parrott's Point, was followed by a prayer meeting which lasted until 2:00 A.M. Fifteen persons were present, and five souls "were set at liberty" (saved) during the night. Garrettson wrote ecstatically: "The Lord was with us in truth. . . . His presence filled the room."

These 1778 meetings and another in 1779, during which William Watters preached for two days in the barn on Parrott's farm, were the foundation stones for Sardis Chapel, the original Methodist church in St. Michaels.

The first of Asbury's forty-three visits to Talbot County over a period of thirty-five years was in September, 1779, when he stopped in at Talbot Court House to visit his impetuous young friend Joseph Hartley. Hartley was in jail at the time, having refused to take the oath of allegiance to Maryland on grounds he had already taken one to the state of Delaware. He was enjoying himself, preaching through the bars of his cell window

Some vanished Easton churches. *Top left*, Trinity Methodist Church South, Harrison and Goldsborough streets. *Top right*, Calvary Methodist Protestant Church, Washington and Bay streets. *Bottom left*, Ebenezer Methodist Episcopal Church (now an office building), South Washington Street. *Bottom right*, First Baptist Church, photographed about 1935, in Harrison Street structure originally built for Easton's first Protestant Episcopal church, 1803.

to crowds which gathered daily, intrigued by the spectacle of a preacher spouting the gospel from a jail cell. Asbury, who himself had been forced to hide out from authorities in a cypress swamp near Sudlersville, was currently barred from preaching in Maryland. Asbury advised Hartley to make bail, "as I thought he would have no trial. All that the opposers wanted, was to prevent his preaching in the county." Asbury also advised Hartley, who wanted to get married, at least to postpone the wedding until he got out of jail.

Hartley took his mentor's advice, and was released on bond of five hundred pounds, guaranteed by James Benson, father of Perry, and Thomas Harrison. He was freed when the grand jury failed to bring in a true bill, and went temporarily to Kent County, where he capitalized on his experience by preaching from the text: "Persecuted but not forsaken; cast down but not destroyed." In December he married a young lady from Miles River Neck, and reportedly settled there at Dundee. He died, still a young man, in 1785; but his work lived on in two Talbot Methodist churches. Many of those who had come to jeer at the "preaching jailbird" went away convinced, and the Easton Methodist Society formed in the fall of 1779 was the forerunner of the old Ebenezer Methodist Church and of today's St. Mark's United Methodist Episcopal Church. The Dundee Chapel, founded in 1784 and said to have been "a child of his preaching," lasted for a century before it gave way to the present church at Tunis Mills.

Soon societies were formed throughout the county, and small, simple chapels were built everywhere. The earliest was probably at Bolingbroke, where a meeting house existed before 1780. Asbury preached at many of them, and made illuminating notations in his journal. Reporting backsliders at Bolingbroke, he lamented: "O how does the power of religion decline!" It was the same in Easton. "Death! Death!" he wrote after a sparsely attended meeting there in 1787. ". . . We held a watch night meeting, and the gentry had a ball." But a year later "the power came" while he was preaching at Easton. The congregation had "a noble shout" and he was "greatly comforted." Wye Mills had "a good new chapel" when he preached there on the first official Thanksgiving Day, November 23, 1789. Trappe's Lebanon Methodist Church, which he visited in 1805, was "the neatest on this shore." Perhaps one reason was that the workmen who had built it had a special incentive to do a good job; church records reveal that they were allotted a gallon of whiskey when they finished.

After a separate Methodist Episcopal Church in America was formally established at a memorable conference in Lovely Lane Chapel, Baltimore, on Christmas Day, 1784, the movement grew rapidly in

A typical "camp meeting" site of the nineteenth century.

Talbot. In 1782, 719 members had been reported in the county; by 1786 the number had increased to 1,601, including 524 blacks. At that time Talbot County had the largest membership of any circuit in America, with more than five percent of the national total. After a decline in the 1790s, a massive revival of interest in 1801-1802 brought membership to 2,417, its highest level of the early period.

While permanent membership fluctuated after that, the intense excitement whipped up by the great camp meetings held every summer kept interest high. These gatherings, at least in the beginning, were emotional eruptions whose effect has been likened to "the sweep of a mighty tornado." Thousands gathered at designated grounds to live in tents, eat oxen, pig, and corn roasted on communal fires, and indulge in a week of preaching, praying, and repentance.

Henry Bochm, first secretary of the Methodist Camp Meeting Association, penned a memorable account of the first such meeting ever held at Wye Camp Grounds just north of Wye Mills, in the summer of 1807. It opened on Friday night, July 29, with a prayer by the Reverend Solomon Sharp. "The work of revival went on all night. Many were converted, and the grove echoed with loud hallelujahs. Sunday was a great day, great crowds, great preaching, great power under the word." That night a fresh relay of preachers was scheduled, but "the work (of salvation) broke out so under the prayer offered at the stand, and such were the cries of distress, the shouts of triumph, that the preaching had to be dispensed with. But the work went on gloriously." According to another account, the shouting and screaming at such events could be heard at a distance of three miles.

The ecstasy continued all week long. The second Sunday, August 5, "was a day of wonders. Eight thousand people were on the ground. The multitude ... looked astounded, it was visible in their countenances."

Summing up, Boehm decided that a final count of how many really had been "born again" would have to wait until a census could be taken in heaven. "But they were many.... This was the greatest meeting I have ever attended. Almost every sinner on the ground was awed to reverence."

Meanwhile the tradition-bound Episcopal churches were in sad straits. Their official tax support had been stripped away at the start of the Revolution, and their membership greatly reduced by defections to the Methodists. Many of their former clergymen had gone back to England, never to return. At the war's end there were only five Anglican clergymen in all of Maryland, and only two of these—including the Reverend Samuel Keene, later rector at St. Michaels—showed up when the Reverend Dr. William Smith issued a call for a convention at Chestertown in 1780 to settle the postwar status of the church in Maryland. However, a later convention under Dr. Smith's leadership was more successful, and adopted the name of The Protestant Episcopal Church in America for the "separate but equal" branch on this side of the Atlantic.

Lack of funds continued to plague the Episcopalians for many years. St. Luke's Chapel at Wye Mills fell into disuse and became a stable for cattle; it was not restored until after 1847. The old chapel in eastern Talbot County, from which Chapel District took its name, had long since been abandoned. Even Old Whitemarsh Church was used less and less frequently after the new church at Easton was consecrated in 1803.

Both the Quakers and the early Methodists had strong commitments against slavery, and one effect of the rise of Methodism was to stimulate a wave of slave manumissions which became very marked in postrevolutionary Talbot County. Maryland Quakers had been forbidden to own slaves since 1777, and the Methodists adopted an equally strict ban shortly afterward. A resolution approved at a Baltimore meeting in 1780, with Asbury in the chair, declared that "slavery is contrary to the laws of God, man, and nature, and hurtful to society; contrary to the dictates of conscience and pure religion, and doing that which we would not others should do to us and ours." Later conventions set up rules for immediate expulsion of any person who bought, sold, or gave away slaves "except for the purpose to free them." The Methodist church later retreated from this position, and by 1836 was opposed to any interference with "the civil and political relation between master and slave." But its militant early stand brought freedom to many blacks in Talbot.

Hundreds of manumissions were recorded in the county in the postwar years. By 1800 Talbot had more free blacks than any other county in Maryland, and probably more in proportion than any similar area in the entire slaveholding South. The trend continued, and on the eve of the Civil War there were almost as many free blacks in Talbot County as slaves.

By no means all the manumissions, however, were for reasons of conscience. Many freed their slaves simply to get rid of them, finding them an economic burden. In a wheat-dominated economy, which required less hand labor, blacks who had been imported to work in the tobacco fields no longer were profitable to their masters.

However, in the nineteenth century's first decade, military rather than moral or economic issues occupied the attention of many Talbot Countians. England was taking advantage of the young American nation on the high seas, and each new incident brought a fresh burst of patriotic fervor in Talbot County. When an uproar arose in 1807 over British insistence on the right to seize and search American vessels, *Republican Star* editor Thomas Perrin Smith called for an indignation meeting with a notice which is a classic of bombastic chauvinism:

> Your independence, the legacy of the heroes of '76, has been attacked by a band of sea robbers and pirates. You are now called upon to assemble around the standards of your country and adopt measures that will convince the cowardly assassins that we are descendants of those heroes who once drove them from our country, and that we are willing and ready to do it again or perish with our constitution.

Brigadier General Perry Benson, who had actually fought the British and had a withered arm to prove it, presided at the meeting which adopted equally fiery resolutions about what Talbot County would do if the British didn't back down. There is no record that London was unduly frightened by these threats—but Talbot Countians felt better.

From then on Talbot was busy with preparations for the war which finally was declared in June, 1812. A number of militia companies were reactivated under General Benson's leadership. In Easton these included the Easton Fencibles, the Light Infantry Blues, the Talbot Volunteer Artillerists, and a band of older citizens, headed by Thomas J. Bullitt of Bullitt House, who called themselves the Town Guard. Elsewhere there were the St. Michaels Patriotic Blues, a cavalry company known as the Independent Light Dragoons or the Talbot Patriotic Troop, the

"Easton, at the Thos. Atkinson's, November 26, 1816." A drawing from the Journal of William E. Bartlett.

Hearts of Oak (from the Royal Oak vicinity), and others. In 1811-12 a new brick armory was built at the back of the Court House in Easton to replace the old revolutionary war powder magazine which stood midway between Washington and Harrison streets.

As usual, however, Talbot County opinion was far from unanimous on the war issue; in fact, a majority appears to have opposed it. In the fall elections of 1812 the antiwar Federalists, who had been having little success in recent years, carried all four Talbot seats in the Maryland General Assembly, and the county gave a majority to an elector pledged to DeWitt Clinton in opposition to the "war president," James Madison.

The war came home to Talbot, as no other conflict has done before or since, in 1813. In the spring a British fleet under Admirals Warren and Cockburn invaded the Chesapeake, ravaged numerous towns and cities, and among other things occupied Sharp's, Tilghman's, and Poplar islands. There were serious fears Easton would be attacked. Earthen fortifications, the outlines of which can still be found, were erected near Easton Point at what was called Fort Stoakes for James Stoakes, a local shipbuilder and Methodist preacher. The gold in the Easton bank was hauled by wagon to a place of safety in Lancaster, Pennsylvania. Militia companies were mustered. But no invasion force appeared; a convoy of what were supposed to be British warships turned out to be local cargo vessels carrying lumber up the Tred Avon River.

On Sharp's Island a landing party under Admiral Warren captured the owner, Jacob Gibson, who had come out to remove his cattle, sheep,

The Cannonball House, St. Michaels. According to tradition, when St. Michaels was shelled by the British in a night attack in 1813, the town was "blacked out," and lanterns were hung in the tree tops to lead the attackers to believe the town was on a high bluff. A cannon ball was said to have hit the chimney of this house and rolled down the stairway.

and hogs. They seized livestock valued at $225, for which they paid him in cash and treasury notes, and let him go. He later donated the money to the state and national governments, but at the same time was accused of trading with the enemy.

On his way back to St. Michaels the fun-loving Gibson decided to play a practical joke on his fellow Talbot Countians. He hoisted on his barge a red banner which looked at a glance like the British Union Jack, set a servant in the hold to beating on an empty rum barrel in the manner of a martial drum, and proceeded up Broad Creek toward the San Domingo landing as if he were the vanguard of an enemy invasion force.

On shore there was instant panic. Still fresh in people's minds was the shameful British behavior at Hampton, Virginia, where Admiral Cockburn had permitted his troops to indulge in an orgy of rape, looting, and arson. Men hastened to gather their wives and daughters, intending to send them inland to safety. Cavalrymen dashed here and there with the latest word on the approach of the "enemy." The St. Michaels Patriotic Blues and other militia units prepared for action.

When the "invaders" turned out only to be Jacob Gibson and a few black servants, the panic turned to fury. Enlisted men of the Patriotic Blues had to be restrained by their officers from killing Gibson on the spot. He was subjected to indignities, and forced to make an abject public apology for his unfunny joke. Later, in further amends, he presented the town with two handsome cannon which were used to good effect when the British really did assault St. Michaels later that year.

On August 6, 1813, the British landed approximately two thousand troops on Kent Island, and reports filtered out that they were planning an attack on St. Michaels, where half a dozen vessels were under construction, including at least one barge being built for use as a war vessel. About five hundred militia from all parts of the county were assembled for defense by General Benson. A boom composed of logs chained together was thrown across the mouth of the harbor, and batteries of cannon stationed at strategic locations. The fort on Parrott's Point, which had been dedicated in May with presentation of a "handsome flag" made by the ladies of St. Michaels, was manned night and day by soldiers who had promised "to defend it with their lives."

Shortly after midnight on the dark and drizzly morning of August 10, eleven barges carrying about three hundred British marines and soldiers slipped up the river on the Miles River Neck side, away from the town. They then crossed over and moored as close as possible to the sandy shore. At 4:00 A.M. troops began disembarking just upstream from the Parrott's Point battery.

Most of the little fort's defenders immediately fled in panic across a cornfield to the main part of town; but according to a well-authenticated report a one-armed black man named John Stevens did not run away with the others. He managed to turn one of the fort's guns on the attackers, and fired at point-blank range a deadly load which included a cannonball, chain shot, pieces of china, spike nails, lead bullets, and broken glass. Nineteen British troops reportedly were killed by this one blast, more than the British fatalities in all the rest of the engagement put together. Stevens then raced to safety.

The British party spiked the Parrott's Point guns and went back to their barges, taking their dead and wounded with them. They did not attempt any other landing. There then ensued an artillery duel between waterborne British cannon and American shore batteries which lasted into the morning. Later that day the attackers returned to Kent Island. The British losses were estimated at thirty killed and an unknown number wounded; the militia had no casualties of any kind except—if tradition can be believed—a rooster whose leg was broken by a cannonball as he climbed on a stump to welcome the morning by crowing.

On August 26 the British put another landing party ashore at Wades's Point, about six miles from St. Michaels. They burned a few buildings, seized some clothing, and began marching toward the town; but militiamen effectively harassed them from the cover of the heavy woods along the road, and they turned back about halfway.

Almost immediately began the "second battle of St. Michaels" which was over what had happened during that dark and rainy night—who among the raw militia had shown courage and who had shown abject cowardice. Tough old General Benson, enraged by what he had seen, ordered a number of courts martial, but these were later dropped. For years the story persisted that the "Hearts of Oak" Company, at the first sound of enemy guns, had run all the way back to Royal Oak, without losing a man. Certainly, as Dr. Harrison wrote in his account of the affair, far more blood was shed in tavern arguments after the event than could possibly have been lost during the battle. "Many were the black eyes and bloody noses of the warriors of St. Michaels," he commented.

One story which gained currency in later years, although not mentioned in any contemporary account, was that the townspeople had "fooled the British" by placing lanterns in the treetops so that the enemy guns overshot the town. Another was that the only house hit was one on Mulberry Street, where a mother was carrying her baby daughter down a flight of stairs when a cannonball crashed through the wall and went thumping past them to the main hall. This still extant structure is known locally as "Cannonball House."

On other fronts, meanwhile, Talbot Countians were distinguishing themselves in a variety of ways. At Fells Point in Baltimore, Talbot-born Thomas Kemp, who had learned shipbuilding in the yards around St. Michaels, was turning out swift commerce raiders which were the scourge of the British navy and among the few things America had to cheer about in a generally disastrous war.

Most famous of his "Baltimore clippers"—which some say should have been named "St. Michaels clippers"—was the *Chasseur*, launched in December, 1812. *Chasseur* has been described as "the most beautiful vessel that ever floated on the ocean"; and certainly, with her rakish lines and topheavy sail, she was one of the fastest ships ever built up to her time. In three notable cruises as a privateer she captured scores of British merchant ships, outsailed the entire British navy, and whipped the armed British schooner *St. Lawrence* in a fierce battle off the island of Cuba. At one point her commander, Captain Thomas Boyle, sailed boldly up to the coast of England and declared a one-ship blockade of the entire British Isles. The British Admiralty sent half a dozen men-of-

St. Mary's Square, St. Michaels. A Revolutionary War cannon reflects the historic character of The Green, now highlighted by the St. Mary's Square Museum. The main building is a restored and furnished colonial house moved from the Maritime Museum Road site originally patented to John Hollingsworth in 1659.

war on a fruitless chase after her, and naval insurance rates at Lloyd's of London shot sky high. From then on she was nicknamed "the Pride of Baltimore." The modern *Pride of Baltimore*, the city's floating ambassador of good will, was inspired by her and built along her lines.

After the war Kemp came back to Talbot and built a handsome house at Wade's Point on Chesapeake Bay. It is still occupied by members of the Kemp family.

Craft built in the St. Michaels area shipyards were almost as famous. The 301-ton schooner *Surprise*, which carried a crew of 120 and ten big eighteen-pound guns, captured forty-three prizes in high seas encounters. The *Caroline* captured thirty, the *Lawrence* twenty-two. Altogether, twenty-eight Talbot schooners operated against British shipping in the years between 1807 and 1814.

In the middlewest, United States Navy purser Samual Hambleton of the Martingham Hambletons achieved lasting renown by designing a battle flag bearing the slogan, "Don't Give Up the Ship," during the battle of Lake Erie September 10, 1813. Stationed aboard Commodore Oliver Hazard Perry's flagship, Hambleton was technically a

An oil portrait of Samuel Hambleton of St. Michaels, first purser of the United States Navy, by John Beale Bordley, 1820. The desk is Chippendale with Federal inlay made by John Shaw of Annapolis in 1786 for Captain John Stevenson of Talbot County.

batant, but volunteered for active duty and was put in charge of two guns which performed effective service in the American victory. His flag has a place of honor today at the United States Naval Academy in Annapolis. After he retired Hambleton built a house just outside St. Michaels which he named Perry's Cabin for his friend and commanding officer, Commodore Perry.

And as mentioned earlier, Francis Scott Key, whose wife was the former Mary Tayloe Lloyd of Wye House, was inspired by the sight of the American flag still flying over Fort McHenry after a night of savage battle in Baltimore harbor September 14, 1814 to write the verses which became *The Star-Spangled Banner*.

As the misnamed War of 1812 finally ground to an inconclusive halt in 1815, a rosy future for Talbot County seemed assured. Its agriculture, now firmly based on wheat and corn, had prospered greatly from the world demand for foodstuffs during the long years of Napoleon's European wars. Its main town, Easton, had the Eastern Shore's only bank, founded in 1805 by a group composed largely of local men. Although this was at first named the Eastern Shore branch of the Farmers' Bank of Maryland, it had from the beginning operated entirely independently of the Western Shore branch at Annapolis. It was truly an Eastern Shore bank, dedicated to safeguarding the interests of local farmers and merchants against the "monied power" of Baltimore, which even then threatened to gobble up everything worth having on the Shore. Its first and longtime president, Nicholas Hammond, was Talbot's leading attorney as well as a banker, and played a dominant role in the county's economic, political, and social affairs for many years. After 1810 the bank's headquarters were located on the same corner at Washington and Goldsborough it later occupied as the Easton National Bank and which today is occupied by its successor, the Maryland National Bank.

In 1815 another enduring institution arose in Easton when Samuel Groome, a storekeeper and the bank's teller, built the Eastern Shore's first real hotel across Washington Street from the bank. This was truly a marvel of its time; it was constructed of brick and had private rooms for guests, in contrast to the rival taverns where everybody slept together in communal bedrooms. First known as the Easton Hotel, and later as the Brick Hotel to distinguish it from the Frame Hotel across the street, it was Easton's—and the shore's—leading hostelry through most of the nineteenth century. Remodeled and converted to stores and offices, it is now known as the Stewart Building.

Another harbinger of things to come was a strange looking little vessel called the *Surprise*, which first appeared in Talbot waters in 1816.

The Brick Hotel, built in 1815 by Samuel Groome, was the Eastern Shore's first real hotel. It is now an office building.

Surprise had sails, but its chief means of propulsion was a crude steam engine which turned a paddle wheel on its side. When the *Surprise* first churned up Third Haven Creek, as the Tred Avon then was called, it is said that crowds gathered on the banks to watch it move steadily against wind and tide at the astonishing speed of three miles an hour. The *Surprise* was soon supplanted by the steamboat *Maryland*, bigger, faster, and more reliable, and between the two of them they heralded the beginning of a century now looked back on nostalgically as the Steamboat Age.

With all this in Talbot County's favor, her leaders could hardly be blamed for looking toward the future with optimism, even confidence. But things did not turn out that way. The long boom was over, and an even longer depression was at hand. America's face was turning westward; in the decades to come Talbot County and the entire Eastern Shore would be left behind.

EIGHT

The Long Depression

HARD times hit Talbot County and the entire Eastern Shore almost immediately after the War of 1812. The basic cause was not hard to find: after thirty years of wars and revolutions, there was peace in Europe at last. The Congress of Vienna in 1815 did more than simply redraw the map and reshuffle the crowned heads of the continent; more importantly to Talbot, it sent European farmers back to their fields to produce grain in competition with the white wheat which had become the lifeblood of the Eastern Shore's economy.

The unnamed author of a letter which appeared in an Easton paper in 1819 gave clear warning of the depression that was to come. After commenting on the good years when Talbot products had been in great demand in Europe, he added:

> Those prosperous days are over. Europe reposes in peace. Thousands have exchanged implements of war for those of peace. From consumers they have become producers, and our farm products are not needed. Farmers must now depend on home consumption. . . . Our income will be reduced.

The truth of his message was already becoming clear. Wheat had sold for $2.50 a bushel in 1817; by 1819 it was down to $1.20, with corn and oats at 50 cents. At one point in 1821, wheat dipped below 75 cents. The results of this worldwide peace were not only lean years for Talbot's farmers, but ruinous conditions for everyone else. Talbot was preeminently a farming community, and its merchants and artisans could not prosper if the farmers had no money to buy their goods. The fallacy of the notion that the Eastern Shore, isolated as it was, was impervious to world conditions was never better illustrated than by the example of what the fall of Napoleon, and the subsequent peace agreement in Europe, meant to the lives and fortunes of nearly every Talbot County family.

"These were long and weary years of agricultural depression," Dr. Harrison wrote of the period between 1820 and 1840, ". . . years when poverty seemed to be the lot of the small farmer, and debt that of the large.... The value of lands in Talbot County declined, and population diminished or was stationary."

Statistics from the United States Bureau of the Census bear him out. Talbot's population decreased by 2,286 persons between 1820 and 1840, and increased by only 406 during the whole period between the end of the War of 1812 and the beginning of the Civil War. White population in particular was hard hit as younger men and women left for the new American frontier in search of a better life. The tide of empire was sweeping westward, leaving Talbot stranded with its memories.

On the farms trouble was followed by more trouble. Farmers' woes were increased by the ravages of the "Hessian fly," an insect pest named for the hated mercenaries of the Revolution, which in some years devoured almost the entire wheat crop. An invasion of caterpillars in 1826 didn't help matters. Nor did the cutworms which infested the corn.

Agricultural methods were little improved from those used in biblical times. Grain was still planted by hand; baskets "for sowing wheat and dropping corn" were advertised as late as the 1850s. Wheat was cut with sickles, or the heavier, more efficient cradles, and left to dry. Then it was spread out on the ground and horses or mules driven over it in an endless circle, treading the grain to separate it from the straw. Afterwards the grain was winnowed—fanned by hand to blow away the chaff. Finally it had to be scooped up and put into containers. Crop rotation, use of improved types of seed, and liming and fertilizing, although long advocated by agricultural experts, were slow to catch on in Talbot County.

To combat such backwardness, leading landowners of the area founded the Agriculture Society of the Eastern Shore in 1818 as a branch of the Maryland Agricultural Society. (An earlier society, formed in 1805, had not long survived.) This group promoted progressive farming methods and improved stock breeding, but its members were chiefly gentlemen farmers rather than dirt farmers. It is uncertain how much impact their teachings had on the average farmer with his small acreage and mediocre land. First president was Nicholas Hammond, Easton's leading banker, and board members included such men as Edward Lloyd, Henry Hollyday, Perry Benson, Tench Tilghman (grandson of the hero), and Robert H. Goldsborough, known as "the Chesterfield of Maryland" for his smooth manners, fine clothes, and enjoyment of life's pleasures.

In and around St. Michaels, shipbuilding fell off dramatically with the end of the war. There was no longer a demand for the light, swift vessels in which St. Michaels craftsmen and their Fells Point colleagues

Nicholas Hammond

had specialized. The shipping world was turning to heavier, slower cargo carriers of a type the shipyards of New England could produce much more efficiently.

The last—and probably the finest—large oceangoing vessel built in St. Michaels was the 283-ton brig *John Gilpin*, launched in 1831. In 1837 she set a mark of fifty-six days, four hours for the transpacific crossing from Callao, Peru, to Lintin, China, a time which stood as the world's record for eight years.

A few smaller brigs and schooners were turned out in Talbot yards during the postwar period by master builders operating on a part-time basis. Among those active were Joseph Robson, Spry Denny, the St. Michaels firm of Joseph Kemp and John A. Horney, Wrightson Jones, Perry Spencer, and his brother Richard. Most of the craft were described in registry records as "sharp built," which meant they were of the rakish Baltimore clipper type. In the postwar years these had but two ready markets: some were used for opium smuggling in the China Sea, and others were fitted out for the hideous slave traffic, in which Maryland-built vessels operating under ostensible foreign ownership played a leading part. The same speed which had served the country so well in time of war enabled these vessels to outrun a blockade of the African coast by the British, who were trying unsuccessfully to halt slave running with its attendant evils of overcrowding, disease, and death. Some craft of the St. Michaels area, including the *Perry Hall*, also known as the *Perry Spencer*, almost certainly finished their careers in this gruesome traffic.

Model of the brig *John Gilpin,* from drawings by the late R. Hammond Gibson.

At the same time, St. Michaels shipbuilders faced another problem: after more than a century, the ready supply of white oak, cedar, and other fine timbers needed for construction of wooden vessels was running low in Talbot. From the 1820s on, the bulk of the industry on the Eastern Shore shifted to Dorchester County and other less heavily exploited areas on the lower Chesapeake.

With its industrial mainstay gone, St. Michaels faced a grim period. Like the rest of Talbot County, the town declined in population as its master craftsmen moved elsewhere. Those who remained scratched out a meager living by harvesting oysters—then sold only in local markets—by crabbing and fishing, or as storekeepers trading with nearby farmers. According to Dr. Harrison: "These ten years from 1820 to 1830 were years of privation and actual suffering. There was much poverty and destitution, particularly among the aged, the infirm and the weaker sex."

The community seemed to have lost its spark. From the 1820s to 1848 it did not even bother to elect the town commissioners entitled by law. The 1805 market house in St. Mary's Square was no longer used for that purpose; it was converted first into a storage shed for War of 1812 cannon, and in 1835 into the town's first schoolhouse. Through these lean years St. Michaels was sustained by its pride, which grew with every retelling, in having been the town that whipped the British, by its abundant supply of oysters, and by its preoccupation with religion, which was overwhelmingly Methodist.

Easton was not much better off. Things got so bad there that in 1823 a soup kitchen to feed the starving, to be operated by the Charitable Society of Easton, was seriously considered. The town's early promise was not being fulfilled; it had degenerated from the bustling business center of the 1790s into a drowsy southern community of weed-grown walks and rutted dirt streets, ringed by malarial marshes which made it one of the unhealthiest towns on the Eastern Shore. Dr. Harrison wrote vividly of the conditions he had observed as a boy in the 1830s:

> Within my recollection to come to Easton and remain for a few days was certain illness, and possible death, in the fall of the year. Strong healthy men were carried off by bilious attacks in a few days, and women who lived within doors were often the victims....
>
> A population of thin cadaverous people, in the autumnal months, crept about their daily duties... with a langour and indifference that betokened a carelessness of life.

Touring troupes of stage players and opera singers no longer bothered with Easton. Almost the only traveling performances advertised in local papers in twenty years were a waxworks museum in 1823 and a "zoological exhibition," predecessor of the circus, which pitched its tents on a vacant lot next to the Union Hotel on Goldsborough Street October 9 and 10, 1835. The animal exhibit, which included gnus, lions, hyenas, a pelican, and a pony act, was preceded by a parade through Easton streets featuring "the celebrated Tremont Military Band from Boston." Admission to the show was twelve and one-half cents.

With outside sources drying up, Talbot Countians created their own amusements. The Eastern Shore's first cattle show was held in 1822; and annual fairs with prizes for the best cattle, hogs, sheep, and other farm animals, as well as awards for sewing, garden produce, jellies and jams, pickles, and baked goods by local housewives, soon became popular. The first of hundreds of church fairs in the county was staged in 1831 for the benefit of Easton's Christ Episcopal Church.

Entertainment of a sort was provided by the stocks and whipping post which until well into the nineteenth century stood in front of the jail, then located much nearer Washington Street than the present one. Culprits in the stocks were forced to sit facing the street, so that they offered convenient targets not only for rude insults but for rotten fruit, eggs, dead cats, and any other refuse bypassers might happen to have in hand.

The Bullitt House, built in 1801 by Thomas J. Bullitt.

Only "boys and low people" indulged in this sort of amusement. The "better classes" had more refined interests—for instance a concert on the pianoforte announced by Dr. Robert H. A. Koch, a German-born professor of music, in August, 1838. Dr. Koch also sang, played guitar, and gave lessons on the piano, harp, flute, violin, and in vocal renditions. Another music teacher, Vincent A. Schmidt, offered instruction in 1839 on these instruments plus the clarinet and in "Sacred Music."

Styles were changing, and pantaloons for men—trousers so tight they sometimes made the wearer appear deformed—were rapidly replacing the knee breeches and long stockings worn during the Revolution. When pantaloons first appeared Bishop Asbury had bitterly opposed them as wearing apparel for Methodist ministers. He saw in them an instrument of the devil which, if not checked, would bring about the ruin and eventual dissolution of his beloved church. But younger preachers took to wearing them anyway, and somehow Methodism survived.

In Easton the last man to wear knee breeches, with silver buckles on his shoes, was said to be Thomas J. Bullitt, president of the Easton bank from 1830 to his death in 1840. He was a familiar sight, and the source of some amusement, as he strolled from Bullitt House, which he had built in 1801, up Dover Street and along Washington to the bank building.

Another, and even stranger, echo of the past appeared in the 1830s on Oxford Neck. A solitary Indian—the last of his race in Talbot—built a cabin in the woods there and lived in it for a number of years. What tribe he came from or why he happened to choose Talbot County for his home has never been explained.

For many Talbot Countians, by far the favorite form of entertainment during this period was the game of politics. This, of course, was strictly for white men; although property requirements for voting had been eased, women and blacks were still denied the ballot. Only a few local offices were elective—county commissioners, most judges, the clerk of court, and register of wills all were appointed from Annapolis until 1851, and even the governor was not elected by popular vote until 1837—but the contests for Congress, the General Assembly, and president provided excitement, free food, and plentiful drinks.

Fish feasts, forerunners of today's bull roasts, were popular in Talbot's early years. These were staged in groves along the water, where seineloads of drum, perch, rock, and other fish could be hauled in, cleaned, and fried on the spot over open fires. Oysters were provided by the barrel, along with liberal quantities of hard cider, applejack, rum, whiskey, and other spirits. As a rule there was a good deal of vulgar fun and roughhousing, along with a few fistfights, to go with the inevitable partisan oratory. As fish became less abundant, hams and whole roasted oxen joined the oysters on the menu.

What was probably the greatest political rally in Talbot history came during the famous "log cabin and hard cider" campaign of 1840, when William Henry Harrison, known as "Tippecanoe" for his victory over the Indians along that Indiana river, was the Whig presidential candidate against Martin Van Buren, the incumbent Democrat. The occasion was a monstrous meeting of all Maryland Whigs on the grounds of what is now Spring Hill Cemetery in Easton, and the open fields that then surrounded it. Nine steamboats from Baltimore and other Maryland ports converged on Talbot, and the crowd in attendance was estimated at fifteen to twenty thousand. Water was provided by the spring from which the cemetery later took its name, and whole trees were uprooted

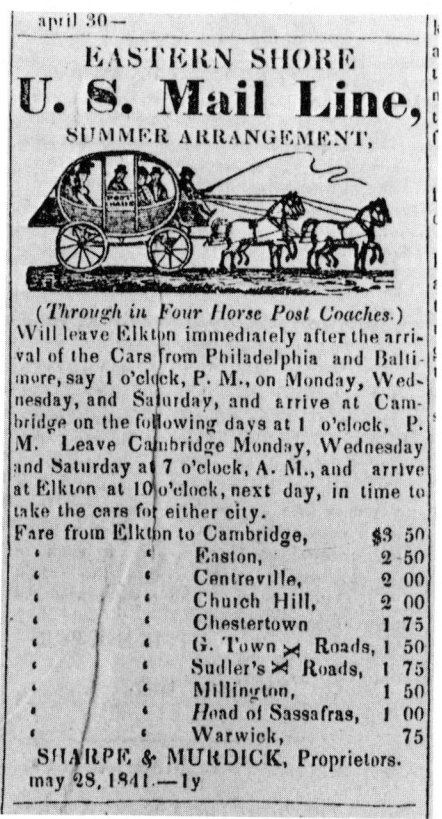

from nearby groves and replanted to provide shade in the rally area. Scores of long tables piled high with Eastern Shore delicacies were provided free for the general public.

Henry Clay and Daniel Webster, famous orators at a time when oratory was considered the highest form of human expression, sent their regrets; but a battery of nationally known speakers was on hand to cajole, amuse, and rouse the crowd with their fiery eloquence. Star of the show was "Old Crit"—J. J. Crittenden of Kentucky, "a man who could beat the world on the stump." He so charmed Talbot Countians with his flowery compliments, homely face, and flamboyant speaking style that they voted Whig in the election that November. So did the rest of the country; Harrison won in a landslide. But unfortunately his presidency was the shortest in American history. He caught cold during his inauguration, and died of pneumonia after only thirty-one days in office. The Whigs soon disintegrated as a major political force both in Talbot and in the nation.

Next to politics, Talbot's favorite outdoor sport during the depression years may have been to go down to the wharves to watch the steamboats come in. Steamboats were not only the heralds of the future, but solid proof that the Eastern Shore had not been abandoned by the outside world. They brought in manufactured goods, food, liquor, news, and traveling salesmen, and took Talbot Countians to booming Baltimore and other centers on the more sophisticated and less depressed Western Shore for shopping trips and social visits.

The little *Surprise*, first steamboat to come to Talbot, made regular runs to Miles River Ferry in 1817 and 1818, but was damaged by fire during her second summer. She was soon replaced by the larger *Maryland*, financed principally by Talbot capital, which began operations between Baltimore, Annapolis, and Easton June 15, 1819. Unlike the *Surprise*, the *Maryland* came up the Tred Avon and docked at Easton Point, much more convenient for Easton travel.

In the company's advertising, the *Maryland* was described as "extremely beautiful" and unexcelled in "elegance, convenience, and security"; but in fact she was a crude little flat-bottomed boat with only a faint foretaste of the true elegance of the steamboats to come. She was steered by an open tiller mounted on the stern, and powered by a paddle wheel on the side. She carried a bowsprit but no sail. Her helmsman passed signals to the engineer below by stomping on the deck. In bad weather passengers, freight, stacked cordwood, boiler, and machinery all were crowded into her shallow hull; if the weather permitted, the passengers usually stood on deck along with the livestock. She also had space for horses and carriages.

For all her crudeness, the sturdy little *Maryland* continued to serve Talbot County and other Eastern Shore localities for many years. She was probably the only steamboat in this service that actually made a profit for her builders; all the later ones were beset by ruinous competition as soon as they were launched. The Maryland Steamboat Company, which built and owned her, had interlocking directors with the Easton bank; until his death in 1830 Nicholas Hammond was president of both. In the 1830s the company planned to replace her with a larger and more modern craft, and a model of a boat to be called *Maryland Junior* was built and put on display in the lobby of the bank; but bad business conditions caused the proposal to be dropped. Later she was sold, but stayed in Chesapeake waters, making runs to Chestertown, Centreville, and Denton at various times. Her oaken beams still sound, she was taken over in 1861 by the federal government for use as a troop transport. She finally burned in 1865 while in service around New York harbor.

Other and more elaborate steamers appeared soon after the *Maryland*. The *Albemarle* began regular service to Cambridge in 1823, with a stop at Howell's Point in Talbot County. The *Paul Jones* came along in 1839, the *Osiris* in 1845, the *Cambridge* in 1846, the *Hugh Jenkins* in 1850, and the "new and fast" *Champion*, commanded by Captain Strandberg, in

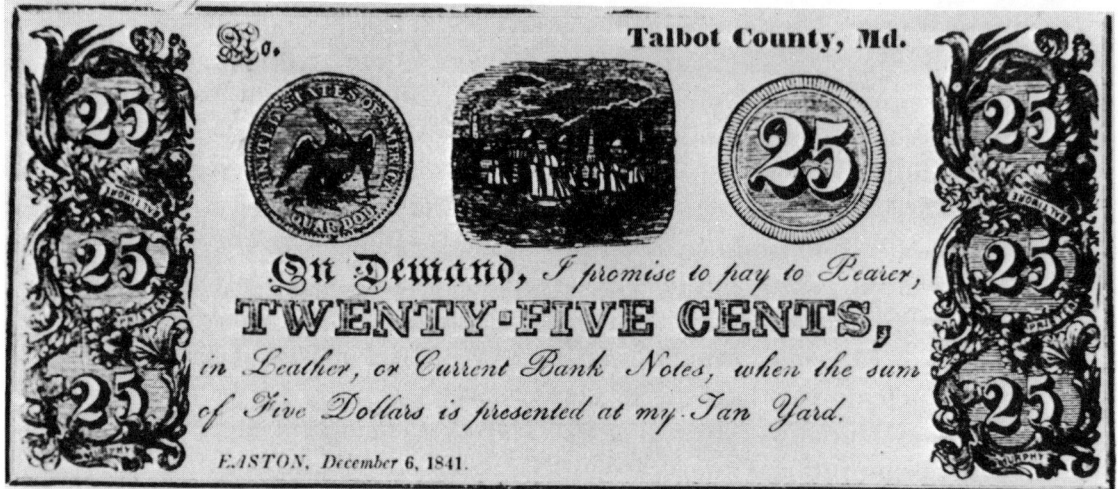

A shinplaster

1851. The *Balloon*, later used to carry federal troops to Talbot and to transport slaves from Miles River Ferry for service in the Union Army, was acquired by the Eastern Shore Steamboat Company in December, 1860.

During the hard times of 1820-40 Talbot County's ever present problem was money—or rather the lack of it. Hard cash in the form of gold and silver was almost nonexistent, and even nickels, dimes, and copper pennies quickly vanished into strong boxes. To make change for their customers, business firms such as Spry Denny's Easton tanyard issued their own paper money in denominations as small as three cents.

These were called shinplasters for their resemblance to a popular patent medical remedy. They were crudely printed on ordinary newsprint, and struck off in large sheets by Baltimore printers, who supplied them in blank form to local merchants. When small change was needed, the storekeeper simply cut the relevant amount from the sheet, signed it, dated it, and handed it to the customer. Most carried a promise of redemption in "good bank notes" when five dollars had been accumulated; but as often as not when that time came the storekeeper didn't have a five-dollar bill to redeem them. Customers collected shinplasters by the boxful, and presented them in payment of bills run up at other stores, despite the objections of the larger merchants. In 1838 and again in 1841, the Easton Merchants and Traders Association passed resolutions declaring that after a certain date its members would accept no more shinplasters; but their use persisted.

Much business necessarily had to be done on credit or by barter. Even morticians were no exception; an Easton undertaker advertised

FASHIONS for 1847.

THE subscriber begs leave to inform his numerous customers that he has just received the latest New York SPRING FASHIONS and would invite the public generally to call and see him, if they want any thing in his line of business, as he is prepared, to make work in a way that cannot be surpassed on the shore, and he warrants all work made in his shop to fit, and to be made in good style, and done according to promise. Garments of all kind cut with the same care as if he was to make them. A deduction made for cash payments, and prices to suit the times.

that "country produce will be exchanged for work at market prices." When customers failed to pay their bills, there was trouble all around. One Easton merchant, pleading for settlement of past due accounts, urged those who owed him money to "come forward immediately or I shall have to retire from business." The *Gazette* carried a page one notice warning that "we want money and must have it" and threatening to take the law to subscribers and advertisers who didn't settle at least part of their accounts promptly. The postmaster, having given credit for postage, admitted he was in hot water with authorities in Washington. His notice read:

> PAY UP—All persons indebted for postage are particularly requested to settle their accounts without delay that I may be enabled to meet my engagements with the Department. Those failing to attend this notice will be required to pay *cash* after this date.

Riding with the times, the Talbot County Commissioners cut spending to the bone. In 1843 county taxes were 30 cents per $100 of valuation, and total county revenue was just over $14,000. Of this, $200 was paid out for wood to heat the Court House, $44.37½ for bounties on crows' heads, $18 for Talbot's share of the cost of repairing the Hillsborough bridge, and $650 in subsidies for the Miles River and Oxford ferries. Total cost of all road repairs for the entire county during the year came to $1,446.43.

Every issue of the papers carried notices of sheriff's sales, and many persons lost homes that had been in their families for generations. Fine old tidewater estates were selling at ridiculous prices. The Easton bank, having foreclosed on the heirs of Jacob Gibson, sold his Marengo farm for $35 an acre. Peachblossom, 392 acres on the creek by that name, went for $8,000. In 1854 James Dixon bought the Miles River Farm, later renamed North Bend, for $21 an acre. Other less well situated land brought as little as $10 an acre.

But there was one compensation: if farm prices were low, the cost of living was low also. In 1852 the first local spring shad reached the Easton market March 13, and sold for twenty-five cents each. A little later a fine pair could be had for twenty cents. Butter was twenty-five cents a pound, eggs a dime a dozen, chickens two for a quarter. A full quarter of spring lamb cost only sixty-two and one-half cents. Wood for heating sold for two to four dollars and fifty cents a cord, with hickory in greatest demand. Coal for fuel, just being introduced, was still too expensive for the average household. So was a new product called "coal oil" (kerosene) for lighting homes with lamps. But both coal oil and sperm whale oil, used by the more affluent, were far safer than the product called "etherial oil," an explosive mixture of alcohol and turpentine. Many Talbot homes, however, continued for many years to be lighted only by home-made tallow candles.

Wild ducks, seafood, berries in season, and other local products were plentiful and cheap. With no closed season or bag limits, Violet Hopkins was able to advertise ducks at almost all times at her Easton market, along with terrapin, oysters, beefsteaks, pig's feet, and baked goods. Market gunners brought in mallards and black ducks in spring and summer, the luscious canvasbacks in fall and winter. In October, 1854, a haul of five hundred drum fish was taken by one seine in the bay, and the paper reported that the net had contained twice that many, but couldn't be pulled up until half were dumped out to lighten the load. A 200-pound sea turtle, captured off Poplar Island, was made the basis for a gala turtle dinner at the Union Hotel in Easton.

Most of this information appeared in the Easton newspapers, which were still the strongest on the Eastern Shore although papers were published in other Eastern Shore countyseat towns beginning in the 1820s. For a time, Easton had three newspapers at once: the *Republican Star*, dating from 1799; the *Gazette*, founded December 15, 1817, by Alexander Graham; and the *Eastern Shore Whig and People's Advocate*, launched September 9, 1828, by a consortium to support the presidential hopes of Andrew Jackson against John Quincy Adams. Two other newspaper ventures, the *People's Monitor* and the *Maryland Censor*, had expired after brief careers.

Despite its name, the *Whig* was anything but a Whig party supporter. It backed the radical wing of the Democratic party; its name had been

The *Gazette*, with staff. The newspaper was founded December 15, 1817, by Alexander Graham.

chosen to honor the Whigs, or patriots, who had opposed the Tories during the Revolution, before the word Whig emerged as the name of a new national party. Its editor, George W. Sherwood, despised everything the national Whigs stood for.

In the early 1830s the chief rivalry for Talbot newspaper supremacy was between the *Whig* and the *Gazette*, which had begun as a pro-Federalist paper and now supported the Whigs. The *Republican Star*, Easton's first successful paper, had lost much of its prestige and circulation. After the death in May, 1832, of its founder-editor, Thomas Perrin Smith, the *Star* went out of business. However, when fire destroyed the *Whig* printshop in the spring of 1841, editor Sherwood saw an opportunity to get rid of the hated word "Whig" on his masthead. He resumed publication a month later under a new name, the *Eastern Shore Star*, soon shortened to the *Easton Star*. Only the word *Star*, and not its policies or traditions, was taken from Thomas Perrin Smith's old publication, which had perished nine years earlier. Thus it is only by glossing over history that the present *Star-Democrat* can claim descent from the original *Republican Star*; it is really a continuation of the *Whig*, and properly dates from 1828, not 1799.

Printers and pressroom of the *Easton Star*, progenitor of the present-day *Star-Democrat*.

In their desperation for new sources of income, Talbot Countians were willing to try almost anything. Two get-rich-quick schemes which would seem incredible today had widespread support in the 1830s and 1840s. They have come down in history as the *Morus multicaulis* mania and the Great Poplar Island Black Cat Fur Farm.

Morus multicaulis was the so-called scientific name for the south sea island white mulberry tree. On the leaves of these trees silkworms fed as they spun cocoons from which the Chinese had been producing fine silks for thousands of years, said one Samuel Whitmarsh, a Pennsylvanian who happened to be in the business of producing and selling shoots of the south sea island white mulberry. According to Whitmarsh, the tree was admirably suited to the soil and climate of the Eastern Shore of Maryland. All the farmers needed do was to grow a few trees, introduce silkworms to their leaves, and then sit back and wait to reap a bountiful reward.

Soon salesmen-disciples of Whitmarsh came to the Eastern Shore from Pennsylvania with bundles of *Morus multicaulis* shoots in their carts. They sold these seedlings to farmers, who in turn used them to produce new seedlings, which the farmers then sold to others. At this stage the scheme undoubtedly was profitable, at least to the salesmen and those who got into seedling production early.

To promote the product, silk companies were to be chartered for the stated purpose of buying up all the cocoons which were going to be produced by all the silkworms which would eat all the leaves which would grow on all the *Morus multicaulis* trees. The companies would then convert the cocoon fibers into fine silk cloth, literally worth almost its weight in gold, and everybody would be rich and happy. At least three of these companies were established in Talbot County—one at Wye Mills, one at St. Michaels, and one near Easton. The Wye Mills firm apparently never got beyond selling stock, and the St. Michaels company did put up a building with the five thousand dollars it collected from investors; but the Easton operation actually established a cocoonery at its headquarters, located at what was appropriately named Mulberry Hill. All three companies, however, devoted most of their time and energy to selling mulberry seedlings.

Talbot Countians bought up the seedlings by the thousands. According to Prentiss Ingraham's *Land of Legendary Lore*, the silkworm mania "seized nearly everyone who could raise even a few dollars, while some even mortgaged their farms. . . . Every available spot was used for setting out their plants. Farmers planted down their fields, and citizens of the town (Easton) filled up their gardens. Everybody expected to be rich in a very short time."

One Easton paper estimated that by 1839 one hundred thousand trees had been planted within a mile of the town. Some eight thousand seedlings were snapped up in a week at thirty-five cents each that September, and then resold again and again at ever increasing prices which reached as high as one dollar per shoot. The county fair added a "domestic silk" section with prizes for the best sewing silk and the best homemade silk stockings. A state silk convention was held in Annapolis.

Then the bubble burst. Somebody had made the dreadful discovery that in order to produce silk it was necessary not only to grow trees but to cultivate silkworms and extract fibers from the cocoons without destroying the fiber. And this was an extremely difficult art developed by the ancient Chinese, requiring great skill and much delicate handiwork. The Eastern Shore's unskilled farm laborers simply could not master the art.

As fast as it had arisen, the market for *Morus multicaulis* trees collapsed. Farmers ripped the shoots out of their fields and, sadder but wiser, went back to growing wheat and corn. Town gardeners replanted the plots where the "money trees" had grown in flowers and vegetables. By the summer of 1841 the silk companies were out of business, and Mulberry Hill and its cocoonery were up for sale.

Only a few years later, an even more fantastic scheme drew attention in Talbot. In December, 1847, R. O. Ridgeway advertised that he would pay twenty-five cents each for one thousand female black cats "when delivered at Poplar Island or my store." Ridgeway was acting as agent for Charles Carroll, grandson of the signer of the Declaration of Independence, who then owned Poplar Island. Carroll had heard there was a market in China for black cat fur, and decided that Poplar Island was a perfect place to produce it. The cats could be fed on fish, and could run at large since the island was far enough from the mainland to prevent escape by swimming. A supply of black toms was already in hand; once enough black females were secured everything seemed set to introduce the two sexes and get ready to harvest the resulting thousands of black kittens.

All went well, especially for the tomcats, until the weather turned severely cold late that winter. Ice soon formed a natural bridge between the island and the mainland. "As soon as the cats found this out," one account said, "they took off for their former homes without waiting for another meal of fish. Probably the Shore has never seen such a migration of felines." And that was the unhappy end of the Great Poplar Island Black Cat Fur Farm.

Another scheme for improving the Eastern Shore's sick economy, although less nutty than raising silkworms or marketing black cat fur, also ended in at least temporary failure. This was the dream, enthusiastically promoted by Talbot Countians, of building a mainline railroad down the spine of the Delmarva peninsula and bringing the impoverished region back into the heart of American economic progress.

As envisioned in the early 1830s, this railroad was to be the chief trunk line of the entire eastern seaboard, carrying through traffic between the prosperous cities of the north and the newly rich cotton states of the Deep South. There was at that time no such trunk line on the Western Shore; the railroad linking Baltimore to Wilmington and Philadelphia was not completed until 1837. Whichever section of Maryland got its bid in first, it seemed clear, would reap enormous financial benefits. Why shouldn't it be the neglected and—in the words of the *Easton Gazette*—"poor and despised" Eastern Shore that secured this boon, rather than the heavily favored Western Shore, for which millions in state funds had been spent already on canals and railroads?

The General Assembly, although somewhat skeptical, went along with the idea, and in 1833 voted $1 million as a capital stock grant for the Eastern Shore railroad. Much more than that would be needed, however, and the line's promoters set out to raise it from private capital. After a branch connecting the main trunk line with Easton was authorized in 1836, an investment office was opened in Easton for stock sales, with such prominent men as William Hughlett, Edward N. Hambleton, John Leeds Kerr, and William H. Tilghman as local promoters. The company's brochure painted a glowing picture: fifty to sixty thousand people a year traveled by boat from Charleston and Savannah to New York and Boston, and most of them "undoubtedly would prefer to travel by railroads." The new railroad would be shorter, and therefore cheaper to build and operate, than those proposed for the Western Shore; it would be an all-Maryland line from the Delaware border near Wilmington to Eastern Shore Virginia; it would bring prosperity, progress, and industrial development to Talbot County and the entire shore.

Unfortunately, those who bought stock lost their money. The dream quickly ran into harsh economic realities. Investment capital dried up in the face of a national fiscal collapse known as "the Panic of 1837," and in any case hardheaded Baltimore bankers saw no reason to put money into a scheme which would favor the Eastern Shore at the expense of their own area. Thomas Emory of Queen Anne's County, who spent most of 1837 in England trying to interest British capitalists in the venture, got nowhere. The company's charter lapsed for lack of funds, and when it was revived in the 1850s the proposed main line ran not through Maryland but through Delaware. Under the leadership of General Tench Tilghman, grandson of the Revolutionary War hero, a ceremonial ground breaking for the Easton branch was staged in 1856; but it remained just a hole in the ground until after the Civil War.

Linked directly with the railroad project was another longtime Eastern Shore dream: secession from Maryland to join Delaware and Eastern Shore Virginia in a new state encompassing what is now called Delmarva. This idea was taken very seriously by Talbot Countians in the early days of Maryland statehood; the right to secede had been proposed in the 1776 state constitutional convention, but had been voted down. It reached fever pitch again in 1833 when the Delaware legislature formally proposed a new state combining the territories which were naturally linked by geography. There was speculation that Easton would be its capital.

Many Talbot Countians welcomed the proposal. In a letter to the *Gazette* published March 2, 1833, "H. H." (probably Henry Hollyday of Ratcliffe Manor) pointed out that the interests of the Eastern and Western shores were "often totally dissimilar and not infrequently conflicting." He said sarcastically that the Western Shore should welcome secession "to judge from their frequent assertions of our being on them a tax and burden."

At the heart of the issue was Eastern Shore resentment over being forced to pay out tax money for internal improvements, such as the

Chesapeake & Ohio Canal and the Baltimore & Ohio Railroad, which appeared designed solely to benefit the Western Shore. It was in answer to these complaints that the legislature later that year voted $1 million for the Eastern Shore Railroad.

The same 1833 legislative session came very near to voting in favor of Eastern Shore secession. A resolution to implement it was approved by the House, forty to twenty-four, and was killed in a Senate committee by the slender margin of only five to four. Thus a change of just one vote in committee might well have lost the Eastern Shore to Maryland forever, an outcome which even today many Eastern Shore residents think would have been something less than a disaster.

The issue remained a hot one, especially after proposals were made to reform the electoral system and give Baltimore more representation in the legislature at the expense of the smaller counties. There is no doubt that the system then in effect was unfair to Baltimore by the modern standard of "one man, one vote." The city's big and growing population had proportionately far less legislative strength than the small and shrinking counties of the Eastern Shore and southern Maryland; and in addition the Eastern Shore by law had to have one of the two United States senators and by custom usually was awarded the governorship every other term. But the reform proposal brought angry roars from Eastern Shoremen. The *Easton Gazette* saw in it just another plot to make the small counties "the victims and prey . . . of their lusty, overgrown neighbors" in power mad Baltimore, and another argument in favor of secession.

In 1842 and 1850 secession came up again, but each time it was voted down by Western Shore legislators. Still it long remained an appealing idea to Eastern Shoremen. It was revived as recently as 1949, when a letter in the *Baltimore Sun* suggested only half jokingly that instead of going to the expense of building the proposed Bay Bridge, Maryland should just "give the Eastern Shore to Delaware" and thereby save $42 million.

Undoubtedly a contributing factor to Talbot's woes through the years of the "long depression" was the public's emotional adherence to the institution of slavery long after it had shown itself to be economically unsound. Dr. Harrison thought this was the main reason for the economy's slowness to recover. "In the midst of social and political unrest all seemed to be so dazed and blinded as to be incapable of seeing the cause why their fertile fields yielded but the crops of sterility and their labor and economy were paid with the wages of sloth and wastefulness," he wrote in his essay on the life of Edward Lloyd VI (1798-1861). In another essay, published in the *Easton Star* in April, 1877, he condemned the county's long "infatuation . . . for the system of slavery, which hideous and monstrous as it was, we caressed and embraced, as something as dear to us as life."

But his was a voice crying in the wilderness. While a good many Talbot Countians did free their slaves, the majority clung to the institution as to a sacred cause—and many were ready to die for it when war came.

Among those who recognized that slavery was a problem, many thought the solution was to send the blacks to Africa. The Maryland Colonization Society, founded in 1817, had strong support in Talbot County. One of the most important single contributions to the black colony known as "Maryland in Liberia" was the gift of a ship, the *Mary Caroline Stevens*, as a bequest in the will of John Stevens of Talbot County, and there were many other benefactions.

Eventually the colonization scheme failed, not for lack of white enthusiasm, but because the blacks themselves refused to accept it. They considered themselves not Africans, but Americans; their leaders argued with considerable justice that their ancestors had lived in Maryland just as long as whites whose forebears had come from England, Scotland, Ireland, or Europe. This was especially true in Talbot County, where mass importations directly from Africa had never been an important part of the slave picture, and where most nineteenth century blacks were descended from slaves who had lived in the county for generations. As far as is known, no Talbot blacks ever willingly migrated to Maryland in Liberia in the half century of the colony's existence.

Many Talbot Countians solved the problem of what to do with their surplus slaves in a more brutal, but at the same time more practical, fashion. In the 1820s hordes of slave buyers from the Deep South, where blacks were in great demand for work in the cotton fields, invaded the Eastern Shore with tempting offers of "Cash! Cash! Cash! for Negroes." Hundreds of Talbot blacks were separated from their families and "sold South," never to be heard from again. By one estimate, fifteen percent of all young black males in Talbot County suffered this fate in the peak years between 1818 and 1835. Also in demand were mothers with children, and even boys and girls as young as six and seven.

Tradition among white families insists that of course *their* families never dealt with the slave traders, but the records tell a different story. One trading firm alone, headed by Austin Woolfolk, a Georgian operating out of Baltimore, bought at least two hundred ten slaves in Talbot County in nine years (1823-31) plus scores more at Woolfolk's Baltimore slave pen. Nearly all were shipped to New Orleans for sale on what was

Frederick Douglass as a young man.

then the world's largest slave market. The list of those who dealt with Woolfolk or others of the estimated eighty traders who operated on the Eastern Shore reads like a who's who of Talbot's elite families: Edward Lloyd, Henry Hollyday, Rachel Kerr, Nicholas and Charles Goldsborough, Peregrine Tilghman, Edward N. Hambleton, William H. D'Courcy, James Lloyd Chamberlaine, and William Hayward, among many others.

Some slaveholders found a different answer: they kept ownership of their blacks, but bought cotton lands and transported them south as workers. A notable example was Edward Lloyd VI, who had inherited a huge estate and more than five hundred slaves—but also a huge debt—on the death in 1834 of his father, Edward Lloyd V, who had been famous for his lavish and expensive entertainment at Wye House. The younger Lloyd was not the colorful figure his father had been, but he was a far shrewder manager. He quickly saw that cotton was where the money was, and in 1837 purchased a large plantation in Madison County, Mississippi. To work it he transported some two hundred slaves south—some voluntarily, but others as punishment for being "difficult" or "uppity." The plantation paid high profits, and Lloyd later bought much additional acreage in Louisiana and Arkansas. By this means, Dr. Harrison wrote in his biography of Edward VI, "he was able to maintain the ancient repute of the family for wealth, when it seemed upon the verge of destruction, to disburden his estate of a heavy debt left charged upon it by his father, to aid his brothers when involved in pecuniary difficulties, and even to add largely to his wealth both in land and slaves."

Another who followed the same course was Richard Spencer of Spencer Hall near St. Michaels. Threatened with bankruptcy after he sank most of his money into a disastrous contract for carrying the mails on the Eastern Shore, he moved to Georgia in 1837, taking with him a large number of Talbot-born slaves. There and in Alabama he established prosperous cotton plantations.

To Talbot's blacks, imbued with a deep loyalty to their Eastern Shore homes and families, being shipped south was the ultimate terror, worse even than staying home to be whipped at the whim of their masters or braving the unknown dangers of running away to the north in search of freedom. Frederick Douglass, the Talbot-born slave who rose to become one of America's greatest abolitionist orators and writers, described this feeling vividly in his three widely read autobiographies. He also gave unforgettable vignettes of slave life at Wye House, where he lived for eighteen months as a boy, and of his experiences in and around St. Michaels as a teenager.

Born Frederick Bailey on a Tuckahoe Creek farm in February, 1818, he was the son of a slave mother, Harriet Bailey, and an unknown father believed to have been a white man. He lived for his first six years with his remarkable grandmother, Betsey Bailey, and then, after his stay at Wye House, spent much of his youth in Baltimore, where he taught himself to read, write, and do arithmetic. Later he spent three years, 1833-36, in the St. Michaels area as the slave of Thomas Auld, a storekeeper and the town's postmaster.

At the age of twenty, in 1838, he escaped north and took the name of Frederick Douglass to evade possible recapture. Eventually he achieved world renown as an anti-slavery writer, orator, and editor, and as a fighter for women's rights and other "radical" causes. As the acknowledged spokesman for the nation's blacks, he was as much a symbol in the nineteenth century of the struggle for civil rights as Martin Luther King, Jr. has become in the twentieth century. At Douglass's death in 1895 it was said of him that he was better known in Europe than any American since Abraham Lincoln. His career scaled heights unknown to any black American before him: he dined with Queen Victoria; was wartime adviser to Lincoln, and later to other presidents; served as United States Marshal and Recorder of Deeds for the District of Columbia, and as

Top, the Strand, Oxford, about 1880. *Bottom,* Eastford Hall, summer hotel, in an 1878 stereoscopic view. The hotel later became the dormitory of the Oxford Military and Naval Academy.

minister to the Republic of Haiti; and achieved a substantial private fortune as a highly paid speaker on the lecture circuit. After the Civil War he returned several times to Talbot County, where in general he was treated with the respect and honor due to the county's most famous native son.

By the 1840s Talbot County was beginning to show signs at last of shaking off the economic doldrums. Oxford was awakening from its slumber of seventy years. The ferry was resumed about 1836, with a subsidy of three hundred dollars a year from the county; it has been operating continuously since then. The postmastership was restored in 1849, and in 1852 election of town commissioners was resumed after a lapse of many years.

A key development was the establishment in 1847 of the Oxford Military Academy, with buildings on Morris Street, one of which—known as Academy House—survives. Sponsored by General Tench

Morris Street and Town Creek, as seen from Eastford Hall in Oxford, 1878. From a stereoscopic view by Professor Janvier.

Tilghman, an 1831 graduate of West Point, the academy had as first superintendent Lieutenant John H. Allen, a Tilghman classmate. Allen instituted a four-year curriculum and launched operations with a class of thirty-three boys. Unfortunately, the principal academic building burned in 1855, and the school went out of business soon afterward.

Two new churches, the first ever for Oxford, were started in the 1850s. A Protestant Episcopal church building was begun in 1853, though not completed until 1892, and St. Paul's Methodist Episcopal Church was built in 1856. But Oxford still had a long way to go; its 1850 population was reported as only ninety-one persons, just about what it had been in 1800. The town's real revival did not come until after it became the terminus of the Maryland & Delaware Railroad in 1871.

In Easton there were changes which foretold modern times. An iron foundry, one of the town's first manufacturing industries, was launched by the Oxenham brothers in 1840 to make plows and other agricultural implements. An "ice cream saloon" was opened in 1844 by H. I. Strandberg, who also did business as a fruit grower, cattle raiser, and steamboat captain. A photographer, W. K. Wolcott, took rooms at the Misses Fedderman's on Washington Street in May, 1845, and announced he would "take LIKENESSES of such as desire them." Presumably he used the process perfected just six years earlier by Louis Jacques Mandé Daguerre of Paris. Adhesive postage stamps came along in 1847, easing the credit problems of the Easton postmaster. The Talbot Medical Society was reactivated in 1848, with Dr. Sydenham T. Russum, who lived under the big oak tree in Wye Mills, as president. The physicians published a price list, virtually unchanged since 1818, which included such charges as fifty cents for bleeding, one dollar for extracting a tooth, two dollars for a minor operation, and ten dollars for a normal childbirth. The cost of housecalls depended on how far the doctor had to travel; it ranged from one dollar for a local visit to twelve dollars for a trip of twenty to twenty-five miles, with a double charge "for riding in a storm or rain."

In 1843 the town finally took steps to rid itself of the unhealthy marshes which virtually surrounded it. Proposals were made at a meeting June 17, and later a drainage canal twelve feet wide was cut through the marsh on the northwest side of Easton, running down to the Tred Avon. (It's still there, although it appears now to be an attractive willow-fringed pond and stream flanking Bay Street.) A large section of marsh to the southeast was also drained. After that the health of Easton residents improved, although typhoid fever remained a serious problem until a sewage system was installed just before World War I.

As of January 1, 1849, keeping swine within the town limits was forbidden. The "standing" of stallions to service mares, a frequent sight on early Easton streets, was also banned. But cattle still roamed at large, doing damage to gardens and lawns in their wanderings. Another ordinance cracked down on boys who played games within the enclosed Court House green.

Gaslights and street numbers soon followed. The first published mention of street numbers appeared in the *Gazette* of June 23, 1855, when Philemon Floyd announced that his Easton band would accept engagements at weddings, excursions, and other affairs, and gave his address as "# 23 Wash. St." He didn't say whether it was North or South Washington. Gaslighting was first proposed at a meeting September 17, 1857, and by December, 1858, a private firm, the Easton Gas Light Company, was making artificial gas in a plant on West Street. Most of its early customers were downtown stores and other businesses; the Easton bank, for instance, ordered four gas burners, which it didn't replace with electricity until 1915. Gas street lights, attended by an official lamp lighter, were installed at strategic locations in the town.

Out in the country, farmers were beginning to use the new laborsaving devices known as reapers and "thrashing" (actually "threshing," although nobody pronounced the word that way) machines. The first reaper ever seen on the Eastern Shore had been demonstrated by its

The Bratt or Academy House, built about 1848 as the officers' quarters of the first Oxford Military Academy.

Cincinnati inventor, Obed Hussey, in 1836, and was awarded a medal by the Eastern Shore Agricultural Society after it whacked through wheat, oats, and barley fields on General Tilghman's Plimhimmon estate at twice the rate of the old method in which heavy cradles were wielded by hand. The first horse-powered "thrasher" appeared in 1838, and was so efficient that a premium of one or two cents a bushel was paid for "machine wheat" as opposed to that trod out by human or equine feet in the old-fashioned way. With whiskey by the barrel only eighteen cents a gallon, every harvest worker drank on the job; it was widely believed that a drink of cold water could kill a man who had been working in extreme heat unless it was diluted with alcohol. Each summer Easton stores advertised "common whiskey, brandy, gin and rum suitable for harvest" along with their other wares.

The village of Trappe had grown steadily, if not spectacularly, throughout the lean years; it had suffered less from the depression than any other Talbot community. By 1850 its population had reached 198 (not counting slaves), and it ranked third in the county behind only Easton and St. Michaels. It had at least eight storekeepers, three doctors, five shoemakers, seven carpenters, two tailors, a bricklayer, tanner, carter, and even a hotel. By 1858 it also had four churches—Methodist Episcopal, Methodist Protestant, African Methodist, and the new St. Paul's Protestant Episcopal, completed that year.

Early in 1856 it was granted a charter by the General Assembly as an incorporated town, and on March 31 the town commissioners met for the first time. They voted to install wooden sidewalks (some of which lasted almost until World War I), and set a town speed limit of eight miles an hour (which also lasted well into the automobile age). Another bylaw, adopted April 12, provided that a curfew horn should be sounded at 9:30 each night, after which "quiet shall be restored within the limits of the town." On Saturday nights people could stay up until 10:00. Violators, if white, were subject to a fine of fifty cents, if black to ten lashes on the bare back. Wrestling, boxing, dancing, gaming, and banjo playing in the streets were forbidden. Under such rules Trappe existed for many years as a quiet, peaceful little country town—which it still is today.

St. Michaels, meanwhile, was starting a modest comeback. Major shipbuilding never revived, but at least two builders—Edward Wiley and Robert Lambdin—kept the art alive by turning out small schooners, pungies, and other craft. Oyster harvesting, at first only for local consumption, became a bigger source of income after the Chesapeake & Delaware Canal was opened in 1829, providing access to the Philadelphia and New York markets. Election of town commissioners was resumed in 1848, and a resurvey of the town completed that same year. A

William R. Hughlett. From a painting by Thomas Coke Ruckle, showing the Hughlett shipyard at Jamaica Point at right, 1850.

chapter of the Odd Fellows lodge was established in 1846, and a Masonic lodge in 1857. Also in 1857 the St. Michaels Female Academy was opened in an abandoned church building on St. Mary's Square; it flourished for many years, until the county schools began providing secondary education for girls.

In the 1830s Talbot County established the rude beginnings of a public school system, a task it had neglected for its first two centuries. Under the spur of a state law passed in 1834, one-room elementary schools were established throughout the county. They were open only to whites, and most of the early teachers were men; but they gave sound training in the famous "three R's"—reading, 'riting, and 'rithmetic. Education beyond the grade school level remained strictly in the hands of private schools until after the Civil War.

The Mexican War (1846-47), which added Texas and the southwest to the American empire, gave people something to cheer about, even in far-off Talbot County, and incidentally helped the economy by temporarily doubling wheat prices. Even more exciting was the discovery of gold in 1848 in California. Scores of Talbot youths went west to seek a fortune, though few found one. A Talbot mariner, Captain Haddaway, did better. He took the brig *Bloomfield*, built at the Tred Avon shipyard of the Bartlett-Dixon family, to Baltimore, loaded it with knockdown houses, sailed around the southern tip of South America to San Francisco, and sold the houses at a handsome profit to forty-niners desperate for places to live. The *Bloomfield*, named for the Bartletts' ancestral home, is believed to have been the last Talbot-built vessel to make a commercial voyage "round the Horn."

Another Talbot shipyard in operation about the same time was at Jamaica Point on the Choptank. There William R. Hughlett, Jr., and his master shipwright, Nathaniel Leonard, produced a number of schooners and at least one brig, the *Argyll*, completed in 1856. This was one of the last brigs ever built on the bay and probably the last commercial oceangoing vessel ever constructed in Talbot County. Sailing craft would continue to be used for cargo hauling on the bay until World War II; but the days of the tall ships were over.

The political storms which rocked the state and nation in the 1850s touched Talbot only lightly. For some years citizens of Baltimore and much of Maryland were caught up in a vicious political movement called the Know-Nothings, so-called because when questioned about their secret rituals members were instructed to say: "I know nothing." The movement in essence was a hate-cult dedicated to eradicating, by force if necessary, the influence of foreigners, Roman Catholics, Jews, and all other un-American elements in Maryland. Its members used strong-arm tactics to gain control of Baltimore—eight were killed and more than two hundred fifty injured in election riots there in 1856, their peak year—and gained control of the Maryland legislature.

In Talbot County the Know-Nothings' stronghold was in St. Michaels District, still populated largely by the rough workmen-turned-watermen who earlier had given the area a bad name. In the 1856 presidential election, St. Michaels gave a solid majority of 279 to 147 to Millard Filmore, the Know-Nothing candidate running under the banner of the short-lived American party. All other Talbot districts favored his more moderate—and victorious—opponent, James Buchanan. No rioting was recorded in Talbot, however, and by 1860 the Know-Nothings had been buried under a rising tide of reform.

By then Talbot Countians had more immediate things to worry about than whether the pope wanted to take over America, as the Know-Nothings had claimed. The American nation itself was threatened with dissolution, being torn to pieces between Free Soil party northerners and proslavery southerners; and every county resident soon would have to decide on which side to take a stand.

NINE

The Civil War Era

JOSIAH BAILEY was a Talbot Countian of the 1850s: twenty-nine years old, tall and strong, a natural leader, described by contemporaries as "a man of more than ordinary parts, both physically and mentally, . . . civil and polite in his manners, and a man of good sense."

He was also a slave, employed as foreman at the farm and shipyard of William R. Hughlett, Jr., at Jamaica Point on the Choptank. Hughlett was considered by the blacks to be a moderate and fair master, as slaveholders went, although like others of his class "he was in the habit of flogging his slaves—females as well as males" for petty offenses.

One day in the autumn of 1856, Bailey later told questioners, he was stripped naked and "flogged very cruelly by his master" because he had quarreled with a fellow slave. Bailey's mind was made up. From that moment on he had "an unswerving determination to leave slavery or die."

Under cover of darkness, he rowed across the Choptank to the Dorchester County home of Benjamin Ross, father of Harriet Tubman, who had been given the code name of "Moses" for her heroic work in leading her people out of bondage to freedom in the North.

"Next time Moses comes, let me know," he told Ross. Soon the word came back: Moses was there. Bailey gathered together three companions, again crossed the Choptank, and with Mrs. Tubman leading the way started on the perilous journey north. It was a route she knew well—up through Caroline County along the marshes on the Choptank's eastern bank, across into Delaware, north to Wilmington, and over the Delaware River bridge into New Jersey and Pennsylvania, where they would be relatively safe.

But pursuers were everywhere. Hughlett and the owners of the other slaves had publicly offered rewards totaling $2,600 for their recapture—$1,500 for Bailey, the rest for his fellow escapees. Mrs. Tubman herself was worth more than $20,000 to anyone who could

> **$100 REWARD.**
>
> RANAWAY from the subscriber on the night of the 27th August, a negro man calling himself JOE MOORE—said negro is about 19 years of age—5 feet 8 inches high, dark complexion, and has a down look. He had on when he went away, a dark frock coat, with yellow plaid lining, and check pants.
>
> The above reward will be given for his apprehension, if taken out of the State, $50 if out of the county, and $25 if in the county, in either case to be lodged in jail either in Baltimore city or Easton, Md
>
> JOHN H. CAULK.
> St. Michaels, Sept. 4, 1847—3t

capture her. They hid in potato holes by day, while white posses passed within a few feet of them, and did their traveling by night. Sometimes they had to separate; sometimes they wore disguises. At the Wilmington bridge a friendly Quaker got them through lines of police and gangs of slave catchers by hiding them in the bottom of a wagon carrying bricklayers home from a day's work.

Eventually they reached Philadelphia, where their stories were recorded by the Vigilance Committee of the Pennsylvania Anti-Slavery Society. Then it was on north toward Canada; under the tough Fugitive Slave Law of the 1850s, nowhere in the United States were escaped slaves really safe. Only in Canada, which Queen Victoria had declared to be free territory in 1839, could runaway slaves find sanctuary.

Years afterward Harriet Tubman remembered Josiah Bailey, recalling his height, his "splendid muscular development," and in particular how he lost heart as they traveled north through New York state. He was sure they would be caught, especially since by that time they were traveling openly by train. Even at Niagara Falls, New York, Bailey refused to join the others in celebrating. When the train reached the high point of the suspension bridge over the Niagara River and started down the Canadian side, Mrs. Tubman rushed over to him, shook him hard, and exclaimed: "You've shook the lion's paw. You're in Queen Victoria's dominions. You're a free man."

> **$30 REWARD.**
>
> RANAWAY from the subscriber on Saturday the 18th inst. a Negro Man called **ISAAC,** who is about 24 or 5 years of age, 5 feet 4 or 5 inches high, of rather a yellow complexion with a flat face, and full set of teeth, he has a large scar on one of his cheeks. ISAAC is stout and pretty well made somewhat bow leged and limps when he walks in his right leg, and also has a large scar on his ham on the same side, he has a pleasant countenance when spoken to, if he dont stutter, he very often makes a stammer before he can get out a word.
>
> The above reward will be given if taken up out of the State, and twenty dollars if taken in the State, and secured in the Easton Jail. JOHN ARRINGDALE.
> Oct. 28

Only then, she related in an 1869 reminiscence, did he react. "His head rose up, he raised his hands on high, and his eyes, streaming with tears, to heaven, and he began to sing:

> Glory to God and Jesus too.
> One more soul got safe.

When last she saw him that day, he was surrounded by friendly Canadian whites and fellow blacks, still waving his arms and singing "Glory to God and Jesus too" at the top of his voice.

Josiah Bailey and the others stayed on in Canada, becoming part of the large American black colony at St. Catharine's, Ontario. It was a hard life—seven months of winter a year—and he had been forced to leave his wife, Anna, and three daughters behind in Talbot County. But Harriet, who visited him often, reported he was "happy and industrious" in his new life. And best of all, in the words of a later black leader, he was "free at last . . . free at last."

Harriett Tubman

That was one face of Talbot County in the 1850s. The face presented by the white majority was quite another. Whites were deeply committed to the perpetuation of slavery, and resentful of anything which interfered with it. Not the least of their objections was the success of the Underground Railroad, by which hundreds of slaves from Dorchester, Talbot, and Caroline counties fled north to freedom. These escapes hit the whites where it hurt most—in the pocketbook. To slaveholders, slaves were not human beings, but property, duly declared to be so by edict of the United States Supreme Court in the Dred Scott decision, and confirmed by Congress in the Fugitive Slave Act. They were worth hard cash in the marketplace—Josiah Bailey, for instance, was valued at $2,000 by his master, Hughlett—and when they were helped to run away by northern abolitionists, it was considered a most despicable kind of theft.

To make matters worse, the two most famous black leaders of the Underground Railroad, both of whom were regarded as heroic figures

Frederick Douglass, in later years.

in the North, were natives of the small mid-Shore area traversed by the Choptank River.

At the lower end was Dorchester-born Harriet Tubman, whose mysterious comings and goings and miraculous feats made her a saint among blacks and a devil among slaveholding whites. In eleven years after her own escape in 1849, she made at least nineteen trips back to the Eastern Shore and led more than two hundred slaves, including her parents and several brothers, north to freedom without being caught.

At the upper end was Talbot-born Frederick Douglass, "superintendent" of the Underground Railroad's northern terminus in Rochester, New York. His role was to find hiding places there for the escapees while he arranged transportation for them to St. Catharine's or other Ontario communities. In their modest home in Rochester, where he was by then the struggling editor of an abolitionist newspaper, Douglass and his wife, the former Anna Murray of Caroline County, gave temporary shelter to hundreds of fleeing blacks. He too was never caught, although at times slave-hunting posses with police protection roamed Rochester's streets.

It was a distinction of which Talbot Countians might have been proud, although few of them were: that the two best known blacks in pre-Civil War America were a man and woman born within twenty miles of each other on opposite shores of the Choptank.

Almost all Talbot Countians regarded abolitionists like Douglass, William Lloyd Garrison, and their cohorts as villains. They were "stirring up the slaves to be discontented with their lot"; they might even bring on that most horrifying of prospects, a slave revolt like Virginia's bloody Nat Turner Rebellion of 1831.

The large population of so-called free blacks, who by the 1850s almost outnumbered slaves in Talbot, made matters worse. They were not really free by any fair standard; they were denied the vote, had no rights in court, no schools, and few job opportunities beyond those of day laborer or kitchen servant. Even their religious gatherings had to be supervised by a "responsible person"—in other words, a white. In 1860 they constituted more than twenty percent of the county's population: poor, ignorant, without incentives for self-improvement, and undisciplined by the tough supervision which kept slaves in check. They were regarded by the whites as a potential source of "infection" for those who remained slaves—and with some justice, since many "free colored" did everything they could to aid escaping slaves and served as conduits for antislavery information. Then or later, not even the most favorably disposed Talbot Countians seemed to have any idea of how to make this large segment of the population a viable part of the county's economy, a situation which endured into modern times and is still not entirely a thing of the past.

Blaming its troubles on "abolitionist propaganda," Maryland during this period enacted tough censorship laws making it a crime punishable by ten to twenty years in prison to take part in the preparation or circulation of printed matter "having a tendency to stir up discontent among the slaves." After that no newspaper editor, no matter how he felt personally, would dare print any article or letter in the slightest way critical of the institution of slavery or of local slave conditions, and as far as this writer knows, none of them did. Postmasters were instructed to refuse to deliver any of a long list of publications, including the *New York Tribune* and the *Christian Advocate*, an official organ of the northern wing of the Methodist Church, which were considered subversive. A black could be arrested even for picking up his mail if he knew it contained abolitionist material, and constables were authorized to search the houses of persons suspected of possessing this literature.

Under this law a Dorchester County lay preacher, Samuel Green, was sentenced to ten years in prison in 1857 when a posse of whites who suspected him of aiding Harriet Tubman conveniently "found" a copy of *Uncle Tom's Cabin* in his house. He served five years before it was revealed that the book had been planted there by the posse members.

In Easton, however, the law backfired after Circuit Judge Richard Bennett Carmichael, later famous for being beaten up in court by federal marshals, gave instructions to the 1860 Talbot grand jury to see to its strict enforcement. Constables were sent out to order all county postmasters not to deliver copies of the *Tribune* or the *Christian Advocate*.

Easton postmaster Charles Robinson flatly refused to obey the edict. Summoned before the grand jury, he said bluntly that he was an officer of the federal government, and not answerable for his official conduct to state courts, and that as postmaster it was his duty to deliver any mail which came properly addressed to his post office without inquiring into its contents.

Surprisingly, in view of their dislike for abolitionism, Easton's citizenry backed the postmaster and not the judge. They disliked state-enforced censorship even more. "The people considered it an infringement of their rights. . . . Much indignation was excited," Dr. Harrison wrote in his account of the affair. The grand jury reported back to Judge Carmichael that the law as he had laid it out for them could not be enforced. Reluctantly, he told them to back down.

Nevertheless, the temper of the times led inevitably to overreaction when rumors of a slave revolt spread through the county. In the spring of 1855 reports of an impending uprising during the Easter holidays caused great excitement in both Dorchester and Talbot. At a crowded meeting in Easton, steps were taken to suppress "the schools and meetings illegally held by blacks," where it was feared revolt plans were being made. Resolutions were adopted requesting slaveholders to keep their servants at home. The *Gazette* commented that the rumors were probably false, but said the gatherings of blacks "have become an annoyance, and it is about time the law was strictly enforced." The *Cambridge Democrat* also denounced the reports as a hoax, and when Easter Sunday came and went peaceably, the excitement died down.

News of John Brown's raid at Harper's Ferry in October, 1859, roused the rumormongers again. The story spread—and was widely believed—that Brown had wandered through southern Talbot County dressed as a woman, seeking recruits for the insurrection he planned. Among other places, he was supposed to have appeared at such Trappe District estates as Boston, Crosiadore, Howell's Point, and Compton. According to the papers there was little doubt that someone had been traveling through the county in disguise, but no proof that it had been Brown.

There was great alarm. A militia company called the Smallwood Guard was mustered; vigilante groups were formed; and patrols were sent out at night to keep strict surveillance over blacks. At least one black was killed; patroller Jerome B. Bennett told authorities he had come upon several Negroes holding what he believed to be an illegal meeting after the Easton town curfew had sounded, and when he challenged them they fled from their meeting house through a rear door. He ran after them, firing his pistol; a black named Philip Garner was shot and killed. No charges against Bennett were filed.

Then on November 27, an anonymous letter was found in St. Michaels, supposedly revealing that an immediate insurrection by blacks was being organized. The word flashed around the county that "an awful revelation had been made by a colored woman at William Townsend's, to Mrs. Townsend, advising her to leave home and that something terrible was going to take place that night."

Immediately arms were taken from the armory behind the Court House and distributed to the citizens. Both the Smallwood and Home guards were put under rigid drill. In effect, Easton was placed under martial law, and all that night patrols marched the streets ready for action when the "terrible" uprising occurred. Again nothing happened, and they went home at sunrise, weary and a little let down. Soon it became evident that the St. Michaels letter had been a forgery, and that the conversation between the black woman and Mrs. Townsend had never taken place.

Even so, the vigilantes continued for some time to patrol Easton's nighttime streets; and the Smallwood Guard was kept under muster, although its ranks steadily diminished due to what the *Gazette* called "a lack of military spirit in Easton." When it was finally disbanded on March 24, 1860, only fifteen of the forty-five volunteers remained.

The mood in which Talbot Countians approached the fateful presidential election of 1860 is difficult to assess today. It has been blurred by time and a tradition—which arose *after* the Civil War—that "practically everybody" favored secession and the confederacy at the start of the war. This is manifestly not true, unless by "everybody" is meant only the members of the well-to-do slaveholding families who had held political power in Talbot for so long, and who had a major financial stake in slavery.

A more accurate assessment is probably that a majority of Talbot whites hoped the whole controversy would go away. They wanted to preserve both slavery *and* the Union, and believed this could be achieved if only the contending parties would show more willingness to compromise. This viewpoint was well expressed in a resolution adopted April 10, 1860, by a large group of conservative citizens. They refused to identify themselves either with the Southern Democrats or the Northern Republicans, and acknowledged "no allegiance but to the Constitution and the Union." On slavery, the resolution said:

> While we are determined to maintain our rights in slave property, we are opposed to all agitation whatever upon the slavery question, believing that our interests can be more successfully secured by consolidating and strengthening the Union than by destroying it.

Results of three elections held between November, 1860, and November, 1861, show clearly that there was no overwhelming sentiment for secession at that time. Rather they reveal that opinion was divided almost exactly evenly, with just about as many eligible voters favoring the Union as favored the Confederacy.

In the 1860 presidential race four candidates were in the field. Three of them—Stephen A. Douglas, John Bell, and Abraham Lincoln—favored the Union, although only Lincoln was regarded as definitely antislavery. The fourth candidate, John C. Breckinridge, was the darling of the Southern Democrats and of the secessionists. In much of the nation the contest was between Lincoln and Douglas, but in Maryland the only two who mattered were Breckinridge and Bell. A vote for Breckinridge was seen as a vote for solidarity with the Deep South, come what may; a vote for Bell, who campaigned on a vague platform of constitutional unionism, was seen as a vote to preserve the Union without destroying slavery.

Breckinridge carried Talbot County with 897 votes to Bell's 792. Douglas received 98 votes, and Lincoln 2. Thus the combined pro-Union ballots, 892, almost exactly equalled the prosecession total of 897. Breckinridge also won Maryland, but Lincoln, of course, gained the presidency in a four-way split of the electoral college.

Just who the two renegades were who voted for Abraham Lincoln remained a matter of great interest in Talbot County for years. In 1883 the *Easton Ledger* named them as Washington R. Melson of Oxford Neck and John W. Blades of St. Michaels. However, Dr. Harrison said at least one member of the Cowgill family of Miles River Neck voted for Lincoln and that as a result the Cowgill family "was driven out of the county by threats." If so, they came back immediately after the war. In 1870 John Cowgill, who had been a Union army colonel, headed a body of armed and uniformed black troops who rode into Easton to make sure that black voters were not molested when they cast their ballots for the first time ever in the congressional election of that year. The family also helped former slaves who had fought in the Union army to found Unionville, long regarded as a model black community.

In January, 1861, a call was issued for a convention in Baltimore to decide whether Maryland should join the Confederacy along with South Carolina and other states of the Deep South. A referendum was held in Talbot County February 4 to test public opinion on two questions—whether such a convention was a good idea, and if one was held, whether Talbot's delegates should be for or against joining the Confederacy. The issue was clear-cut: a vote to hold the convention was considered a vote for secession, a vote against it one for the Union; and opposing slates of pro-Union and prosecession delegates were listed on the ballot by name.

To almost everyone's surprise, the Union side won handily. The convention proposal was rejected, 847 to 666; and the Union delegate ticket of John Harper, Thomas H. Leonard, and C. C. Cox won by even wider margins over their three opponents. Brigadier General Tench Tilghman, probably the most outspoken of all Talbot County secessionist leaders, ran dead last in the field.

Dismayed southern supporters insisted the referendum proved nothing except that Talbot voters did not favor a convention at that particular time. "Nobody is happy about it but darkeys and Quakers," sneered the rabidly prorebel *Easton Star*. But the fact remains that in this test vote far more Talbot Countians sided with the Union than with the Confederacy, no matter what people came later to believe.

The referendum also gave a clear picture of where in the county the relative strength of the opposing forces lay. Easton District, which included the large slave estates on Miles River Neck, was secessionist by more than two to one. St. Michaels District, which included many non-slaveholding families, was even stronger for the Union, with 301 ballots against the convention to only 90 in favor. Trappe District also opposed the convention, and when word arrived in Trappe that it had been defeated, the Stars and Stripes were flown from the cupola of the town hall, a thirty-four gun salute was fired, patriotic speeches rang out, and an impromptu celebration was held, with the boys' drill team called the Trappe Blues leading the way.

Soon afterward St. Michaels figured in a unionist rally said to have been the largest ever held there in numbers and enthusiasm. A pole was erected one hundred-feet high, painted red, white, and blue, and topped by a gilded eagle. A mammoth American flag was presented to the "old defenders"—venerable men who had defended the town against the British in 1813—and while a band played *The Star-Spangled Banner*, the veterans hoisted it to the top of the flagpole.

Just then a live eagle flew over the crowd. What people who were not there believed about what happened next depended on which newspaper they read. The pro-Union *Gazette* reported the eagle had hovered overhead for some time, "appearing to look upon the procedure in admiration," and then sped southward toward South Carolina, where it "no doubt hung its head in shame to see that the rattlesnake had taken its place." The pro-South *Star* claimed that as the flag reached the top of the pole it hit a snag, which tore off two stripes and ten stars, "emblematical of the ten states that have perfected the work of secession from the Union." As for the live eagle, said the *Star*, "it sped away Southward to carry the news . . . to Jefferson Davis."

By that time, however, far more ominous matters were afoot. Fort Sumter had been fired on, and the shooting war was underway. On April 20 word reached Easton that New England federal troops, on their way to Washington by train, had clashed with a secessionist mob in Baltimore in a bloody battle the day before.

A crowd quickly gathered at the Court House to cheer pro-Southern orators who denounced what they called a "Yankee invasion" of Baltimore. Joining in were uniformed members of the Easton Horse Guard, the Town Guard, and the Easton Band, who happened to have been drilling nearby. Thomas P. Williams, a wealthy North Carolinean, offered to charter the steamer *Pioneer*, which had brought the news, and pay expenses for all who would volunteer to go to the rescue of what had been pictured as the besieged city of Baltimore. About one hundred men, most of them armed militia, took up his offer, and set off across the bay aboard the *Pioneer*. But when they reached the city next morning, they found that police had brought the mob under control, the troops had continued on their way, and calm reigned once more in Baltimore.

Shortly afterward the secessionists made a determined effort to take over Talbot County in the name of the Confederacy. At a meeting April 23 resolutions were passed declaring that Maryland's "destiny is with the South" and calling for an immediate session of the legislature for the purpose of seceding. A "Committee of Safety" composed chiefly of the county's leading secessionists was set up, and the county commissioners were requested to levy a special tax of twenty thousand dollars for its expenses. A Confederate flag was raised near the home of Dr. Samuel Harper, chairman of the meeting, who had publicly dragged the American flag in the dust a few days earlier. (The next night, however, it was cut down by "persons unknown.")

According to Dr. Harrison, the Committee of Safety "took it upon themselves to govern the county even to the utmost minutiae of conduct." Citizens were commanded to stay at home; stores were ordered to

General Tench Tilghman

be closed; all expressions opposing the Confederacy were suppressed; and blacks were placed under rigid surveillance. When *Gazette* editor William H. Councell protested, a handbill signed "Many Citizens" was published demanding that he be haled before the grand jury to face a criminal libel charge for claiming Unionists had been threatened with personal violence and warned to leave the county.

All this secessionist activity alarmed federal authorities in Baltimore. On Sunday, June 9, a detachment of four hundred United States troops raided the armory at Easton and seized all the weapons and ammunition stored there. The ammunition included flintlock muskets, cannons, and sabres which had been placed in the armory after the War of 1812. The troops said they had been told the Committee of Safety intended to use the arms to aid the Confederacy, and that they had expected to find four or five hundred rebel soldiers under arms in Easton. The weapons, including two old cannons used in the defense of St. Michaels in 1813, were taken to Fort Meade. A number of local people were arrested, but were soon released.

The raid did not set well with Talbot Countians. Even Union supporters thought it high-handed and probably unnecessary. From that date on federal actions proceeded to arouse deep resentment and turned Union sympathizers into advocates of the rebel cause.

Plimhimmon, the Tilghman family estate at Oxford.

The next such action came in September, when two companies of the Second Delaware Regiment arrived at Easton Point aboard the *Pioneer*. A guard of ten men under Captain Rickets marched to Plimhimmon, the home of Major General Tench Tilghman, searched the premises, and found some muskets reportedly hidden by his daughter in a well. General Tilghman was arrested September 26 and taken to Cambridge for interrogation by Brigadier General Henry H. Lockwood, Union commander on the Eastern Shore.

There was no doubt where General Tilghman's sympathies lay. He had been quoted as boasting of his belief in "the equality of the States and the inequality of the races," and had described his political position as "a little to the southward of the South." Because of Tilghman's extreme partisanship, Governor Hicks had voided his commission as major general of the Maryland militia that May; and while the legislature restored his rank June 19, it did not give him back his command. The New York papers had carried reports that Tilghman was gathering arms at Plimhimmon and enlisting recruits for the South. According to a report in the *New York Herald*, he was about to take command of a large body of troops at Accomac on the Virginia Eastern Shore to promote the secessionist cause.

Tilghman denied all this, and insisted the guns found on his property were only some old muskets which had been used in drill by cadets at the Oxford Military Academy in the 1840s. He was released on parole October 4 after pledging to do or say nothing henceforth in opposition to the Union. He scrupulously kept his parole, making no public appearances and seldom leaving Plimhimmon for the duration of the war.

His arrest antagonized still more Talbot Countians; after all, he was the grandson of the Revolutionary War hero, and had served the county in a variety of capacities, including his long but so far unsuccessful efforts to bring a railroad to Easton.

However, the third election in which Talbot voters had an unhampered chance to express their viewpoint—the gubernatorial contest of November, 1861—showed the two sides still almost exactly even. Benjamin C. Howard of Baltimore, the states' rights candidate, carried the county by one vote, 906 to 905, over Unionist Augustus W. Bradford of Harford County. Again the pattern was as in 1860; Easton was strongly for Howard; St. Michaels was strongly for Bradford; and the rest of the county was divided.

But by this time Talbot, and especially Easton, were out of step with general Maryland sentiment. Howard won only three other counties, all in southern Maryland, and Bradford swept the state by more than two to one. A pro-Union legislature also was elected, and Maryland's adherence to the Union was assured.

By this time also, federal troops were stationed in Talbot. A body of cavalry set up what was called Camp Quaker near the Third Haven Meeting House, just outside the Easton town limits. They were not exactly popular, especially when, after receiving their first pay October 2, some of them "indulged too freely in liquor," and had to be locked up.

In the winter of 1861-62 barracks were built on Dover Road outside the town at what was first named Camp Kirby for Major William Kirby, its commander, and later renamed Camp Hicks for the first wartime governor. Three companies of the First Eastern Shore Volunteer Regiment were assigned there—Company H, composed of local men who had been recruited at Trappe, Company E from Caroline County, and Company I, from Baltimore city. Soon there was friction, climaxed by what became known as "the Battle of Cow Landing."

THE CIVIL WAR ERA

On January 21, 1862, Thomas K. Robson, the aggressively pro-South editor of the *Easton Star*, published an article lampooning the action of Major Kirby in arresting a man named Reese who had been involved in a fight with two Camp Kirby soldiers at Easton Point. Robson datelined it "Cow Landing," the ancient name for the point. He ridiculed the soldiers as "Caroline County sand diggers," and "Mr. Lincoln's pet lambs." According to Robson, Reese's "crime" had been to make remarks about the Union which the soldiers had resented and to flaunt his disloyalty by eating some "sesech candy," a peppermint stick striped with red and white but lacking the blue of the federal government.

Major Kirby overreacted with characteristic vigor. He ordered Robson to be arrested and brought before him. After receiving a stern lecture, Robson agreed to sign a parole pledging that he would not "publish in the *Star*, anything personal hereafter, calculated to offend the said command," meaning Major Kirby. But he carefully added two provisos: that he was signing the parole under duress; and that nothing in it should be considered "to debar me of my editorial privilege of commenting upon the actions of wrong doers, be they in the army or otherwise."

Thereafter, although he did not criticize any of the troops personally, he lambasted federal policies and Talbot Countians who supported them even more severely than before. Local Unionists became "eavesdroppers, spies and informers" for the hated federals. Each Confederate military victory—and there were many at that stage of the war—became a triumph for the cause; the few Union successes were played down or ignored in the pages of the paper.

Then came an incident so shocking that it focused the attention of the nation on Easton, and polarized public opinion in Talbot County. On May 27, 1862, Circuit Judge Richard Bennett Carmichael was dragged from the bench and brutally beaten by federal marshals while he was conducting a trial in the Talbot County Court House. He and three other men were arrested and hauled off to Fort McHenry on a charge of treason, punishable by death, while two companies of federal troops occupied the court house green, prepared to put down any reprisals.

Immediately there rose a tide of angry protest among southern partisans throughout Maryland. Judge Carmichael became an instant hero, and the treatment he received an example of the "brutality" with which federal authorities were keeping the state in the Union camp by armed force. Even the staunchest Union supporters were revolted by the spectacle of a judge, no matter how misguided, being beaten and arrested in his own court. The Judge Carmichael affair has been called the most important single nonmilitary event of the war in Maryland; and it certainly was the most dramatic event in turning Talbot public opinion against the Union. Robson in the *Star* denounced it as "a tragedy to surpass in atrocity the most infamous deeds in history," and even the *Gazette* had to admit the action of the federal marshals had been "unnecessarily violent."

In the hue and cry, the background of the arrest was virtually forgotten. As in the case of General Tilghman, there was no doubt of Judge Carmichael's partisanship for the South; he had issued ruling after ruling which made this evident. As he saw it the United States Constitution itself placed the powers of the states above those of the federal government.

The immediate issue which brought about Judge Carmichael's arrest stemmed from an incident in the November, 1861, election campaign. A Unionist rally in Chapel District was broken up by hecklers. The Unionists appealed to the commander of the federal troops stationed in Talbot to prevent election violence, and consequently three men were arrested on federal charges of interfering with the election process. Judge Carmichael, however, instructed the Talbot grand jury that the arrests were in themselves crimes, and the military men who had made them were indicted, along with Talbot's Henry H. Goldsborough, who had been principal speaker at the Union meeting.

This was an act of defiance going directly to the heart of the conflict about which the Civil War was being fought. Judge Carmichael was asserting that the states' civil powers were superior to those of the federal government. When he went even further early in May by failing to mention in his charge to the grand jury a new "treason bill" enacted by the Maryland legislature to crack down on southern sympathizers, the federal authorities decided to remove him from the bench.

On May 24 deputy United States Marshal John S. McPhail and special officer John L. Bishop arrived in Easton with papers instructing them to arrest Judge Carmichael and Talbot's state's attorney I. C. W. Powell as traitors, on authority of Major General John A. Dix, federal commander of the Maryland military district. On Tuesday, May 27, after troop reinforcements had reached Easton, McPhail, Bishop, and other federal officers went to the Court House and informed Judge Carmichael, who was in the midst of hearing a civil case, that he was under arrest.

Exactly what happened next is still a matter of dispute after more than a century. The *Star* and the *Gazette* gave conflicting versions, though both claimed to have gotten their stories from eyewitnesses. But they agreed on the basic facts: officer Bishop attempted to take Judge Carmichael into custody; the judge resisted; Bishop hit him on the head with the butt of his pistol; other federal officers rushed forward to help Bishop, swinging their pistol butts; and Judge Carmichael was knocked to the floor, bleeding and semiconscious. Several local men who tried to help him were also beaten. Among them was attorney John Bozman Kerr, one of the Eastern Shore's most outspoken supporters of the Union.

Throughout the county, people were horrified as word of this brutal affair spread rapidly. There was talk of striking back, but no one dared challenge the federal troops platooned with guns at the ready around the Court House. After Judge Carmichael's wounds were dressed, he was taken to Fort McHenry aboard the steamer *Balloon*. Later he was removed to Fort Lafayette, and then to Fort Delaware. No trial was held, and on December 4, 1862, he was unconditionally released. He did not resume his place on the bench, and thus the federal intention of silencing him was accomplished; but as a symbol of resistance to what secessionists called "the despot's heel" on Maryland, he did far more damage to the federal cause than he could ever have done by judicial rulings.

The next federal crackdown on a Talbot dissident came in May, 1863. Robson had continued to denounce the government, and especially President Lincoln, in the *Star*. In July, 1862, he published a poem by a Talbot youth, John N. F. Martin, entitled "Noble Ashby," which eulogized the fallen Confederate hero, General Turner Ashby. This and Robson's anti-Lincoln editorials were such an annoyance that federal officials decided he, like Judge Carmichael, would have to be silenced.

On the evening of May 8, 1863, Robson was arrested in the *Star* office on a warrant signed by President Lincoln. He was given fifteen minutes to pack a trunk and say goodbye to his family, then hustled aboard the *Balloon* and taken to Fort McHenry. From there he was taken under military guard to Harper's Ferry, conducted at night through both Union and Confederate lines, and dumped into the middle of the Shenandoah Valley by his guards. In the words of a contemporary, "there they left him seated, cooling his heels on his trunk, in the middle of a bare, winding road, dust-filled and desolate."

Robson was soon picked up by a rebel patrol and, after questioning, allowed to make his way to the Confederate capital at Richmond. He remained there for the duration of the war, working as a clerk. At one point he was drafted into the Richmond defense forces, but got out of it on grounds he was an "exile" entitled to "asylum in a friendly nation." After the war he returned to Easton, as unreconstructed and as violently racist as ever, and resumed publication of the *Star*, which had been suspended at the same time he was arrested. He continued as the paper's editor-publisher until his death November 20, 1888.

Admiral Franklin Buchanan, from a painting by Rembrandt Peale.

Other Talbot County men served the Confederacy in more conspicuous capacities. Captain (later Admiral) Franklin Buchanan (1800-1874) had already had a distinguished naval career when in May, 1861, he resigned his commission in the United States Navy and cast his lot with the Confederacy. A career officer, he had helped to establish the United States Naval Academy at Annapolis, and had served as its first commandant from 1845 to 1847. He had seen active duty in several battles of the Mexican War. In 1853, as top aide to United States Commodore Matthew C. Perry, he was literally the first American to set foot on Japanese soil as Perry's fleet sailed into Tokyo Bay and opened Japan to American commerce. At the time of the Civil War's outbreak he was commandant of the Washington Navy Yard. Although a native of Baltimore, he made his permanent home at The Rest on the Miles River in Talbot; his wife was the former Ann Catherine Lloyd of Wye House.

In the Confederate navy his career was equally distinguished. In August, 1862, he was captain of the first Confederate ironclad ship, the *Virginia* (known to Northerners by its former name, the *Merrimac*), at the time of its historic battle with the little turret-topped Union ironclad, the *Monitor*. Wounded during an earlier phase of the action, Buchanan was not aboard the *Virginia* when she was disabled and driven back to Norfolk harbor by the *Monitor*; but his "ability and bravery" during the battle were commended.

Later, with the rank of admiral, he was given command of rebel naval forces in Mobile Bay. It was against his squadron that Admiral David G. Farragut issued his famous order during the Battle of Mobile Bay in August, 1864: "Damn the torpedoes—full speed ahead!" Buchanan again was severely wounded, and this time taken prisoner.

After the war Buchanan eventually resumed his residence at The Rest. Among his notable guests was Jefferson Davis, former president of the Confederacy, in 1867.

Another relative of the Wye House Lloyds, Brigadier General Charles S. Winder, was one of the South's early war heroes as right-hand man to the famous Thomas "Stonewall" Jackson. Winder's mother had been Elizabeth Tayloe Lloyd, Mrs. Buchanan's elder sister. General Winder was in command of Jackson's Stonewall Brigade, but was killed at the Battle of Cedar Mountain, August 9, 1862. Both Admiral Buchanan and General Winder are buried at Wye House.

Brigadier General Lloyd Tilghman, born at Rich Neck, was another early Confederate hero who was killed in battle. He died while commanding rear guard troops in the retreat from Vicksburg in July, 1863. In the Vicksburg National Military Park is an equestrian statue depicting him in action at the time he was fatally wounded.

Three sons of General Tench Tilghman, the silenced secessionist of Plimhimmon, served the Confederacy. Oswald, twenty years old in 1861, fought with Terry's Texas Rangers, was captured in Mississippi in July, 1863, and spent two years in a northern prison camp at Johnson's Island, Ohio. Later he was transferred to the Union prison camp at Point Lookout, Maryland. After the war he became a leading Talbot County attorney and lifelong proponent of the "Lost Cause" legend which for so long held currency in Talbot. He died at Foxley Hall in Easton June 17, 1932.

John Leeds Tilghman also was in the Confederate army. But it was Tench Francis Tilghman, who joined the rebels as a civilian, who had the most dramatic experience; he helped Jefferson Davis evade pursuing Union troops after the Confederacy collapsed in the spring of 1865, and came home to Plimhimmon with a share of gold from the Confederate treasury to prove it.

Tench Francis had slipped through federal lines into Virginia in 1863. He was assigned to civilian duty, rounding up horses in North

The Rest, the home of Admiral Franklin Buchanan, from an 1880 photograph.

Carolina for the rebel forces. After the fall of Richmond and General Lee's surrender, he and several companions headed south for Florida. In Charlotte, North Carolina, on April 19, 1865, they agreed to act as escorts to Davis, who was fleeing southward with a few followers, the Confederate archives, and about twenty-five thousand dollars in gold which was all that remained of the rebel treasury. Tilghman had charge of Davis's personal wagon.

On May 6 Davis left the wagon train in Georgia and rode on ahead. A few days later the group learned he had been captured. They decided to split up and make their way home. The archives were buried in the barn of a Florida plantation, and the gold divided among the survivors. Tilghman's portion was 400 gold sovereigns, valued at $1,940. He reached home June 24, 1865.

There were heroes on the Union side as well, though none with such glamorous names as Lloyd or Tilghman. James C. Mullikin signed up with Company H of the first Eastern Shore Volunteer Regiment in 1861, at the age of twenty. He served for the duration, fought in the Battle of Gettysburg, and came home in 1865 as a twenty-four-year-old lieutenant colonel, one of the youngest in the Union army.

The unsung heroes of the war were the scores of Talbot blacks who volunteered for the Union army after President Lincoln finally opened the doors to them in the summer of 1863. They received low pay, could

Artist's conception of the sinking of a wooden frigate by the first Confederate ironclad ship, the *Merrimack (Virginia)*, commanded by Admiral Franklin Buchanan at Norfolk, Virginia, 1862.

not advance beyond the ranks, and were hurled into the fiercest fighting as cannon fodder in battle after battle. The South made it clear that if captured they would be shot, hanged, or sold back into slavery; and even the North for some time gave them lower pay and allowances than whites. Only in the right to die were they granted equality. But they were promised freedom when they got home—if they got home—and that was reward enough.

Slaveholders saw it differently. They complained bitterly that federal recruiters were stealing their property, and that there would be no one to till the fields if all the strong male slaves went off to war. Oxford became the principal embarkation point for mid-Shore area blacks departing for Camp Stanton in Charles County, where they received basic training. James Dixon, Talbot Quaker and leading businessman, recorded in vivid terms the scene as more than two hundred slaves left the Oxford wharf aboard the steamer *Champion* on September 18, 1863:

> The owners and others stood silent and thoughtful upon the wharf and beach, and as the steamer moved off, the colored people on board, waving their hats in good bye, broke out into one of their jubilant hymns such as they were accustomed to sing in their religious meetings, for having no patriotic songs those hymns were converted into songs of deliverance from slavery.

Many Talbot Countians who had supported the North in the beginning turned their backs on it as the war became more and more a crusade to end slavery rather than simply to preserve the Union. They did not

Farm workers unloading bags of grain from a mule drawn cart on to a boat for ferrying to a waiting schooner bound for the Baltimore market.

want the end of slavery; and more especially they were repelled by the growing talk about "black equality" which was being heard in some parts of the north and even in Baltimore. If opinion on the war had been divided about evenly at the start of the war, that was far from the case by 1864. Dr. Harrison estimated that not more than two hundred "hard core" white Unionists—only about ten percent of the voting population—stood firmly with the Republican party when black civil rights became the dominating issue.

In fact, however, the rebellion itself played a leading role in destroying slavery. Some Eastern Shore Union newspapers went so far as to say that Jefferson Davis, not Abraham Lincoln, should be called "the Great Emancipator," as slavery was abolished in vast territories of West Virginia, Kentucky, and Missouri. Said Denton's *American Union*: "Slavery, because of this Rebellion, has received a mortal stab from those professing to be its best friends."

Uncertainty over the war's outcome, and loss of markets in the Deep South, sent the prices brought by slaves sold in Talbot County plummeting. Dr. Harrison, who attended the last slave auction ever held in Easton, on August 26, 1863, noted that the average price paid for sixteen slaves from the estate of the Reverend Thomas Bayne was only $184. Eight years earlier a similar auction had brought bids as high as $1,125 and an average price of $752.

THE CIVIL WAR ERA

In the absence of an official slave market, these auctions were held at the Court House door. They had been a familiar part of the Easton scene for many years.

Talbot men who volunteered for the Union's First Eastern Shore Regiment had an uneventful first two years. They had been recruited strictly as a "home guard," under a widely publicized pledge by the secretary of war that they would not be assigned to duty off the Eastern Shore. The one hundred men of Trappe's Company H got no farther away than Eastern Shore Virginia until the spring of 1863. But then General Lee boldly sent his army north to invade Pennsylvania and Maryland, and all promises were called off. On the early morning of July 3, 1863, Trappe's youthful volunteers found themselves in the midst of a roaring inferno at Culp's Hill near Gettysburg, participants in the greatest battle the world had ever known. At 7:00 A.M. they were ordered to advance over the crest of Culp's Hill.

Then followed one of those unbelievable coincidences which set the American Civil War apart from almost all others in history. On the other side of the hill they met troops of the First Maryland Confederate Regiment, which included a number of Trappe area men who had slipped away to Virginia to join the rebel army. The color sergeant for the Confederates was P. M. Moore of Trappe; the color sergeant for the Union was his cousin, Robert W. Ross, also from Trappe. For long minutes as the struggle raged they stood almost face to face, while all around them boyhood friends from Trappe tried desperately to kill each other.

Sergeant Moore, fatally wounded, was taken prisoner by the Union men. He died a few days later. Other rebel casualties are unknown, but ten Company H men were wounded. Andrew Satterfield died shortly afterward; William H. Price and James E. Price each lost an arm; William R. Chaplain, James H. Gossage, Robert Giles, C. H. Gester, William T. Reed, Samuel Matthews, and James H. Scott all suffered wounds. It was a fearful price to pay for the only battle in which Company H took part during the entire war.

In the quiet woodland of Culp's Hill today are two monuments, one to the First Maryland Confederates, the other to the First Eastern Shore Union Volunteers.

Visitors to Easton who see another monument, the statue of a rebel soldier on the Court House grounds with the inscription, "To the Talbot Boys 1861-1865 C.S.A.," are likely to get the impression that most area men served the Confederate cause. This is far from true. The monument's sides carry the names of 85 men, with an additional 11 listed

Dusk on Papermill Pond, the southeast reach of the Tred Avon River at Easton Point.

underneath as "Citizens After War," whereas a special census enumeration of Union veterans or their surviving wives made in 1890 listed 334 from Talbot County. Those are probably fair estimates of total participation on both sides in the Civil War. The monument was erected in 1915-16, at a time when wartime passions were still strong and the county was dominated by persons of Southern sentiment. A proposal to dedicate the monument to both sides was turned down.

As Talbot opinion crystallized, almost no one found it possible to remain neutral on the great issues of the war. Even churches were drawn in. A pro-Union Trappe correspondent complained in the *Gazette* in May, 1862, that the ministers of both the Methodist Episcopal and Methodist Protestant churches there "are carefully negligent of praying for the government" in deference to what he called the "disunionists" in their congregations. The Episcopalians were almost entirely pro-Confederate, the Quakers pro-Union, the Methodists split (they later divided into separate North and South churches, and stayed that way for many years).

Easton's women were especially strong in advocating the "secesh" cause. With society still ruled by the old-line slaveholding families, it became the fashionable side to be on. Secession "was understood to constitute a passport to select social circles," said Dr. Harrison, who did not admire the trend. "Even those who had loyal husbands and brothers" favored the South.

They let their sentiments be known in unmistakable ways. The *Gazette* complained of "those who when they meet a soldier on the street, turn up their nose and make their faces look as though they were drawn out of shape by a severe spasm." When Thomas A. Wollaston, who was Union provost marshal, hung a large American flag outside the hotel he operated at the corner of Washington and Goldsborough, many Easton women refused to walk under it, crossing to the other side or even picking their way through the mud of the dirt street. In November, 1862, Wollaston replaced it with a much larger flag, attached to a rope which ran all the way across the street so that the flag hung from the middle. Reporting this, the *Gazette* commented: "We hope those of the fair sex who have hitherto taken to the middle of the street to avoid walking under it—or to make a display of their ankles— . . . will now be able to wend their way without molestation or hindrance."

Pro-Union women formed the "Ladies Union Relief" to provide food and medicine for sick men at the federal military camps near Easton. They got little help from their Easton sisters; most of their contributions came from St. Michaels and Trappe. Nevertheless, they did much good; a card in the *Gazette* of January 10, 1863, from the steward of the military hospital acknowledged the "many comforts and delicacies" they had provided the sick soldiers, and thanked them for their "personal attendance" at the hospital.

Wollaston's Union Hotel, at the site of the Nevius building (but not in the present structure, which was built later), figured in another controversy which involved Robson and the *Star*. On November 3, 1862, Henry H. Goldsborough, who by that time held the rank of brigadier general and had charge of Talbot military affairs, issued an order barring the sale of liquor within five miles of Camp Hicks, the former Camp Kirby. Three weeks later men "dressed in military uniforms" raided the *Star* office next door to Wollaston's hotel, pushed over the forms, presses, and other equipment, and scattered the type up and

Washington Street, Easton, circa 1880.

down Goldsborough Street. Investigation indicated that they had been drinking, and that they'd gotten their liquor at Wollaston's hotel.

On Goldsborough's order, Wollaston was arrested and charged with illegal liquor sales. Secessionists thought it was hilarious that the first man arrested under Easton's first prohibition law should be the chief marshal of Union forces in the area, responsible for keeping the civilian population under control. Wollaston denied the charge and was released, but later lost his post as provost marshal. Although Goldsborough had promised a thorough investigation of the incident, none of those responsible for wrecking the *Star*'s office was ever arrested. Friends and small boys helped Robson pick up his type in Goldsborough Street, and admirers contributed about six hundred dollars to help him repair the damage. The next week's issue of the *Star* was printed as usual.

Before he lost his position as provost marshal, Wollaston also took part in a much more serious affair. On a tip, he led a raid on a stable at Royal Oak and found five men hiding there who were alleged to be Union deserters being helped to go home by rebel sympathizers. They were brought to Easton under guard and placed on a steamer to be taken to Baltimore. At Cambridge, first stop on the way, one of the men jumped from the boat and ran. Guards Joseph Raisin and Stephen Houghland pursued him. They later said they called on him to halt, and when he did not, Raisin fired three shots and Houghland two. The man fell dead.

THE CIVIL WAR ERA

There was an uproar about the incident. The guards were exonerated, but as late as 1873, Dr. Harrison said, many people in Talbot County still regarded Raisin as a cold-blooded murderer.

The wartime draft, instituted in October, 1862, was extremely unpopular. It was also unfair; as had happened in the Revolution, men who could afford it could hire substitutes to serve for them. This quickly became a racket, since the substitutes had to stay in camp only ten days to collect bounties ranging from three hundred to seven hundred dollars. Many hung around just long enough to get their money, then skipped out to appear as volunteers elsewhere.

Funds were collected from private sources to provide substitutes for deserving but poor men. One who contributed was James M. Seth; he put up enough money in 1864 to buy all the substitutes needed for Bay Hundred District, where he lived.

By that time the county was in the substitute buying business on an organized scale. The commissioners voted fifty thousand dollars in 1864 to pay volunteers as substitutes for drafted men, and made a contract with a Baltimore agent to supply them at three hundred dollars a head. But as events turned out, few were needed. So many blacks were volunteering that only a handful of white draftees was required to fill the Talbot quota for 1864.

On the economic front, retail shortages appeared. By February 20, 1862, merchant James H. Grace of Easton was advertising "dandelion coffee" and "roasted rye" as substitutes for the real thing. The Easton bank looked with doubtful eyes at paper money from both sides, since neither type had anything more substantial behind it than a cheerful promise to win the war. For a time the bank refused to accept either federal or Confederate paper; its divided board of directors, split six to five in favor of the Confederacy, followed the war news anxiously, waiting to see which way to jump. The balance of power was held by Quakers such as James Dixon, whose family would play a key role for the next century in the Easton National Bank's affairs. They condemned both slavery and war. Hot debates were held behind closed doors until moderates led by Dixon and William H. Groome convinced the partisans that the bank was in business to make money, not to support political passions on either side. They proved right; bank deposits quadrupled between January, 1861, and May, 1865. Some of this stemmed from inflation, but most of it came from the prosperity brought to the long depressed Eastern Shore by the war.

Much as some Talbot Countians hated to admit it, there were rich profits to be made from federal domination of the Shore. Everything the area produced—grain, livestock, foodstuffs, seafood, bay schooners, and other boats—was in demand for the Union army. Some clandestine trade was carried on with the Confederacy, largely by log canoes which slipped at night past Union gunboat patrols, but it was comparatively small. "Boards of trade," set up late in 1862 at Oxford and St. Michaels, required an oath of allegiance from any trader who wanted either to bring goods into Talbot County or ship them elsewhere. At first none was established in Easton for fear of reprisals by the "disaffected," but by January, 1863, one was also in operation there.

By contrast, huge orders were placed by federal authorities hungry for supplies. Early in 1861 the government advertised in Easton papers for 100,000 oak spokes for army wagon wheels. Ships loaded with grain departed regularly from ports on the Wye, Miles, Tred Avon, and Choptank. Not all of them made it; the schooner *Minnesota*, carrying 1,700 bushels of grain, sank in the Miles during a storm in the bitter winter of 1862-63.

Market prices skyrocketed. Wheat went from $1.50 a bushel at harvesttime in 1861 to $2.90 in June, 1864. Before the war ended best quality white wheat topped $3.00. Corn and oats increased proportionately. In 1864 pork was selling for 18 cents a pound, chickens for $1.00 (compared with two for 25 cents before the war). A fat goose at Christmastime that year brought $5.00.

Luckily, wages also doubled. Pay in 1860 had averaged $4.00 to $5.00 per week for "helpers," $9.00 for blacksmiths, $8.00 for such skilled workmen as carpenters, shipwrights, painters, and harness makers. By 1865 the range was $10.00 to $18.00 for these same categories.

But the secessionists, especially in Easton, saw to it that pro-Union merchants didn't profit too much from the good times. "Disloyal" ladies boycotted merchants whose stores did business with the Union soldiers, or who advertised in the *Gazette* to show their Union sympathies. After the *Star* was suppressed Arthur Brown, a pro-rebel *Star* printer, started a paper called the *Easton Journal* to give secessionists a guide to stores and something to read. Under its later name of the *Easton Ledger*, it survived until 1917.

In the war's early stages, secessionists were jubilant as Southern armies scored victory after victory. Even unfounded rumors brought wild celebrations. When reports spread on July 5, 1862—a Saturday—that General McClellan had offered to surrender the entire Army of the Potomac to General Lee, an excited crowd gathered in Easton. There were cheers for Lee and Jeff Davis, shouts that the Confederate armies soon would take over Washington. Unionists' faces were glum. All weekend (there was no telegraph to Easton then) the crowd waited anxiously for papers to arrive with the expected confirmation of Lee's triumph, and the impending end of the war. But when "Bob's messenger," a courier who brought papers down from Queenstown on days when there was no steamboat to Easton, reached Easton Monday morning with the latest journals from Baltimore and Philadelphia, the news was just the opposite. Far from surrendering, McClellan had outmaneuvered Lee and defeated him "with great slaughter." "Those who came from the country discovered they had no further business in town, while those who had lined the sidewalks and occupied the street corners were suddenly reminded that pressing engagements required them elsewhere," the *Gazette* reported with ill-suppressed glee.

As the tide of war turned, it was the Unionists who did the cheering and the secessionists whose faces were glum. Pro-Northerners celebrated the twin victories of Vicksburg and Gettysburg in July, 1863, by firing off cannon and whooping it up on Easton streets. Rebel partisans simply refused to believe the Union victories had occurred. They also ignored a Union celebration on July 4, 1864, when troops of the One Hundred and Forty-ninth Ohio Volunteers who were quartered at the Court House paraded to the music of Benny's Annapolis Brass Band. A stand in front of the Court House was decorated with flags and streamers. Artillery salutes boomed out, flags flew, the Ohioans marched, and an American flag was presented by Miss Lizzie Nicols to Sergeant Lamkin of the ordnance department. At 2:00 P.M. the Declaration of Independence was read by Reverend T. E. Martindale and an oration "full of patriotic ardor" was delivered by Dr. C. C. Cox. But many of the townspeople stayed in their homes; to them July 4 that year was just another Monday.

Two momentous elections were held in the fall of 1864. In both, all who expressed Confederate sympathies as well as those who had actually aided the South were barred from voting. On October 12, those who were eligible balloted on a "radical" new Maryland constitution. Its most controversial provision was for immediate emancipation of the state's slaves, who had not been affected by Lincoln's Emancipation Proclamation of 1863 since the state was not among those in rebellion. Even with all southern sympathizers supposedly disenfranchised, Talbot voted against the new constitution, 1,020 to 430. So did the entire Eastern Shore; and a preliminary count showed the constitution defeated in Maryland, 29,536 to 27,541. However, the courts permitted votes cast by soldiers in camp to be counted, and they put the constitution over by a margin of 375 votes. It was declared effective at once, and Maryland's slaves were freed as of November 1, 1864.

On November 8, balloting was held for president. Again it was meaningless as a true test of Talbot sentiment. Voting restrictions were applied even more rigidly than before; secessionists charged that many who had been permitted to vote on the constitution were barred this time. Lincoln carried the county, 578 to 267, over General George McClellan, a northern "copperhead" who called for an immediate end of the war and a negotiated peace with the Confederacy. Lincoln also won Maryland, and a second term as president.

News of the fall of Richmond, which arrived April 3, 1865, brought wild excitement to Easton Unionists and deep despair to the secessionists. "The Court House bells have rung, cannon jar the earth, bonfires blaze and illuminations prevail," Dr. Harrison recorded. Said the *Gazette*: "While the face of every Union man was beaming with delight, Rebel countenances became so elongated that they might almost have been measured by the yard."

Announcement of Lincoln's assassination was made in churches Sunday, April 16, the day after he died. In some it was greeted with cheering and applause. At one Trappe church "not a few of the women attending service expressed their joy at the atrocious act of the assassin," Dr. Harrison wrote. When services for Lincoln were held on Wednesday, April 19, Easton was officially in mourning, with business suspended, houses draped in black, and special services in some churches—but not all.

Then the rebel soldiers began drifting home, to be treated as heroes by many, as traitors by some. The *Gazette*, bitter to the end, fumed because they did not seem to realize they had been beaten. "They return with an air as defiant and pompous as if they were perfect heroes," editor Councell wrote. "They should be taught that they are conquered, not conquerers—that they have no rights in the loyal states." Councell called for an indignation meeting, but none was held.

The war was ended, and so was slavery, after two hundred years. Now it was time, not for indignation meetings, but for the work of picking up the pieces.

TEN

The Age of Steam

TECHNOLOGICALLY speaking, the last third of the nineteenth century was the age of steam in Talbot County. On the water, steamboats became ever bigger, faster, and more luxurious; on land, the railroads finally arrived, reshaping the economy, creating new wealth, new industries, new towns. Steam sawmills replaced the colorful but less efficient water-powered mills of an earlier day; steam-powered "thrashers" appeared on the farms, steam-driven factory machines in Easton. A steam printing press enabled the *Easton Gazette* to outstrip its rival newspapers, turned out on old-fashioned handpresses little changed since Gutenberg's time. Even the first automobile ever to travel down the Eastern Shore is said to have been a Stanley Steamer driven by Thomas A. Edison's son, W. L. Edison, in 1899.

But if it was the age of steam, it was the age of much else also in Talbot: croquet, lawn tennis, bicycling, and baseball; church socials, county fairs, and family picnics; busy villages and small towns, jammed on Saturday nights with farmers' wagons; resort hotels and summer boarders; waves of "foreign invaders," rich northerners who bought up Talbot's fine old waterfront estates and endured their former owners' haughty snubs. It was the age, too, of the oyster, rockfish, terrapin, crab, and canvasback duck, the watermelon and "roasting ear," the great peach orchards with their bountiful harvests hauled to railheads in wagon trains a mile long, and all the other Eastern Shore delicacies which would become scarce too soon. There was a kind of shining innocence about this age, when children entertained themselves with made-up games, youths courted young girls at church suppers and hay rides, and adults thought the height of pleasure was an ice cream soda at the corner store.

Many of these things would endure into the twentieth century; Talbot, more than most parts of the world, was slow to change. But they arose in the last years of the nineteenth, and that is where they properly belong.

A Buffalo-Pitts tractor engine pulling a threshing rig along Talbot Street in St. Michaels en route to a nearby farm, 1905.

Almost the first order of business for Talbot County, once the terrible fratricidal war was over, was completion of the railroad which had been promised for so long. As early as October, 1865, grading for a line which would run from a junction with the main north-south railroad at Clayton, Delaware, to Easton and Oxford was underway. The Maryland & Delaware Railroad Company, which was building it, was largely financed by Talbot capital and headed by Talbot men. General Tench Tilghman, whose prewar dream it had been, served as president, although he was ousted temporarily by E. L. F. Hardcastle, also a Talbot man. Both eventually lost out to the contractors to whom the company was deeply in debt even before the first train reached Easton. Tilghman's son Tench Francis was the line's chief engineer until his death in 1867, and his friend John W. Scott, who had accompanied him on the "flight into oblivion" with Jefferson Davis in 1865, was general agent and treasurer for many years.

As the rails crept past Goldsborough and Greensborough, excitement mounted in Talbot County. Weekly bulletins in the newspapers kept the public informed of progress—or, in some weeks, lack thereof.

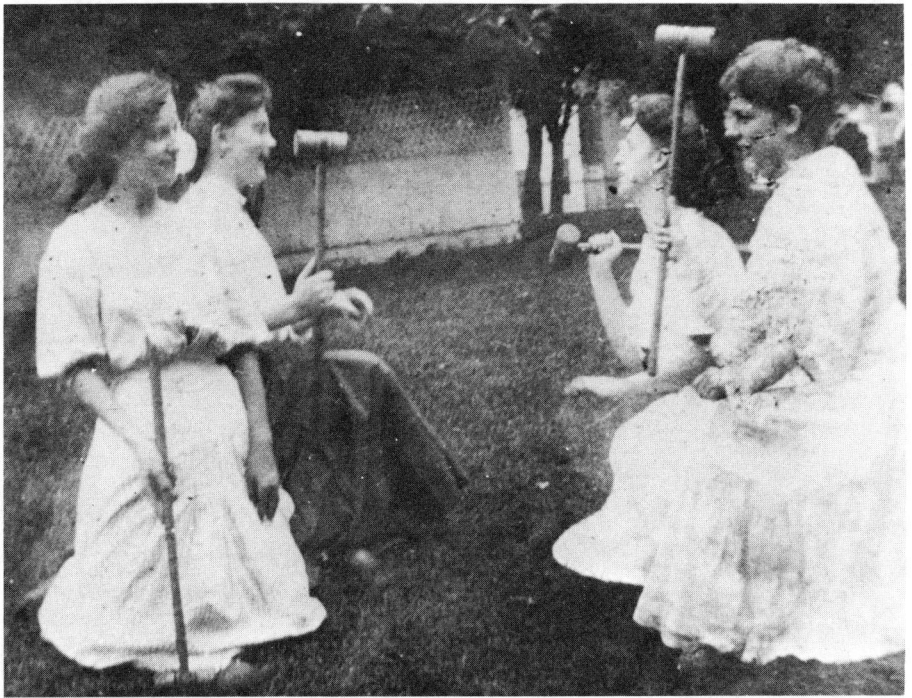

A game of croquet on the lawn of a home near Trappe. Photo from an anonymous family album, 1890.

By January, 1869, the tracks were laid almost to Hillsborough, and fifty laborers were at work on clearing and grading in northeastern Talbot. There was a temporary halt when the company ran out of money and couldn't pay its workers, but the county commissioners came to the rescue with fifty thousand dollars in taxpayers' funds.

A bitter dispute arose in Easton over how the railroad should enter town. Downtown merchants wanted it to run through the middle of West Street, thus helping business at their stores on "Front Street," as Washington was called for a brief time. The surveyors and engineers insisted that a route along the eastern edge of Easton, with a depot near Dover Road, would be cheaper and better. They won out, thus saving Easton despite itself from the blight of having a railroad run through the middle of town.

By April 20 track had been laid as far as Lloyd's Creek in Chapel District and a wooden bridge was under construction there. Trains were running to the new town of Ridgely in Caroline County, and a daily stage service from Easton took travelers there in time to board the 9:00 A.M. New York train. By August the tracks were just four miles northeast of Easton; hundreds of Talbot Countians journeyed up to Woodenhawks Bridge on August 2 to admire the new locomotive, called the Easton, and

J. W. Seemer's Hotel Avon coach, which met steamers and trains. The Bullitt house is at right, and the steps and porch of the hotel at left.

enjoy an eleven-hour excursion into Delaware. On August 14 a train got as far as Chapel Road, a mile and a half outside town. On August 31 the Easton hitched up to a line of cars and hauled thousands of bushels of peaches, then Talbot's chief fruit crop, up to New York, where they were selling at far higher prices than in Baltimore. After delays for smoothing out the roadbed, daily passenger service from Easton began November 15. A person could board the train at 6:00 A.M. and be in Philadelphia at 11:45, in New York City at 4:00 P.M. It seemed a miracle. With a change of cars at Clayton, the trip to Baltimore took eight hours, no faster than the steamboats but more dependable in wintertime.

From Easton the line pushed on southwest, reaching its terminus on the Oxford waterfront in 1871. By then a second locomotive, the Talbot, had been added, and the Easton depot was in place on the eastern town line. (It's still there, now occupied by a grocery, although the town has grown far beyond it and the trains are gone.)

Top, Pennsylvania Railroad Station, Easton, 1910, a postcard view. *Bottom*, the steamer *Cambridge* and a freight train at Claiborne, 1907.

A passenger train crossing Trippe Creek bridge enroute to Oxford, 1930

For Talbot Countians, the railroad meant far more than just fast travel to and from the big cities. It created a cash market for a host of previously unsaleable products. Blackberries, huckleberries, and wild cherries were shipped in quantity; partridges (bobwhites), wild ducks and geese, rabbits and rabbit skins, dressed and live poultry all went to market on the railroad. Eggs packed in straw, bran, or oats were shipped by the barrel. Talbot turkeys were highly esteemed in New York, where they sold at premium prices. Shipments of peaches (until blight destroyed the orchards in the 1880s) and other perishable fruits and vegetables increased enormously. Seafood production, especially the canning and pickling of oysters, became a major industry.

The railroad also created new towns, and changed the complexion of life in others along its route. Queen Anne owes its existence to the railroad; its site was a cornfield on the farm of Colonel Charles Nichols until 1867, when officials decided to put a railroad station there instead of at nearby Hillsborough. Mrs. S. J. Barton, by then owner of the Nichols farm, divided it into lots and sat back to await a town which was sure to grow up around the railroad depot. Soon it had a granary, a general store, houses, a flour mill, canneries, a lumber mill, and a milk cooling station. In 1896 it became a two-depot town when another railroad, the Maryland, Delaware & Virginia, ran tracks across the Eastern Shore from Rehoboth and Lewes, Delaware, to Love Point on Kent Island.

Cordova also grew out of the 1869 railroad. Only a crossroads hamlet called Thimbletown existed there until the rail station was built. The

Miles River ferry, used while second bridge was being built, 1913.

story goes that its first stationmaster, told to find a more attractive name, thumbed through a geography book until he found one he liked: the ancient Spanish city of Cordova, famed for its fine leather. At any rate Cordova prospered, although not as fast as its enthusiasts had hoped. Its big boost came in 1906, when the county's largest canning plant, the Talbot Packing & Preserving Company, was established near the many farms to process and pack peas, sugar corn, tomatoes, lima beans, succotash, and applesauce.

Other small towns in Talbot gained impetus indirectly from the railroad. As farm prosperity increased, these towns became the shopping centers of the horse-and-buggy era, each serving the community around it for a radius of five miles, about as far as a farmer and his family could conveniently travel by team. The post-Civil War period was the golden age of villages and small towns; nearly all of them were much busier and more populous than they would ever be again.

Wye Mills was an example. In the 1880s it had a population of nearly three hundred, scattered along its two main streets. It boasted three churches, five general stores, an ice cream parlor, two blacksmiths, two carpenters, a shoemaker, butcher, wheelwright, oyster dealer, and miller, in addition to the meeting house of Grange 99 of the Patrons of Husbandry, a farmers' organization which was the forerunner of today's Farm Bureau.

Trappe old-timers still recall the days when there were as many as eighteen general stores in the area, and "the town was so crowded on Saturday nights you could scarcely walk in the streets." Its merchants provided everything a farm family could want, from crackers in a barrel to flannel underwear and ladies' dresses, from candy for the kids to machinery for dad and stoves for mom, from fancy millinery to mattresses. At Sewell's steam flour and sawmill a farmer could bring in his

The Ocean City Flyer nearing Royal Oak

own grain, and while he waited have it ground into his private brand of flour or corn meal. Barter was standard practice; a farm wife could swap eggs, milk, butter, poultry, meat, or fresh garden produce for sugar, coffee, clothing, or a new hair ribbon. The town had three drugstores (one more than downtown Easton has today), several resident physicians, a "hair cutting and shaving saloon" where a shave and haircut cost the traditional two bits, and after 1903 its own library, staffed by volunteers and furnished with books contributed by the townspeople. Over the years, it even had three newspapers—the *Index*, the *Trappe Enterprise*, and the *Talbot Times*.

Despite all this enterprise, Trappe was by no means "modern" as the nineteenth century drew to a close. Its streets were paved with oystershells, and lighted dimly by a few widely spaced kerosene lamps; its main corner, distinguished by a town pump and the official weighing scales, was a favorite hangout for goateed loafers; its residents, happily ignorant of sewage disposal, used outdoor privies and bathed, if at all, in portable tubs set on the kitchen floor and filled with steaming water heated on cast-iron stoves. Nor was it beloved by all who lived there; Mary Hart, longtime Trappe correspondent of the *Star-Democrat*, recalled a barber who used to say that if he owned both Trappe and Hell, he'd sell Trappe and live in Hell. But it was a good small town in a good time for small towns.

Royal Oak, an ancient community, gained momentum when the steamboats and railroads began bringing summer visitors in droves to spend their vacations in Talbot. Half a dozen old homes opened their doors to paying guests. Best known was the Pasadena Inn; it was started in 1901 by Fred Harper, who had decided to stay home and build his own "Pasadena" when other family members went West and wrote back

The Valliant packing plant, Bellevue, as it looked about 1914.

glowing reports about the beauties of Pasadena, California. He advertised in the Baltimore and Washington papers for "summer boarders—$5 a week—children half rates." They came in sufficient numbers to make the inn a thriving Harper family business for more than half a century.

At its peak Royal Oak had other attractions—two saloons to complement its two churches, five stores, two blacksmith shops, a barbershop, and a business which combined the unlikely functions of carriage salesroom and undertaking parlor.

It also had a national reputation as "the healthiest place in America," although this was unearned if not necessarily undeserved. It resulted from a newspaperman's idea of a joke. In 1874 the coeditor of the *St. Michaels Comet*, stuck for something good to say about a piece of Royal Oak property being advertised for sale, wrote "according to unpublished statistics the health centre of the United States is a circle with Royal Oak as the centre and a radius of four miles." This was pure fiction; no survey had ever been made. But the item was picked up by metropolitan papers and published and republished, embellished and exaggerated throughout the United States for the next twenty years, even appearing in the *Manila Times* on the Philippine Islands. Finally in 1899 the hoax was exposed in an article in the *Baltimore Sun*. Even so many Royal Oak area people continued to believe it, taking the view that if it wasn't true it ought to be.

Seafood processing plants at Pier Street, Oxford. Also shown are an engine manufacturing plant, railroad terminal, and the rail line running parallel to the Oxford-Easton road, 1931.

Some "towns" launched in this era never got off the drawing boards. Bellevue was laid out in streets and lots by Oswald Tilghman, and named for his wife, the former Belle Harrison. He hoped it would become a resort center rivaling Ocean City, but instead it remained just "the place on the other end of the ferry from Oxford." At one time it did boast a thriving packing plant operated by W. H. Valliant, but that was about its only claim to fame.

Oxford, on the other side of the Tred Avon, did much better, thanks to the railroad. Its reincarnation really dates from the establishment of the rail terminus in 1871. In the next ten years its population jumped from 277 to more than 750, and it shot past Trappe to become the county's third largest town.

Sparking the growth were two steamboat wharves, one at the foot of Morris Street in the oldest part of town, the other at the south end, where a large pier to link rail and boat services was constructed in 1875. Oyster shucking houses and packing plants soon grew up in both areas, and two smaller wharves on Town Point, where the Tred Avon Yacht Club now stands, were leased to various commercial shipping firms. An oyster shucking and packing house was located there as early as 1877; later there was a tomato canning plant manned in the peak season by Bohemian immigrants from Baltimore who lived in shacks alongside the main building. A two-story icehouse was built to store blocks of ice shipped down from as far north as Kennebec, Maine, and packed in straw or sawdust to keep them cold.

A third center of activity was at the northeastern end of the Strand, then called Front Street. William P. Benson and Nathaniel Leonard, master builders at William R. Hughlett's Jamaica Point shipyard in the

Oxford Boatyard, 1930. "The Point," at the upper left, was frequently inundated at high tide, and the Strand was unpaved.

1850s, moved their operation to a site on Town Creek in 1866 in partnership with Henry E. Bateman. After three years Leonard withdrew to become proprietor of the nearby steam sawmill, but Benson continued to turn out vessels of various types for many years. Between 1879 and 1892 he launched at least five bugeyes, the sailing workboats which followed the log canoe and preceded the skipjack as watermen's favorites for dredging the oyster bars. (Ask any two old-timers where the word "bugeye" came from, and you'll get at least two different answers, and maybe more; but they usually carried two round spots which looked like bug's eyes on opposite sides of the bow.)

Vancouver or Kerr's Island in Town Creek, once slated to be the site of public buildings and a church which never materialized (see Chapter 3), was joined to the mainland in 1882 by a causeway connecting it with the Strand. A brick vault with an iron door was built there in 1883 to hold the explosive fuel called gasoline, used for the town's streetlights. Electric streetlights didn't arrive until 1921.

Town Park on Morris Street, which also dated from early colonial times, became the object of beautification efforts in the 1880s. Thirty linden trees were planted, and protected by whitewashed wooden tree boxes. Baseball playing in the park was prohibited in 1887. The town's first school, moved from a site on Oxford Neck in 1876, was located at the north end of the park; a second building, constructed later, served as Oxford High School.

Oxford got its first brick sidewalks in 1864, its first post office—in the Morris Street residence of Miss Mary Stewart, who served as postmistress for sixty-three years—in 1877, its first bank, the Oxford Savings Bank, in 1890. A newspaper, the *Oxford Enterprise*, was published in 1880 and perhaps later, although how long it lasted is uncertain. Only part of one issue, dated November 13, 1880, and owned by the Oxford Museum, is known to have survived.

The town's cool summer breezes, relaxed atmosphere, and convenience for sport sailors and fishermen attracted flocks of summer visitors. The old house where Robert Morris had had his residence and office, at the foot of Morris Street, became a favorite vacation spot; enlarged and equipped with a mansard roof, it was known as Riverview House. A bowling alley was next door. The Eastford Hall Hotel, farther up Morris street, was another favorite until it burned in 1894. Smaller guesthouses included Sinclair House and the Grapevine House, named for a huge grapevine, still extant, said to have been grown from cuttings brought from the Isle of Guernsey in 1798 aboard the brigantine *Sara and Louise*, and planted by John Willis, then collector of customs.

In 1885 Oxford became the site of one of the most ambitious educational undertakings ever projected for the Eastern Shore—the Oxford Military and Naval Academy, which its sponsors hoped would become the equal of the academies at West Point and Annapolis. A square-rigged sailing ship was acquired for cadet training, and the school catalogue claimed an enrollment of 254 boys. From the beginning the academy had problems. The first superintendent left after a year at the invitation of the trustees, and his successor, Major Armes, fared even worse. The *Easton Star* reported in March, 1887, that the school was "about up the spout," and that Major Armes was "certainly not the right man in the right place." The term had started with about 175 students, the *Star* said, but "so many are displeased with Major Armes' administration and have left, that only some 25 or 30 remain.... It is not to be expected that such young gentlemen ... would submit to be treated like common soldiers."

That was the academy's final year. Eastford Hall, which had been its headquarters, went back to taking in paying guests. The school's assets were acquired by Oswald Tilghman, who evidently hoped to start another academy; but he never did.

Claiborne was also a community long associated with the railroads, although actually it was launched—at least on paper—fifteen years before it saw its first train. It was the brainchild of three local residents, Theophilus Cockey, Frank Turner, and Joseph B. Seth. About 1875 they laid out a town on Turner's Addition, a parcel of land south of Rich

The ferry dock at Claiborne with cars being unloaded from the *Gov. Emerson C. Harrington*, first of the Claiborne-Annapolis ferries, about 1915.

Neck Manor, where Seth lived, and north of the present village. A plat of it which appeared in an 1877 county atlas was imposing—nearly two hundred lots on eight main streets with such names as Rich Neck Road, Leeds, Ward, Progress, Monument, Tilghman, and Dom Pedro (whoever he was). At its center was Henry Clay Square, a large area reserved for public buildings. Joseph T. Tunis, who ran the local steam sawmill and sold real estate on the side, provided a slogan: "Young man don't go West, but to Claiborne."

Northwest of Turner's Addition, on Tilghman's Creek facing the Miles, lay the real Claiborne of that day, or what there was of it—Tunis's sawmill, the Claiborne Oyster Company, a boatyard, a few homes, and a landing for steamboats on their way up the Miles River. At the foot of Rich Neck Road, where the village is today, was a general store.

The new town was to be called Bay City when it got big enough, but it never made the grade. Eleven years later, when Seth, by then a militia general, succeeded in getting a charter for the railroad from the legislature, it was still waiting to be born. The railroad was a combined operation, with steamboats bringing passengers from Baltimore and trains whisking them on to Ocean City by way of St. Michaels, Easton, Salisbury, and Berlin, with crossroads flag stops in between. Officially named the Baltimore, Chesapeake, and Atlantic (B C & A), it was better known to Talbot Countians as the Before Christ & After or the Black Cinders &

Sharp's Island Hotel, built in the 1890s.

Ashes line. It began operations in 1890, but unluckily for "Bay City," its steamboat landing, for engineering reasons, was placed on the bay side of Claiborne, not the Tilghman's Creek side. Few of its passengers tarried long in Claiborne; they were as anxious to get on to Ocean City then as the weekenders on Route 50 are today. A layover hotel for rail employees called Railroad House, a not-very-successful waterfront hostelry, the Bellefont Hotel, and a few oyster houses struggled for what transient dollars there were.

Nearby, however, private boarding houses for summer vacationers flourished as visitors from Baltimore and elsewhere discovered the pleasures of the Eastern Shore. One of the best known and longest lasting was Maple Hall, a mile or so up the Miles from Tilghman's Creek in what is known today as Old Claiborne. Started by John Cockey, uncle of Theophilus, and his wife, the former Sarah Catherine Tunis, it began taking in paying guests in 1875 and lasted until 1967.

Another boarding house was Wade's Point, the handsome structure built in the 1820s by the famous Fells Point shipbuilder, Thomas Kemp (see Chapter 8). Mrs. Joseph Kemp, the young wife of a Thomas Kemp descendant, had so many summer visitors that she started charging them for their board. They paid up happily, and so did generations of guests who followed. Today Wade's Point is still a summer guesthouse.

There were many others as the era of the summer boarder got into full swing: the Roost, run by Tilson Cockey and his wife, Louise; Safety

Beach; Breezy Point, and a string of places all the way down the bay shore to Tilghman Island, where the venerable Chesapeake House was opened in 1875.

Out on Sharp's Island, already wasting away from erosion, a three-story, six-gabled resort hotel was built in the 1890s, apparently as a recreational center for the Young, Creighton, & Diggs Boot & Shoe Manufacturing Company of Baltimore. Hotel, company, and island all vanished before many years. After 1900 the firm ceased to be listed in Baltimore City directories; and when an Easton group, the Alforetta Fishing Club, used the island for an outing in 1905, they found the hotel's furnishings were gone and the building in bad repair. By 1918 it was in a state of collapse. But, by then the island itself was almost gone. Estimated at 700 acres in 1660, it had shrunk to 438 acres in 1848 and had only 53 acres in 1910. Today nothing remains of it but a warning light in Choptank Bay.

On Tilghman, a little less remote and partly sheltered from erosion, life bloomed in the 1880s and 1890s. The island's people were almost all watermen, as many of them still are. To them the bay and its products were their entire livelihood.

Active boat builders were numerous. Most specialized in log canoes and, later in the nineteenth century, in bugeyes. Perhaps the first log canoe produced in the area was the *Sharp's Island*, launched in 1856 by Thomas Bruff at his Sharp's Island yard. Built the same year was the *Kuddle*, by William Covington. Sid Covington, William's son, produced a number of noted racing canoes, among them the *Island Bird* (1882), the *Island Blossom* (1892), and the *Sweet Potatoe* (1895). Other well-known builders included James Lowery, John B. Harrison, and John T. Harrison. Altogether at least forty-five log canoes, including both racers and workboats, were handicrafted with skill and care in the century between 1856 and 1954. Known bugeyes totaled thirty-nine, the most notable being the *Edna E. Lockwood*, launched in 1889 by John B. Harrison, which is still a showpiece of the Chesapeake Bay Maritime Museum in St. Michaels.

Life on Tilghman Island in the 1880s and later had its own sparkle and flavor, dictated by the islanders' isolation and their sense of being allies against the elements and the world. A post office was set up in 1883, but mail deliveries were uncertain, depending on when a boat arrived, until regular land-based service from McDaniel started in 1896. A bridge of sorts across Knapps Narrows, connecting the island with the mainland, had existed since 1775, but not until a new county bridge was installed in 1869 was there room for two-way traffic. Even then the bridge didn't have a draw; boats with high cabins had to wait for low tide, and those with fixed masts had to sail around the south end of the island. It lasted until the present bridge was built in 1932.

One of Tilghman's few exciting moments came in 1887 when a balloon appeared overhead, riding a south wind from Norfolk toward Baltimore. Its pilot waved and dropped a note, which was promptly forwarded to its Baltimore addressee by the new and little-used telegraph line, strung down from McDaniel the year before. It read: "Should arrive in about nine hours, weather good all clear and safe. Signed, G. L. Armings." Islanders never learned whether the balloonist got where he was going, but they hoped he did.

There was more excitement in 1890, when Hode Taylor set up a merry-go-round in a field, for which the charge was five cents a ride. It was powered by a white horse which often got dizzy from continually going round and round, and had to be spelled by a substitute. A second merry-go-round, imported by Ira Harrison about 1909, took a dunking when the boat bringing it to the island sank in a storm. Fished out of the water, it ran as good as new. Its gasoline motor was considered a great improvement over the horse; at least it didn't get dizzy on the job.

A telephone connecting with McDaniel and the outside world was installed at Harry R. Howeth's store in the 1890s. People made their calls from there until 1902, when Howeth added a switchboard permitting service from several other phones. But there was no formal telephone company for many years.

By 1908 Tilghman even had a movie theater of sorts. Ira Harrison, the merry-go-round entrepreneur, set it up in a tent in front of the firehouse. It had coal-oil lighting and a hand-turned projector. The films were of the nickelodeon type, with handsome heroes, damsels in distress, and leering villains. Since the hero always won, the films soon got to be boring. Therefore, Harrison varied his fare by running them upside down or backward, to great applause from the audience. Admission was ten cents for children, fifteen cents for adults.

Other forms of entertainment were equally simple: box socials, at which lunches prepared by the ladies were bid for by the men, who didn't know until they turned the box over whose company for the meal they had won; straw—not hay—rides to Sherwood or Wittman pulled by horses bedecked with bells, and accompanied by much laughter and song; sleigh rides in winters if there was snow; berry picking, husking bees, oyster roasts, fish fries.

Ladies were fascinated by laborsaving devices such as the sewing machine, hand operated by a wheel at the side, brought home in 1887 by Mrs. Margaret Sinclair. The first washing machine (1895) was also hand operated; it had big wooden paddles to beat the clothes clean. It be-

Knapps Narrows, Tilghman Island, showing watermen's harbor, 1975.

longed to Mrs. S. K. Wilson, whose physician husband imported the first phonograph in 1898. When wound up this would produce squawking music from cylinder-shaped records through a tall, curved horn.

Other material progress came slowly, if at all. A steamboat wharf was built in 1892. The first gasoline-powered workboat, in 1904, was a log canoe owned by Sid Covington; for better handling, the motor was installed in the bow and the boat operated back-end-to. The first automobile to run on Tilghman's oystershell roads didn't come until 1910, when Fletcher Covington acquired a new Studebaker. Elsewhere by then the automobile age was well underway.

The island had several oyster shucking and packing firms, but its major industry was the Tilghman Packing Company, founded in 1897 by brothers S. Taylor and J. Camper Harrison. It packed oysters, crabmeat, fish, and roe. A few years later the brothers added the Tilghman Canning Company to put up tomatoes, corn, and other vegetables. Operated for many years by Taylor Harrison's son, George T. Harrison, the company gained a national reputation for its fine frozen seafood.

Other Talbot communities mushroomed around country stores, new churches, or light industries. Tunis Mills, first known as Oakland Mills, grew out of the steam saw and planing mills established on Leeds Creek by W. W. Tunis and brothers. McDaniel acquired a post office, school, church, at least two stores, and a mill. Wittman topped that; it not only had a post office but three churches and two schools, one for white children, one for blacks. Villages like Matthewstown in Chapel District and Bozman on Broad Creek Neck were not only shopping centers but rallying points for community pride. Bozman in particular showed its

Finest product of the steamboat age was the magnificent *Talbot,* launched in 1912. She was 192 feet long, had steam heat, running water, electric lights, even private baths, but competition from automobiles soon drove her out of business.

mettle when, in the midst of the horrendous blizzard of March, 1888, more than fifty persons gathered for a gala dinner to celebrate the inauguration of daily postal service from St. Michaels despite the fact that the mailman couldn't get there because of the snow. Those who made it ate a huge meal of oysters, ham, turkey, roast goose, wild ducks, vegetables, and ice cream. A before-and-after weighing revealed that one man had gained fifteen pounds. Leftovers were sold to benefit the proposed library that Bozman hoped soon to have.

Ancient Hole-in-the-Wall had a brief resurgence in the limelight before succumbing to the obscurity of its being called Hambleton, a name thrust upon it by unimaginative officials when it was granted a post

Tilghman Packing Company's plant, with Avalon Island and the mainland facilities, Tilghman, 1935.

office. Hambleton was the site of the county fairgrounds and race track until the annual county fairs were moved to Idlewild, just south of Easton, in the 1880s. In 1888 the village achieved another distinction: the "Social, Literary & Musical Club of Hambleton" was incorporated with the grand purposes of acquiring a hall, establishing a library, holding musical soirees, and setting up billiard tables. No one now remembers if any of these ever came to pass.

Black communities—Unionville, Ivyville, Williamsburg, Hopkins Corner, Copperville, and others—were built around churches and schools by exslaves, many of whom had earned their freedom by fighting for the Union in the Civil War.

For Talbot blacks, the half freedom of the postwar era was not much improvement over conditions under slavery. Blacks were held in virtual peonage by white refusal to sell them farmland and white reprisals against those who tried to operate their own stores. Frederick Douglass's son Lewis, who visited St. Michaels in 1865 during a short-lived attempt to set up a school for blacks on Ferry Neck, wrote his father that St. Michaels was "one of the worst places in the South" for race relations, and that a meeting of blacks to talk about opening their own stores had been mobbed and broken up by angry white storekeepers. He described the unwritten agreement by which blacks were kept in the status of servants in these terms:

> The white people will do everything they can to keep the blacks from buying land. Large tracts of woods that the whites will neither use nor sell to the blacks lie idle and wasting.... The whites think to control the labor by not selling land to blacks. The highest price paid a farm hand here is fifteen dollars a month. A large number of colored men make from eighteen to twenty dollars a week oystering. They have surplus money and can't use it to any advantage around here; and they do not want to move away.

Young Douglass's observations on black wages are borne out by records kept on Talbot County farms during the postwar period. On the farm of William A. Kirby in Trappe District, Morris Trippe, listed as a laborer, was paid at the rate of $100 a year in 1880, but was docked 50 cents a day for any day he missed. He also received a "lay-in" consisting of twelve bushels of cornmeal, five bushels of wheat, and six gallons of blackstrap molasses. Charges for butter, tobacco, bacon, and other supplies were deducted from his wages, so that the net cash paid to him during the year was only $71. Adeline Hopkins, who worked as a kitchen servant, received $4 a month in 1886. Alexander Hopkins was employed at $120 a year, but was charged $50 in annual rent for the house he lived in. These were typical rates of pay, not especially low ones, and for ninety-five percent of Talbot blacks the only other choice was to migrate to the slums of Baltimore and Philadelphia.

Race relations were strained by the virulent campaigns staged by Easton newspapers after blacks were guaranteed the right to vote in elections for federal office by adoption of the Fifteenth Amendment to the Constitution. In the election of 1870, the first since 1801 in which blacks had been permitted to cast ballots, both the *Easton Star* and *Easton Journal*, Democratic papers, pictured the election as a crusade for "white supremacy" and against "negro equality." The *Star* openly called the Republicans the "nigger party" and described Republican meetings as "nigger fandangos." The election itself went off quietly and without incident, and the Democrats won a narrow victory despite a heavy, and solidly Republican, black turnout. The *Star* crowed in headline type: "Victory! Victory! . . . the Nigger Party routed . . . the Cause of White Man Vindicated," and the *Journal* said: "All Honor to those who peacefully and quietly crushed out radicalism and negro equality in Talbot." However, the Republican *Easton Gazette*'s turn came two years later when its party carried the county for General Grant over Horace Greeley by 142 votes. For the rest of the century Talbot presidential elections were extremely close, with neither party winning by more than a few votes, although the Democrats kept firm control of local offices.

Washington Street at the Talbot County Court House as Easton's Centennial was celebrated with gala festivities in 1888.

In the 1870s big city writers "discovered" the Eastern Shore as a prime source of colorful copy, sure to intrigue metropolitan readers weary of the crime and grime of the cities. Articles in such national magazines as *Harpers, Scribner's, Lippincott's, Century,* and the *Nation* extolled the Shore's virtues and especially its remoteness, only a few hours from New York by train and yet quaintly different. Albert Bushnell Hart in the *Nation* labeled the Shore "a Southern Arcadia, ... as yet innocent alike of summer boarders and of tourists." Another writer described the sands of Ocean City, just then emerging as a resort, as "like velvet on the feet." Marylander John Williamson of *Century Magazine* penned a romantic account of the past glories of Wye House, the Villa, and other estates which made up in nostalgia for what it lacked in historical fact. In these articles, depending on the writer's choice of topic, most Eastern Shore people were either hard-bitten oystermen wresting a living from the water or the gracious descendants of the squires and ladies of colonial manor houses.

Such glowing tributes as the latter helped swell a tide which was already going on—the influx of rich northerners who bought up old Talbot estates and converted them into summer residences. This "Yankee invasion"—which, of course, is still continuing—had started even before the war ended. Spurred by publicity which pictured the Eastern Shore as a prostrate territory whose slaveholders would be forced to sell their land at ruinous prices for lack of blacks to work it, a wave of northern buyers arrived as soon as the new constitution abolishing

The Villa

slavery in Maryland took effect. "In many cases farms have already changed hands," the *Gazette* reported December 10, 1864.

These first "foreigners" received a hostile reception in Talbot. Wartime passions were still strong among the slaveholders who owned most of the choice estates; northern money might be welcome, but northern people were not. They were "carpetbaggers" come to take advantage of the South's defeat. And in any case, the old Talbot families clung to their land as a symbol of their aristocracy. "It has been held to be more 'aristocratic' to possess a thousand heavily mortgaged than a hundred free acres," a correspondent for *Harper's* wrote from the Eastern Shore in 1871. "Large estates belong to 'blood,' which is still a word of great potency in this world."

Most of the early buyers sold out at a loss and went back north, but a new wave started in 1875. This time the *Gazette* pleaded with Talbot Countians not to snub the newcomers nor treat them with contempt, but to "show that we harbor no suspicion." The *Star* retorted that "no such prejudice or hostility exists. . . . A Northern man or woman settling here will be received at what he or she may be worth." Talbot Countians might be slow to make social calls on outsiders or invite them to their homes, said *Star* editor Thomas K. Robson, but that was natural reticence, not deliberate insult.

At any rate the invasion continued, and even increased. Eventually most of the fine old waterfront estates were in the hands of "foreigners" from Baltimore, Philadelphia, New York, or Pittsburgh. A list of estate sales which appeared in the *Easton Ledger* March 30, 1905, illustrated the trend, as well as what were considered enormous prices in that era. Headed "High-Priced Talbot Farms," it contained these examples:

Ellenborough, to Charles C. Nickerson of Delaware, $30,000.
The Anchorage, to Charles A. Chipley of Philadelphia, $12,000.
The Rest, former home of Admiral Buchanan, to Charles E. Henderson, vice-president of the Reading Railroad, $15,000.
Eastman, on the Miles River, to J. J. Speck of Pittsburgh, $12,200.
The L. W. Trail farm to Clifton Wharton of Pittsburgh, $28,000.
M. T. Goldsborough farm on the Tred Avon to M. J. Bell of Philadelphia, $10,000.
The Villa, to J. Lockwood of New York, $25,000.
Ratcliffe Manor, the Hollyday estate, to A. Hathaway of Milwaukee, $19,700.
Marengo, the old Jacob Gibson estate, to William P. Hall of Baltimore, $16,500.

One "foreigner" who became the target of local prejudices was Simeon Brady, a New Yorker who purchased The Villa on Glebe Neck in 1875. This ornate mansion already had a colorful history; it had been built in a lavish style in the 1840s by Richard Fortune, Maryland's "lottery king," who lost his immense wealth when lotteries were outlawed and died a pauper. Events which either did or did not happen in the spring of 1876—no one is yet sure which—added immeasurably to its legend.

Neighborhood gossip reported mysterious goings-on at The Villa. Suspicion grew that it was being used as a hide-out by the notorious William M. (Boss) Tweed, then the object of a nationwide manhunt with a $10,000 reward for his capture. Tweed had escaped jail while under arrest for allegedly looting the New York City treasury of $125 million or so in graft. Brady, the rumors said, was a Tweed employee who let his boss hide in The Villa's three-story tower until it was safe for him to continue his flight down Chesapeake Bay in a mysterious "black yacht." Brady's grandson, W. O. Collier, later denied the whole affair, saying his grandfather was a shy man of independent wealth who didn't even know Tweed, and that the story was concocted by malicious locals who resented Brady as a Yankee. But members of the Bartlett family, who were living at The Villa as boarders that spring, insisted that a stranger was hiding in the mansion's tower while they were there, and they continued to ask the question: "If it wasn't Boss Tweed, who was it?" Tweed, who was later captured in Cuba, never did reveal his whereabouts during the months he was being sought.

Not all the northerners who found Talbot County attractive were wealthy industrialists. Many were dirt farmers from rural Pennsylvania and upstate New York who brought with them improved farm machinery and methods. Productivity went up; the *Star* reported in November, 1878, that Robert Hough, of Knightly on Miles River Neck, had "raised 350 barrels of corn on a 40 acre field, which is 45 bushels to the acre." The *Star* thought this was "an excellent yield, and shows what Talbot County land can do." (Today's Talbot farmers have gone far past that—200-bushel yields are possible in good corn years—but Hough's record was a lot better than the 5 bushels to the acre common in the early 1800s.)

The county's two largest towns, St. Michaels and Easton, both showed healthy growth. In 1880 Easton climbed past the 3,000 mark for the first time in its history. Overall, Talbot County's population increased by 3,630 persons between 1860 and 1880 after virtually standing still for half a century. In 1900 the county's population stood at 19,736, its all-time high until the Bay Bridge was built.

Talbot County's influence in Maryland politics remained far stronger than might be indicated by its population or economic position in the state. Much of this was due to the prestige still accorded the Lloyds of Wye House and other aristocratic families which had been leaders since colonial days. During the nineteenth century, four native Talbot Countians and three other men with close Talbot family connections served as governor. Altogether they were in office for more than twenty-five of the century's one hundred years.

Edward Lloyd V was named governor by the General Assembly for two one-year terms, 1809 to 1811. He also served as United States Senator, Congressman, and in both houses of the state legislature. Lloyd's grandson, Dorchester-born Henry Lloyd, was governor from 1885 to 1888, and another descendant, Lloyd Lowndes, a native of Clarksburg, West Virginia, was governor from 1896 to 1900.

Samuel Stevens, Jr., of Compton in Trappe District, governor from 1822 to 1825, was a colorful character who gloried in his "country boy" image. His favorite costume was a swallowtail coat and trousers made of blue jeans material spun and woven on his Talbot farm. It was during his administration that the ancient law barring Jews from voting in Maryland was repealed, and all religious qualifications for holding office were eliminated.

Another Trappe District man, Daniel Martin of The Wilderness, was governor from 1828 to 1829 and again from 1830 to 1831. He died in office, and family tradition says he predicted his own death from a series of dreams in which his deceased mother told him he would soon be "called home."

Philip Francis Thomas of Easton, one of the first governors to be elected by direct popular vote, served from 1847 to 1850. A Southern sympathizer during the Civil War, he was named United States Senator in 1866 but was refused his seat on grounds of disloyalty. He was later elected to the House of Representatives.

In addition Dorchester County's Charles Goldsborough, Jr., governor in 1818 to 1819, was married to a cousin, Elizabeth Goldsborough of Myrtle Grove in Talbot County; and his mother was the former Anna Maria Tilghman.

More people and more money meant more churches, for Talbot's social and emotional life in this era centered around the church. Throughout the county, new church buildings went up. In Easton, Roman Catholics, who had attended mass in a rented hall, laid the cornerstone of SS. Peter and Paul Church in 1866, completed in 1868. Also in 1868, Easton became the see, or cathedral city, of the newly created Protestant Episcopal Diocese of Easton, with the Right Reverend Henry Champlain Lay as bishop. The first cathedral was a small frame building, long since gone, on the grounds of the present edifice; but later a cathedral congregation was developed and funds raised for a more suitable structure. The handsome stone Trinity Cathedral on Goldsborough Street was formally opened for worship July 5, 1891.

Much of the church proliferation, however, developed not from postwar prosperity but from wartime bitterness which split the Methodist Episcopal Church into two seemingly irreconcilable camps. This was the second division of Methodist ranks in less than forty years; a struggle over local autonomy versus church control by the traveling preachers and bishops had led many members to walk out in 1829 and form congregations of the Methodist Protestant Church in Easton, St. Michaels, and Trappe.

This time the schism was over an even more emotional issue: North versus South, freedom versus slavery, whites versus blacks. Those who found the parent church's support of the Union and opposition to slavery during the war intolerable broke away in 1866, and joined the Methodist Episcopal Church South which was dedicated to keeping alive states' rights and white supremacy traditions of the Confederacy. Churches of this denomination were soon built in Easton, Trappe, Royal Oak, and Wittman. However, at Oxford's St. Paul's Methodist—where pro-South members during the war had entered and departed through windows to keep from walking under the American flag which hung over the doorway—dissidents formed a branch of the Methodist Protestant Church rather than joining the Methodist Episcopal South.

Black Methodists also were divided. A minority remained loyal to the African Methodist Episcopal Church, which had black leadership, while the majority formed churches within the fold of regular Methodism, which was led entirely by whites.

Through all these vicissitudes, the original Methodist Episcopal Church—sometimes erroneously called the Methodist Episcopal Church North—maintained its position as Talbot County's dominant religious group. All the dissidents put together had far fewer members. An estimate made in 1876 by the Reverend Robert W. Todd, at that time head of the Talbot circuit, gave this breakdown of church membership in the county:

Methodist Episcopal Church South, 300.
Methodist Protestant, 383.
African Methodist Episcopal, 300.
Methodist Episcopal (the parent church), 2,290, including 1,500 whites and 790 blacks.
Total Methodists, 3,273.

The Reverend Todd did not give estimates for non-Methodist denominations, but the total probably did not exceed 1,500, with the Episcopalians (about 900) and Roman Catholics (about 500) heading the list. Few other denominations were yet established in Talbot.

No matter how they were divided on doctrine, the churches were the centers of Talbot's social as well as religious life. Church suppers, fairs, sewing bees, and other activities provided outlets for women's energies, especially in the dreary winter months. Wednesday night prayer meetings punctuated the week. Church shows, such as the "Grand Illustrated Musical Entertainment" staged in 1883 at Trinity Methodist Episcopal Church South in Trappe, took the place of today's movies and bars. Church moral leadership, spearheaded by the Women's Christian Temperance Union, sparked the drive toward prohibition which led Easton and most of Talbot County to go dry under local option in 1874.

Church influence even spilled over into outdoor sports. The jousting tournaments staged at St. Joseph's Catholic Church near Cordova beginning in 1868 proved so popular that they became annual events.

Crazes for other outdoor activities swept the county in successive waves. Baseball, played by soldiers of both North and South in wartime camps, was introduced in Talbot County in 1866. By 1867 there were organized teams in Easton, St. Michaels, and Trappe. Over the years, the Easton Independents, the St. Michaels Osceolas, and the Idlewild Baseball Club played scheduled games with teams of picked players from

Frank ("Home Run") Baker

Cambridge and Federalsburg. At the turn of the century, Trappe's young Frank Baker, born in 1886, was making unbelievable catches and hitting home runs "so far out into the cornfield that nobody could find them." These talents later got him into baseball's Hall of Fame as "Home Run" Baker of the Philadelphia Athletics.

Croquet and quoits came into vogue in the 1870s. Lawn tennis courts were introduced on Talbot estates in the 1880s, and tennis clubs were formed in Easton and Trappe. By the gay nineties the universal passion was bicycling. There were organized races throughout the Eastern

An excursion boat docks at Oxford, 1930.

Shore, and riders balancing themselves on bikes with forty-four-inch front wheels zipped so carelessly along town sidewalks that laws were passed to protect pedestrians.

Regardless of the trains, steamboats were still "the way to go" to Baltimore and other Western Shore points. They combined the acme in comfort and even luxury with convenience no railroad could match. In 1878, for instance, the Maryland Steamboat Company's *Highland Light* and *Kent* between them provided nightly service to and from Baltimore, with stops at Easton Point, Double Mills, Goldsborough's Wharf, Oxford, Clora's Point, Cambridge, Chancellor's Point, Jamaica Point, Secretary Creek, and Medford's Wharf. Three days a week these ships went on to Denton by way of Dover Bridge and Kingston. The *Champion* and the *Olive* served the Miles River area, and twice a week the *Olive* visited Wye River points all the way up to Wye Landing on Skipton Creek. About the same time the little *Minnie Wheeler* and the *Chesapeake*, screw propellered boats rather than paddle wheelers, stopped at Trappe Landing and then chugged up Tuckahoe Creek to Wayman's Landing, the port for Queen Anne and Hillsborough. No place in Talbot County was more than a short buggy ride from a steamboat stop.

In the 1880s came the *Avalon,* the *Tred Avon*, built in 1884, and the sister ships *Ida* and *Joppa* (1885). The *Joppa* stayed on the Choptank run intermittently until 1921.

THE AGE OF STEAM

The final word in luxury was provided by the *Talbot* and *Dorchester*, sister ships launched in 1912. They were the grandest—and last—of all the steamers on the bay. Each had three decks, steam heat, running water, electric lights, and call bells, eighty-five staterooms plus several "parlor staterooms" with private baths, and total accommodations, including chair seats, for 400 passengers.

Talbot County old-timers recall the "steamboatin' days" with fondness. "Going to Baltimore by steamboat was the greatest thrill in the world," said Mary Hart in a 1976 interview. "You always had dinner on the boat, and it was perfectly delightful—seafood, cornbread, Maryland fried chicken, salads, cakes and pies, all you could eat for $1.25." Nearly always there was a passenger who could play the piano, and the travelers could dance the night away, or take a romantic stroll on the moonlit decks. An added dividend for many was that while Talbot County was dry, Baltimore certainly was not, and rye whiskey in brown bottles could be brought home or shipped to order at two dollars a gallon. That was important at a time when, as one visitor lamented, not even a "wink at the soda fountain in the drug store" could get a thirsty man anything stronger than sarsaparilla, and even hard cider was frowned upon.

St. Michaels' postwar resurgence, even more than that in Oxford and Tilghman, was keyed to the oyster and the log canoe. Oystering had always been important to the town's economic life, but in the 1880s it reached new heights. The fleet which set out daily from the harbor was larger than it had ever been, and new devices such as drags and scrapes brought up a more plentiful harvest than could be gathered with simple tongs. "Buy boats," chiefly schooners and pungies, waited in the harbor to bid for the daily catch and haul it to the Baltimore market. But much of this harvest stayed at home; shucking houses and packing plants dotted the waterfront. St. Michaels oysters were said to be in demand as far away as Cheyenne, Wyoming.

The fleet by this time was composed almost entirely of log canoes, modernized and stabilized by addition of a centerboard from the old, swift but tipsy craft. Captain Robert Lambdin, who had kept St. Michaels shipbuilding alive through its leanest years, was credited with this revolutionary development. In 1872 he experimentally added a centerboard to a canoe called the *Mary*. The idea caught on. In the years that followed Lambdin built sixty-eight centerboard log canoes and remodeled fifty others by adding a centerboard.

Writing in 1882, Dr. Harrison penned a lyric tribute to the St. Michaels oyster canoes, "marine beauties, . . . graceful in their lines, resplendent in their colors, light in their structure, swift and aerial in

Top, log canoes, Navy Point, now the site of the Chesapeake Bay Maritime Museum, St. Michaels, 1890. *Bottom*, log canoes racing, St. Michaels, 1890.

their movements—the very butterflies of sea. . . . No more beautiful sight, of the kind, can be offered to the eye, than is witnessed upon every fine morning in the fall of the year, when this miniature fleet of more than a hundred sail boats start from the harbor of St. Michaels for the oyster grounds."

Log canoe racing, a sport that developed out of impromptu contests as the oystermen sped home hoping to be first to sell their catch, soon took on importance of its own. Early racing was dominated by Captain Giles Jump; his *Dashaway*, built by Lambdin in 1877, never lost a race in its career. Others were almost as swift; in 1893 Lambdin and George West took the log canoe *Chesapeake* by water and rail to the Columbian

Top, log canoes racing, St. Michaels, 1981. *Bottom*, bugeye *Hugh Orem* dredging oysters and two tongers in their engine-powered log canoe.

Top, Miles River Yacht Club, St. Michaels, 1980. *Bottom,* Regatta Weekend, Tred Avon Yacht Club, Oxford, 1980.

Exposition in Chicago, greatest of the early world's fairs. The first log canoe ever seen west of the Chesapeake, she easily outsailed any of the Great Lakes craft she raced against.

With the advent of gasoline and diesel engines, the log canoe lost out as a practical workboat. For dredging it was replaced by the sturdier bugeyes and skipjacks, for tonging by the motorized "bay builts," long, flat craft easy to handle and inexpensive to operate. In any case oystering soon lost its importance when the seemingly inexhaustible oyster beds began to give out from overharvesting and lack of reseeding. Soon St. Michaels and Oxford declined as oystering centers and gained new status as ports for sport sailing. Few new canoes were built, but the log canoe was kept alive by socialite yachtsmen. Some of those still racing today out of the Miles River Yacht Club, founded in 1920, and the Tred Avon Yacht Club, founded in 1931, were launched by Lambdin and his rival Tilghman Island builders in the 1880s.

Behind the beautiful facade of the oyster sailing fleet of 1882 lay an ugly reality: life for many Chesapeake Bay watermen was cruel and sometimes even murderous. Many oyster boat captains recruited their crews from the drunks and loafers who infested the Baltimore docks, with no thought except how to get the cheapest possible labor and exploit it to the utmost. Agents who received two dollars a head for recruits waited outside jails, flophouses, and cheap saloons, and lured men who knew nothing about oystering with glib promises about pay and working conditions which would never materialize. When it was necessary to fill contract quotas, men were picked up or shanghaied aboard boats.

Four to five thousand men a year were rounded up this way in Baltimore. Many were non-English-speaking foreigners. Agents' fees and the cost of clothing and other supplies were deducted from the victims' meager wages, often at exorbitant rates. Those who got sick or were injured received no medical treatment until the voyage, sometimes of several weeks, was ended. Those who died were simply dumped overboard or buried without ceremony on a deserted shore. Each year the beaches on the bay from Claiborne to Tilghman Island produced a grim harvest of watermen's bodies. Sometimes a captain, nearing the end of his voyage, would "accidentally" let the boom get loose and knock a crewman overboard so that the captain could pocket his unpaid wages.

State officials, shocked when they learned of such atrocities, sought reforms in the late 1880s, but the legislature took no action. Only the swift decline of the oyster beds, which began about 1900, brought an end to these evil practices.

For Easton, the postwar era saw growth and development, though there was less economic progress than local businessmen would have liked. Much of the present downtown area, sometimes mistakenly called colonial, dates from this period. Buildings constructed in the 1870s and 1880s have remained intact primarily because merchants were too poor

Easton's first public telephone in the wooden booth at the left, a market day scene in Court House Square, 1915.

during the first half of the twentieth century to tear them down and build uglier, modern ones.

The telegraph came to Easton in May, 1872. Reporting that the line had been completed to Clayton, Delaware, and the first telegram sent, the *Easton Journal* of May 30 said demand for a telegraph line had been strong since the new railroad's first major train wreck, March 2, in which the locomotives Tilghman and Easton collided in a snowstorm with several minor injuries.

The first telephones soon followed, but they were strictly local lines designed to serve Easton businesses. The *Star* of March 4, 1879, reported that a private line had been hooked up between the downtown office of R. B. Dixon & Company and its coal and lumber warehouse at Easton Point. A week later another was in operation from Goldsborough's Drug Store to the railroad depot.

The Easton National Bank building under construction at the corner of Washington and Goldsborough streets, 1894.

Long distance service of a sort was inaugurated in December, 1885, when the Talbot County Telephone Company was formed with connections to Longwoods, Skipton, Wye Mills, Kent Island, Queenstown, Centreville, Chestertown, and Cecil County. There was no local exchange; all long distance calls were made from the phone in the store of J. C. Henry & Brother, which was known as the "Easton instrument." The *Star* commented February 2, 1886, on how marvelous it was that "one can stand in Henry's back room and hear people in Centreville talking politics." Later on, Easton and all Talbot towns were served by the Diamond State Telephone Company, and "central" was in Hillsborough. There was still no local switchboard, and it was easier to talk to someone in New York City than it was to talk to your next door neighbor.

Although the first electric line was installed in 1887, Easton merchants and residents were slow to accept electric lighting. According to Elliott Buse, the Easton National Bank's historian, the bank did not have electricity until 1915, "and then it was the desire for electric fans that inspired the installation."

Several changes were made in the old 1794 Court House and the square surrounding it. Fireproof vaults were installed at a cost of three thousand dollars for storage of court records and wills, and the front door was remodeled to make it more difficult for loafers and "brute beasts" to get in at night. In March, 1873, workmen began clearing ground for a new iron fence and an eight-foot brick sidewalk around the Court House grounds. This inspired what might be called Easton's first environmentalist protest. The *Journal* of March 13 said many citizens were "highly indignant to see the outer line of large old trees which surround the Court House being dug up . . . to make room for the pavement." To placate them, the commissioners planted new trees inside the fence; many of them are there today, now fine old trees in their own right.

The Court House, first remodeled in 1858, was remodeled again in 1898 at a cost of ten thousand dollars. That year the town clock which tells more or less accurate time in four directions was installed in the tower as a gift from public-spirited citizens. A new jail—still in use 102 years later—was constructed in 1881.

In 1870 the old open market house which had stood on Market Space alongside the Court House since 1805 was torn down. It was replaced by an enclosed brick building with the market on the lower floor and town offices above it. But on October 1, 1878, one of the most disastrous fires in Easton's history destroyed the new market house along with numerous shops and stores along Court Street and the Odd Fellows Temple at the corner of Court and Washington. The Court House roof caught fire, but the building was saved by a bucket brigade. At the Methodist Church on Washington Street, later named Ebenezer Methodist Episcopal, members of the congregation gathered and prayed in relays that the building not be destroyed. Their prayers were answered when the wind shifted, saving the church and the three-story brick building next to it.

Eventually much good came of this disaster. A new and far superior structure replacing the market house was completed in 1879. It was three stories high, with market stalls on the ground floor, a six hundred-seat auditorium with dressing rooms for performers on the second, and several music rooms on the third. Known as Music Hall, it served as the town's entertainment center and later its movie house for the next sixty years. From 1940 to 1976 it housed the Talbot County Free Library. Today it is headquarters for the district court of Talbot County.

In addition the Easton Fire Department was reorganized, equipped with a steam-powered pumper known as the "Little Giant," and provided with a new engine house on the west side of Harrison Street. This is still in use as a town office building. A new three-story Odd Fellows building was constructed, another three-story structure (now the Lockhart building) went up between the lodge and the church, and new stores were built all along Court Street.

Washington Street at Court and Dover streets, looking east from The Music Hall. Photograph taken about 1920.

Another by-product of the 1878 fire was construction of Easton's first piped water system to replace the wells and pumps which had been the town's only source of water for fighting fires as well as the source of water for drinking and household use. The Easton Waterworks Company, financed by a special tax assessment of five cents per one hundred dollars of valuation, was chartered in March, 1886. A pumping station was built on north Washington Street at Tanyard Branch (the current name for the north fork of the Tred Avon), a standpipe erected on Hanson Street at Mill Place, six artesian wells drilled to supply the water, and mains laid throughout town, connected with fifty-four fire plugs at strategic locations. On September 18, 1886, the big wheel controlling the flow of water into the mains was ceremoniously turned by Miss Kate Norris, daughter of innkeeper James C. Norris.

Other changes in downtown Easton were numerous. In 1869 the old Easton Hotel, built in 1815, was remodeled, given a third story and a mansard roof, and reopened under the proprietorship of Colonel Norris with a formal dinner at Christmastime. From then on it was called the Brick Hotel. Across Washington Street stood the Frame Hotel, built in

1866 on the site of the old Union Hotel, where display of the American flag had so disturbed the rebel-minded ladies of Easton during the Civil War.

By the 1890s both of these hostelries were driven out of business by the lavish new Hotel Avon, completed in 1891 at the Harrison-Dover corner where the Tidewater Inn now stands. The Avon had all the latest comforts for travelers—steam heat, dumbwaiters, and even hot and cold running water in the more expensive rooms. Seemer's omnibus, a splendid carriage drawn by four white horses, met steamboats at Easton Point and trains at the railroad station. The Brick Hotel became an office building known as the Moreland Block (now the Stewart Building); the Frame Hotel housed Nevius Hardware, operated by Simon A. Nevius and later his sons, Ronald and Carl Nevius, from 1897 until the hardware store was closed in 1982.

May 4, 1881, was a gala day for Easton as the new Masonic lodge building on North Washington Street was dedicated by members of Coats Lodge of Easton, assisted by officials of the Grand Lodge of Maryland and other dignitaries from Baltimore, plus the membership of Granite Lodge, St. Michaels. Featured were a parade to and from Easton Point, where the visitors arrived by steamer, music by the Easton Mozart Band and Pick's Band of Baltimore, solemn ceremonies in front of the lodge hall, and an "eloquent address" at Music Hall on the principles of freemasonry.

Public education took a great step forward when Talbot's first high school was opened in what is now the Academy of the Arts building October 1, 1866. The school ran through the tenth grade (the eleventh grade was not added until the early 1900s, and the twelfth not until modern times). Boys and girls were taught separately. Those admitted had to be white, at least twelve years old, of good moral character, and able to pass an entrance examination. In addition to compulsory courses in mathematics, history, Greek, Latin, and science, the boys studied military tactics and the girls domestic economy (cooking, sewing, etc.).

By the beginning of the twentieth century Talbot had four high schools—at Easton, St. Michaels, Trappe, and Oxford—plus fifteen graded primary schools and fifty-one one-room schools. A fifth high school, known as Tri-County, was added at Queen Anne in 1913 to accommodate pupils from Talbot, Queen Anne's, and Caroline counties, and a sixth, at Tilghman, in 1916. There was no way for black children to go to high school in Talbot County until Moton High School was completed in 1937.

The 1880s were a great period for Easton newspapers, at least in numbers, if not in profits. At one point there were four of them—the

Top, Easton's Hotel Avon, completed in 1891. *Bottom,* Hotel Queen Anne and annex, Dover Street, Easton, 1910.

Fourth of July in St. Michaels, circa 1908.

Gazette, the *Star*, the *Ledger* (formerly the *Journal*), and the *Democrat*, which had started life in 1885 as the *Easton Independent*. In addition there were three others in the county—the *St. Michaels Comet*, the *Oxford Enterprise*, and the *Talbot Times* in Trappe. Obviously this was too many newspapers, especially since all except the *Gazette* gave their political support to various factions of the Democratic Party. By 1896 the *Star* and the *Democrat* were in deep financial trouble. Editor-publisher Wilson M. Tylor of the *Gazette* bought both of them and resold them immediately to J. Frank Turner, a former *Star* owner, who merged them into the *Easton Star-Democrat*.

As the last decade of the nineteenth century approached, Easton's leaders once again enjoyed rosy dreams of the town's economic future. In the words of historian James C. Mullikin:

> It appeared that Easton had never been more prosperous. The ten-year period between 1880 and 1890 had been one of considerable civic progress. . . . Easton's position as the Eastern Shore's most important and most progressive town appeared to be impregnable . . . Easton had been the dominant town of the area for nearly a century, and there was nothing to indicate it would not continue to be so.

But the town, and the entire county, were in for a rude awakening. The census of 1890 showed that Easton was losing population, and by 1900 it had dropped to fourth place among Eastern Shore towns, behind Cambridge, Salisbury, and Crisfield, with Chestertown only a shade smaller. The county, too, was beginning to lose population again, as it had in the 1820-1840 period. The next four decades would be a time of economic stagnation and increased isolation.

ELEVEN

The Gasoline Revolution

"**T**HE OLDSMOBILE IN EASTON," trumpeted a front-page headline in the *Easton Gazette* September 7, 1901. The accompanying article went on to indicate that J. H. K. Shannahan, Sr., prominent Talbot County well driller, had taken delivery of a 1901 model Olds runabout from Shannahan & Wrightson's Washington Street hardware store. He had given it a "speed trial" to St. Michaels, dashing along the twelve miles of "exceedingly rough and muddy roads" in just forty-five minutes, an average speed of sixteen miles an hour. The Olds, said the *Gazette*, was capable of doing as much as twenty-five per hour on straightaways. As the paper went to press, Shannahan was off on a daring motor trip to Chestertown and perhaps even beyond, to Middletown, Delaware.

Engineering details made fascinating reading for Talbot Countians who weren't even quite sure that the bicycle was destined to stay. The Oldsmobile was powered by a five and a half-horsepower engine which consumed a gallon of gasoline every forty miles. It weighed 550 pounds. The motor was started by "turning a little crank at the side of the front seat," and locomotion was achieved by means of a friction-clutch lever. Speed could be controlled by another lever. For nighttime driving, "a 25 candle power acetylene gas lamp throws a brilliant light 50 feet ahead." This particular model had an adjustable "dos-a-dos" (back-to-back) seat with foot rest, so that four passengers in addition to the driver could ride at one time. It was, the *Gazette* reported, "elegant in appearance," with "all of the operating parts so placed as to cause wonderment at the ease of control."

Needless to say, it was the talk of the town. "It may be asserted that this machine attracted more comment and more visitors, in a short time, than any vehicle that ever came to Easton," the *Gazette* added. There had been other horseless carriages in Easton, but they were just what their popular name implied—carriages equipped with motors, so that all their working parts hung out in the open. This was a true automobile.

VOL. 85. NO 40.   EASTON,

THE OLDSMOBILE IN EASTON.

After a delay of some weeks caused by fire in the factory and the general mechanics strike, the Oldsmobile ordered by J. H. K. Shannahan through Shannahan & Wrightson Hdw. Co., arrived in Easton on Saturday. It may be asserted that this machine attracted more comment and more visitors, in a short time, than any vehicle that ever came to Easton. The fact that a number of prospective automobile purchasers in this county have awaited the arrival of the Oldsmobile before purchasing, leads THE GAZETTE to give a brief description of it. It is called the Oldsmobile because it is built by The Olds Motor Works, of Detroit, Mich., and is the pattern known as a "runabout." Elegant in appearance, weighing only 550 pounds, all of the operating parts so placed as to cause wonderment at the ease of control, makes every feature trim and neat in appearance.

And well it might have been a source of wonder; for in that 550-pound frame, that five and a half-horsepower engine, lay the germ of a social revolution which would shake Talbot County, and all America, to their foundations. The gasoline engine was as truly revolutionary a force as the Paris mobs or the discovery of electricity. It would change literally everything about how Talbot Countians lived and how they thought about themselves. Eventually it would bring ruin to the steamboats and railroads, kill the prosperity of the small towns, free the farmers and their wives, motorize the oyster tongers and crabbers, transform the school system, force creation of a paved highway network, and bring the world to Talbot County by way of the great Bay Bridge.

But all that was not even a speck on the horizon in September, 1901. Talbot County was heading complacently into the twentieth century, confident it could cope, as it always had, with whatever the future had to offer. The county might be poor and backward by big city standards, but it was withal a pretty good place to live. If it lacked factories, it also lacked the accompanying dirt and slums, the crime and graft, and the poorly assimilated masses of European immigrants that were characteristic of the great metropolitan centers. If pay was low—the average wage in Talbot in 1900 was $260 a year—so was the cost of living. "We were too busy being happy to realize how poor we were," one lifelong resident was later to recall of his boyhood days before the First World War.

In any case, Talbot County was by no means ready for the automobile age. Of its four hundred miles of public roads in 1900, about twenty were paved with oystershell; the rest were just mud and sand. "Most of the roads out from Easton have been shelled for a few miles and make smooth, comfortable highways," state geologist William Bullock Clark reported. "The majority of the dirt roads have been shaped with a road machine for a width of 12 to 15 feet."

The road from Easton to St. Michaels was probably the best in the county. It had been shelled for most of its length. But the north-south road between Easton and Skipton, with a bed of sand and clay, had a number of eight to ten percent grades where streams were crossed by primitive bridges. Total county spending for roadwork of all types, including shelling, repairs, bridges, and replacing the old wooden drains with tile drains, averaged only a little more than $14,000 a year. There were no state or federal highway systems.

Easton businessmen might be intrigued by Shannahan's "merry Oldsmobile," but they showed no signs of realizing what lay ahead. In the same *Gazette* issue which reported the car's arrival, the Shannahan & Wrightson store published a large advertisement which didn't even mention that their firm was in the business of selling automobiles. Instead it promoted their good old standbys—Auburn steel axle farm wagons, South Bend and Oliver plows, disc harrows, handsome carriages, surreys, phaetons, and buggies, fine harness, horse sheets and dusters, new and secondhand bicycles.

Compared with automobiles, which cost from $750 to $2,000, horse drawn vehicles were cheap. James A. Spence had on sale ordinary runabouts marked down to $36.54, cushion-tire runabouts at $66.42, Concord wagons at $44.22, wire-wheel ball bearing runabouts with 1¼-inch tires at only $100, and standing top surreys at $98.22. Of course, the horse was optional at extra cost, and good horses cost anywhere from $200 to $500. But they didn't break down, belch forth noise and fumes, or consume scarce and expensive gasoline, which cost as much as 40 cents a gallon provided the motorist could find some.

Up and down the Eastern Shore, hot debate was going on between enthusiasts for the horse and for the machine. The *Kent News* of Chestertown, which favored the automobile, reported August 12, 1899, that "a trip of 720 miles, from Cleveland to New York, over all kinds of country roads, has actually been made in a gasoline carriage." It continued:

Lane's Machine Shop, Easton, carriage making and repair.

All the arguments (are) in favor of the automobile and against the horse. It is ready without having to be hitched up. It can more easily be stored, no stable being necessary. No coachman is required. It is safer, can be guided with greater accuracy and turned in less space. It doesn't have to be hitched when left standing.

In the writer's view, the only question was whether the power source should be steam, electricity, or gasoline. There were advocates of all three. Steamers were clean, noiseless, and unbelievably fast, but required a long time to work up steam. When they did get going, the flame under the boiler often was blown out by the wind. Electrics were popular in cities—New York, said the *Kent News*, had a fleet of a hundred electric taxicabs—but their usefulness elsewhere was limited by their extremely short range. In the end gasoline won out, smelly, expensive, and dangerous though it was.

Within a few years automobile travel was becoming common on major roads of the Eastern Shore. Farmers complained that autos racing at speeds of thirty-five to forty miles an hour frightened livestock with their noise and raised unpleasant clouds of dust. The highway division of the Maryland Geological Survey, which handled road problems until

Top, repair shop of The Eastern Shore Automobile Company, the Ford agency on Dover Street, Easton, July 5, 1920. *Bottom*, a family and their family car, Trappe.

the State Highway Commission was formed in 1908, seriously considered—but luckily rejected—two suggested methods of curbing speed: artificial ridges built into roads at frequent intervals, high enough "to absolutely deter the most rabid 'scorcher' from more than one attempt to maintain an excessive speed," and governors in the gearing "so that excessive speeds are impossible." Eventually the state settled for posted speed limits, which everybody ignored.

In 1908 the Salisbury grand jury took official note of the dangers of motoring. Cars sailing along at forty miles an hour, it said, were going at "twice their safe speed," scaring horses, and causing frequent runaways. But the jurors—and the farmers—were flying in the face of progress; already it was evident that the future belonged to the automobiles and the "go-devils" who raced them along quiet country roads. In Easton the H. E. Clark Company all that summer ran front-page ads for Detroit's newest marvel, the Model T Ford, which weighed only one thousand pounds but could outrun costlier cars weighing three times that much. In November, 1908, Nevius & Frampton announced they had taken the agency for the Maxwell for the coming year. They kept it, the late Ron Nevius recalled, for several years. When the giant General Motors Company was formed, Shannahan & Wrightson expanded its Oldsmobile franchise to include other cars in the GM line. Its showroom was on Washington Street in the building now occupied by Rowen's Stationery and the "bird cages" next door. People built sheds called "garages" and learned how to pronounce the old French word. Filling stations appeared. Auto licenses, issued by the secretary of state, at first were simply numbers painted on leather and nailed onto the wooden frames of cars. Later metal plates were used. Drivers' tests were as yet unheard of.

In 1909 Talbot County had only four highways under the state's newly established "good roads program." These ran from Wye Mills to Easton, from Easton to Trappe, and from Easton westward to St. Michaels and eastward to Dover Bridge. The first of these to be paved with concrete under state financing was the stretch from Easton to the Queen Anne's county line near Wye Mills. Completed in October, 1913, its paved area was only twelve feet wide; when two cars passed, one or both had to drive on the gravel shoulder with their outer wheels. Eventually this road, which connected with the highway to Centreville, Chestertown, and Wilmington, became part of the federal system. First known as "the Eastern Shore Trail," it later was designated U. S. Route 213. Reduced to the status of a back road when Route 50 was built, it is now State Route 664.

Also completed in 1913 was what was regarded at the time as a miracle of modern engineering—a new concrete and steel drawbridge across the Miles River to replace an old wooden structure dating from before the Civil War. It had a forty-foot bascule draw of the most improved type, which was floated down by barge from Baltimore. The bridge contained nearly five thousand tons of reinforced concrete piles, floor slabs, abutments, and piers. Engineers from Delaware and Virginia as well as all parts of Maryland came to watch it go up and to marvel at its construction details. At the time it was said to be the longest and largest span over a navigable river in Maryland, and the first concrete bridge of any size with a modern bascule draw, which went up and down instead of swinging sideways as most drawbridges did then.

When the bridge opened for traffic November 1, 1913, the first person to cross it officially was Miss Anna Earle of the Anchorage, driving a cutaway carriage and accompanied by Henry Wilcox, chief construction engineer. But eleven-year-old Clarissa Tilghman Goldsborough had beaten Miss Earle to it. Even before the formal ceremony began at 7:30 A.M., she rode across the bridge on her bicycle. With her was her dachshund, Dewlip, who pulled a wooden cart containing her doll.

The cost of the bridge, $58,440, was borne half by the state and half by the county. (By contrast a 1983 replacement cost approximately $4.9 million.)

At the dawn of the twentieth century, Easton badly needed a face-lift, or even major surgery. It had lost its proud place as leader of the Eastern Shore, and was barely holding its own in population, while Cambridge, Salisbury, and Crisfield raced ahead. Worried town businessmen, firm believers in the doctrine which equated progress with commerce, factories, and jobs, launched a program to bring in new industries. But it was a peppery little merchant and insurance man, Trappe-born Martin M. Higgins, who almost single-handedly succeeded in "getting Easton out of the mud" and back on the road to progress and prosperity.

Higgins advocated paved streets, a mayor and council system to replace the antiquated town commissioners, a sewer system to halt the yearly epidemics of typhoid fever, and municipal ownership of the town's utilities. Eventually he got them all, although not without some humbling setbacks along the way.

In 1904 he published a series of paid advertisements advocating a new town charter to replace the one which had been in effect ever since the town was founded in 1786, and a mayor and council system with broad executive powers for the mayor. He urged that the town bond itself to build a complete sewer system, which no Maryland municipality had yet done, take action to pave its main streets, and establish a modern

The Miles River Bridge of 1913 was being replaced by a higher draw span seventy years later when this photograph was made in 1983.

fire department. He deplored the poor service provided by the privately owned waterworks and electricity plant, and suggested municipal ownership if improvements were not made.

Higgins's aggressiveness, rigid honesty, and inflexible determination caught the public fancy. The new charter was drafted, and he lobbied to get it enacted by the General Assembly in 1906. At the town election in May he became Easton's first elected mayor.

In the next two years he worked out plans for bond issues to build a sewer system and municipal power plant. Ordinances providing for these were approved by the town council February 25, 1908. But in a vote held April 2, 1908, both bond issues were overwhelmingly rejected by the Easton electorate, largely on grounds they would cost too much. The margin against the sewer system was 301 to 138, against the municipal power plant 256 to 178. And, in the mayoralty election in May, Higgins was defeated by William P. Chaffinch, who was accused of being the candidate of the private water company, although he denied it. Easton had spoken, it seemed, on how it felt about "progress"—if progress was going to cost money.

However, Higgins was undaunted. For the next two years he kept up a constant bombardment for his improvements and against the "forces of corruption" which held them back. In 1908 he was restored as mayor and in 1911 finally won approval of the sewer system bond issue.

From that point on, Easton came to be regarded as a model community in Maryland. The sewer network, in operation by 1914, was the first complete system in any Maryland municipality. The waterworks was purchased that same year. A municipal electric plant was started in 1915, replacing the private company which since 1888 had provided power only from dusk to midnight, and not always even then. The new town-owned plant was one of the first in the world to supply alternating current (AC) instead of the direct current (DC) then in vogue. When the town acquired the gasworks in 1923, ending complaints that housewives trying to cook Sunday dinner could hardly even bring a pan of water to a boil, Easton became the only municipaltiy in Maryland to own all its utilities.

Town leaders who had launched a drive in 1899 to bring industry to Easton had less success. Two small plants were enticed to locate in the town—an enameling works which employed about forty people and a mattress factory employing ten. Both suffered disastrous fires and went out of business after a few years.

The one major industry which did grow up in this period—the Easton Furniture Manufacturing Company, for many years Talbot's largest private employer—was strictly a local affair, financed, organized, and operated by Talbot Countians.

Founded in 1899 by a group of businessmen, it lasted under one form or another until 1942. Prime movers in its organization were Robert B. Dixon, William P. Chaffinch, and William H. Kemp, whose family still operates a prosperous furniture-making firm in North Carolina which is an outgrowth of the Easton plant. Under their leadership Easton Furniture grew rapidly. Capital stock investment, which had

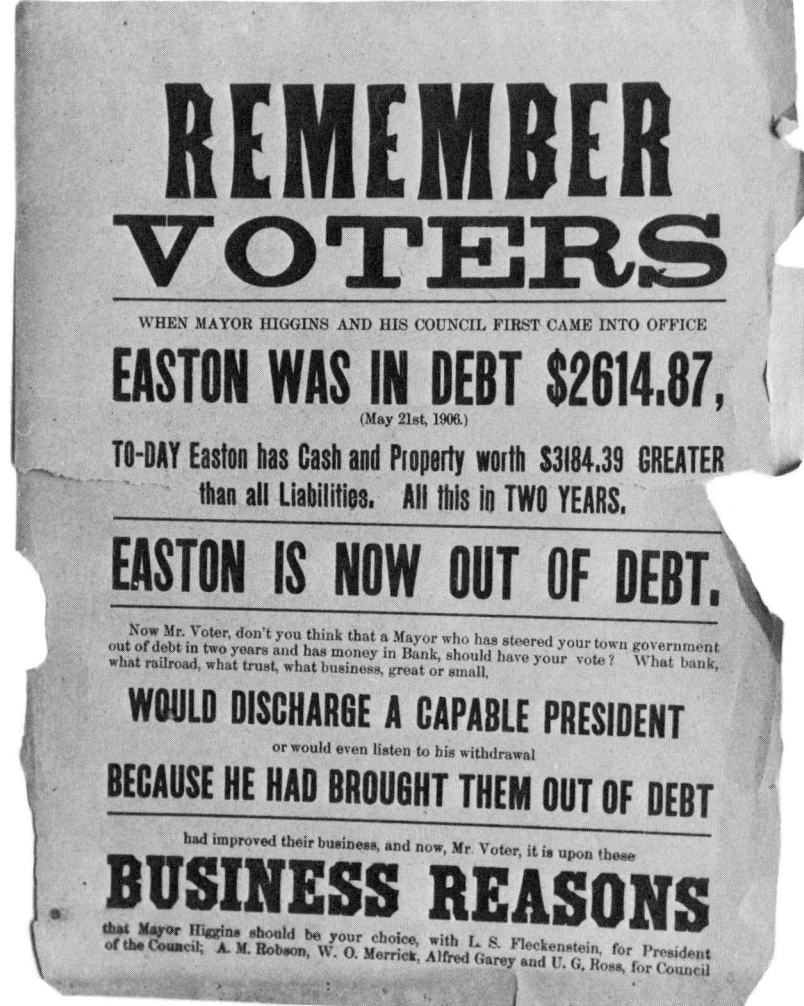

started at $25,000, increased to a peak of $500,000 in 1921, when the company had nearly three hundred employees.

Throughout these early years the company specialized in quartered oak dining room furniture and oak bedroom furniture. But oak went out of style in the 1920s, and the company began to flounder. It tried furniture styles with veneered walnut and mahogany without much success; all its raw materials had to be shipped into the area, and the finished products shipped out again, a costly process. By 1929 it was virtually out of business. William P. Kemp, son of William H., took over the firm, and in 1931 moved it to North Carolina, where good lumber was more readily available, and wage rates were lower.

In Easton, meanwhile, efforts were made in 1931 to revive the original Easton Furniture Company in order to utilize its large plant on

TOWN OF EASTON.

OFFICIAL BALLOT.

Election, held May 4th, 1908.

Draw a black line through the names not voted for.

For Mayor:
Vote for one only.
WILLIAM P. CHAFFINCH.   *336*
MARTIN M. HIGGINS.   *225*
maj 111

For President of the Council:
Vote for one only.
CHARLES W. ADAMS.   *351*
LEONARD S. FLECKENSTEIN.   *212*
maj 139

Facing page, 1908 campaign poster urging reelection of Mayor Higgins. However, as tally above shows, Easton voters rejected him and his reform government by a wide margin.

Brookletts Avenue near the railroad and give employment to at least some of its long-time workers. John W. Noble, one of the new incorporators, set out to raise $100,000 in fresh capital, but recalled later that he was so doubtful about the venture's success that he advised veteran employees against sinking their life savings into it. He proved to be right; the firm got only about fifty thousand dollars in investments, never made any money, and went out of business again within five years.

The corporation was finally dissolved by action which received state approval May 12, 1942. It was not quite bankrupt even then; all taxes and debts had been paid, and stockholders eventually got back about one dollar for every twenty-five dollars they had put into the corporation.

All this was far in the future as Easton and Talbot County faced the problems and needs of the twentieth century from the vantage point of

Easton Furniture Manufacturing Company, founded in 1899, and for many years Talbot County's largest employer, 1930 photo.

1900. One factor holding back growth and development was the persistence of what has been called the "Lost Cause" syndrome—the tendency by people to look back on the Civil War era instead of forward toward the future. By this time it was widely believed in the county that Talbot had been solidly Confederate in its sympathies during the so-called "War Between the States," and was held in check only by the "despot's heel" imposed by federal troops. This myth was fostered by the former slave-holding families who were still Talbot's social leaders in the early 1900s. The legend was reinforced by the negative attitude exhibited by most of the county's whites toward the North on the issues of black freedom and black civil rights. It reached its apex in 1913 when a proposal was made to erect a monument on the Court House green to Talbot's Confederate veterans, ignoring those who had fought for the Union. The idea provoked angry debate, and a committee was formed to raise funds for a countermemorial to the "Talbot boys in blue." It was also suggested that a single monument honoring both sides would be more suitable. But, the "unreconstructed rebels" were in full control; the statue finally erected in May, 1916, was the bronze figure of a young Confederate soldier, and the names of ninety-six Talbot men who had served the Southern cause were listed on its base. More than three hundred Union veterans from the county were forgotten; the fact that many of them had been blacks was reason enough, in the view of many.

Race relations were strongly affected by this Southern tradition. To most Talbot whites, blacks were "darkies"—comical figures at best, petty criminals at worst. "Good" race relations meant that the blacks stayed in their place, "bad" ones that blacks wanted something more than status as common laborers or servants. As a result of this one-sided arrangement hundreds of blacks left the county for Baltimore and other metropolitan centers between 1900 and 1940. The black population decreased during that period by 1,734 persons, a net loss of 23 percent.

Those who remained in the county were kept in their place by rigid segregation, which was almost as strong in Talbot County and the rest of the Eastern Shore as anywhere in the Deep South. Not only were schools and churches segregated, but so was every aspect of life. A black could not eat in a "white" restaurant, sit in the "white" section of a movie house, buy a Coke at a soda fountain, or even get an ice cream cone unless the storekeeper was willing to hand it out through a window. Some Easton stores refused to sell anything to blacks; some doctors' offices had separate doors for black patients, and separate chairs in which they were to sit. Any approach by a black to a white other than a servile one was strictly taboo.

Talbot County never had a lynching, as did Salisbury and Princess Anne on the lower Shore, but it came very close. Only firm leadership on the part of the white establishment averted it.

The situation arose in 1919 when Isaiah Fountain, a Trappe area black, was accused of raping a white high school girl. He was arrested in Chester, Pennsylvania, and lodged in the Baltimore city jail until time for his trial because of threats that he would be taken from the Easton jail and lynched. On the first day of the trial a crowd which had gathered around the Court House tried to grab Fountain as he was being escorted to the jail after the girl, testifying from a wheelchair, identified him as her attacker. Sheriff James L. Stichberry and his deputies stood them off, but in the melee Fountain escaped.

Trial judge Adkins of the circuit court immediately offered a $5,000 reward for Fountain's capture, to be paid only if he was returned unharmed. That sent Baltimore police, sheriff's deputies, and private citizens scurrying in all directions, hoping to capture Fountain before a mob could lynch him. He was found on a farm in Delaware and brought back safely to Easton, where 250 volunteer deputies backed by a National Guard company and a dozen Baltimore police were mobilized to make sure there was no further violence. Fountain was convicted and sentenced to hang, but won a new trial after Baltimore papers charged the jury had been intimidated by the mob. Again convicted, this time by a Towson judge, he was hanged in the Talbot County jail July 23, 1920.

Along with muddy streets, outdoor privies, germ-suspect water, flickering power, and low gas pressure, the Easton of 1900 suffered from another weakness—lack of a hospital, essential to any modern community. In this as in other ways it had fallen behind its rival towns on the Eastern Shore. Hospitals had been founded in Cambridge and Salisbury

Top, Emergency Hospital was organized and opened January 28, 1907 in the former hotel building on the left in this view of Washington Street, 1910. *Bottom*, the "new" Emergency Hospital, dedicated on the present site of Memorial Hospital at Easton, November 23, 1915.

as early as 1898, and funds were being collected for the purpose in both Crisfield and Elkton. But in the entire mid-Shore area, seriously ill or injured patients had no place to receive care except at home, in doctors' offices, or by a long trip to Baltimore.

In 1906 a group of dedicated volunteers set out to fill the need. Several of the leaders were women, notable among them Mrs. Cata Davidson of Easton, Mrs. Oswald Tilghman, Mary Bartlett Dixon of Bloomfield, and Elizabeth Wright, later Mrs. James Dixon. There were men as well; General Joseph B. Seth, who was president of the Maryland Senate, secured a $2,000-a-year appropriation for the venture from the legislature, and served as president of the hospital board of directors from 1906 to 1912.

With support from numerous private donors, the institution known as Emergency Hospital of Easton opened its doors January 28, 1907, in the upper two floors of a rented building on South Washington Street which formerly had housed the Norris Hotel. Dr. Charles F. Davidson was first chief surgeon and Dr. Phillip L. Travers his principal assistant; both remained closely identified with the hospital until the 1920s. With the addition of Dr. William N. Palmer, who joined the surgical staff in 1911, and Dr. William T. Hammond, who came in 1912, the nucleus of a staff was formed which would serve the community for many years.

From the beginning, Emergency Hospital emphasized that it would serve surrounding counties as well as Talbot, and that its doors would always be open to blacks on an equal basis with whites. Its first patient, in fact, was a black girl from Preston in Caroline County, and Dr. Davidson's first surgery was performed on a black woman from Oxford. In deference to white prejudice, blacks were segregated in separate wards, but the medical attention they received was equal to that given whites.

The little hospital, which had space for only thirty-two beds, was soon overcrowded; but it took a major fire in 1913 to awaken the community to the need for a larger building away from the downtown Easton area. The fire broke out in a meat and provisions store on Court Street on the afternoon of August 27. It quickly spread to other Court Street structures and to the Odd Fellows building at the Washington Street corner. Only heroic efforts by volunteer firemen saved the hospital from destruction, while equally heroic work by staff nurses saved the patients from being trapped in the fire. All nineteen were removed to nearby stores and homes.

Almost immediately after the fire a drive was launched for public donations to pay for a new and larger hospital building away from the downtown area. A total of $43,000 was raised, and after a bitter fight over where it should be located, the new Emergency Hospital was dedicated on Memorial Hospital's present site November 23, 1915. It retained the name of Emergency Hospital until 1943, when it was renamed Memorial Hospital at Easton in honor of the area's service men and women and the hospital's early doctors, nurses, and volunteers.

The onset of World War I put many young Talbot County men in uniform and roused the local citizenry to heights of patriotic fervor. The Germans were pictured in propaganda cartoons as savage Huns gleefully driving their bayonets into Belgian babies. Everything connected with Germany and German culture was despised; even sauerkraut was renamed "liberty cabbage." Meanwhile nothing was too good for the American boys "over there," even if over there was only a training camp in North Carolina or Tennessee. Red Cross volunteers rolled hundreds of bandages, women knitted socks by the hundreds for soldiers; the local Red Cross chapter collected so much money that it wound up with a surplus of $20,000, which it gave to the hospital for a nurses' home after the war.

The war's worst impact on Talbot County was the calamitous influenza epidemic which swept the world in 1918, killing an estimated 20 million people, including 548,000 Americans. At its peak so many people were dying in Talbot County that undertakers reported difficulty in getting sufficient coffins. The Easton town council passed an emergency ordinance closing all schools, churches, theaters, billiard parlors, and bowling alleys. The public was warned not to congregate, and to keep children at home. Even the hospital was quarantined. Every doctor and every nurse was stricken with the flu, and at least one student nurse died. All the patients except two or three who could not be moved were sent home.

But the flu epidemic, tragic though it was, had its lighter moments. Raymond D. Smith, who was working for the B C & A Railroad as a telegrapher at Claiborne in 1918, recalled that the company routinely issued a bottle of aspirin and a quart of whiskey to employees as a flu preventive. They were advised to take several aspirins a day and have a sip of whiskey at bedtime; but some reversed the prescription, taking several slugs of whiskey a day and one aspirin tablet at night. And, as far as Smith knew, none of the railroad employees succumbed to the flu.

A colorful dividend of the steamboat age was the showboat. Beginning about 1914, James Adams's Floating Theatre made annual visits to Talbot towns and wharves, staying for a week and performing such hits as *The Girl of the Golden West, Ten Nights in a Barroom,* and *East Lynne,* along with comic sketches and concerts.

The boat which housed the theater was a huge, bargelike craft named *The Playhouse.* This could seat seven hundred, had eight beddressing rooms, a nineteen-foot stage, and drew only twelve inches of water. Motive power was provided by two towboats, the *Elk* and the *Trouper,* which also carried the orchestra when they toured nearby creeks and coves playing sprightly music to let people know the showboat had arrived.

Stars of the shows were Adams's sister, Beulah, billed as "the Mary Pickford of the Chesapeake," and her husband, Charles Hunter. Novelist Edna Ferber spent a week aboard the boat in 1924 gathering material for *Show Boat,* although she switched the scene to the Mississippi River and the time to the 1890s for her novel. Ferber's *Show Boat* was later made into a hit Broadway musical and an even more successful movie. By 1930 the automobile had made movie theaters available to people in the remotest areas, and the wharves where the Adams's *Playhouse* docked soon rotted from lack of use. Adams finally sold his enterprise to a St. Michaels woman, Mrs. Nina Howard, who changed the name to the Original Floating Theatre and continued to operate it until 1939.

Equally popular in the century's early years were the annual Talbot County fairs, held each September at Idlewild Park, then outside the southern limits of the town. Earlier fairs had been staged at Hole-in-the-Wall (renamed Hambleton); but in 1886 the newly organized Talbot County Fair Association, a private company, built a racetrack, grandstand, and other buildings in the open field which it named Idlewild. To make access easier from downtown Easton, the association cut a new road at a cost of five hundred dollars, extending Harrison Street through Earle's Addition, the newest part of town, to a junction with the Trappe Road at the park. Its first fair, September 21-24, was a huge success, and from then on for a number of years the county fairs attracted big crowds. They featured both harness and flat racing, and sometimes even tricycle racing, along with exhibits of farm machinery, prize livestock, fancy needlework, jams, jellies, and other choice creations of farm kitchens, and unusual specimens of farm produce.

Professional entertainment was provided; in 1903, for instance, top billing went to Miss Lillian Hoffman, "the World's Greatest Horsewoman," who rode two swift horses around the track with one foot on each horse. The first airplane most Talbot Countians ever saw was a rickety Curtiss biplane which was a featured attraction in 1914. Although billed as an "aerial exhibit," it had difficulty most days in getting off the ground. Shortly after that the fair association ran into financial difficulties and discontinued the fairs after 1915.

The annual Chautauquas also drew large crowds, especially since they combined moral uplift and self-improvement with magic acts, music, dramas, and other forms of entertainment. Started in 1874 in upstate New York as a Methodist Bible-study camp meeting, the Chautauqua movement expanded into a national lecture and entertainment circuit of immense popularity.

In Easton, which joined the circuit in 1911, the summer sessions were held in a large tent on the grounds of Easton High School, then on Hanson Street. Undoubtedly, the high point for local Chautauqua entrepreneurs came September 3, 1913, when an overflow crowd of 1,700 from all parts of the Shore jammed the tent to hear a stirring oration by

Harness racing at the Talbot County Fair Grounds, Easton, 1895.

William Jennings Bryan, the religious fundamentalist and three-time loser as the Democratic Party's nominee for president. At the time Bryan was secretary of state in the Wilson cabinet, and so his words carried added weight when he assured his audience that progress was being made in the moral and intellectual disciplines throughout the world and that war, famine, and disease soon would be eradicated by an enlightened human race. (Just eleven months later, World War I began.)

Only one mishap marred Bryan's triumphal journey through Talbot County, which included a motor trip from Claiborne to Easton in E. McNeal Shannahan's open touring car while crowds gathered to cheer him at every stop along the way. Outside St. Michaels a motorist—no doubt a Republican—raced around the official car and pulled away "at a rate which covered the passengers with dust," according to the *Star-Democrat*. Bryan brushed himself off and insisted he was "feeling fine." The 1,700 people in the tent made up for this unfortunate incident when they greeted him with a standing ovation and a mass waving of handkerchiefs, considered the highest honor in the Chautauqua world.

After World War I came the Roaring Twenties, although it must be admitted that gangsters, tommy guns, jazz, speakeasies, and other manifestations now associated with the prohibition era were far away from

The grandstand, Talbot County Fair, 1898.

Talbot County. There were illicit stills tucked away in Talbot's woods where "white lightning" was produced, but there always had been. On dark nights trucks sometimes rolled up to deserted country wharves where launches were waiting with cases of booze "right off the boat," but they sped quickly off toward Baltimore or Philadelphia. The county's leading bootlegger, reportedly Buck Bryan of Trappe District, was not exactly considered a criminal; in fact he was honored by having a road named for him. One county sheriff, Raymond Carroll, did get elected on a pledge of "cleaning up the bootlegging trade." Since his margin of victory was just one vote, it could hardly be considered a mandate; anyhow, he never got around to his cleanup campaign. One of the few raids ever staged by "revenooers" in Talbot was in 1929 on Poplar Island. Five were arrested and a one thousand-gallon still broken up.

Talbot Countians were more interested in sports: gunning, golf, sailing, baseball. The Talbot Country Club and the three yacht clubs—the Chesapeake Bay Yacht Club, Tred Avon Yacht Club, and Miles River Yacht Club—were where the well-to-do gathered to relax and socialize. The oldest of these, the Chesapeake Bay Yacht Club, had been an Easton institution since 1885. It was unique in that it had no anchorage; its

William Jennings Bryan speaking at the railroad station in Easton on October 23, 1900.

headquarters from 1911 on were in downtown Easton, in a Washington Street building which had served as a residence, printshop, and post office for Thomas Perrin Smith not long after he founded the *Republican Star* in 1799. Nevertheless, its members included many of the eastern seaboard's most prestigious yachtsmen. Regattas were—and are—held jointly with the Tred Avon Yacht Club, founded in 1931.

For the less affluent the place to go was Federal Park, located west of the Court House, where St. Mark's Village is now. There professional baseball was played beginning about 1922. Easton's teams, known at various times as the Farmers, the Brownies, and the Yankees, played in the Class D Eastern Shore League, which had an on-and-off existence for almost thirty years. The teams were well stocked with talent, chiefly youngsters being groomed for possible stardom by the major league clubs.

One of the notable moments in Eastern Shore sports history came in the summer of 1924, when a Sudlersville-area farmer, Dell Foxx, paid a visit to Frank ("Home Run") Baker, who had retired as a player and was managing the Easton Farmers. Foxx wanted Baker to give his sixteen-year-old son, Jimmie, a chance to play with the Farmers. Baker did, and young Foxx, then a catcher, responded by batting .296, including a flock of home runs. Baker then persuaded his former manager, Connie Mack, to sign Foxx for the Philadelphia Athletics; and the strong boy from Sudlersville went on to challenge Babe Ruth with a lifetime total of 534

Frank Baker, the celebrated home run king, who managed the Easton Farmers team at Federal Park, is seated at center. Behind him is his 1924 discovery, Jimmie Foxx of Sudlersville. Foxx subsequently challenged Babe Ruth's home run record in the major leagues, and both he and Baker were elected to the National Baseball Hall of Fame.

home runs, and win membership in the National Baseball Hall of Fame. Baker also achieved this honor, even though he had won his nickname in the dead ball era by hitting only eleven or twelve homers a year.

The Eastern Shore League's career was sporadic. It folded during the Depression, was revived from 1937 to 1941, closed again in World War II, and had a last brief fling from 1946 to 1949, when Easton was a New York Yankee farm club. Then came TV, and baseball fans would no longer pay to watch a bunch of minor leaguers when they could see the major leagues free in the comfort of their homes. The Shore League, and most other minor leagues, quietly died.

Throughout the period, outsiders continued to find Talbot County and its environs the place where they'd most like to live if they didn't have to earn a living. Some who weren't satisfied with what they found remade the social and cultural scene into what they would like it to be.

In 1922 the "Mad Stewarts," Jacqueline and Glenn, came from New York and bought a point of land opposite St. Michaels. She was Ireland-born, he a native of Pittsburgh; both were independently wealthy, although no one knew exactly how they had acquired their fortunes. They built a Moorish castle of pink stucco on the estate they named Cape Centaur. It had walls almost three feet thick, doors of steel plate overlaid with oak, narrow slits for most of the windows, and a three-story tower. Both Stewart and his secretary-caretaker, Adolph Pretzler, slept with loaded Colt revolvers under their pillows. Surrounding the estate were a high wire fence and a wide strip denuded of all shrubs and trees, and patrolled by mounted men armed with shotguns and giant Irish wolfhounds, of which Mrs. Stewart at one time owned thirty-two. The Stewarts didn't want to be disturbed.

Eventually they bought up most of Wye Island, tried unsuccessfully to raise Percheron horses and sheep there, and finally turned it into a western style cattle ranch complete with gun-toting cowboys. In downtown Easton they bought the ancient Brick Hotel, more recently called the Moreland Block, remodeled it completely, doubled it in size, and renamed it the Stewart Building.

One day Glenn Stewart, who wore a patch on one eye as the result of the explosion of a homemade bomb while he was at Yale, stepped aboard his black yacht *Centaur*, sailed off for Nassau, and never returned. Jacqueline stayed on; after her death in 1964 appraisers searching the castle found more than $160,000 in cash, much of it in gold, along with diamonds, emeralds, bushel baskets full of jewelry and coins, and trunkfuls of sterling silver flatware, not to mention a 1931 Duesenberg convertible, a crossbow, and a Steinway grand piano. A share of her estate went to Pretzler, who continued to live at Cape Centaur.

An outsider of an entirely different sort was Arthur A. Houghton, Jr., founder of the Steuben Glass Company, president of Corning Glass, and onetime curator of fine arts for the Library of Congress. In 1937 Houghton began buying up land in lower Queen Anne's County, where he established the Wye Institute, world famous for its herd of Aberdeen Angus bulls, but involved as well in a number of other agricultural experimentation and civic betterment projects. His major benefaction in Talbot County was the restoration in 1948-49 of lovely old Wye Church in Wye Mills, originally built in 1721.

In 1928 the "invaders" were moviemakers, an entire Hollywood film crew on location in St. Michaels to make a movie called *The First Kiss*. It dealt with the love life of a waterman and his upper crust girl friend. The stars were Gary Cooper, in his first feature role, and Fay Wray, later famous for being waved aloft from the top of the Empire State Building by King Kong. At the time Cooper was so little known that the *Star-Democrat* at first thought his name was Gary Gopper.

For six weeks the entire cast, including Cooper and Miss Wray, stayed at Royal Oak's Pasadena Inn, where they charmed their hosts, the Harper family, with their quiet ways, hard work, and early hours. Miss Wray's fiancé, film writer John Monk Saunders, came east, and they were married June 15 at Easton's Calvary Methodist Protestant Church, with the Reverend Edgar T. Read officiating.

Eighteen "grizzled watermen" were hired for bit parts, and the entire St. Michaels oyster dredging fleet of twenty-five skipjacks and bugeyes was put under contract. Numerous other Talbot Countians got their faces on camera in one way or another as scenes were shot in St. Michaels, at Easton's Third Haven Meeting House, and on a site described by the Hollywood publicist as "within a stone's throw of the famous Wye House." For the climactic courtroom scene—Cooper played an oyster dredger who turned to piracy to put his three brothers through college—some two hundred Talbot Countians were cast as jurors, and spectators, and the Talbot Court House and jail were used as the setting. Unfortunately, this footage wound up on the cutting room floor; when the movie had its Maryland premier in August at Easton's New Theater (now the Avalon), the real Court House had been replaced by a Hollywood fake and the local players by professional extras.

The First Kiss, among the last of the big budget silent movies (it cost $200,000), was generally rated one of the worst films ever made. New York critics called its plot "impossible and overdrawn" and said of Cooper's acting ability only that "he does a lot of chest heaving." But the moviemaking business paid off for the Harpers at the Pasadena Inn. For decades afterward shopgirls and secretaries from Washington and Balti-

The County Building and Library, Easton, 1940.

more came as summer visitors, hoping to sleep in the same bed that Gary Cooper had slept in. The Harpers, always obliging, assured these visitors that any room which happened to be vacant was, indeed, "Gary Cooper's room."

Two earlier silent movies had also been made in Talbot County. One, called *I Will Repay*, starred Corinne Griffith, and included scenes at the railroad station, the Hotel Norris, and Ratcliffe Manor. The other, *In the Land of Legendary Lore*, was the story of Betty Lowe, a Talbot County belle who according to the plot was wooed and won by Lord Baltimore.

Other well-known personalities had summer homes in Talbot, and helped give the county an air of sophistication lacking in most of the other Eastern Shore counties. Among the big-names were retired heavyweight boxing champion Gene Tunney, who had a retreat near Benoni's Point; Metropolitan Opera baritone John Charles Thomas, who spent his summers in the county and gave numerous benefit concerts for the hospital, the Children's Aid Society, and other charities; and Presidents Roosevelt and Truman, who spent weekends at the Jefferson Island Club on one of the three isles into which Poplar Island has disintegrated. In more recent times, movie star Robert Mitchum, baseball owner Bill Veeck, Democratic presidential nominee George McGovern, and author James A. Michener have all had full or part-time homes in Talbot County.

One victim of the gasoline age was the old-time one room country school. Busing of school children, now an explosive emotional issue in many quarters, began in Talbot as early as 1917, when wartime shortages forced the closing of poorly attended rural schools and transportation of their pupils to larger ones. The 1920s and 1930s saw intensified moves toward school consolidation; in 1900 the county had seventy schools, in 1945 only twenty-five. By that time more than half of all pupils were being bused to classes, and the number of public high schools had dropped from six to three, two in Easton and one in St. Michaels.

With consolidation came more, if not necessarily better, education. The school year was lengthened to 180 days, and a twelfth grade finally added to the high schools. The curriculum was broadened and more student activities encouraged to educate "the whole child"; but many parents complained so much time was spent on athletics, dramatics, and social activities that there wasn't any time for studying. They're still complaining.

Opportunities for adult education were provided through the Chautauquas, the Current Events Club of Easton, other women's clubs, church societies, and the Talbot County Free Library.

The Talbot County Free Library, the oldest public library on the Eastern Shore, was opened in October, 1924, in an empty Washington Street storeroom. By January, 1925, it had 2,100 books, many of them donated by individuals. Spark for the project was provided by Mrs. Caroline Burnite Walker, a Talbot County native who had had extensive experience at the Carnegie Library in Pittsburgh and the Cleveland Public Library, one of the world's greatest open-shelf collections. She served as president of the board of trustees from 1925 to 1936, and as librarian from 1931 to 1936.

When the county commissioners bought the old Music Hall for conversion into an office building, the library was given space in the front of the building. New books, equipment, and janitor service were provided by friends of the library and most operating expenses paid by annual grants from the county and the Easton town council; but the library maintained its status as an independent unit not dominated by any governmental agency.

These quarters were dedicated June 7, 1941, with one of the shortest dedication speeches on record, by Donald S. Ross, then board president. Ross also was president and gave the same dedication speech when the spacious new library building was opened in 1976.

In the long run, the advent of auto, truck, and bus traffic could fairly be blamed for the downfall of the railroads and steamboats. But the rail lines which served the Eastern Shore were in deep financial trouble long before the first auto appeared on Talbot's roads. Badly undercapitalized and beset by much higher than expected construction costs, they fell one by one into the hands of the giant Pennsylvania Railroad system.

First to go was Talbot's own railroad, the Maryland & Delaware, which traversed the county from Queen Anne to Easton to Oxford and was the mainspring of the Talbot economy. Bondholders foreclosed on its original builders and bought it out December 20, 1877, just six years after its Oxford terminus was completed. It was reorganized as the Delaware & Chesapeake Railway Company. In 1882 the entire stock of this firm was acquired by the Philadelphia, Wilmington & Baltimore Railroad Company, a division of the Pennsylvania system. From that time on it was operated as a Pennsy branch line, until the once mighty Pennsylvania itself went bankrupt in the 1970s.

The line known to generations of Talbot Countians as the B C & A, or Black Cinders & Ashes, also was beset by financial woes. Its builder, the Baltimore & Eastern Shore Railroad Company, was forced into receivership, and sold it at public auction August 29, 1894, to outside capitalists closely allied with the Pennsylvania. They organized a transportation conglomerate, the Baltimore, Chesapeake & Atlantic, which included several rail lines and most of the steamboat companies serving the Eastern Shore. The Pennsy acquired controlling interest in the B C & A in 1902, but permitted it to continue to operate under its own name and management. Through the B C & A, the Pennsy in 1905 also took

THE GASOLINE REVOLUTION

over the Maryland, Delaware & Virginia, which ran mostly through Queen Anne's County but had a Talbot depot at Queen Anne.

By 1907 the B C & A controlled not only these railroads but thirty-six bay steamers. Its combined operations that year hauled 517,024 tons of freight and carried 854,908 passengers. Its Claiborne-Ocean City run was a great success, with trains each summer weekend of up to fifteen crowded cars, which sometimes required two engines. But its overall operations were not as successful; the Maryland, Delaware & Virginia lost money from the start, and the steamboats operated at a deficit, especially during severe winters. The winter of 1903-4 was especially bad, as ice halted all bay traffic for nearly a month. That winter also saw the great Baltimore fire, which paralyzed all business dealings in and out of the city. The company faced tax problems both in Baltimore and Salisbury, its Eastern Shore headquarters.

Still the railroad from Claiborne to Ocean City chugged along, scoffed at but beloved by Talbot Countians who didn't care who owned it as long as the trains ran. For three decades the steamer *Cambridge* brought travelers to Claiborne, where they rushed to board the trains. Going east the weekend express was known as the Ocean City Flyer; coming back on Sunday evening it was the Baltimore Flyer. It crossed the peninsula in just over two hours, spewing smoke and fine cinders in its path as it raced through the Talbot countryside at sixty miles an hour.

Year-round local service was not that fast, but still provided transportation comparable to the best that automobiles can do today. The railroad's scheduled run from St. Michaels to Easton took just twenty-one minutes, and trains could be boarded at Riverside, Royal Oak, Kirkham, and Bloomfield along the way. Going east there was equally fast service to Bethlehem, Preston, Hurlock, and Salisbury.

By 1932, the worst year of the Great Depression, the age of steam was over. Autos, trucks, buses, and improved highways to carry them had done their work, and hard economic times completed the job. The beautiful side-wheel steamers lay rusting in Baltimore Harbor or had been sold to finish their careers elsewhere. The *Joppa* had been taken off the Choptank run in 1921, and the *Talbot* put on a sharply curtailed schedule in 1924. Two years later she was reduced to carrying excursionists from Baltimore to points on the Potomac River. All regular passenger service to the mid-Shore area was abandoned in 1932, although there were occasional excursions and cruises until 1939.

On the B C & A, passenger service between Claiborne and Easton ceased in 1931. Only an occasional freight train to McDaniel from Easton remained to remind Talbot Countians of the railroad's past glories, and even those ceased in the 1960s.

The Bullet, a motor train, was the bright spot of railroad service. It operated between Oxford and Easton and Easton and Wilmington from 1930 through 1950.

On the Oxford-Easton line, passenger service lasted until 1949. An attempt to compete with automobile traffic by means of the Bullet, a high-speed one-car gasoline coach, was a failure. The last freight train between Oxford and Easton ran in 1957, and what was apparently the last train on the entire line made a sentimental journey from Greensboro to Clayton, Delaware, February 22, 1983. However, as this is written there is talk that the 115-year-old railroad may once more be revived.

For Talbot farmers, the 1900-1940 period was marked by the emergence of new crops—chiefly tomatoes and other truck produce and dairying—and by gradual emancipation from the shackles of rural isolation. The gasoline revolution played a part in both; truck crops meant exactly that—crops that could be shipped directly by truck to markets—and large scale dairying depended on the availability of facilities for delivering fresh milk daily to the metropolitan centers.

The Model-T Ford, more than any other single item, freed farmers from restriction to the small area in which they could travel by horse and wagon. As a corollary, it also doomed the prosperity of the crossroads villages and small towns whose merchants depended on local farmers. There was no way in which they could compete with the lower prices and wider choice offered by chain stores and other merchants in the larger centers to which farm families now could travel.

Model Ts and other early automobiles, Washington Street, Easton, 1925.

Even the county's bird population was drastically changed by the gasoline revolution. English sparrows and starlings, both imported species, increased in such numbers in the late nineteenth century that they threatened to eradicate all other kinds of birdlife. There were great clouds of them along rural roadways and the unpaved streets of towns. The auto age ended the threat by a simple and inelegant process: it eliminated the horse droppings on which they throve, and so reduced their numbers as rapidly as they had risen.

Talbot's tomato era began shortly after 1900. Soon every farmer was a tomato grower, and every man who could get his hands on a steam engine set himself up in the business of canning tomatoes. (The same plant could be used for distilling moonshine whiskey.) At one time or another there were nearly fifty of these small canneries in Talbot County. Most soon went out of business; but some remained active for many years, producing canned tomatoes under their own or other labels, and switching to other produce when high labor costs for picking ended the tomato boom.

The late Charles B. Adams of Trappe, whose family-owned cannery on Lovers' Lane was founded in 1902 (and is still operating), recalled in a 1976 interview the days when every Talbot farm had four or five acres of tomatoes, and "when they were ripe, the whole family got out and picked them."

Gus Mielke's wheat threshing rig, Wyetown Farm, Miles River Neck, 1935.

Canning season ran from August to early October. The tomatoes were scalded, skinned, and packed into cans by hand. After the lids were soldered on, the tomatoes were cooked in huge kettles of boiling water for forty minutes, then the cans were labeled and crated. Most of the labor was piecework; a good tomato skinner or label paster could make as much as fifteen cents an hour. In the early years most of the work was done by crews of eastern European immigrants imported from Baltimore. Later local blacks were employed.

One Talbot Countian whose progressive ideas benefited both himself and the area's farmers was J. McKenny Willis, Jr. As manager of the family farm, and as a fertilizer salesman for Armour & Company, he had noted that uneconomical buying and selling practices were costing Eastern Shore farmers thousands of dollars annually in badly needed revenue. Fertilizer was bought in individual lots in Baltimore, shipped to Talbot by rail or boat, and stored on the farm until planting time. Wheat and other grains were shipped to Baltimore, their value reduced because good and poor quality grain were mixed in the same schooner. Feed grains grown in Talbot were sold in Baltimore, and the farmers then bought grain produced in the midwest to feed their livestock and poultry.

THE GASOLINE REVOLUTION

In 1930 young Willis, with his father as partner, launched J. McKenny Willis & Son with the aim of correcting these deficiencies. The firm imported fertilizer in bulk, stored it, and for a flat fee let the farmer have it when he needed it. Willis built facilities to grade and store grain locally, which assured farmers of getting higher prices for their better grain, and thus encouraged quality improvement while at the same time eliminating shipment costs. Equipment was installed to grind the grain of livestock producers, and to sell to the farmers only the supplemental elements they could not raise on their own farms. A corn dryer was installed so that corn could be stored on the farm and sold at any time of the year, not just during the peak harvest season. For the first time there was a local market for most of the corn produced in Talbot County.

When broiler production replaced tomatoes and dairying as a mainstay of the Talbot farm economy, the company went into the chicken business. It hatched millions of baby chicks annually and then under the name of Bayshore Foods, Inc., began raising and processing its own broilers. Its chickens, flour, feed, and other products were marketed under the trade name of Shorgood.

All this paid off handsomely both for the Talbot farmers and for Willis & Son. The firm was started in 1930 with $1,500 in borrowed capital in an old sailboat warehouse on Easton Point. When it was sold to Kane-Miller, Inc., thirty-nine years later, it was grossing more than $25 million a year, employed 600 people, and hatched, fed, and processed more than 35 million chickens annually. It was probably the best example in Talbot history of a successful homegrown, home-led, home-based industry built on home-produced raw materials.

Almost as important as Henry Ford's Tin Lizzie in freeing the farmer and his family, and ending the golden age of the small communities, was the rise in the 1920s of installment buying. Anything from furniture to a funeral could be bought on "easy payments" in the larger towns. "Buy now, pay later" was a slogan for which country storekeepers had no answer. So prevalent was the practice that when Emergency Hospital put on a drive in 1927 for seventy-five thousand dollars to pay debts and build a new maternity wing, it was called the "installment plan campaign"—one eighth down and the rest in seven easy payments.

At the same time rural population was declining everywhere as people flocked to the towns and cities, where life seemed somehow more glamorous and there were better job opportunities. (The rush back to the country came later.) Talbot's overall population declined by 7.7 percent between 1900 and 1940, and its rural population even faster. Only Easton and to some extent St. Michaels were growing; everywhere

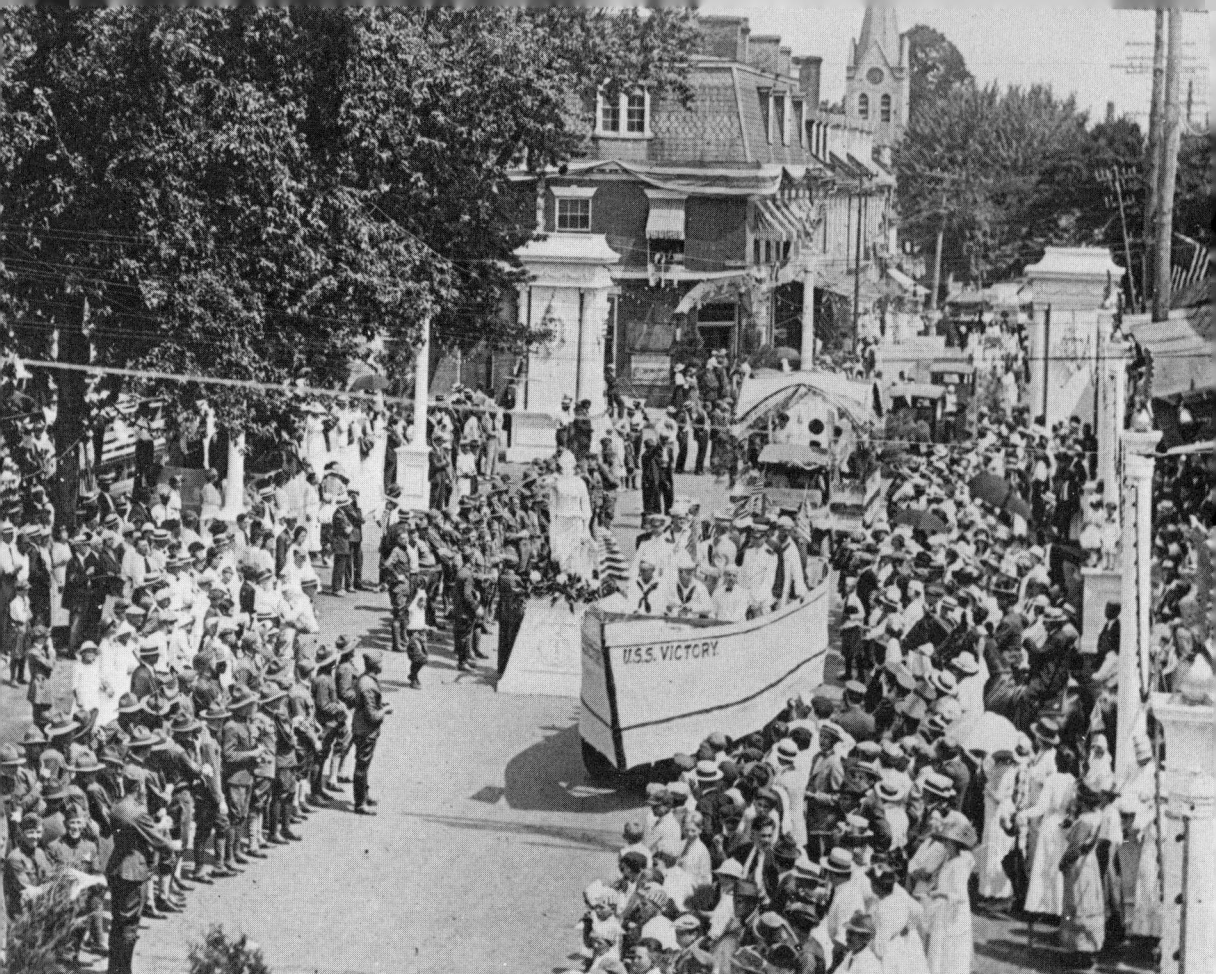

World War I victory parade, Easton.

else people were leaving for the cities. The drain was heaviest on young families. Between 1920 and 1936, Talbot's white birthrate decreased by 23.2 percent. The post-World War I hit, "How You Gonna Keep 'Em Down on the Farm, after They've Seen Paree?" was more than just a popular song; it was the nutshell description of a sociological revolution.

Commercial aviation, another offspring of the gasoline revolution, was pioneered in Talbot County by brothers Malcolm and Stephen Hathaway of Ratcliffe Manor. In June, 1928, they took over a cow pasture near their home, built two landing strips on it, and started the Tred Avon Flying Service with two planes.

Stephen soon dropped out but Malcolm, who had learned flying as a naval reserve pilot, kept the business going until after Pearl Harbor. In 1930 he moved to Webb Field on Dover Road, named for its owner, Dorsey Webb. There he gave flying lessons and conducted a charter business. In 1933 he started scheduled passenger service to Baltimore. But that only lasted about a year; there wasn't enough traffic to make it pay.

On Sundays thousands of people would flock for air shows such as this one in 1928 at Malcolm Hathaway's Ratcliffe Manor field.

In 1929 Hathaway began a long association with H. Robins Hollyday, who enjoyed both flying and photography. One day Hathaway suggested that they combine forces; they got a small aerial camera, and in the next thirteen years Hollyday took thousands of aerial photographs of the area which are now treasured possessions of the Historical Society of Talbot County.

Hathaway's Webb Field operation ended when he went into wartime service, first as a pilot for Pan American air ferries, and then in naval air transport. The present Municipal Airport, built during the war as an emergency measure, with enemy prisoners of war providing the labor, became a commercial field in 1946 when Chesapeake Airways inaugurated a daily schedule between Baltimore and Ocean City, along with an up-to-date flying school, service shops, and hangars.

The Great Depression of the 1930s hit hard in Talbot County, though less so than in the big industrial centers. Talbot had no giant factories to close down, nor skyscrapers from which ruined stock market gamblers could hurl themselves out of windows. People who were already poor simply found themselves a little poorer. Some small plants closed; some jobs were lost; and those who had jobs received substantial pay cuts. However, bank accounts actually rose as individuals fearful of the economic future liquidated their investments and put the money where they could get at it more readily; deposits at Easton National reached $3,098,433.48 on October 3, 1933, an all-time high up to that point.

As for farmers, they already faced depression conditions. Hard times had begun for them in the mid-1920s, when Wall Street was just beginning to ride the great bull market which ended with the crash of October, 1929. Farms, like the schools, were being consolidated as the tractor enabled an individual farmer to handle more acreage, and low prices forced marginal farmers to sell out and move to town.

Talbot Countians turned out en masse for the opening of the Emerson C. Harrington bridge and causeway across the Choptank October 26, 1935. Many saw it as the answer to the depression; it would link the lower and upper shores, bring truck, bus, and tourist traffic through the heart of Talbot County and into downtown Trappe and Easton, generate jobs, stimulate business, and in general bring back that prosperity which for so long had been "just around the corner."

An added attraction was that Franklin D. Roosevelt was on hand in person to dedicate the bridge's drawspan. At approximately 3:30 P.M. he sailed under the bridge in his yacht, *Sequoia*, smiling and waving as hundreds on both sides of the draw crowded forward to get a glimpse of him. FDR and his New Deal were not especially popular in conservative Talbot County—in 1936 he carried the county by just 206 votes over Alf Landon despite what was elsewhere the greatest landslide in American history—but he *was* president; and in a sense he was a Talbot Countian, since he and his Democratic cronies spent leisure time at their Jefferson Island hideout.

The Choptank bridge didn't do all its enthusiasts had hoped; it would take more than a bridge to pull the stricken Eastern Shore out of the depression. But it did change things; within weeks traffic on the main highway tripled as Red Star buses and big interstate trucks rumbled day and night through the streets of Easton, Trappe, and Wye Mills. There was a flurry of accidents—the roadway was only fourteen feet wide—and new demands were made for traffic lights, or some device, to halt "the noise and fast driving of automobiles and trucks through town."

But the merchants liked the new bridge, even if nobody else did. To them traffic in the middle of town was money in the bank, not a nuisance. They fought to keep it, just as they would fight a hard but losing battle to keep bypasses from being built around Easton and Trappe when Route 50 was built after World War II.

By the end of the depressed 1930s Talbot Countians, like the rest of the Eastern Shore, appeared to at least one outsider to be living in self-imposed isolation. They were more suspicious than ever of the outside world—especially Baltimore. Sociologist Frank Goodwin, who studied the Eastern Shore in depth in the period between 1935 and 1939, found its people proudly self-conscious about the area's history and traditions, thoroughly adjusted to rural and small town living, and openly defiant toward any criticism. Both men and women were boosters and joiners; many belonged to nine or more different clubs and societies. They tended to name as their most admired leaders businessmen, politicians, and lawyers, leaving out churchmen and educators. County newspapers, still locally owned, were edited by local men, few of whom had gone to college, and concentrated on church socials, farm news, and the comings and goings of local people.

Almost universally, Eastern Shore residents pitied rather than envied city dwellers. "The Shoreman knows his land is the world's garden-spot and his people are God's people. His is the good life," Goodwin observed.

Unfortunately Goodwin, who was associated with Washington College in Chestertown, did not differentiate among the nine Eastern Shore counties, so there is no way of knowing how precisely his findings applied to Talbot Countians. But it seems safe to assume that they were not too different from their neighbors, and that his study is a reasonably accurate portrait of Talbot County as it appeared in 1940.

Then came World War II, and all the changes it brought in its wake—television, the Bay Bridge, new life styles, the invasion of the "permissive society." Pearl Harbor Day—December 7, 1941—was a landmark date for Talbot history. Nothing would ever be the same again.

TWELVE

After the Bridge

THE evening news on August 14, 1945—V-J night to Americans—touched off what was perhaps the wildest celebration in the history of staid little Easton. For forty-eight sleepless hours, Talbot Countians had stayed home, ears glued to their radio sets, listening to rumors and counterrumors as they waited for word that the Japanese, beaten into submission by the awesome power of two atomic bombs, had agreed to surrender terms. Then, on the 14th, shortly before 7:00 P.M., it came: President Truman walked into the White House pressroom and announced to reporters that Japan had surrendered. The war was over.

In Easton, as everywhere in America, there was jubilation. People rushed into the streets, laughing, shouting, waving flags. Many jumped into their cars and started driving, somewhere—anywhere—honking their horns in steady blasts. Fire sirens blew; the town's fire engines and ambulance drove through Easton, tooting their deep-throated horns and clanging their bells. Impromptu bands gathered at corners. Some used lard cans for drums; others joined in playing and singing victory songs; boys did acrobatic stunts in the streets. Shotguns and pistols were fired; in western Talbot County, it was reported later, the thunder of big guns booming in Annapolis across the bay could be heard distinctly.

"Joy was unconfined," was the way the *Star Democrat* summed it up in its edition of August 17. The paper told of one man who stood in the middle of Washington Street, dressed in a top hat and linen duster, directing traffic. Every so often he set fire to a newspaper, dropped it into a bucket at his feet, and gleefully watched it burn. Another man tried to get a woman to waltz with him in the middle of the street, but she refused, saying, "No, thanks. I want to live to see the rest of this happy night." So, said the paper, he marched off down the street, ringing the doorbell of every house he passed. Still others carried confetti or torn up strips of newspaper, which they showered on bystanders. Most businesses closed immediately, their clerks swelling the crowds and adding to the racket.

Many persons, especially the wives, sweethearts, and parents of servicemen, headed for church. But the din outside was so great that at downtown churches normal services were impossible. At Christ Church the Reverend Durrie Hardin didn't even try; instead he stood at the door greeting parishioners as they entered, and let them compose their own prayers of thanksgiving. At Trinity Methodist there was singing and responsive reading, but the preacher stopped his sermon in the middle because nobody could hear him.

Next day came orders from Washington to cancel wartime rationing of gasoline and of most canned goods at once. By Thursday filling station owners in all parts of the county reported constant lines of people driving in with the almost forgotten order: "Fill 'er up!" Storekeepers immediately started selling all canned goods except milk without ration points; but curiously, there were few buyers. "People around here are funny," said one merchant. "When they find out they can get things, they don't want 'em anymore."

For thirty-four Talbot men, the war's end came too late. They were the dead and missing who, in the words of a *Star-Democrat* headline, "will not return from abroad—they gave their lives."

It had been a long and agonizing uphill struggle from Pearl Harbor December 7, 1941, to V-J Day August 14, 1945. Talbot's first fatality had come even before America was involved; young Eddie Streets of Easton had joined the Royal Canadian Air Force and risen to the rank of captain before he was killed on the island of Malta in 1941. After the war the Easton chapter of the Veterans of Foreign Wars was named the E. E. Streets Memorial Post in his honor.

Pearl Harbor and the early German successes in Europe brought on a wave of hysteria in Talbot which almost amounted to paranoia. Enemy spies were believed to be everywhere; enemy air raids were considered a real and constant menace; even a German invasion aimed at Washington by way of the Eastern Shore was not discounted, especially after some German frogmen were picked up by the FBI as they landed from a submarine on the Delaware coast.

Newspaper headlines added to the hysteria. "Extreme Care is Required to Guard County. Enemy Agencies Are Believed To Be in Our Midst at Present. May Be Expected to Strike Any Time," the *Star-Democrat* reported on page one in June, 1942. The article went on to say that German sympathizers were known to be in Talbot County, and that strangers should be watched very carefully to prevent them "from getting in their dirty work. . . . If you see any suspicious persons . . . or hear conversations that are detrimental to this country, it is your duty to report these at once. . . . We can't be too careful."

The situation was aggravated when Adolf Kappus, a German national who was working at Emergency Hospital as a bacteriologist, was picked up by the FBI immediately after Pearl Harbor and interned for the duration of the war as an enemy alien. Many thought him a spy, although the FBI later cleared him of that charge. His military bearing, German accent, contempt for all things American, and even the fact that he didn't like corn on the cob were cited as "proof" that he had been a Nazi agent. Wild rumors circulated against others of German background; some of the comments got into the papers and had to be retracted.

Almost at once the Coast Guard Auxiliary was mobilized and started patrolling Chesapeake Bay, on the lookout for boats which might carry gasoline and other key supplies to German submarines operating in the Atlantic. Airplane spotters manned lookout posts at strategic points throughout the county twenty-four hours a day, with instructions to scrutinize every plane that passed overhead very carefully to make certain it was "friendly." John W. Noble, in charge of civil defense, directed a series of practice blackouts and simulated air raids. At the hospital student nurses were trained in how to deal with casualties from bombs and flying glass. Because of their proximity to Washington, D. C., Talbot County and the surrounding area were considered to be among the most vulnerable regions in America for enemy air attacks, next only to California and the Norfolk Navy complex.

When no raids occurred, Talbot Countians gradually turned their attention from the enemy in Germany and Japan to what seemed to many to be the enemy in Washington—the government bureaucrats. Gasoline rationing, instituted May 16, 1942, in Maryland and sixteen other Atlantic seaboard states, produced initial chaos and much resentment. Many people knew that gasoline itself was not scarce; it was rubber for automobile tires that was rapidly running out as the Japanese gobbled up Southeast Asia, where ninety percent of the world's rubber was produced. Gas rationing was imposed to control drivers who ignored warnings that when their tires wore out their cars would be off the road.

On the last weekend before rationing, Talbot's roads were jammed with cars as practically everybody in Maryland went on a final joyride to the Eastern Shore and Ocean City. Most filling stations quickly sold out, or put up signs saying "regular customers only" or "50 cents worth only." (That last wasn't as bad as it sounds today; in 1942 fifty cents bought nearly three gallons of gas.) On Sunday the Matapeake-Annapolis ferry was forced to run all night; when its last scheduled trip took off at 8:00 P.M., a line of cars three miles long was waiting to return to the Western Shore.

When ration cards were issued on Tuesday, May 12, it seemed that everybody in Talbot County either used his car to drive to work, was a farmer, or was engaged in some other "essential" business. Everybody wanted an "X" card, entitling the holder to unlimited gas. The situation wasn't helped as word spread that both Maryland senators, Millard Tydings and George L. Radcliffe, had put themselves down for "X" cards. Almost nobody wanted to admit using his car only for pleasure or shopping, and therefore being limited as an "A" card holder to just three gallons a week.

Gradually the confusion over gas rationing straightened itself out as military demands made the fictitious shortage a real one and rationing was extended to the entire country. Eventually nearly all consumer goods were rationed—meats, butter, fats, canned goods of all sorts, sugar, shoes. Even cuffs on trousers were banned, and ladies' skirts became stylishly short to save cloth. Foods were put on a system of red and blue ration stamps, issued periodically to prevent hoarding, and given point values which had to be paid to the store along with cash. Price controls were clamped on virtually everything civilian consumers bought.

For the most part, Talbot Countians took such things in stride; this was one war in which there was complete unity of public opinion—the world simply had to be saved from being overrun by Hitler's Nazis and Hirohito's Japs. But by the summer of 1943 the merchants—and especially the grocers—were being overwhelmed by the mountains of paper work required by Washington. Grocers were required to keep complete inventories of everything in their stores not only in terms of prices but in terms of ration points.

In desperation Albert T. (Doc) Dawkins, proprietor of Dawkins' Market on South Washington Street, dashed off a newspaper ad announcing that henceforth his store would be closed on Wednesday afternoons so that he could catch up on his paper work for the government. To his surprise, the idea spread like wildfire throughout the country. Press dispatches resporting it were published in many major newspapers, including the *Wall Street Journal* and the *Christian Science Monitor*. Editorials lamented the plight of the "little merchant" who had to spend one whole afternoon a week just working for the government. The bureaucrats paid no attention, but other local merchants did. Soon Wednesday afternoon closing in Easton stores was almost universal. The custom lasted for more than two decades.

A critical labor shortage was eased when a camp for German prisoners of war was established north of Easton. The prisoners built an emergency airfield there which later became Easton Airport. Many of them worked in Talbot canneries or on farms, where they were employed in summer cutting hay and barley, or picking cucumbers and other vegetables and fruits, and in fall and winter repairing barns and fences and doing other carpentry work. Some also worked in sawmills.

Doris Rend, then a *Star-Democrat* reporter, gave a vivid account of life at the camp in the summer of 1945. There were then 526 prisoners, very near the capacity of 550. She informed readers that they were heavily guarded, and wore uniforms with PW in large letters stamped on the back. The camp was surrounded by a stockade fence with twenty-one strands of barbed wire topped by an overhang with more barbed wire, and guards armed with carbines and machine guns manned wooden towers outside each corner. As far as is known, none ever escaped.

All this was reassuring to a public which was apprehensive about having such a large number of enemy aliens in their midst. Talbot Countians felt even better when, in October, 1945, the camp was disbanded and the Germans sent to western states to help harvest sugar beets.

Despite the scarcity of industry, several Talbot firms gave good accounts of themselves in the war effort. Tilghman Packing Company of Tilghman Island and Harrison & Jarboe, with plants at Sherwood and McDaniel, both received the War Food Administration's coveted "A" (for achievement) award for their food production. The Oxford Boatyard twice was granted the Army-Navy "E" for excellence; its directors, A. Johnson Grymes, Jr., Robert Goldsborough Henry, Jr., and Sigurd N. Hersloff, were so proud of their achievements that in December, 1945, they took out a full page newspaper ad to boast about them: 126 vessels built and 71 repaired for the United States Navy. The experience, they added, would make them better equipped to handle postwar pleasure boat needs. But a few years afterward, the trio sold out

War's end found Talbot County facing a whole new world. There would be no more isolation, and almost everybody knew it. Nor would the simple prewar standards of life suffice; fifteen frustrating years of depression and war had left the public hungry for everything at once—better schools and roads, more consumer goods, higher pay, job opportunities, improved housing—and the only question was how it would be accomplished.

Most certain of all was that the great Bay Bridge which had been talked about at least since 1908 was going to be built at last. It would

The Tidewater Inn, as it looked in 1980.

transform everything, although whether for good or bad no one knew. Whatever its other effects, it would breach the wall which Eastern Shoremen had built around themselves, and behind which they had lived for a century in insular seclusion.

By 1947 the winds of change were blowing strong. Talbot had never seen anything quite like it.

On January 27 ground was broken for the splendid new downtown Easton hotel, to be called the Tidewater Inn. It was being financed and built by A. Johnson Grymes, Jr. on the site of the old Hotel Avon, which had burned in January, 1944. Like many of Talbot County's benefactors, Grymes was one of those once snubbed outsiders who had invaded the county from the north and had remained to love it. A member of a wealthy New Jersey shipbuilding family, he had lived in Talbot since boyhood, had been a partner in the highly successful Oxford Boatyard during the war, and now was willing to gamble a fortune on the future of Easton and the county. The ninety-four-bedroom inn would be by far

The single span Bay Bridge, 1952.

the largest and most luxurious hotel on the Eastern Shore, and would rival the hospital as the biggest structure in Talbot County.

More than two years in the building, the Tidewater Inn opened for business September 3, 1949, after a daylong open house during which four thousand visitors trooped through it, admiring its spacious lobby, dining and meeting rooms, and neatly furnished modern bedrooms. It quickly became an attraction for tourists and visiting dignitaries, and the center of Talbot's social and business life, especially after a new north wing containing the elegant Gold Room and twenty-eight additional bedrooms was completed in 1953.

In March of 1947 came the long awaited announcement: funds for construction of a bridge across Chesapeake Bay between Sandy Point and Matapeake on Kent Island were included in a five-year, $168 million program for the complete modernization of Maryland's highway system proposed by newly installed Governor W. Preston Lane, Jr., and soon thereafter approved by the legislature. In July Lane announced awarding of contracts for planning, and initial construction.

There was some grumbling about the prospect, but less so in Talbot than elsewhere on the Eastern Shore. Merchants feared their customers would drive across the bridge and do their shopping in Baltimore instead of Easton, but were mollified by discovery that the overall program included construction of numerous modern highways leading to Easton, greatly enhancing the town's chances of becoming a trading center for the entire mid-Shore area.

With the bridge about to become a reality, the ferry and rail services which had served as Talbot's links with the outside world were fading. Old Smokey Joe—actually the steam ferry *Philadelphia*, operated by the

Pennsylvania Railroad—made its last run August 31, 1947. It had been a pleasant way to travel between Love Point on Kent Island and downtown Baltimore; you drove your car to the point, parked it, boarded the ferry, had lunch, and three hours later disembarked at Light Street. Drinks stronger than soda pop were strictly bring-your-own-bottle, but there was always a card game for fairly high stakes going on behind closed doors in a room belowdecks. Many were sorry to see the last of Smokey Joe, but the Pennsylvania was cutting its losses everywhere well in advance of the bridge; two years later, in 1949, it ended all passenger rail traffic to Easton and Oxford.

The Love Point ferry's demise left only two such links between the Eastern and Western shores. Both were state operated. The main run was between Matapeake on Kent Island and Sandy Point north of Annapolis. A secondary line, launched in 1938 for the convenience of residents in western Talbot County, operated between Claiborne and Romancoke near Kent Island's southern tip. From there autos and trucks had to travel by road to Matapeake and board a second ferry to complete the journey. Neither operation was very satisfactory; there were constant demands for more frequent service. But with the shadow of the bridge looming ever larger, nothing was done about it.

At home in Talbot, meanwhile, the biggest building boom in the county's history was underway by March, 1947. The *Star-Democrat* reported that 122 new units had been completed since the war's end or were currently under construction. Included were ninety new homes, eight garages, six new filling stations, five new warehouses, three new stores and five other stores completely remodeled.

At least sixty-two of the new homes were in Easton, nearly double the prewar record for any comparable period. The town was growing fast, and spreading into new areas. Unless some measure of control was applied, the growth threatened to get out of hand, with little subdivisions springing up helter-skelter and new homeowners clamoring for power, water, sewer, and other services.

In February, 1947, therefore, the Easton Town Council took a fateful step by enacting an ordinance regulating future subdivision of land in the town of Easton and—significantly—within a mile of the town limits. Included was a call for a master plan for the development and expansion of Easton, giving the town control not only of its own destiny but of its future growth into unincorporated areas. The mayor promptly appointed a planning and zoning commission to implement the ordinance.

 ͻ was the first such program ever enacted by an Eastern Shore community and the first in Maryland to assert the right of a municipality to control its suburbs and prevent the urban sprawl which had already developed around Washington and Baltimore. The ultimate outgrowth of the Easton council's work would be countywide planning and zoning, which in the next eight years would precipitate the bitterest and most divisive struggle since the Civil War in Talbot. But first it faced an immediate test in a squabble over the location of new industry in Easton.

In November, 1947, Waverly Press, a Baltimore-based firm which published medical and scientific books, proposed to build a new plant near the south edge of town, between South Aurora Street and the Pennsylvania Railroad tracks. The railroad company owned the land and was anxious to sell it to Waverly, which brought its paper in by rail and therefore would be a good customer.

Few denied that Waverly Press was exactly the kind of "clean, light industry" which Talbot County badly needed. It produced no smoke or grime as by-products, had an excellent labor relations record, and promised to train and employ scores of local workers. Since the war Talbot had been losing a significant number of small industries which had provided employment in earlier years—factories in Easton, St. Michaels, and Oxford which manufactured silk hosiery were being phased out by the development of nylon. Small plants making hand-sewn shirts were no longer economically practical in a machine-dominated industry and canning plants were being wiped out by the decline of tomato growing.

So Waverly Press certainly would be welcomed—but the question was: exactly where would it be welcomed? Until the previous February, the railroad would have been free to sell its land to anybody who would buy it; but now with its new zoning powers the town of Easton would have to make the decision.

As soon as the proposal became known, residents along the section of Aurora Street which faced what was then Easton High School (now Idlewild Park) circulated a protest petition against letting the land between Idlewild Avenue and Dutchman's Lane be zoned industrial or commercial. On November 16 about thirty residents appeared before the town council to register their protest. Waverly Press, their spokesman said, would be "a good asset to the community," but Eastonians didn't want it in their neighborhood. A factory backing up against their homesites would "harm the neighborhood and depreciate property values." It might open the door for sale of more railroad land to less desirable types of industry. And anyhow, they argued, there were other sites along the railroad tracks to the north of their area which would be better locations for a factory.

The council thus faced its first dilemma. The railroad, seeking revenue, refused to sell its land for any but commercial purposes. The residents insisted it should be zoned residential. The town and county needed the industry. And the concept of planning and zoning hung in the balance.

To their credit, the council members worked out a compromise which appeared to satisfy all concerned. The railroad agreed not to sell land to any objectionable factory. The town agreed to zone the track area to permit only "smokeless and noiseless industries" with architecture similar to that proposed by the Waverly Press. The residents took a long look at Waverly's building plans, and decided it wouldn't be such a bad neighbor after all. They withdrew their objection, Waverly Press got its building permit, and Easton moved forward. The principle had been established: henceforth the town, and not land buyers and sellers, would decide who built what, where, and under what conditions.

But the *Star-Democrat*, taking a longer view, saw in the objections which had been expressed a latent opposition to letting any sort of industry locate in Easton. In an editorial published November 21, it cited as "well-known" the fact that many residents feared the character of the town would be changed by inviting industries. "One man has stated that if trolley cars were ever run along Washington Street, . . . he and his family would sell out and go some other place to live," the paper noted. The Easton Businessmen's Association was planning an advertising campaign to promote Easton as a good place for small industry, "but before this can be accomplished the people of the community must be united on this plan. . . . If we maintain the attitude prominent in the past that such industries are undesirable, then we can expect to remain as we are."

In a nutshell, the question was: industry, growth, and jobs versus traditional values. It was an argument which soon enough would engulf the entire county, and which to this day has not been entirely resolved.

In many lesser ways, 1947 in retrospect stands out as a year of destiny for Talbot.

It was the year, for instance, in which television reached the county— not exactly in its present scope, but nevertheless recognizable as a potent part of the wave of the future. Here's how it happened:

Leroy M. Royer, a partner in the Easton electrical appliance firm of Royer & Barto, had been tinkering with television ever since 1929. By the summer of 1947 a station in Washington, D. C., was broadcasting regular programs, but the experts said they couldn't be received in Easton because the station's signal had a range of only forty-five miles, ten miles short of the crow-flight distance between Washington and Easton. Royer decided to prove them wrong; he rigged up a homemade TV set with a six-by-eight-inch screen, built a lofty aerial on top of his

Harrison Street store, and invited the public to come in and watch TV. While they waited, he fiddled with seven synchronization and timing knobs at the rear of his set, made delicate adjustments, and got a voice and a lot of snow—but no picture.

So it was back to the drawing board for Leroy Royer. Finally he added another fifteen feet to his aerial tower, waggled his knobs again, and this time pulled in a picture of the opening of the United Nations General Assembly "as clear and free from interference as could be received right in Washington." For the rest of the summer visitors to Royer & Barto could view a six-by-eight-inch version of such events as lawn tennis matches from Forest Hills, prize fights from Madison Square Garden, and British movies (Hollywood moguls wouldn't let their movies be shown on TV, considered an upstart rival). When a station was opened in Baltimore, only forty-five miles away, reception got even better. By the summer of 1948 people all over Talbot County were putting up tall aerials, buying small screen sets, and staying home nights to stare at them.

The year 1947 was also when St. Michaels got around to voting in favor of a town sewer system, and when Trappe and Oxford started talking about one. Trappe's proposal was vigorously promoted by Maurice T. (Possum) Adams, the town's unofficial mayor for many years, but was voted down by more than two to one in a 1949 town referendum. It was not until 1961 that Trappe residents decided a sewer system would be worth the money, and it was 1963 before both it and Oxford's two-lagoon system were completed. The rest of the county managed—and still does, as this is written—on private septic tanks and in some poor areas outdoor privies.

The county's new liberal element arose in 1947 to demand Sunday movies, forbidden ever since the first nickelodeons flickered on screens made out of sail canvas. Churchgoers frowned, but the liberals pressed on; they finally got their Sunday movies in November, 1948, although it took an act of the legislature and a countywide referendum to achieve them.

A knotty problem in 1947—and for several years afterward—was the issue of "God's time versus daylight time," chiefly a struggle between the county's farmers and its urban residents. Daylight saving time, an outgrowth of the war, was being bitterly debated throughout Maryland. City folks liked it, but farmers argued that cows couldn't tell time, and paid no attention when clocks were set forward or back. In Talbot, the situation became ridiculous; Easton adopted daylight saving time from April to October, but the rest of the county, including schools and county offices, stayed on "God's time." For a while, nobody knew what time it was. Eventually, the issue was settled by the legislature, which voted against God and the cows, and in favor of the urbanites and universal daylight saving time.

Finally, late in 1947, the prospect of remodeling the ancient Talbot County Court House arose. Dating from the 1790s, the Court House had undergone only a few modest face-liftings since then. Clearly it was inadequate for modern county government, and its priceless records, some dating from the 1660s, were rotting away or being gnawed by rats in damp basements and attic storerooms.

In December a committee headed by T. Hughlett Henry, Jr., attorney to the county commissioners, recommended construction of a two-and-a-half story addition at the rear of the Court House. It would be attached to the existing building "but in no way alter its historic beauty or the general appearance of the Court House square." Henry thought it could be built for $200,000 and "would be adequate to meet the county's needs for the next hundred years."

The proposal roused a storm of debate which eventually was enmeshed in the larger struggle over what became known as "the colonialization of Easton."

The concept of countywide planning and zoning is so universally accepted today that mention of it brings yawns instead of cheers or groans. But it was not so in the early 1950s. Then talk of zoning brought forth angry cries of "Communists" and "rich four-flushers." Appeals were made to raw human emotions—greed, fear, prejudice, patriotism. Pitted against each other at one stage or another were old-time residents versus newcomers, farmers versus urbanites, poor versus rich, traditionalists versus progressives. Behind the scenes moved shadowy figures, unknown to the public—on one side the powerful "billboard lobby," which opposed zoning, and on the other a crack New York public relations firm which helped mold public opinion in its favor. There were angry protest meetings and jam-packed, emotionally charged debate sessions. At the climax, as he listened to the cheering, booing, shouting, and stomping of an aroused crowd of one thousand people during a showdown hearing in the Easton armory, one lifelong resident shook his head sadly. "Never in all my life have I seen the county split as it is now," he said, "and I hope I never do again."

The classic confrontation dragged on for five full years. But out of it all, somehow, grew modern Talbot County.

Bridge Dedication Day—July 30, 1952—was an occasion to remember, if only because it marked the first and last time Marylanders ever got to ride toll free across the 4.35-mile span.

Actually, two ceremonies were held, and four ribbons were cut in symbolic opening of the bridge. Former Governor W. Preston Lane, Jr., in whose administration construction had begun, and the current Governor Theodore R. McKeldin were both on hand for the festivities which began at 10:30 A.M. with a nineteen gun salute at the western end of the bridge. Simultaneously, they cut two ribbons. Then, after innumerable speeches by assembled dignitaries and the unveiling of a plaque on the administration building's lawn, the governors led a parade across to the eastern side. Behind them marched bands playing martial music and military units from all the services, followed by a long string of official cars. At the eastern end, after more speeches, the two governors did their twin ribbon-cutting act again. The double ceremony lasted nearly four hours.

As soon as it was over, a fleet of state-leased buses started carrying the thousands of spectators back and forth across the bridge for their one and only free ride. Promptly at 6:01 P.M. the tollbooths were opened and regular paid traffic began.

The ferry boats on the parallel line between Matapeake and Sandy Point also gave free rides throughout the day, their final one after thirty-three years. At about 5:30 P.M., ferries pulled out from the two terminals at the same time. As they passed in midbay, they sounded their horns in mournful salute. As soon as they touched shore on the other side, they went out of service for good.

(The other state-owned ferry, between Claiborne and Romancoke, stayed on the job until December 31. Then it too went out of service, with a final free ride which departed from Claiborne at 6:00 P.M. on New Year's Eve.)

Initial tolls were set at $1.40 for cars and up to $5.00 for heavy trucks, with an extra twenty-five cents each for passengers. These tolls were supposed to pay off the $45 million cost of the bridge, which had been raised through the sale of revenue bonds, by 1961. After that, at least in theory, the bridge would become tollfree—although of course that hasn't happened, and doubtless never will.

Everyone who saw the structure, even those who had not wanted it, had to agree that it was quite a bridge. The central suspension span was 1,600 feet long, the overall bridge and causeways 22,990 feet or 4.35 miles. Just to paint it, which was done continuously, required 24,000 gallons of paint. Its curved design gave it a distinctive grace, although the reason behind this design was practicality rather than beauty; the curve was required to bring the abutments of the suspension span precisely at right angles with the Baltimore ship channel which ran between them, and to base the bridge on the most favorable terrain at both ends.

But by their very presence the bridge and the new highways it fed meant potential trouble for the Eastern Shore. Some thoughtful Talbot leaders had watched their progress with a certain amount of dismay. Knowing what had happened elsewhere, they were fearful that completion of the bridge would mean a solid string of honky-tonk cafes, curio stores, filling stations, and the like running all the way from Kent Island to Ocean City, and that the thirty-two-mile Route 50 corridor down the length of Talbot County would become a "tunnel of billboards." Above all, they feared land values would tumble if uncontrolled subdividing and construction of small shopping areas, as was already happening on Kent Island, should spread to Talbot.

Some form of zoning seemed to be the answer. But the state law enabling communities to establish zoning required detailed study and development of a master plan as a preliminary. These could take years.

In September, 1951,—almost a year before the bridge was opened—*Star-Democrat* editor Norman Harrington and T. Hughlett Henry, Jr., concocted an "interim" zoning ordinance intended, in Harrington's words, "to lock the barn door before the horse is stolen." Based solely on the county's police powers and not on the state enabling act, this was

Norman Harrington, editor of the *Easton Star-Democrat*, 1948-1964. The *Star-Democrat* building was originally Bartlett's Mill and now is One Mill Place.

designed to give the county control over developments until a countywide master plan and zoning restrictions could be worked out. The commissioners promptly approved it and named a county planning and zoning commission, with Harrington as first chairman. Other members were Norman Fike of Cordova, Norman Howeth of Tilghman, Maynard Stewart of St. Michaels, and Bertram C. Voshell of Trappe District. All were friends of the zoning concept, and among them they represented every section of the county.

Late in November they presented detailed proposals to the county commissioners. These called for an initial budget of $13,800 and employment of a full-time county zoning clerk, along with a zoning consultant who would develop a master plan for the county's future for a fee of $6,000.

"The opening of the Bridge next July will signal the beginning of a new era," their report said. ". . . The prognosis is toward rapid expansion. . . . Changes in our county's traditional way of life (are) inevitable."

Their long-range aim, they said, was to ensure that the county's inevitable development "be carried forward in an orderly, desirable manner with a minimum of undesirable features." To this end they set two immediate goals:

—Protection of U. S. Route 50 and other new or improved highways against "the mushrooming of taverns, billboards, and other commercial structures." This was essential "if the beauty of the roads is to be maintained and serious traffic hazards to be avoided."

—Protection of the county's unique waterfront area to enhance property values and encourage development "along lines which will (preserve) the basic charm of the area."

As later developments indicated, not all Talbot Countians agreed that planning and zoning were the way to achieve these goals. But the county commissioners went along, and Irving C. Root of the National Park Service was hired as consultant to develop Talbot County's master plan. He came highly recommended, having done similar work for Rockville, Gaithersburg, and Alexandria, Virginia. But in Talbot he was exploring uncharted ground; while some Maryland municipalities had zoning plans, no Maryland county had ever tried it on a full countywide basis.

By this time Harrington, who had served as an Army combat photographer in World War II, had been recalled to active duty as a public relations officer in the Korean crisis. B. C. Voshell, former operating head of the Standard Oil Company of New York who now lived at Belmont in Trappe District, took over as chairman of the zoning commission—and stayed in the post for twenty years. "He is the real father of planning and zoning in Talbot County," Harrington says of Voshell.

There seems no doubt, however, that the countywide zoning ordinance first proposed by the commission in December, 1952, had serious flaws. For one thing, it was needlessly complicated; the text ran to sixty-six pages, much of it in legal language no ordinary property owner could hope to understand. For another, it proposed zoning restrictions for every acre of Talbot County farmland, including areas far removed from major highways or the waterfront. That roused a storm of protest from farmers. Its restrictions on billboards were so drastic that some doubted whether even a homemade sign advertising "eggs for sale" could be displayed.

The zoning proposal was to be considered in segments—one for each of Talbot's five election districts. A hearing on the first one, the Easton District outside the town itself, which had its own zoning plan, was scheduled for January 12, 1953.

It quickly became apparent that this hearing would become a test of sentiment for the entire county, not just Easton District. On January 9 a half-page ad in the *Star-Democrat*, paid for by the billboard interests, warned farmers that the ordinance as written could mean substantial financial loss or higher taxes. It could mean that farm buildings and dwellings along highways would have to be moved back as much as fifty feet, and that owners could not sell or lease their property for a business establishment, tourist court, filling station, advertising display, or any other but a few limited uses. Such restrictions would mean lower prices for land, the ad claimed.

At the January 12 hearing in the County Building auditorium, more than three hundred persons appeared. All seats were taken, there were many standees, and scores were turned away at the doors. Relatively few were from rural parts of Easton District, the ostensible subject of the hearing. Of twenty-nine speakers only three identified themselves as living in that area. Fifteen were from the town of Easton, eleven from elsewhere in the county. No vote was taken, but the majority appeared to feel that, while some sort of zoning was needed, the proposed ordinance was too complicated, and that all restrictions on inland farm areas should be removed.

On January 20, sixty farmers appeared before the county commissioners to emphasize their opposition to any zoning of farmland in the county. Their spokesman, dairy farmer Herbert L. Andrew (father of the 1983 county council chairman), told the commissioners: "We need no one to dictate to us how to build, buy or sell our land. We as individuals consider this an invasion of our rights and an insult to our integrity."

Meanwhile, a bombshell revelation hit the county in February, 1953. Pan American Refining and Transport Company, a subsidiary of Standard Oil of Indiana, was considering Bay Hundred District as a possible site for a giant oil refinery with an eventual cost of $50 million. The plant would bring in a construction force of one thousand workers, and give permanent employment to as many as five hundred people, many of them local residents. On February 27 it was confirmed that the site, one of several under study by the corporation, was on approximately one thousand acres of land at Wade's Point near the northern end of Tilghman peninsula. Crude oil from South America would be shipped up the bay in tankers, off-loaded to the refinery, and refined gasoline, kerosene, and heating oil would be carried out of the area by ship or truck. Because of shallow water near shore, a lengthy channel would have to be dug to deep water dockage facilities located well out in the bay.

More than any other development of the decade, the refinery proposal galvanized public opinion for and against zoning. Here was big industry, seemingly ready to spend millions to transform a remote, poverty-stricken region of poor watermen and small farmers into a modern industrial complex with all the benefits and problems that phrase implied. Was this what Talbot County wanted in its future? Bay

Hundred residents shouted an emphatic yes; most of the rest of the county said no.

In the heat of the argument, people tended to forget that Pan American had never said it definitely wanted to build there, but only that it might do so. Chief spokesman for the proposal, and most determined foe of zoning, was Aldace F. Walker, a Washington-based businessman with Pan American connections whose mother, Mrs. Alonsita Walker, and other family members owned the 823-acre Wade's Point site under consideration and had options on 300 additional acres nearby.

At a public meeting held in the Tilghman schoolhouse March 2, three hundred persons—more than half of them from Tilghman Island—braved sleet and icy roads to register their vigorous disapproval of countywide zoning in any form. What Bay Hundred people did with their land, they said, was nobody's business but their own.

George D. Olds, Jr., a retired oil company executive, presented the case for zoning and against the refinery. He said the plant would use four gallons of water for every gallon of product, and that it was doubtful if the area's water table could stand that kind of pressure. He warned that, no matter what precautions were taken, the refinery would be potentially more dangerous than an explosives plant because a pound of gasoline had the explosive power of ten pounds of dynamite. And pollution could be caused by the human element: "You can get pollution when somebody forgets to close a valve or when crude oil accidentally spills into the water."

Bay Hundred residents who had visited a refinery in New Jersey to observe conditions for themselves scoffed at this. They had seen little or no evidence of air pollution, and had been told that the water which was put back into the Delaware River after use was much purer than that taken out. Vernon Ball, their spokesman, noted that they had seen a pond between two refineries "where there were more ducks in a square mile than we've seen here all this winter."

They also rejected the claim of county tax assessor Lee C. Vinyard that the county would not profit from the estimated $180,000 a year in additional tax revenues the refinery would bring in because most of it would have to be paid out in additional school costs. When a show of hands was taken after nearly three hours of debate, the vote was overwhelmingly in favor of the refinery and against zoning.

With Bay Hundred in revolt, the county's farmers up in arms, and St. Michaels, nearest town to the proposed refinery, defiantly opposed to zoning, the advocates of zoning decided they needed heavy reinforcements. A New York public relations firm was contacted, and Morgan Schiller, a Pittsburgher whose wife was the former Elizabeth Key Lloyd of Wye House, raised five thousand dollars in twenty-four hours in voluntary contributions to pay its initial fee for coming in with advice on how to win over the public.

One of its first recommendations was that zoning advocates, instead of being merely antirefinery, should appear to be proindustry as long as it was of a diversified type. As a front for this, a citizens' committee was quickly formed for the announced purpose of encouraging diversified industrial development. Headed by B. Frank Sherman, this later developed into the Talbot County Economic Development Commission.

Another recommendation was to scale down the scope of the zoning proposal and appease the farmers at any cost. With the public relations men sitting in, a simplified program was developed emphasizing five main points:

—Adequate areas for commercial and industrial expansion in all parts of the county, including Bay Hundred and St. Michaels.

—Control of large billboards on the grounds it was necessary "to promote highway safety."

—Subdivision control only when three or more lots were involved.

—"Reasonable" lot size requirements in waterfront areas, suburbs of towns, and along highways.

—No other restrictions on farmland, except a requirement of building permits for new brooder or broiler plants and slaughter houses.

The public relations experts felt this sugarcoated plan could be sold where the vastly more complicated original program could not. And the prozoners enthusiastically set out to do it. A countywide drive was started under the chairmanship of Easton attorney L. Clark Ewing to get signatures on petitions urging the commissioners to adopt the five-point plan. Speakers before civic groups and clubs pushed the idea of "simplified zoning" as the answer to the county's postbridge ills.

In the *Star-Democrat* Norman Harrington, back as editor after nine months of military service, kept up a steady bombardment against the refinery. The paper reported that at least three other large industries were planning to come in on the heels of the refinery, and that an unnamed real estate firm was said to be buying up options on most of the land in Bay Hundred District. "The whole project would be overwhelming in scope, and all Bay Hundred would be hardly big enough to handle it," the article stated. Ten thousand acres would be needed—"virtually all the land from St. Michaels road to the tip of Tilghman Island." None of this was ever confirmed, nor were the alleged industries identified; but it was effective as a scare tactic.

A preliminary hearing on the simplified plan April 27 in the Easton High auditorium drew 650 people and indicated the zoners were winning their case. Twenty-one speakers favored zoning; only six opposed at least some parts of the new package.

Bay Hundred, however, remained adamant. Spokesman Elmo Granger charged the citizens' committee was using the zoning proposal as a smokescreen to keep the oil refinery out. He asserted that the "so-called rich class, or four flushers" opposed the refinery "for their own personal reasons," and added bitterly: "It is ridiculous to try to keep Talbot County a rich man's paradise."

Other Bay Hundred speakers said they favored any kind of industry, large or small, "because the seafood industry is fast going out as a means of livelihood." The rest of the county had no right to say what went on in Bay Hundred District. "We're capable of telling you what we want," one shouted. "Why should anyone not residing in Bay Hundred have any say?"

Prozoners insisted that zoning had nothing to do with the refinery, and objected to Granger's tactics in bringing the "class issue" into the argument. "Zoning is good if it helps all the people, and this plan does just that," said John W. Noble.

A final hearing on the simplified plan was scheduled for Saturday afternoon, May 16, at the Easton armory. The county commissioners would listen to the arguments, and immediately afterward vote yes or no on the simplified plan. "The future of Talbot County will be in the balance," said the *Star-Democrat*.

In the preceding weeks both sides worked frantically to rouse public sentiment to a fever pitch. The Bay Hundred Anti-Zoning League hired sound trucks to tour the county, booming out a warning that the zoning proposals were "Communist-inspired." (At the same time they claimed zoning was favored by the rich, though how those two were compatible was never explained.) The prozoners worked through the Citizens Committee for Talbot County Development. Their slogan: "Change is inevitable; change without a plan is folly; change with a plan is progress."

The antizoners, in a letter to the commissioners, demanded a countywide referendum before final action was taken. They believed public sentiment was strongly on their side. Prozoners opposed a referendum, ostensibly because the issue was too complicated to be decided by a yes or no vote, although privately they weren't at all sure how Talbot's "silent majority" would react. The commissioners ignored the Anti-Zoning League's request; it seems evident now that their minds were already made up.

The May 16 hearing was by far the largest ever held on a public issue in Talbot. For three hours more than a thousand people sat or stood in sweltering heat, cheering, booing, applauding, or stomping as speaker after speaker brought up every argument—and a few new ones—that had ever been used for or against zoning. Tempers flared. Several antizoners complained that it was "practically impossible to get a good-paying job in Talbot County," and that their sons and daughters were being forced to leave the Eastern Shore in order to make a living. Prozoners stuck to their guns: zoning would not keep industry out, but merely regulate how and where it was established.

The commissioners listened to all this in silence. Then they adjourned to hold a special session in the office of J. McKenny Willis & Son, and unanimously adopted the simplified planning and zoning ordinance. It was "the wish of the overwhelming majority of the people and districts of the entire county," they said in a statement.

That should have ended that, but it didn't.

Shortly afterward, Pan American Refining filed a petition with the newly constituted permanent Planning and Zoning Commission for rezoning from agricultural to industrial of 1,100 acres at the Wade's Point site to permit establishment of the oil refinery if it so wished. Company president L. W. Moore admitted Bay Hundred was only one of ten sites being considered, but said it was high on the list, and had the enthusiastic endorsement of the federal government. The town of St. Michaels joined in the petition. Later Moore and his staff put specific figures on the jobs and money involved: 218 permanent positions would be open to local people; initial investment would be $20 million, with an ultimate prospect of tripling that amount.

The Zoning Commission adopted what the St. Michaels town commissioners charged were delaying tactics, meeting only once in sixty days and raising technical questions to which they said the company did not give complete answers. Demands were made for a public hearing, but none was scheduled. Bay Hundred residents said this proved they had been right, that the commission was determined to keep the oil refinery out; and in retrospect that appears to have been the case.

On September 18 Pan American ended the matter by announcing it would locate the refinery in York County, Virginia. It denied that opposition in Talbot had influenced its decision, saying: "On the whole, we feel that we were given a fair opportunity to present our case." The deciding factor was the relatively high cost of distributing finished products from the Eastern Shore as compared with the Virginia mainland, the company said. Bay Hundred was not convinced—and still isn't.

One more chapter remained to be written before zoning in Talbot County was home free. In March, 1954, a company named the Port of Chesapeake Authority, Inc., of which Mrs. Alonsita Walker was president and Aldace Walker vice-president, filed applications to construct a major seaport facility at Wade's Point, at a cost of $10.5 million. In

December, five members of the Walker family, as Bay Hundred property owners, filed suit in Circuit Court, asking that the interim zoning ordinance under which the land had originally been zoned agricultural and residential be declared invalid on grounds it had been illegally drawn up, and that the zoning ordinance adopted in May, 1953, be declared without force and effect.

In a four-day court hearing before Judge J. DeWeese Carter in March, 1955, company attorneys led by Hyman Pressman of Baltimore alleged that the site in question constituted "the most suitable site for general modern industry remaining along the entire Atlantic seacoast from Maine to Florida." Pressman repeatedly tried to get Harrington to admit that interim zoning had been adopted solely for the purpose of keeping the oil refinery out, and Harrington repeatedly denied it, pointing out that the ordinance had been adopted in 1951, long before the refinery proposal came up.

Judge Carter, in a thirteen-page decision, ruled that Talbot's zoning ordinance was legal and valid. The losers took the case to the Maryland Court of Appeals and finally to the United States Supreme Court, but lost both times.

The way was clear at last for the "light industry only" policy and the tough waterfront zoning restrictions around which modern Talbot County has been built.

Parallel to the battle over zoning, but not a part of it, was the move to "colonialize" downtown Easton which produced another of modern Talbot's hallmarks. Although this grew out of a faulty reading of history, it had laudable—and highly visible—results.

The idea was publicized in February, 1952, when the Maryland Historical Society aired a proposal—never implemented—to raise $2.5 million for the restoration of historic buildings throughout Maryland. Eight of these would be in Talbot County, including most notably the ancient Court House. Others: the old Wye Mill, Third Haven Meeting House, Whitemarsh Church, a chapel at Rich Neck Manor then thought to be of very early date, Clay's Hope near Bellevue, the Lostock house, and Jeremiah Banning's first customs house on Plaindealing Creek.

There had already been talk of turning Easton's public square area into a showplace emphasizing colonial rather than modern architecture. The Talbot County Garden Club was trying to persuade downtown merchants to adopt a colonial motif in remodeling their stores, and offering free architectural advice to anyone who would consider it. Their model was colonial Williamsburg, the Rockefeller Foundation project in Virginia which was then very much in the public eye.

This sketch of early Washington Street buildings, by Dr. Henry Chandlee Forman, precipitated the 1950s campaign to "colonialize" Easton.

Then, in April, 1954, came a dramatic demonstration of the form such a restoration might take. A sketch made by Dr. Henry Chandlee Forman, a distinguished historian and architect who lived near Easton, was published on page one of the *Star-Democrat*. It showed eighteen buildings along Washington Street "as they looked around 1800, soon after the Talbot Court House was constructed . . . to serve as the east capital of Maryland."

The accompanying article said a recreation of the square "in the Georgian and post-colonial styles would be unique in the United States," that it would have both historic and educational values, that it would attract thousands of tourists and have a "great and favorable impact" on the county's economy. "It would be a colonial Williamsburg in miniature, although unlike Williamsburg [most of which had been built from the ground up] much of the original could be retained and utilized in the Easton restoration." Editorially the paper urged the most careful attention to Dr. Forman's suggestion. "Once in a great while an idea is born that captures the imagination and . . . transforms a community," it said.

Actually Dr. Forman's sketch depicted the Easton of about 1820 rather than that of prerevolutionary times. It included the front of the Court House, which was not completed until 1794, a portion of the old

Brick Hotel, which was built about 1815, and the market house of 1805, along with other buildings which certainly did not date from much earlier than that. Neither then nor later did Dr. Forman ever describe it as representing Easton, or rather the village of Talbot Court House which had preceded it, as it might have appeared in colonial times.

But it was the word *colonial* which captured the imagination of town leaders and real estate promoters. They wanted a "colonial Easton" to match "colonial Williamsburg." Dr. Forman's carefully worded description of his sketch was quickly edited to suit their purpose. "Post-colonial" became "colonial," neatly wiping out some fifty years of history, and the fiction of "colonial restoration" became an article of faith in Easton.

Soon everybody was climbing on the bandwagon. Easton was touted as "the colonial capital of the Eastern Shore," blithely ignoring the fact that it had been no such thing. A Citizens Committee for the Colonial Restoration of Easton, with the ubiquitous John W. Noble as chairman and most civic and business organizations represented, was formed in October, 1954. Merchant after merchant fell in line, although some protested that a "colonial" storefront offered very little scope for window displays. Companies which wanted to build or rebuild along modern lines found endless delays in getting building permits; town engineer William H. Corkran, Jr. simply sat on them until the firm changed its plans. Companies willing to "colonialize" got special interest rates from the Easton National Bank.

Then came a Baltimore firm called James W. Rouse & Co. Inc. with a proposal to build a "huge shopping center," to be called Talbottown, at the northern edge of Easton. Rouse, an Easton native, had been a successful mortgage banker, but this would be his first venture into the development field, in which he later achieved international renown. As originally conceived, the sixteen-store, $1 million complex was to be ultra-modern, with lots of glass and chrome; but after being bombarded by local civic leaders Rouse changed his mind. The shopping center—first in Eastern Shore history—opened in the summer of 1955. It was not exactly colonial Williamsburg (as Rouse said, there were no shopping centers then, nor parking areas for five hundred cars), but it conformed basically to the so-called colonial design. Not incidentally, it also did much in ensuing years to push Easton into first place as the mid-Shore area's premier trading center.

Next target of the "colonializers" was the Court House, about which nothing had been done since the 1947 proposal to modernize it with a two-and-a-half story addition at the rear.

"Save the Court House!" became a popular rallying cry. John Noble's citizens committee called it "a never to be replaced example of colonial

John W. Noble, left, with Willard G. Rouse, about 1950. Both men served as president of the Rotary Club of Easton and in other civic groups.

architecture," again ignoring the fact that it hadn't been built until nearly twenty years after Maryland ceased to be a colony. (Many were not even aware that the structure under discussion was not the 1712 Court House but the 1794 one.) The big rear addition would leave it a "mere shell," a desecration sacrificing its historical value on the altar of expediency, it was charged. It should be restored to its "original colonial appearance," and office space for county business provided elsewhere. "Millions have been spent at Williamsburg to build replicas of colonial buildings; in Easton Court House we have an original. Let's think long and hard before we destroy this outstanding symbol of our heritage," the *Star-Democrat* said.

In the wake of these protests the rear wing idea was scrapped, and the Boston architectural firm of Perry, Shaw, Hepburn & Dean was employed by the county commissioners to develop a new design. Described as "the nation's foremost authority on colonial design," they had done the restoration of Old Wye Church and a great deal of work at Williamsburg.

In May, 1956, they came up with what they called an "entirely new approach." The original structure would be preserved and restored, and wings built on either side. Both wings would be connected to the central building by two-story hallways. Architect Andrew Hepburn said this plan would keep the original building dominant, and would be "the best possible design from the standpoint of beauty, efficiency, and economy."

Again there was a howl of protest from the "save the Court House" group. Hepburn's plan would result in "loss of the parklike setting, the appeal of the uncrowded, lovely grass and trees," they said. It would increase the pressure on already inadequate downtown parking spaces. It was incompatible with "the colonial Easton concept." A better idea would be to build an underground vault for record storage and move all county offices except the library to the area of the Hanson Street school.

Although this protest was joined by thirteen major civic groups, including the newly formed Historical Society of Talbot County, of which Dr. Forman was curator, the county commissioners ignored it. On June 19, 1956, they voted unanimously to proceed with construction of the detached north and south wings. The present Court House complex was completed within the next few years.

Almost everything which has happened to Talbot County since has grown out of these controversial developments of the 1950s.

The victory for planning and zoning convinced the affluent outsiders to remain in Talbot County, and encouraged many others to join them in acquiring summer estates or retirement homes. Soon Talbot was *the* place to live if you could afford it; the county was said to have more millionaires per capita than any other county in America. One wealthy television personality who moved here recalled that when he asked a real estate broker about locations on the eastern seaboard, he was told there were only two he should consider—Nova Scotia and Talbot County, Maryland.

Adequate zoning in turn enabled the county to maintain the policy of "controlled growth" which has marked the three decades since the opening of the Bay Bridge. Rural areas were kept rural, urban sprawl was held to a minimum, and existing towns were promoted as centers of population, services, and employment. Most waterfront land was zoned for two- to five-acre developments, which encouraged "quality" construction and "quality" (which meant affluent) newcomers, and by no coincidence drove real estate prices extremely high. The planners aimed at population growth of ten percent every ten years. How well they succeeded is shown by census figures: in the thirty years between 1950 and 1980, Talbot population increased by exactly 30.1 percent, from 19,428 to 25,604. That is remarkable in a time when a megapolis is engulfing the northern East Coast from Boston to Washington, D. C.

Downtown Easton, Washington Street, 1983.

The presence of affluent retirees meant that there was big money to be tapped for worthy causes, and Talbot organizations soon discovered how it was done.

Memorial Hospital's volunteer leaders went after $750,000 in public contributions to enlarge the hospital in 1951—and got $1.1 million. They asked for a little more than $2.3 million in 1964—and raised $2.6 million, two thirds of it from about a hundred wealthy donors. Finally in 1978-81 a fund drive brought in the unprecedented total of nearly $4 million, although by that time hospital costs were so astronomical that most of the improvements had to be financed by an $11 million bond issue.

In 1954 the reunited Methodists raised $700,000 to build the new St. Mark's United Methodist Church, replacing three separate downtown churches in which Methodists had worshiped in stubborn disunion for nearly a hundred years. In 1963 more than $1 million was raised to build the magnificent Oxford Road YMCA, which despite its traditional name (Young Men's Christian Association) provides recreational and educational opportunities for both males and females and is open to all races and creeds. And so it went—almost any worthwhile charitable organization could find the wherewithal to support its aims. Many combined their efforts in the Talbot United Fund, established in 1955-56. And much of the money by necessity came from the same "Yankee invaders" who had been so resented and rebuffed in earlier years.

William H. Corkran, Jr.

Downtown Easton's artificial colonialism gradually evolved into an eclectic blend of architectural styles—neocolonial, federal period, early and late Victorian—which represent the town as it really was, and which give it a grace and charm almost unique among American communities. Historic Easton, Inc., was launched in 1972 in a successful effort to preserve three of four late Victorian houses on North Washington Street scheduled for demolition by town authorities. Later the organization was instrumental in establishing historic zoning for the original area of Easton.

Guardian for almost forty years of the "wall of quality" on which modern Easton prides itself was William H. Corkran, Jr., longtime town engineer and director of public utilities. Corkran's fierce protectiveness toward his native town and his no-holds-barred tactics in fighting for what he considered its best interests earned him such epithets as "Mother Easton" and "the Eastern Shore Grizzly Bear." More than any other person, he was responsible for the town's clean and treelined streets, excellent public utilities, off-street parking, lack of neon signs and garish storefronts, efficient trash disposal, and long-range development plans. He was the man to see in Easton if you wanted something done. If he liked your idea, you were in; if not, you faced a long, hard road. Even the

Mrs. W. Alton Jones with Easton Mayor Sherwood M. Hubbard at the dedication of the Social Center for St. Mark's Ministry to the Aged, April, 1975.

fact that Easton still classes itself as a town and not as a city stems from a Bill Corkran preference. To him the word city smacked of dirt, slums, factories, and daily traffic jams, and so he simply blocked the required change in the town's charter.

If Corkran was the area's grizzly bear, its benevolent great aunt was Mrs. W. Alton (Nettie Marie) Jones. She and her husband, who was president of Cities Service with head offices in New York City, made Cedar Point Farm in Talbot their home base beginning in 1942. Through the W. Alton Jones Foundation, which now has assets of more than $66 million, Mrs. Jones aided a long list of Talbot County causes and individuals. Just a few of her major contributions were to the YMCA, Memorial Hospital, Hog Neck golf course and ice skating arena, the Chesapeake Rehabilitation Center, St. Mark's Village, the Talbot County Historical Society, Third Haven Heights housing development for blacks, the Chesapeake Bay Maritime Museum, and the Talbot Agricultural Center. In addition she gave scholarship aid to scores of needy young people. Nearly always her gifts were in the form of challenge grants; an intensely hard worker herself, she refused to help people or groups that wouldn't help themselves.

Mrs. Anne N. B. Lockhart with Donald S. Ross, center, and William Ditman at booth she was supervising for a Talbot County Chamber of Commerce Flower Mart.

After her husband's death in a plane crash in 1962, Mrs. Jones made her home in Talbot for a dozen more years before moving to Charlottesville, Virginia, in 1974.

Associated with Mrs. Jones in many of these projects was Anne N. B. Lockhart. A Philadelphia native with Eastern Shore roots, Mrs. Lockhart was a Talbot business and civic leader for forty-two years until her death in 1980. As Talbot's first licensed woman realtor, she specialized in projects designed to preserve the county's architectural heritage and to enhance its attractiveness. She was responsible for development of Clifton, a suburb east of Route 50, and Clifton Industrial Park; for rehabilitation of the Stewart Building and the old Hanson Street *Star-Democrat* building (now One Mill Place); for the Villa subdivision; for Court House Alley, and other developments. She played key roles in the Talbot County Red Cross, Humane Society, Chamber of Commerce, and Historic Easton. When Historic Easton was turned down by the Town Council in its 1972 bid to save the so-called Langsdale houses, she filed as a last minute candidate for Council president—and won, first woman ever on the Council and first to head it. She served four years.

The controversial Langsdale houses on North Washington Street about 1970. After a bitter struggle, three were preserved, although two had to be moved to a new location.

In such a congenial atmosphere, cultural and recreational organizations flourished in Talbot.

The Historical Society of Talbot County, founded in 1954, soon afterward bought for its headquarters, with aid from Mrs. Jones, the three-story brick town house on South Washington Street built about 1810 by James Neall and most recently occupied by Dr. James E. Stevens. Today it is the largest county historical society in Maryland, with 1,300 members, more than $1 million in assets, and five historic properties between Washington and West streets. A corps of one hundred twenty-five volunteers, called docents, serve as guides, staff the museum and gift shop, do historical research, and organize educational projects.

Marching soldiers in colonial uniforms provide a fitting foreground for the Museum and early Federal period townhouse of the Historical Society of Talbot County on South Washington Street, Easton. The occasion was the 1982 Delmarva Chicken Festival parade.

The Chesapeake Bay Maritime Museum in St. Michaels, established in 1963 as an adjunct of the Historical Society of Talbot County, became independent in 1968. It acquired its most spectacular showpiece, the century old Hooper's Strait lighthouse, in 1966. Under the leadership of R. J. (Jim) Holt, who became director in 1971, it has blossomed into one of the Eastern Shore's outstanding tourist attractions, with 3,700 memberships from all parts of the bay area, and 100,000 visitors a year to its eighteen museum and exhibit buildings.

Easton's Academy of the Arts, housed in what was once the home of the Easton Academy at Harrison and South streets, grew out of the

Dedication day for the Chesapeake Bay Maritime Museum at St. Michaels, May 22, 1965. Speaking is Jeremiah Valliant of Oxford.

enthusiasm of internationally famous sculptor Lee Lawrie, who lived for many years near Longwoods. Founded in 1958 with about twenty members, it now has a membership of thirteen hundred. Its programs encompass the entire field of dramatic and graphic arts—theater, the dance, music, creative writing, photography, painting and drawing, and sculpture—and it provides both exhibits and instruction classes. Its permanent art collection is outstanding.

Not all Talbot ventures have had such smooth sailing. The Easton Airport, a joint project of the town and county, never has been able to sustain the scheduled passenger service its backers hoped for. Between 1946 and 1956 Chesapeake Airways, All American, and Allegheny Airlines all tried unsuccessfully to generate enough traffic to make daily service to Washington and New York a paying proposition. After that the airport was managed capably for many years by William S. D. Newnam, a World War II marine combat pilot who also operated a

Easton's Academy of the Arts. Bust in the courtyard at right is of sculptor Lee Lawrie who was among the founders of the Academy in 1958.

charter firm, Maryland Airlines; but in 1983 a squabble over Newnam's dual role left his future—and that of the airport—clouded.

Agriculture, still important to the county's economy but no longer dominant, developed along predictable national lines. Dairy farming, truck farming, and poultry raising gave way to corn and soybeans, with wheat running a poor third. Power machinery, chemical crop treatment, close-row corn planting, and other innovations brought skyrocketing yields, until huge grain surpluses eventually forced a government-sponsored reduction in planted acreage. High costs forced more and more farm consolidation; today's Talbot farmer is more likely to farm 1,600 acres than the traditional 160, and to have an investment of several hundred thousand dollars in land and equipment, far more than the average small businessman.

But Talbot has clung stubbornly to the farm family concept even as it lost the family farm. Sons with University of Maryland agriculture degrees still follow their self-taught fathers into farming; daughters consider the best possible life is to be a farmer's wife, as their mothers have been.

Lee Lawrie in his studio at Longwoods. This architectural sculpture for the United States Military Academy at West Point was the last work completed by the internationally known artist.

Talbot County started bravely—and early—on the rocky road to school desegregation following the Supreme Court's 1954 and 1955 decisions which declared racial segregation unconstitutional and called on local school boards to end it "with all deliberate speed."

The first three grades at the Hanson Street primary school in Easton and the Oxford primary school were integrated in September, 1956, on a selective basis, with eight carefully screened black pupils admitted. There were protests and some demonstrations by disgruntled whites, but no major incidents. However, the process bogged down in Talbot, and it was not until 1966 that complete desegregation of the county's

Easton Airport and Industrial Park, 1983.

schools was accomplished. Desegregation of most hotels, stores, restaurants, and other public accommodations was achieved without incident in 1963 at the peak of the bloody rioting which put neighboring Cambridge in the national spotlight.

Again and again in the 1970s national attention was focused on Talbot, not always with complimentary results. Oxford drew both raised eyebrows and applause in 1972 when it rejected a proposed development which would have converted nearby Bachelor's Point into a planned community at an eventual cost of $30 million, and brought hundreds of new residents to swell the town's population of 750. To many the rejection appeared to be refusal to accept progress, but to the townspeople their reasoning was simple. "Oxford wouldn't be Oxford anymore," explained one resident.

A similar issue was raised in 1973 when James Rouse, by this time the famed developer of the planned city of Columbia, Maryland, and numerous other similar projects, proposed a model community on Wye Island, just north of Talbot in Queen Anne's County. Talbot Countians, though not directly involved, watched the ensuing struggle between

Air Show that drew a crowd of five thousand to Easton Airport in 1947

Rouse and those who opposed any kind of development with extreme interest. Eventually Rouse withdrew in the face of long and vociferous local opposition, although he still thinks he could have won if he had persisted. And many Talbot Countians are still wondering whether a planned community on its northern border containing 2,750 people, nearly all of them affluent, with careful attention to environmental protection, would not have been good for Talbot's future.

The nation's media descended in droves on Easton to cover the first post-Watergate congressional election in the country when incumbent Republican Robert E. Bauman was supposed to lose to Democrat Frederick Malkus, thereby signaling the American people's political reaction against President Nixon. Ace reporters from the TV networks, national newspapers and magazines, and even the British Broadcasting Corporation, sipped free drinks in the Tidewater Inn's Crystal Room as they waited for the news that would give them top billing on The Today Show, Good Morning America, or in the *New York Times* and the *Washington Post*. They waited in vain; Bauman won, and there wasn't any story.

Corn being harvested with a self-propelled combine, a machine that reflects the high financial investment required for production in agriculture in the 1980s.

The media was back again in the fall of 1975 for what became known as "the Great Goose Hunt Scandal," in which aircraft manufacturers were alleged to have entertained top Pentagon officials with booze, sumptuous food, and women during goose-shooting weekends at Talbot County hideouts in order to influence billions of dollars in defense contracts. Television crews dashed around getting pictures of geese in flight and seeking quaint watermen to interview. Again the story fizzled; the hideouts turned out to be places like the Tidewater Inn, where many of the guests had stayed during the weekends, and prominent estates in Talbot. No charges resulted from the investigation.

Easton's annual November Waterfowl Festival was launched in 1971 by Dr. Harry Walsh. As a market gunner in the Eastern Shore marshes, Dr. Walsh had helped pay for his own education and had, over the years, acquired an outstanding collection of memorabilia from waterfowl gunning's more prolific days. In his efforts to establish a festival he was aided by Bill Perry, Maryland Natural Resources official and outdoors editor of the *Star-Democrat*, and by scores of enthusiastic volunteers. At first conceived as a means of raising money for Ducks Unlimited, the Waterfowl Festival developed into a nationally acclaimed celebration which supports numerous environmental projects and attracts nearly twenty thousand visitors to Easton each autumn. It remains, as it has been from the beginning, a nonprofit operation conceived and managed entirely by local volunteers.

Canada Geese on a Talbot County farm are symbols of Easton's annual Waterfowl Festival, started in 1971.

Finally, Talbot gained attention as the setting for James A. Michener's best-selling historical novel, *Chesapeake*, published in 1978. Although by no means altogether true to the area's history—Michener himself was the first to point out that it was a work of fiction, not of fact—the book gave more than a million readers their first taste of the rich panorama of life through four centuries in the county he called "Choptank." One result: in the midst of his year-long stay while researching and writing *Chesapeake*, Michener and his wife Mari became so enamored of the region that they bought a five-acre estate on Broad Creek south of St. Michaels and became part-time Talbot residents.

Totting up its assets and liabilities from the vantage point of 1983, Talbot County has good reason to be proud of its achievements. It has advanced remarkably from the basically poor and rural county of the 1930s, but without destroying the best of its historical and cultural

Top, Memorial Hospital at Easton in 1983 when a $13.5 million expansion and modernization project was undertaken. *Bottom,* the Talbot County YMCA on Oxford Road at Easton, 1983.

heritage. In many ways it is as good a place to live as exists in modern America.

Among its tangible assets:

—An excellent modern hospital and a skilled, well-qualified medical corps, including numerous specialists.

—A better than average public school system and two good private schools—the Country Day School, which goes through the eighth grade, and SS. Peter and Paul Roman Catholic School, which offers all twelve grades—plus a nearby public junior college.

—Cultural organizations, such as the Academy of the Arts, the Historical Society, and the Maritime Museum, which are unusually strong for a community of twenty-five thousand people.

Top, new satellite generating plant of the Easton Utilities Commission, 1979. *Bottom*, ice skating at Hog Neck Arena, 1980.

—A fine public library, housed in a $2 million building dedicated in 1976 and designed for expansion to meet the county's needs well into the twenty-first century. The Eastern Shore's best collection of historical and genealogical materials is contained in its Maryland Room.

—Two modern shopping centers within half an hour's drive of almost any part of the county, and a revitalized, attractive downtown Easton shopping area.

—A complete absence of traffic jams and daily commuter problems. (In Talbot a traffic jam is defined as any time more than three cars are waiting for the light to change at Route 33 and the Easton bypass.)

—A modern highway system offering easy access to the most remote parts of the county.

—A sound if very conservative county government, based on the council and manager system, which was adopted in the early 1970s to replace the ancient county commissioner system.

—The Eastern Shore's finest hotel and several good modern motels.

—Good restaurants, three good movie houses, a few live entertainment centers, and even a summer dinner-theater.

—Outstanding public recreational centers (though few public parks) in the Hog Neck golf course and arena and the Talbot YMCA.

—A unique combination of land and water—more than 600 miles of tidal shoreline, said to be the most in any United States county, to only 279 square miles of land. Among other things this produces excellent waterfowl gunning, especially for Canada geese, superb sailing, water-skiing, and crabbing, good fishing, and access to fresh locally caught seafood.

—Fine fire fighting, rescue, and ambulance facilities provided without direct cost to the taxpayer by seven volunteer fire companies in towns and villages throughout the county. The Easton Volunteer Fire Company, dating from 1808, is the oldest and largest of these. Others are in Oxford, Trappe, St. Michaels, Cordova, Tilghman, and Queen Anne.

—Generally good police protection by the Maryland State Police, with barracks on Route 50, the Talbot County sheriff's department, and police forces of modest size in Easton, St. Michaels, Trappe, and Oxford.

—A number of job-generating light industries, exemplified by the Black & Decker plant, Waverly Press, and small plants which have filled two industrial parks and are rapidly expanding in the Airport Industrial Park northwest of Easton.

—A population which combines a healthy mix of affluent newcomers and old-time Eastern Shore elements.

But there are also drawbacks, some of them serious ones to which Talbot County should be paying more attention. An informal survey by this writer drew these comments:

—"Ordinary people can't afford to live in Talbot County; it's snobbish and exclusive."

—"If it's going to develop as a retirement community (Talbot now has more retirees per capita than any other Maryland county), that's fine for those who are wealthy enough to retire here. But who are going to be

Talbot County's present claim to national baseball fame, Harold Baines of the Chicago White Sox. Among the Sox's top 1983 batters, Baines was first seen by owner Bill Veeck in the St. Michaels Little League at age twelve. "Remarkable person, remarkable player," said Veeck, then a Talbot County resident.

the janitors, the laborers, the store clerks, the volunteer firemen? Rich retirees won't fill those jobs."

—"There aren't enough job opportunities for young people." (This from a fairly recent Easton High School graduate.) "Most of the people in my graduating class went away to work, and I haven't seen them since. The opportunities are in the cities, not here. Everybody can't go into the real estate business, and what else is there?"

—From a black community leader: "Opportunities for minorities are almost nonexistent. If you think it's tough being young and white and ambitious, try being young and black and wanting to get somewhere.

The Oxford-Bellevue Ferry, winter, 1978.

Talbot is still living in the early part of the century with its race relations. The dominant attitude is paternalistic, and not unkind. But anything approaching real equality is a long way off."

—"The County Council has been a bunch of stick-in-the-muds. Their idea of good government is to do as little as possible. They're not interested in tackling this area's real problems—and if they were, the taxpayers wouldn't support them. Maybe the new council members will do better. I hope so."

—"There's no place to live if you're of low or moderate income. Housing is just too terribly expensive. Many people I know have to live in Caroline or other neighboring counties and commute to work in Talbot. They can't afford to rent or buy in Talbot County."

Those are the criticisms: snobbishness, too much a retirement community, too few job opportunities, especially for blacks, too high a cost of living, too little government involvement in community problems.

Are they valid? And are they dangerous to Talbot's future well being?

Time will tell.

347

Notes on Sources

FOOTNOTES are useful to scholars, but anathema to many readers. Therefore, because this book is designed for general readership rather than scholarly study, they have been omitted here. Instead we offer guides to further reading in two categories—an annotated bibliography, covering works of broad range which are cited repeatedly throughout this history, and chapter by chapter references indicating the sources considered most reliable for particular accounts of people and events.

ANNOTATED BIBLIOGRAPHY

Andrews, Matthew Page. *History of Maryland: Province and State.* Garden City, N. Y.: Doubleday, Doran, 1929.
   A concise modern history useful in providing background on Maryland events which influenced Talbot County. Hereafter cited as *Andrews*.

Archives of Maryland. 72 vols. to date. Baltimore: Maryland Historical Society, 1883—.
   A lifetime of reading won't exhaust all the material in this vast collection containing official Maryland records from the earliest colonial times through the Revolution. Hereafter cited as *Archives*.

Buse, Elliott. *150 Years of Banking on the Eastern Shore.* Easton: no pub., 1955.
   Much broader in scope than its title suggests. Basically a history of the bank, founded in 1805, which became the Easton National Bank, but contains excellent detail on Talbot County's economic life and the rise of Easton. Hereafter cited as *Buse*.

Clark, Charles B., ed. *The Eastern Shore of Maryland and Virginia.* 3 vols. New York: Lewis Publishing Co., 1950.
   The format of having each chapter by a different author makes the quality of this work uneven, but it is a good general guide to Eastern Shore history. Of special interest is the chapter on Talbot County by Homer Bast (2:943-90). Hereafter cited as *Clark*.

Emory, Frederick. *Queen Anne's County, Maryland.* Baltimore: Maryland Historical Society, 1950. (Originally published in *Centreville Observer*, 1886-87.)

This scholarly history of a county which was part of Talbot until 1707 contains much of interest, both for the early period and later. Hereafter cited as *Emory*.

Footner, Hulbert. *Rivers of the Eastern Shore: Seventeen Maryland Rivers*. New York: Farrar & Rinehart, 1944. Reprint ed. Cambridge, Md.: Tidewater Publishers, 1964.

Highly readable account of Eastern Shore history, with chapters on the Choptank, Tred Avon, Miles, and Wye rivers, Oxford, St. Michaels, and the Lloyds of Wye, along with much else of interest to Talbot readers. Hereafter cited as *Footner*.

Ingraham, Prentiss. *Land of Legendary Lore*. Easton: no pub., 1898. Reprint ed. Easton: no pub., 1979.

Fascinating blend of fact and legend, although the distinction between the two is not always made clear. Hereafter cited as *Ingraham*.

Maryland Historical Magazine. 78 vols. to date. Baltimore: Maryland Historical Society, 1901—.

Rich source of historical, anecdotal, and genealogical material on Talbot County and Talbot Countians. Individual articles are cited by volume and year of publication.

Scharf, J. Thomas. *History of Maryland from the Earliest Period to the Present Day*. 3 vols. Baltimore: no pub., 1879. Facsimile edition. Hatboro, Pa.: Tradition Press, 1967.

Scharf's access to original source material and great attention to detail make this by far the most valuable study of early Maryland history, although his pro-South bias mars his treatment of the Civil War era. Hereafter cited as *Scharf*.

Talbot County Records: Land Records, Wills, Accounts, Inventories, etc. Easton: Talbot County Court House, 1661—. (Also available at Maryland Hall of Records, Annapolis.)

An inexhaustible source of data on Talbot County and Talbot Countians from earliest times to the present. Hereafter cited by individual categories, as *Talbot Land Records*, etc.

Tilghman, Oswald, comp. *History of Talbot County Maryland 1661-1861*. 2 vols. Baltimore: Williams & Wilkins, 1915. Reprint ed. Baltimore: Regional Publishing Co., 1967.

Not written by Oswald Tilghman (see Preface), and not really a history, but a collection of essays chiefly by Dr. Samuel A. Harrison. Nevertheless, the one indispensable work for any detailed study of Talbot history. Hereafter, for want of a better identification, cited as *Tilghman*.

NOTES BY CHAPTERS

One: *A Shore Dimly Seen*

Captain John Smith's own account of his 1608 explorations of the upper Chesapeake first appeared in *The General Historie of Virginia, New England, and the Summer Isles* (1624), volume 1, chapter 5, under the title of "The Accidents that Happened in the Discovery of the Bay of Chisapeake." The text is reprinted in full in *Scharf* 1:6-10. An excellent modern account is in *The Three Worlds of Captain John Smith* (1964), by Philip L. Barbour.

For a discussion of earlier bay explorations see chapter 1 of *Clark* 1, by Robert L. Swain, Jr.

William Claiborne's Kent Island settlement and his struggles with the Calverts are superbly chronicled in *Virginia Venturer* (1951), by Nathaniel Claiborne Hale. Readers are warned against relying on earlier Claiborne biographies, which misidentified Claiborne and misinterpreted his early life, or on early Maryland historians, whose pro-Calvert bias led them to dismiss Claiborne as a scoundrel and his thriving colony as a mere trading post.

Even Hale, however, has little to say about "Popeley's Island." For that important precursor to Talbot history it is necessary to dig deeply into Claiborne's own records and accounts. For easy reference, Daniel Cugley is mentioned as hog keeper in 1632 in *Maryland Historical Magazine* 28:35 (1933), and the 1634 planters on the island in 27:106 (1932). Identification of 1637 as the year in which Richard Thompson's family was massacred by Indians appears in Liber F, Maryland Land Office Records, under date of September 7, 1640.

Thomas Hawkins's will and inventory are taken from *Archives* 54:99-102.

The descriptive material on Talbot County as the first settlers found it has been pieced together from many sources. The letters of Henry Callister, eighteenth century Oxford merchant, are a treasurehouse of information on early Talbot. Four unpublished volumes of his letters have been preserved at the Episcopal Diocesan Library in Baltimore, and a complete set in photostat is available in the Maryland Room of the Talbot County Free Library. A study of Atlantic coast hurricanes between 1492 and 1870 by David M. Ludlum is also in the Maryland Room. The Dutch missionaries who marveled at the ducks and geese, Jaspar Dankers and Peter Sluyter, are quoted in *Scharf* 2:3-4. The story of the bear hunt is from "Narrative of a Voyage to Maryland, 1705-1706," by an unknown author, which lay undiscovered in the British Museum for two centuries before it was found and published in the *American Historical Review* in 1907. Also from this source is the tale of the "rattlesnake supper" at York Court House, recounted in Chapter three. The story of the woolly mammoth comes from James Cope of Easton, whose collateral ancestor was the Philadelphia professor who identified the remains.

The one statement in this chapter that seems most likely to be challenged is my assertion that there were no settled Indian villages in present-day Talbot when the English arrived. But I challenge the challengers to produce any evidence of such a village; there were Indian towns both to the north and south, but there is no record of one in this county.

Two: *First Settlers*

The story of Captain William Mitchell, mainland Talbot's scandalous first landowner, is spelled out in unsavory detail in *Archives* 2 and 10. For some details, however, I am indebted to the late James C. Mullikin, Talbot-born newspaperman and historian, who was working on a history of Talbot County at the time of his death in 1964. Mullikin's papers are on deposit in the Maryland Room. He in turn was relying heavily on the unpublished notes and annals of Dr. Harrison at the Maryland Historical Society. I cheerfully confess to having cribbed freely from both. Mullikin is also the source of most of the material on land surveys in Talbot by year and location.

Complete records of what little is known about the formation of Talbot County, and minutes of the county court from 1661/62 to 1674 have been published in *Archives* 54:353-609.

Information on the Talbot Quakers comes principally from minutes of their meetings, which are extant beginning in 1676, and their records of births, deaths, and marriages, which date from 1664. The story of Wenlock Christison is adapted from Dr. Harrison's biographical essay in *Tilghman* 1:103-32. Quotations from George Fox are from *The Journal of George Fox* (1952), edited by John Nickalls.

Dr. Harrison is responsible for most of the biographical material on Edward Lloyd I (*Tilghman* 1:132-46) and Alexander D'Hinojosa (*Tilghman* 1:521-31).

Three: *Building a County*

The tragic story of the Eastern Shore Indians and what became of them is worth a volume in itself. They were among the first Indians in North America to be systematically exterminated or reduced to vassalage. But no historian has ever set out to put it together from the Indians' point of view. Only a few have done much at all in this area. William B. Marye was first to suggest that the Indians identified by Captain John Smith as the Ozinies were really the fierce Wicomesses, and to track some of their subsequent wanderings on the Eastern Shore until they were exterminated in a genocidal war. The chapter by C. A. Weslager in *Clark* (1:39-72) is useful; and the departure of the Matapeakes is described in *Scharf* 1:137-38. Much additional Indian history can be found in *Scharf*, although it is not organized as such; but for most of the story, the student must work systematically through early volumes of the *Archives*.

The account of Talbot's first court house at York comes principally from Dr. Harrison's essay in *Tilghman* (2:200-45) and from Mullikin's booklet, *Ghost Towns of Talbot County*. *Archives* 8:13, and several other sources, including my own *Wye Oak: The History of a Great Tree*, supplied information on the celebrated drinking bout at York. Details of the arrest and trial of Poh Poh Caquis are found in *Archives* 17:176-79, 186-87, 193-95, and 224-30. They are repeated with some errors in *Tilghman* 2:35-39.

Dr. Harrison's essay on "The Town and Port of Oxford," first published in 1882 and republished in *Tilghman* 2:332-74, Jane Foster Tucker's *A Port of Entry: Oxford Maryland* (1968), and various volumes of the *Archives* all were consulted in reconstructing Oxford's early history. The story of Doncaster or Wye Town is chiefly from Mullikin's *Ghost Towns*. The complicated political maneuvering in which the court house was moved from York to Oxford and finally to "Armstrong's Old Field" (the site of Easton) is partially covered by Dr. Harrison's 1878 essay (*Tilghman* 2:218-28), but for the full story *Archives* 27, covering proceedings of the General Assembly from 1707 to 1710, was consulted.

Four: *King Tobacco*

Much has been written about the tobacco era in Maryland. Good sources for further reading include Arthur Pierce Middleton's *Tobacco Coast* (1953); Aubrey C. Land's *Colonial Maryland: A History* (1981); Raphael Semmes's *Captains and Mariners of Early Maryland* (1937) and *Crime and Punishment in Early Maryland* (1938); *Scharf* 2:1-103; Matthew Page Andrews's *History of Maryland: Province and State* (1929) and *The Founding of Maryland* (1933); and numerous volumes of the *Archives*. The quotation from King James I on the evils of tobacco first appeared in *Counterblast to Tobacco*, published anonymously in 1604. That from George Alsop on tobacco culture was in his 1666 booklet, "A Character of the Province of Maryland." The survey demonstrating the extent to which seventeenth century Talbot County servants were whites is based on my own study of early inventories. Data on the materials alloted to freed servants is from the *Archives* and Thomas Bacon's *Laws of Maryland* (1765), a handsome copy of which is available in the Talbot Library's Maryland Room. A modern edition of Ebenezer Cooke's *The Sot-Weed Factor* is also available at the Library, as is Barth's novel.

For background on the Church of England in Talbot, see *The First Parishes of the Province of Maryland* (1923), by Percy G. Skirven; *Maryland's Established Church* (1953), by Nelson Waite Rightmyer; *Contributions to the Ecclesiastical History of the United States*, 2, *Maryland* (1839), by Francis L. Hawks, D.D.; and parish records in the Maryland Room. Governor Nicholson's reference to James Clayland as "scandalous and unqualified" appears in *Archives* 25:580, and his questioning of the credentials of both Clayland and Leech in *Archives* 20:141 and 149-50. Material on John Lillingston, abstracted from the *Archives*, is summed up in *Emory* 154-56.

Details on Philemon Lloyd's storekeeping activities were gleaned from *Talbot County Inventories* 1:322 ff., and on the personal wardrobe of Henrietta Maria Lloyd from *Inventories* 1:389 ff.

Statistics demonstrating Talbot County's high place in Maryland's economy at the turn of the eighteenth century have been put together from several sources. Details of censuses taken in 1701, 1704, 1710, and 1712 appear in *Archives* 25:255-59. Although not altogether reliable, these show clearly that the balance between the eastern and western halves of the colony was about even, and that the Eastern Shore, led by Somerset and Talbot counties, had more whites and fewer slaves. The information on shipbuilding comes from a report requested by the Council of Maryland in May, 1697, and published in *Archives* 25:595-601.

More has been written about Henrietta Maria Lloyd than about any other Talbot woman. It was Hulbert Footner who first called her (at least in print) "the great ancestress of the Eastern Shore." See *Footner* 273-75. Dr. Harrison

NOTES ON SOURCES

provided biographical details in his essay on her second husband, Philemon Lloyd (*Tilghman* 1:147-50), including the quote from an unidentified source about her support of American Catholicism. The story of her celebrated ring appears on page 181 of *The Hollyday and Related Families of the Eastern Shore of Maryland* (1962), by James Bordley, Jr. Bordley also lists many of her descendants, although in a sometimes confusing fashion, and gives details of her family background. It should be noted that the assertion that her mother, Ann Neale, had been lady-in-waiting to the queen is based on questionable family tradition rather than known fact. But the ring itself is real, however it came into possession of Henrietta Maria Lloyd.

Five: *Golden Years*

Two excellent primary sources help give authenticity to this chapter—the salty observations of Jeremiah Banning (1733-1798), Oxford mariner whose adventurous life and comments on the Talbot scene are preserved in *The Log and Will of Jeremiah Banning*; and the letters of Henry Callister (see notes on Chapter One). The original of Banning's log and a facsimile edition published by a descendant are in the Maryland Room, and his life is admirably summed up in a booklet, *Jeremiah Banning: Mariner and Patriot* (1977), by Jane Foster Tucker. Regrettably, Callister's letters have never been published in full, although quotations from them are cited by almost every historian of Maryland or the Eastern Shore.

Details on the rise of Dover are taken largely from James C. Mullikin's *Ghost Towns of Talbot County*, although his interpretation of the struggle between Dover and Talbot Court House as merely an intracounty rivalry (see Chapter Seven) seems to me unrealistic. Mullikin's notes for an uncompleted history of Trappe District, on deposit in the Maryland Room, cite *Social Life in the Time of Queen Anne* (author unnamed) as the source for his statement that Talbot's Hole-in-the-Wall was named for a London tavern, said to have been "on Chandos Street, where Du Vall, a noted highwayman, was taken while drunk."

Details on Talbot Countians' reading habits, such as they were, are from *Clark* 1:349-60 and a 1940 article in *Maryland Historical Magazine*, "Books Owned by Marylanders 1700-1776," by Joseph Towne Wheeler (35:338-41). Dr. Harrison's account of early Talbot schooling, including the Talbot County Free School, appears in *Tilghman* 2:457-76. John Adams's low opinion of the Maryland aristocracy is quoted from *The Adams Papers*, 2:261. The lampooning of Edward Lloyd V as "Lord-Cock-de-Doodle-Do" appeared in a series of crude satirical articles in the *Herald and Eastern Shore Intelligencer* in August and September, 1802. Matthew Tilghman's letter on the Oxford races is quoted from *Tilghman* 1:430-31, and the details on the Lloyd stable's Nancy Bywell are from *Blooded Horses of Colonial Days* (1922), by Francis Barnum Cutler. The story of Mary Tayloe Lloyd's hair curlers comes from *Francis Scott Key* (1937), by Edward S. Delaplaine.

For a more complete account of the life of Richard Bennett III, early Maryland's almost forgotten "first tycoon," see my *Wye Oak: The History of a*

Great Tree (1972), 21-34. And for detailed biographies of all the Lloyds from Edward I to Edward VII, see Dr. Harrison's essays in *Tilghman* 1:132-228. The contrasting picture of how black slaves lived in colonial Talbot County is drawn from my *Young Frederick Douglass: The Maryland Years* (1980).

Mary Starin's 1980 monograph on the Reverend Dr. John Gordon; *Maryland's Established Church* (1956), by Nelson Waite Rightmyer; *Chronicles of Colonial Maryland* (1913), by James Walter Thomas; *Tilghman* 1:276-77; the correspondence of Governor Horatio Sharpe (*Archives* 9 and 14); a manuscript history of St. Peter's Parish, compiled about 1842 by an unknown author; and many other sources were consulted in putting together my brief account of the eighteenth century Church of England clergy in Talbot. For material on the Reverend Thomas Bacon, I relied chiefly on Dr. Harrison's essays (*Tilghman* 1:272-300 and 2:477-95), Henry Callister's letters, and Bacon's sermons as republished in an edited form by William Meade in *Sermons Addressed to Masters and Servants* (1813), and *Sermons, Dialogues, and Narratives for Servants* (1836). Ironically, the same sermons which were considered dangerously radical when Bacon delivered them in the 1740s were held up as models for the use of pro-slavery preachers a century later. Governor Sharpe's letter indicating that Bacon's famous charity school had only a brief existence appears in *Archives* 9:415.

My brief sketch of Robert Morris relies on Dr. Harrison (*Tilghman* 1:66-83). Good material on the English-French wars of the 1740s and 1750s is found in the chapter on "Intercolonial Wars" in *Clark* 1:369-84, augmented by numerous other sources.

Six: *The Revolution*

The basic material from which this chapter has been shaped comes from Dr. Harrison's lengthy chapter on "The Revolution in Talbot" (*Tilghman* 2:48-132), from *Scharf* 2, from the writings of Jeremiah Banning, and from chapters 17-19 of *Clark* 1. Some modern studies, such as *The Background of the Revolution in Maryland* (1940), by Charles Albro Barker, and *A Spirit of Dissension* (1973), by Ronald Hoffman, help fill out the picture. *Tench Tilghman: The Life and Times of Washington's Aide-de-Camp* (1982), by L. G. Shreve, is the definitive biography of that colorful Talbot-born figure. I wish there were as good a biography of his father-in-law, Matthew Tilghman, but despite his vital role in pre-Revolutionary Maryland affairs, Matthew lacked the flamboyance to inspire biographers.

For life on the home front, a superb source is in the letters of Henry Hollyday (1725-1789), who built Ratcliffe Manor and who sat out the Revolution as an unflinching British loyalist. More than one hundred of his letters, most of them written to his brother James, who lived at Readbourne in Queen Anne's County, have been preserved at the Maryland Historical Society, and typed transcripts are available at the Maryland Room of the Talbot Library. Some of the letters are quoted in *The Hollyday and Related Families on the Eastern Shore of Maryland* (1962), by James Bordley, Jr.

NOTES ON SOURCES

Seven: *The Rise of Easton*

From the time of the establishment of the *Maryland Herald and Eastern Shore Intelligencer* in 1790 and the *Republican Star* (with various subtitles) in 1799, Talbot County always has had one or more weekly or daily newspapers. From this point on, therefore, I have relied more heavily on contemporary newspapers in compiling this history than on any other single source. Most issues of most early Easton newspapers can be consulted at the Maryland Room, the Maryland Historical Society, the Enoch Pratt Free Library in Baltimore, or the Library of Congress.

The story of the legislative maneuvering by which the town of Easton was created, the threat of Dover disposed of, and the second Talbot County Court House financed and built is taken in large part from Dr. Harrison's essay on the Court House (*Tilghman* 2:200-45), his unpublished notes on the rise of Easton as abstracted by James Mullikin, and William Kiltie's *Laws of Maryland* (1800), in addition to a search of extant issues of the *Maryland Herald*. (Very useful digests of the Easton newspapers between 1790 and 1824 have been published in *Maryland Eastern Shore Newspaper Abstracts*, 4 vols. to date, by F. Edward Wright.)

Details of Charles Willson Peale's romantic interlude with Molly Tilghman are recounted briefly in *Footner* 294-95, and more fully in *Charles Willson Peale: A Biography* (1969), by Charles Coleman Sellers. The bit about the ghost comes from Tilghman family members. For more on Jacob Gibson see *Tilghman* 1:231-56 and 2:415-34. Dr. Harrison's essays on St. Michaels history (*Tilghman* 2:381-414) are the best source of information on that town up to 1883. His account of the battle of St. Michaels and related Talbot events, reproduced in *Tilghman* 2:148-77, was first published in the *Easton Ledger* in June and July, 1882.

I used a number of sources in reconstructing the rise of Methodism: *Tilghman* 2:297-310; a manuscript history of Methodism in Talbot (1876), by Robert W. Todd, on deposit at the Maryland Hall of Records, Annapolis; *Methodism of the Peninsula* (1886), by the same author; *The Garden of Methodism* (1948), by E. C. Hallman; Francis Asbury's journals; *The Shaping of Religion in America* (1980), by Norman Harrington; "St. Michaels Methodism," mss, (1894), by Thomas H. Sewell, on microfilm at the Hall of Records and the Talbot Maryland Room; and several others.

A good account of Thomas Kemp and his famous clipper, the *Chasseur*, appears in *The Fells Point Story* (1976), by Norman G. Rukert, and more on Purser Samuel Hambleton can be found in *Tilghman* 1:455-76. Much more detail on the founding of the bank in Easton, and on its early leaders, is presented in *Buse*.

Some readers may look askance at my statement that the Easton Hotel (now the Stewart Building) was built in 1815 rather than the generally accepted date of 1812. My dating is based on an exhaustive study of Talbot Land Records of the period, which shows conclusively that Samuel Groome did not even acquire the land on which to build the hotel until 1815, and did not complete it until later that year or perhaps not even until 1816.

Eight: *The Long Depression*

Evidence to support my characterization of this era as "the long depression" comes principally from *Buse* and the essays of Dr. Harrison, backed up by study of the Easton newspapers of the time. *Buse* is my authority for material on wheat prices, early steamboats, shinplasters, credit and barter, low land values, and the cost of food. Dr. Harrison's comment on "the long and weary years of agricultural depression" appears in his essay on Edward Lloyd VI (*Tilghman* 1:213), and his remarks on suffering in St. Michaels between 1820 and 1830 in his essay on St. Michaels history (*Tilghman* 2:375-414). My source for saying some St. Michaels-built ships went into the African slave trade is *The Search for Speed Under Sail* (1967), by Howard I. Chapelle, and my own study of Port of Baltimore custom house records at the National Archives. See also *Young Frederick Douglass* 145-47.

The story of the great 1840 Whig rally in Easton comes principally from *Ingraham* (235-36) and Emory (469). The bit about the Indian on Oxford Neck is from a memo in Dr. Harrison's unpublished papers.

I must take responsibility for blowing the whistle on the *Star-Democrat's* proud claim of being a direct descendant of the *Republican Star,* founded in 1799. This is embarrassing since I served as chief editor of the paper's "175th anniversary edition" in August, 1974; but I've since become convinced that the facts don't support the claim. Dr. Harrison didn't think so either; in an essay on Talbot newspaper history published in the *Easton Star* in 1870, he commented: "The present *Easton Star,* is by no means the successor of the *Republican Star,* except that it came after and is of the same political faith and similar name." The claim was made, and arguments given to substantiate it, by James C. Mullikin in *Story of the Easton Star-Democrat* (1949).

Ingraham 238, *Buse* 51-52, the *Encyclopaedia Britannica,* 20:665, and contemporary newspapers all provided information on the story of the great silk worm bubble in Talbot. *Buse* 75 is the source of the tale about the Poplar Island black cat fur farm. There are discussions of early efforts to build a railroad in *A Centennial History of the Pennsylvania Railroad* by George H. Burgess, (1949), 398-99, and *Buse* 50-51. A detailed description of the 1856 groundbreaking ceremony in Easton appears in *Tilghman* 1:632-33. An excellent summation of the related issue of Eastern Shore secession, by Mullikin, can be found in *Clark* 1:453-84.

For more on the sale of slaves from Talbot County to the Deep South, see *Young Frederick Douglass: The Maryland Years* (1980) 74-80; *Slave Trading in the Old South* (1931), by Frederic Bancroft; "Slave Trader in a Slave Economy: Austin Woolfolk, A Case Study," by William Calderhead, in *Civil War History Journal,* September, 1977; and *Talbot County Land Records,* where slave sales were recorded. All the names listed in my brief summary are taken from the Land Records on file in the Talbot County Court House. Scores of other sellers are also listed. Details on Edward Lloyd VI's transfer of slaves to cotton plantations are from Dr. Harrison's essay in *Tilghman* 1:210-21. Much more about Frederick Douglass and his youth in Talbot will be found in my *Young*

NOTES ON SOURCES

Frederick Douglass, as well as in his three autobiographies, of which the best for this purpose is *My Bondage and My Freedom* (1855).

For Trappe's emergence, see my *Trappe: The Story of an Old-Fashioned Town* (1976). The story of the Jamaica Point shipyard also appears there; the tale of the brig *Bloomfield* comes from a memoir of James Dixon (1810-1890) possessed by his descendants.

Nine: *The Civil War Era*

One of Dr. Harrison's major projects was the compilation of a detailed history of events of the Civil War era in Talbot County. It runs to more than a thousand pages of handwritten manuscript, but unfortunately it has never been published. In my reconstruction of the Civil War era, I have tried to present a balanced view by judicious use of items from Dr. Harrison's manuscript, which is among his papers at the Maryland Historical Society, while filling out the picture with other accounts of major events.

The story of Josiah Bailey, one of hundreds of slaves from Talbot and Dorchester counties who escaped north in the 1850s, is pieced together from *The Underground Rail Road* (1871, modern edition 1970), by William Still, and *Harriet Tubman, the Moses of Her People* (1886, reissue 1961), by Sarah H. Bradford. Still was secretary of the Vigilance Committee of the Pennsylvania Anti-Slavery Committee. The role of Frederick Douglass in the underground railroad is best described in his third autobiography, *Life and Times of Frederick Douglass* (1892, reissue 1962), 266-67. Details on Maryland's efforts at censorship appear more fully in my article, "Censorship, Maryland 'Justice' and Slavery," in the *Baltimore Sun* Sunday Magazine, November 6, 1977.

Election statistics on the balloting of February 4, 1861, are from Dr. Harrison's manuscript history. Results of other elections are quoted from *Clark* 1:541, 547, 550, and 553.

For the "battle of Cow Landing" and details of the arrest and banishment of *Easton Star* editor Thomas K. Robson, I relied chiefly on James C. Mullikin's *Story of the Star-Democrat*. My interpretation of the arrest and beating of Judge Carmichael comes from study of many sources, among them Dr. Harrison; *Scharf* 3:489-91; contemporary issues of the *Easton Star* and *Easton Gazette*; *Clark* 1:542; *Emory* 503-9; *Andrews* 359; and a two-part series in the *Queen Anne's Record-Observer* May 24-31, 1962. My own ambivalent impressions were summed up in an article, "Heroic Figure or Traitor?" in the *Baltimore Sun* Sunday Magazine June 10, 1973.

Tench Francis Tilghman's diary, with its revealing story of the last days of the dying Confederacy, is in large part unpublished. Some segments have been quoted in the *Florida Historical Quarterly* 17 (1938-39): 160-80, and in *Flight into Oblivion* (1938), by A. J. Hanna. The complete diary is in the Southern Historical Collection at the University of North Carolina, Chapel Hill, and typescripts are available at the Talbot County Historical Society and the Maryland Room. A history of Trappe's Company H, compiled by James C. Mullikin, was published in the *Easton Star-Democrat* April 10-May 22, 1959.

Most of my information on the wartime Talbot economy comes from *Buse* 88-98, while noneconomic items are from Dr. Harrison's manuscript. For more on the contribution of blacks to the Union victory, see *The Sable Arm: Negro Troops in the Union Army, 1861-1865* (1956), by Dudley Taylor Cornish, and the *Official Army Register of the Volunteer Forces of the Army for the Years 1861-1865*, part 8.

Ten: *The Age of Steam*

Details on the completion of the railroad to Easton and Oxford, and much else in this chapter, were taken directly from contemporary issues of the *Easton Gazette, Easton Star,* and *Easton Journal. Buse* 105-8 provided material on the railroad's effect on the economy; information on the rise of such small towns as Queen Anne, Cordova, and Royal Oak appeared in the anniversary edition of the *Easton Star-Democrat* (August 21, 1974). Readers of *Trappe: The Story of an Old-Fashioned Town* (1976) will recognize the summary of that community's golden age; in this case, as in many others, I've cribbed shamelessly even from myself. Much of the story of Oxford's comeback is from Dr. Harrison's essay (*Tilghman* 2:332-74) and Jane Foster Tucker's *A Port of Entry: Oxford, Maryland* (1968). Interesting plats of Claiborne, Bellevue, Trappe, and other towns as they appeared, or were envisioned, in the 1870s were published in an *Atlas of Talbot and Dorchester Counties* by Lake, Griffing, and Stevenson (1877) and republished in *The 1877 Atlases and Other Early Maps of the Eastern Shore of Maryland* (1976). An excellent series on the era of the summer boarders, by a group of local authors, was carried in the *Star-Democrat* in the autumn of 1982. For the delightful details on Tilghman Island life I am indebted to *The Tilghman's Island Story, 1659-1954*, by Raymond R. Sinclair.

My picture of black conditions in the postwar period comes from numerous sources. I found Lewis Douglass's revealing letter to his father in the Frederick Douglass Collection, Moorland-Spingarn Research Center, Howard University, Washington, D. C. Data on black pay scales is from account books of William A. Kirby, lent by a descendant. Details of the 1870 election campaign are directly from the newspapers quoted.

For a few of the many articles in national publications dealing with the postwar Eastern Shore, see Bayard Taylor in *Harper's New Monthly Magazine* (October, 1871); the Reverend Robert Wilson in *Lippincott's Magazine* (July, 1876); Albert Bushnell Hart in *The Nation* (April 23, 1891); and John Williamson Palmer in *Century Magazine* (December, 1894.)

A great deal—probably too much—has been written about the "Boss" Tweed episode, one of the sturdiest myths in Talbot history. Those who want to rehash it once again are referred to *Ingraham* 183-84, the *Baltimore Sun* for June 8, 1930, the *Easton Star-Democrat* for January 9, 1953, *Footner* 257-58, and my article, "If That Wasn't Boss Tweed at the Villa, Who Was It?" in the *Tidewater Times* of August, 1978.

For those who wish to know more about Talbot's nineteenth century governors, material on Edward Lloyd V appears in *Tilghman* 1:184-210 and in

NOTES ON SOURCES

Young Frederick Douglass: The Maryland Years 45-48. A sketch of the life of Samuel Stevens, Jr., is in *Tilghman* 1:622-25, and one on Daniel Martin in *Tilghman* 1:228-31. Brief biographies of all the governors are in *Governors of Maryland* (1908), by Heinrich E. Buchholz.

No one that I know of has put together a history of the Methodist Church South or the Methodist Protestant Church in Talbot. Both would be excellent subjects for a thesis. For the Methodist Episcopal Church itself, see my notes on Chapter Seven.

Much of my material on the steamboat age is from *Buse*; *Chesapeake Bay: A Pictorial Maritime History* (1953), by M. V. Brewington; *This Was Chesapeake Bay* (1963), by Robert H. Burgess; research in contemporary newspapers; and interviews with Talbot residents quoted in *Trappe: The Story of an Old-Fashioned Town*. Dr. Harrison's comments on the log canoe oyster fleet of the 1880s appear in *Tilghman* 2:393-94. My primary source for the vicious conditions on oyster dredge boats is the *First Biennial Report of the Bureau of Industrial Statistics and Information of Maryland* (1886), submitted by Thomas C. Weeks, chief of bureau, 65-72. See also *The Oyster Wars of Chesapeake Bay* (1981), by John R. Wennersten.

Far too many sources went into my study of post-Civil War Easton for listing here item by item. Among them were contemporary newspapers; *Buse*; notes made by James C. Mullikin for the history of Talbot County he never got to finish; Mullikin's *Story of the Easton Star-Democrat* (1949) and *History of the Easton Volunteer Fire Department* (1962); various articles on Easton hotel history; and Homer Bast's chapter on Talbot County in *Clark 2*.

Eleven: *The Gasoline Revolution*

In this chapter I relied mainly on contemporary newspapers, recollections of residents, *Buse* 128-51, James Mullikin's two books cited above, and Bast's chapter in *Clark 2*. Martin M. Higgins' book about his role, *The Reincarnation of Easton*, proved disappointing. Much of my information on the Easton Furniture Manufacturing Company came from incorporation papers on file at the Court House, personal recollections of William P. Kemp, who moved the firm to North Carolina in 1931, and John W. Noble, who was active in the attempt to revive it in the 1930s.

My interpretation of race relations in the pre-World War II era is based on talks with many older residents, black and white, extensive reading in Easton newspapers, population statistics, and a study of Eastern Shore life and characteristics in the 1930s by Frank Goodwin, which was published as a doctoral dissertation in 1944 by the University of Pennsylvania under the title of *A Study of Personal and Social Organization: An Exploratory Survey of the Eastern Shore of Maryland*. Dr. Goodwin's main theme was not black-white relations, but his discussion of the subject, on pages 45-53, is especially revealing with its quotations from whites that there was "no race problem" in a decade when savage lynchings occurred on the Eastern Shore.

Much more detail on the origin and history of the hospital at Easton is available in my *75 Years of Caring: A History of the Memorial Hospital at Easton, Md.* (1982). More on the Floating Theatre can be found in my book on Trappe, among other sources. An account of William Jennings Bryan's visit to Easton appeared in the *Star-Democrat* September 6, 1913, while my information on "Buck" Bryan is from the recollections of friends.

The best account of the activities of Glenn and Jacqueline Stewart is in *Wye Island* (1977), by Boyd Gibbons, 90-101. Although this book deals primarily with the attempt by James Rouse to build a planned community on Wye Island (see Chapter Twelve), it offers fascinating insights into other Queen Anne's and Talbot County personalities. For the full story of *The First Kiss* see the *Star-Democrat* for February 7, 1973, and the *Baltimore Sun* Sunday Magazine for May 20, 1973. *Star-Democrat* writer Bill Perry was helpful in providing information on the old Eastern Shore baseball league. Mrs. Elizabeth Carroll, former librarian, furnished details on the founding of the Talbot County Free Library.

A number of sources provided bits and pieces on the twentieth century railroads and their decline. Among them were *Buse* 145-47, *Rails Along the Chesapeake* (1979), by John C. Wayman, contemporary newspapers, and recollections of residents, including the late H. Robins Hollyday, a railroad buff as well as photographer. Information on agriculture came principally from talks with farmers or dealers in farm products. The quotations from Charles B. Adams were obtained for a segment in *Trappe: The Story of an Old-Fashioned Town*; the details on Bayshore Foods directly from company founder J. McKenny Willis, Jr. The story of Talbot's first airfield is from Malcolm Hathaway, who operated it.

Twelve: *After the Bridge*

For events in Talbot County since World War II, my guide and mentor has been Norman Harrington. As editor of the *Star-Democrat* from 1948 to 1964, and the *Talbot Banner* from 1973 to 1979, and in his current post as managing director of the Historical Society of Talbot County, Harrington has held a unique position both as observer and participant in Talbot County affairs. He in his turn undertook a thorough review of newspaper files to refresh his memory on key developments, so that the picture presented in this chapter reflects not only his recollections but details as they were reported at the time. I might add that Harrington's other contributions to the book have been immense; he has read the complete manuscript and made suggestions for improvement, and in his role as picture editor has produced the illustrations which bring Talbot's history vividly to life.

Others who have helped, both on this chapter and preceding ones, include William H. Corkran, Jr.; Mrs. Marguerite Harvey, successor to the late Mary Starin as curator of the Library's Maryland Room; Keith Harrington, who aided his father in picture production; Pat Emory, assistant editor of the 1973 anniversary edition of the *Star-Democrat*; J. McKenny Willis, Jr.; J. R. Holt, director of the Chesapeake Bay Maritime Museum; Donald S. Ross; John G. Earle; Hugh Bailey, editor and publisher of the *Tidewater Times*, in which my contributions on "Talbot Yesterday" have appeared for more than ten years; and numerous others.

Illustration Credits

John G. Earle, 55, 192 (*top*), 218, 235, 258, 259 (*bottom*), 286, 287

H. Chandlee Forman, F. A. I. A., illustration from *The Architecture of the Old South,* Harvard University Press, 1948, reprinted with permission, 49, and reconstruction drawing of Easton's Court Square from *Tidewater Maryland Architecture and Gardens,* Architectural Book Publishing Company, 1956 (original drawing in collection of Historical Society of Talbot County), 326

The Frick Collection, 216

Norman Harrington, 17, 20, 27, 75, 79, 82, 89, 90, 91 94, 110, 116, 126, 131, 135, 136, 151, 154, 156, 158, 164, 167, 168, 174, 176, 195, 211, 222, 245, 250, 259 (*top*), 260, 276, 292, 309, 310, 330, 331, 332, 333, 334, 335, 336, 337, 339, 341, 342, 343, 344, 347

The Historical Society of Talbot County Collection, 32, 51, 66, 83, 86, 95, 118, 122, 123, 125, 145, 163, 190, 192 (*bottom*), 193, 197, 216, 231, 242, 249, 273, 300, 318, 340

H. Robins Hollyday Collection (at the Historical Society of Talbot County), 103, 124, 142 (*top* and *bottom*), 143 (*top*), 170, 220, 224, 230, 232, 233, 234, 236, 238, 239, 241, 247, 256, 262, 263, 272, 280, 288, 289, 296, 297, 298, 301, 338

Mrs. Barbara B. Lassiter, 105

Michael Luby Collection, 267, 282 (*top*)

The Mariners Museum, A. Aubrey Bodine Collection, 246

Maryland Historical Society, 53, 96, 135, 148

Maryland Historical Trust, 61

Memorial Hospital at Easton, 282 (*bottom*)

National Baseball Hall of Fame and Museum, 255

John W. Noble family, 328

Dickson J. Preston, 47, 76, 108, 237, 268

The Star-Democrat, 346

Talbot County Free Library. Archives of The Maryland Room, 4, 6, 8, 9, 37, 81, 97, 113, 130, 142 (*center*), 143 (*bottom*), 147, 149, 160, 173, 178, 180, 181, 183, 184, 200, 201, 202, 203, 210, 219, 265, 270, 278, 279, 316

Henry Francis Du Pont Winterthur Museum, 87

Index

A

Ababco, Choptank king, 52
Abbot's Mill, 71
Aberdeen, University of, 96
Abolitionists, 204
Academy House, Oxford, 192; *illus.*, 195
Academy of the Arts, 266, 335-36, 343; *illus.*, 337
Acadians, 106-7
Accomac, Virginia, 212
Accomack Indians, 21
Act of Religious Toleration, 34, 66
Adams, Beulah, 284
Adams, Charles B., 297-98
Adams, James, 284
Adams, John, 85, 151
Adams, John Quincy, 182
Adams, Maurice T., 314
Adams, Samuel, 112, 119
Adams Floating Theatre, 284-85
Adkins, Judge, 281
African Methodist Episcopal Church, 254
African slave trade, 173
Agricultural Society of the Eastern Shore, 172, 196
Agriculture: tobacco planting, 60-63; size of plantations, 92; shift to wheat, 105; planting by hand, 172; truck and dairy farming, 296; tomato era, 297-98; 1920s farm depression, 302; decline of family farm, 337; *illus.*, 230, 298, 341
Airport Industrial Park, 345; *illus.*, 339

Albemarle, steamboat, 179
Alborn, Joseph, 144
Aldern, William, 54
Alforetta Fishing Club, 243
All American Airways, 336
Allegheny Airlines, 336
Allen, Lieutenant John H., 193
All Saints' Parish, 102
Alms House Road, 102
Alsop, George, 60
American Party, 198
American Union, newspaper, 220
Anabaptists, 65
Anatchcom, Indian, 40
Anatomy of Melancholy, The, 59
Anchorage, The, estate, 251, 275
Anderson, David, 30
Anderton, estate, 25, 71
Anderton, John, 25
Andrew, Herbert L., 320
Anglican Church. See Church of England.
Anglo-French wars, 106-8
Annapolis, 24, 28, 54-56, 96, 120, 137, 169, 315; as "giddy capital," 87; 1765 stamp riot, 111; burning of *Peggy Stewart*, 112; first ferry service, 150
Annapolis Jockey Club, 86
Annapolis Naval Academy, 216, 240
Anne Arundel County, 34-35, 60, 72, 92, 97-98
Appalachian Mountains, 18, 19
Archives of Maryland, 28
Argyll, brig, 198
Armes, Major, 240

Armings, G. L., 243
Armour & Company, 298
Armstrong, Philemon, 58
Armstrong's Old Field, 57-58, 60
Arnold, Benedict, 92
Artesian wells, 19
Articles of Association of the Freemen of Maryland, 119
Asbury, Francis, 145, 157-59, 176-77
Ashby, General Turner, 215
Auld, Thomas, 191
Automobiles: first on Eastern Shore, 229; arrival in Easton, 269-70; impact of Model-T Ford, 296; gas rationing, 1942, 306-7; *illus.*, 270, 273
Avalon, steamboat, 256

B

B C & A Railroad. See Baltimore, Chesapeake & Atlantic Railroad.
Bachelor's Point, Oxford, 339
Bachelors' tax, 106
Bacon, Anthony, 80
Bacon, Mrs. Elizabeth. See Bozman, Elizabeth.
Bacon, Reverend Thomas, 80, 84, 92, 96-103; sermons on slavery, 93, 99; charity school, 99-100, 102; aids Acadians, 107; *illus.*, 96
Bahia de Madre Dios, 6
Bahia de Santa Maria, 6, 7
Bailey, Anna, 201
Bailey, Betsey, 191
Bailey, Frederick. See Douglass, Frederick.
Bailey, Harriet, 191
Bailey, Josiah, 199-201
Baines, Harold, *illus.*, 346
Baker, Frank, 255, 288-90; *illus.*, 255, 289
Ball, Vernon, 321
Balloon, steamboat, 180, 215
Bally, Mary, 12
Baltimore, 72, 85, 86, 88, 134, 186, 187, 191, 256, 282; rise as port, 105; shipbuilding, 155, 166; Methodist Church organized, 159-60; election riots, 198; rail service to, 232; summer visitors, 242; fire of 1904, 295; as grain market, 298-99; air service to, 301; ferry terminal, 311
Baltimore, Chesapeake & Atlantic Railroad (B C & A), 241-42, 284, 294-95
Baltimore, ship, 114
Baltimore & Eastern Shore Railroad Company, 294
Baltimore & Ohio Railroad, 187-88
Baltimore clippers, 155-56, 166-68
Baltimore County, 72
Baltimore Sun, 188, 237
Banning, Benoni, 117
Banning, Jeremiah, 80, 84, 89; 109-11, 116-17, 137, 325; on Robert Morris, 102-3; names Easton streets, 139-40; on Easton's growth, 144; lament for Oxford, 153-54; death and burial, 155; *illus.*, 116
Banning, Robert, 155
Barbados, 62, 93
Barbour, Philip L., 8
Barker, John, 80
Barker Creek, 80
Barnaby, Captain, house, *illus.*, 126
Barnett, Mary, 29
Barroll, William, 152
Barth, John, 63
Bartlett-Dixon family, 198
Bartlett family, 33, 251
Bartlett's Oak. See Royal Oak.
Barton, Mrs. S. J., 234
Baseball, 254, 288-90
Bateman, Henry E., 239
Bauman, Robert E., 340
Bay Bridge, 188, 270, 308, 310, 315-17; *illus.*, 310, 316
Bay Hundred (also called Bayside), 18, 24, 36, 157, 225, 320-25
Bay Hundred Anti-Zoning League, 323-24
Bayne, Reverend Thomas, 220
Bayshore Foods, Inc., 299
Beadnell, Father James, 107
Beck, Rachel, 100
Belchier, Reverend John, 100-1
Bell, John, 207
Bell, M. J., 251
Bellefont Hotel, Claiborne, 242

INDEX

Bellevue, 238, 325; *illus.*, 237
Belmont, estate, 319
Bennett, Jerome B., 206
Bennett, Richard II, 73
Bennett, Richard III, 50, 68, 73-76, 88-90
Bennett, Susannah, 74
Bennett's Point, 73
Benny's Annapolis Brass Band, 224
Benoni's Point, 117, 293
Benson, James, 159
Benson, Perry, 137, 150, 159, 162, 172; role in Revolution, 129-30; defense of St. Michaels, 165-66
Benson, William P., 238-39
Berry, William, 33, 66
Bethlehem, 295
Betty's Cove, 36-38, 57, 84
Beverly, estate, 155
Binghamton, New York, 42
Birckhead, Colonel Christopher, 132
Bishop, John J., 214-15
Bishop, Tom, Choptank Indian, 43
Bishope, George, 33
Black & Decker, Inc., 345
Bladen, Governor Thomas, 97-98
Blades, John W., 207
Bloodworth Island, 13
Bloomfield, brig, 198
Bloomfield, estate, 198, 282, 295
Boehm, Henry, 160-61
Bohemia, estate, 107
Bolingbroke Methodist Chapel, 159
Bonaparte, Napoleon, 153, 171
Bordley, John Beale, 124-25, 128, 133-34; *illus.*, 125
Boston, estate, 205
Boston, Massachusetts, 33, 34, 112, 115, 187
Boston Tea Party, 112
Boyer, Andrew, 146
Boyle, Captain Thomas, 166-68
Bozman, 245-46
Bozman, Elizabeth, 100-1
Bowen, Mr., waxworks, 147
Bowie, Reverend Dr. John, 132, 150, 153
Bowling, *illus.*, 78
Braddock, James, 114-15, 155

Bradford, Augustus W., 212
Brady, Simeon, 251-52
Brandywine, Battle of, 129-30
Brascup, Joseph, tavern, 114
Breckinridge, John C., 207
Breezy Point, summer hotel, 242
Brick Hotel. See Easton Hotel.
British loyalists, 111, 117-18
Broad Creek, Kent Island, 44
Broad Creek, St. Michaels, 67, 155, 164
Broad Creek Neck, 156, 245
Brooke, John, 5
Brookes Forest, 5; *illus.*, 6
Brown, Arthur, 226
Brown, John, 205
Browne, Johnson, 30-31
Browning, Thomas, 107
Bruff, Joseph, Jr., 144
Bruff, Joseph, Sr., 84, 127, 140
Bruff, Mrs., 147
Bruff, Richard, 56
Bruff, Thomas, 49, 243
Bruff's Island, 56
Bryan, Buck, 287
Bryan, James, 44
Bryan, William Jennings, 285-86; *illus.*, 288
Buchanan, Franklin, 216-17, 218, 219, 251; *illus.*, 216
Buchanan, James, 198
Buchanan, Mrs. Franklin, 216, 217
Bugeyes, 239, 243, 260-61
Bullen, estate, 25
Bullen, Thomas, 25
Bullet, train, *illus.*, 296
Bullitt, Thomas J., 162, 176-77
Bullitt House, 162; *illus.*, 176, 232
Burton, Robert, 59
Buse, Elliott, 263
Bussey, Thomas, 51
Butler, Elizabeth, 10
Butler, Francis, 56

C

Cabot, John, 6
Callister, Henry, 14, 84, 85, 92, 101-2, 105-7

Calvary Methodist Protestant Church, 291; *illus.,* 158
Calvert, Benedict Leonard, 64, 68
Calvert, Caecilius (second Lord Baltimore), 9, 22, 23, 25, 26-27, 34, 35, 45, 64, 75
Calvert, Cecil, 100
Calvert, Charles, 26, 36, 40, 52, 53-54
Calvert, Philip, 25, 40
Calvert Cliffs, 33
Calvert County, 60
Calvert family, 95
Cambridge, ferry, 295; *illus.,* 233
Cambridge, Maryland, 43, 104, 127, 179, 224, 268, 275; first baseball team, 254-55; steamboat service, 256; hospital founding, 281-82; desegregation riots, 339
Cambridge, Massachusetts, 116
Cambridge, steamboat, 179
Cambridge Democrat, 295
Camden, North Carolina, 129
Camp Hicks (also called Camp Kirby), 212-14, 224
Camp Quaker, 212
Camp Stanton, 219
Canada, 106, 200-3
Cannonball House, 166; *illus.,* 164
Canterbury Mannour, 25
Cape Centaur, 290
Carmichael, Judge Richard Bennett, 205, 213-15
Carney, Thomas, 129-30
Caroline, War of 1812 raider, 168
Caroline County, 32, 129, 132, 140, 203, 213, 266, 283; creation, 78, 213; tories in, 133; slave escape route, 199, 202; first railroad, 231
Carpender, Francis, 30
Carroll, Charles (of Carrollton), 121
Carroll, Charles (1840s), 186
Carroll, Mrs. Charles, 86
Carroll, Raymond, 287
Carter, Judge J. DeWeese, 325
Castellux, General de, *illus.,* 135
Cecil County, 91, 107, 263
Cedar Mountain, battle of, 217
Cedar Point, estate, 32, 38, 332
Centaur, yacht, 290

Centreville, Maryland, 46, 64, 83, 149, 179, 263, 274
Century Magazine, 249
Chaffinch, William P., 277
Chamberlaine, James Lloyd, 120, 127-28, 190
Chamberlaine, John, 92
Chamberlaine, Samuel, 92
Chamberlaine, Samuel, Jr., 132-33
Chamberlaine, Thomas, 128
Chamberlaine family, 91-92
Champion, steamboat, 179-80, 219, 256
Chancellor's Point, 25, 45, 256
Chapel District, 161, 231, 245
Chapel Road, 232
Chaplain, William R., 221
Charity Working School, 99-102; *illus.,* 103
Charles County, 219
Charles I, King, 75
Charleston, South Carolina, 112, 187
Charlotte, North Carolina, 218
Charlottesville, Virginia, 333
Chase, Samuel, 87, 121
Chase-Lloyd House, Annapolis, 87-88
Chautauqua movement, 285-86, 293
Chesapeake, log canoe, 258-60
Chesapeake, novel, 342
Chesapeake, steamboat, 256
Chesapeake Airways, 301, 336
Chesapeake & Delaware Canal, 196
Chesapeake & Ohio Canal, 187-88
Chesapeake Bay, 3, 5, 6-7, 9, 13, 19, 28, 45, 104-6, 174; Claiborne-Calvert struggle, 10; British invasion, 163-66; cruelties in oyster fleet, 261; bridge funds voted, 310; bridge dedication, 315-17
Chesapeake Bay Maritime Museum, 243, 332, 335, 343; *illus.,* 336
Chesapeake Bay model, 44
Chesapeake Bay Yacht Club, 287-88
Chesapeake House, summer hotel, 242
Chesapeake Indians, Virginia, 45
Chesapeake Rehabilitation Center, 332

INDEX

Cheshill, Martha, 29
Chester, Kent Island, 106
Chester Hill. See Centreville, Maryland.
Chester River, 5, 12, 16, 21, 28, 39, 46, 53, 54, 78, 104
Chestertown, Maryland, 53, 56, 83, 85, 97, 104, 115, 127, 161, 179, 263, 268, 269, 271, 274, 303
Cheston-on-Wye, 25
Chew, Richard, 149
Chincoteague Bay, 6-7
Chipley, Charles A., 251
Choptank Bridge. See Emerson C. Harrington Bridge.
Choptank Indians, 20, 40, 42-43, 52; origin of word, 45
Choptank River, 5, 6, 12, 18, 20, 28, 37, 38, 42-43, 45, 50, 53, 67, 72, 78, 80, 138, 199, 201-2, 256, 302
Christ Episcopal Church, Easton, 149, 150, 161, 175, 305; *illus.*, 158
Christian Advocate, 204-5
Christian Science Monitor, 307
Christison, Wenlock, 33-34
Church Neck, shipyard, 156
Church of England, 34, 64-66, 74, 94-99, 133, 157
Cities Service Corporation, 332
Citizens Committee for the Colonial Restoration of Easton, 327-28
Citizens Committee for Talbot County Development, 323
Civil War in Talbot: slave escapes, 199-204; 1859 martial law, 206; 1860 election, 207; 1861 referendum, 208; aid to Baltimore, 209; prorebel takeover, 209-10; raid on Armory, 210; arrest of General Tilghman, 211-12; federal troops, 212; "Battle of Cow Landing," 212-13; beating of Judge Carmichael, 213-15; Editor Robson's exile, 215; Confederate heroes, 216-18; Union troops, 218-19; clash at Gettysburg, 221; feminine support for South, 223; economic conditions, 225-26; opposition to emancipation, 227; Lincoln's assassination, 228; Confederate monument, 221-22, 280
Claiborne, town, 23, 106, 240-41, 261, 284, 286, 295, 311, 317; *illus.*, 233, 241
Claiborne, William, 8-11, 44; *illus.*, 9
Claiborne Oyster Company, 241
Claiborne's Island. See Sharp's Island.
Clark, William Bullock, 271
Clark Company. See H. E. Clark Company.
Clay, Henry, 178
Clayland, James, 64
Clay's Hope, 325; *illus.*, 61
Clayton, Delaware, 230, 232, 262, 296
Clifton Development, 333
Clifton Industrial Park, 333
Clinton, DeWitt, 163
Clora's Point, 256
Cloverfield, 25
Clow, Cheney, 133
Clymer, John, 30
Coast Guard Auxiliary, 306
Coats, Dr. John, 144-46
Coats Lodge, Masonic Order, 266
Cockburn, Admiral George, 163-64
Cockey, Mr. and Mrs. John, 242
Cockey, Mr. and Mrs. Tilson, 242
Cockey, Theophilus, 240-41
Cock fighting, 86
Cole, Josias, 31
Coleman, Josiah, 110
Collier, Thomas, 54
Collier, W. O., 251
Colston, Jeremiah, 127-28
Columbia, Maryland, 339
Columbian Exposition, 258-60
Company H, Union volunteers, 218, 221
Complete System of Revenue in Ireland, A, 99
Compton, estate, 205, 252; *illus.*, 82
Concord, Massachusetts, 115
Conestoga Indians, 44
Conestoga wagons, 44
Congress of Vienna, 1815, 171
Constitutional Convention of 1776, 119, 121
Continental Army, 116, 125-26

Continental Congress, 42, 112-13, 114, 119, 120-22, 124, 150
Cooke, Ebenezer, 63
Cooper, Gary, 291-92
Cope, Professor Edward, 19
Copperville, 247
Cordova, 107, 234-35, 254, 318, 345
Corkran, William H., Jr., 327, 331-32; *illus.*, 331
Corner, Solomon, tavern, 147
Corning Glass Company, 291
Cornwallis, General Charles, 134
Corsica Creek, 53, 78
Councell, William H., 210, 228
Country Day School, Easton, 343
Coursey, Henry, 25, 26, 51-52
Coursey, John, 25
Coursey, William, 16, 25, 26, 40, 46
Court House Alley, 333
Court House Square, Easton, *illus.*, 262
Coventry Parish, Somerset County, 98
Covington, Sarah, 83
Covington, Sid, boatbuilder, 243, 245
Covington, William, boatbuilder, 243
Cowan, James, 144, 152-53
Cowgill, John, 207-8
Cowgill family, 207-8
Cow Landing. See Easton Point.
Cowley, George, 46
Cox, Dr. C. C., 208, 227
Crayford, estate, 10
Crisfield, 268, 275, 282
Crittenden, J. J., 178
Cromwell, Oliver, 25, 35
Cromwell, Reverend Joseph, 157
Crookshanks, Charles, 114
Crookshanks, Elizabeth, 29
Crosiadore, 25, 46, 122, 205; *illus.*, 124
Crouch's Island. See Bruff's Island.
Cugley, Daniel, 10
Culp's Hill, Gettysburg, 221
Cunliffe, Foster, firm, 80, 84, 103-5
Curley, Monsieur, 148-49
Current Events Club, 293

D

Dashaway, log canoe, 258
Dauphine, ship, 6
Davidson, Cata, 282
Davidson, Dr. Charles F., 283
Davis, Jefferson, 209, 217-18, 220, 230
Davis, John, 156
Dawkins, Albert T. (Doc), 307
Dawson, Impey, 155
Daylight Saving Time, 314-15
D'Courcy, William H., 190
Declaration of Independence, 120-23
Delahay, Henry, 128
Delaware, 42, 133, 187, 199
Delaware & Chesapeake Railway Company, 294
Delaware Bay, 28
Delaware Indians, 5, 19
Delaware River, 199, 200, 321
Delmarva Peninsula, 19, 129, 157, 186
Democratic Party, 151, 177
Denham, Massachusetts, 33
Denny, Spry, tanyard, 173, 180
Denton, 179, 256
DePeyster, Betsey (Mrs. Charles Willson Peale), 147
Depression of 1930s, 295, 301-2
D'Hinojosa, Alexander, 36
Diamond State Telephone Company, 263
Dickinson, James, 80, 104
Dickinson, John, 122-24; *illus.*, 125
Dickinson, Walter, 32
Dickinson, William, 46, 73
Dickinson Bay, 25
Dickinson family, 25, 122
Ditman, William, *illus.*, 333
Dividing Creek. See Trappe Creek.
Dix, Major General John A., 214
Dixon, James, 182, 219, 225
Dixon, Mary Bartlett, 282
Dixon, Robert B., 262, 277
Dixon family, 33
Dixon's Creek, 38
Dockery's livery stable, 83
Doncaster (lost town), 18, 24, 46, 49, 53, 56-57, 64, 67, 74, 75, 107

INDEX

Dorchester, steamboat, 257
Dorchester County, 5, 32, 36-37, 42, 78, 91, 120, 140, 174, 202, 204-5, 252, 253
Double Mills, 256
Douglas, Stephen A., 207
Douglass, Anna (Murray), 203
Douglass, Frederick, 191-92, 247; *illus.*, 190, 203
Douglass, Lewis, 247-48
Dover, Delaware, 122
Dover Bridge, 256-274
Dover ferry, 45
Dover (lost town), 57, 78, 80, 102, 138-39, 140; *illus.*, 81
Dover road, 78, 80
Draft, military, 132, 225
Ducks Unlimited, 341
Dundee Methodist Chapel, 159
Dyer, Mary, 34

E

Eastern Bay, 6, 23, 56
Eastern Shore, 3, 5, 6-7, 12, 13, 18, 39, 133, 138-39, 146, 171, 302-3; tobacco, 57; 1700 population, 71-72; tobacco merchants, 104; Catholics, 107; Methodist sweep, 156-61; salt riots, 127-28; British loyalists, 132-34; Revolutionary War "navy," 134; silk worm mania, 184-85; secession demands, 187-88; railroads, 186-88, 230-34, 294-96; automobiles, 271-74; pride of residents, 302-3; effects of Bay Bridge, 317
Eastern Shore Automobile Company, *illus.*, 273
Eastern Shore Baseball League, 288-90
Eastern Shore Star. See *Easton Star*.
Eastern Shore Steamboat Company, 180
Eastern Shore Trail, 274
Eastern Shore Triumverate, 96
Eastern Shore Whig and People's Advocate, 182-83
Eastford Hall hotel, 240; *illus.*, 192
Eastman, estate, 251
Easton, 18, 54, 79, 80, 103, 138-51, 162, 182, 185, 186-87, 253, 294, 299-300, 345; town laid out, 139-40; named Easton, 140-41; early growth, 144-45; entertainers, 147-49; attack fears, 1813, 163; malarial marshes, 175, 184; great Whig rally, 177-78; comeback of 1840s, 193-94; last slave auction, 220-21; votes dry, 1874, 254; arrival of railroad, 230-31; first telegraph and telephone, 262; electricity, 263; major fires, 264, 283; piped water, 265; automobiles, 269-70; rebirth under Higgins, 275-77; effects of Choptank bridge, 302; V-J Night, 304-5; 1947 zoning, 311; downtown "colonialization," 325-29; *illus.*, 224, 265, 297, 330. See also Talbot Court House, Talbot County Court House, Civil War in Talbot.
Easton, locomotive, 231-32, 262
Easton Academy, 335
Easton Airport, 301, 308, 336-37; *illus.*, 339, 340
Easton Armory, 163, 206, 210, 323; *illus.*, 142
Easton Businessmen's Association, 313
Easton Democrat, 268
Easton District, 208, 319-20
Easton Farmers, 288; *illus.*, 289
Easton Fencibles (militia), 162
Easton Fire Company, 150, 264, 345
Easton Furniture Manufacturing Company, 277-79; *illus.*, 280
Easton Gas Light Company, 194
Easton Gazette, 181, 183, 187, 188, 194, 206, 209, 210, 222-23, 226, 227, 228, 266-68, 271; founded, 1817, 182; on need for railroad, 186; on slave revolt rumors, 205; on Judge Carmichael, 214-15; on "secesh" women, 223; on fall of Richmond, 228; steam printing press, 229; supports Grant, 248; welcomes "Yankees," 250; on first Oldsmobile, 269; *illus.*, 163
Easton High School, 266, 285-86, 312, 322-23, 346

Easton Horse Guard, 209
Easton Hotel (also called Brick Hotel): built, 1815, 169; remodeled, 1869, 265-66; becomes Stewart building, 290; *illus.*, 183
Easton Independent. See *Easton Democrat.*
Easton Independents, 254-55
Easton Journal, 248, 262, 264. See also *Easton Ledger.*
Easton Ledger, 207, 226, 251, 268
Easton Merchants and Traders Association, 180
Easton Methodist chapel, 159
Easton Mozart Band, 266
Easton National Bank, 34, 163, 177, 179, 281-82, 301; 1805 founding, 169; Civil War split, 225; installs electricity, 263; supports "colonial Easton," 327; *illus.*, 263
Easton Point, 107, 141, 150, 163, 179, 211, 213, 256, 299
Easton railroad station, 293; *illus.*, 233
Easton Star, 183, 189, 208, 209, 213, 226, 262, 268; relationship to *Whig*, 183; on Judge Carmichael, 214-15; 1862 raid, 223-24; suspension, 215; on black voting, 248; on "foreigners," 250-51; on long distance phones, 263; merged with *Democrat*, 268; *illus.*, 184. See also *Eastern Shore Whig, Easton Star-Democrat.*
Easton Star-Democrat, 236, 268, 286, 304-5, 308, 311, 319-20, 328, 341; longevity claims, 183; support for zoning, 313, 317-18, 322-23; promotes "colonial Easton," 326; *illus.*, 316, 318. See also *Easton Star.*
Easton Town Council, 311-13, 333
Easton Utilities Commission, *illus.*, 344
Easton Waterworks Company, 265
Ebenezer Methodist Episcopal Church, 159, 264; *illus.*, 158
Eden, Governor Robert, 86, 117
Edison, Thomas A., 229
Edison, W. L., 229
Edmondson, John, 32, 37-38, 46, 53, 66

Edmondson, Pollard, 126
Edmondson, Sarah, 32
Edmondson (Edmundson) Neck, 32
Edna E. Lockwood, bugeye, 243
Education: in colonial times, 84-85; first public schools, 197; first high schools, 266; busing and consolidation, 293; modern school system, 343. See also Charity Working School, Talbot County Free School, Quakers.
Elizabeth, ship, 72
Elizabeth River, Virginia, 34, 45
Elk River, 5
Elkton, 282
Ellenborough, estate, 251
Emergency Hospital. See Memorial Hospital at Easton.
Emerson C. Harrington Bridge (Choptank bridge), 302
Emerson family, 82-83
Emerson's Landing, 67
Emory, Thomas, 187
Endeavor, schooner, 114
Endicott, Governor, 33
Ewing, George, 85
Ewing, L. Clark, 322
Experiment, barge, 134

F

Fairview, estate, 80, 82; *illus.*, 83
Falconer, Patrick, 63
Farmers' Bank of Maryland. See Easton National Bank.
Farragut, Admiral David G., 217
Fausley, Tench Tilghman birthplace, 117
Federalist Party, 151, 152-53, 163
Federal Park, 288
Federalsburg, 254-55
Fells Point, Baltimore, 155, 156, 172
Fendall, Josias, 35
Ferber, Edna, 284-85
Ferguson, George, 73
Ferry Neck, 156, 247
Fike, Norman, 318
Fillmore, Millard, 198
Finney, William, 50
First Baptist Church, *illus.*, 158

INDEX

First Eastern Shore Regiment, 218, 221
First Kiss, The, movie, 291-92
First Maryland Confederate Regiment, 221
Fishbourne, Ralph, 33, 73
Fitzhugh, William, 86
Floyd, Philemon, 194
Foote, Hardin, *illus.,* 130
Forman, Dr. Henry Chandlee, 56, 326, 329; *illus.,* 49, 326
Forman, T. H., 152
Fort Delaware, 213
Fort Frederick, 106
Fort LaFayette, 215
Fort McHenry, 169, 213, 215
Fort Meade, 210
Fort Ninety-Six, South Carolina, 129-30
Fort Stoakes, 163
Fort Sumter, 209
Fortune, Richard, 251
Foster, Elizabeth, 36
Foster, Seth, 11, 12, 25, 26, 29, 36, 46
Fountain, Isaiah, 281
Fox, George, 31, 33, 36-38, 84; *illus.,* 37
Fox, Henry, 23
Fox hunting, 70
Foxley Hall, Easton, 217
Foxx, Dell, 288
Foxx, Jimmie, 288-90; *illus.,* 289
Frame Hotel, Easton, 169, 265-66
Francis, Tench, 92
Franklin, Benjamin, 13
Frederick County, 102
Free Soil Party, 198
French and Indian War, 106, 108
French fur traders, 7
French Revolution, 149, 153
Frith, Henry, 58, 78

G
Gaine, Ann, 29-30
Gale, Harry, 134
Garey, Alice, 33
Garner, Philip, 206
Garrettson, Reverend Freeborn, 157
Garrison, William Lloyd, 204
General Court of Maryland, 138
George III, King, 110, 111, 133
Gester, C. H., 221
Gettysburg, Battle of, 218, 221, 227
Gibson, Jacob, 152-53, 163-65, 181-82, 251
Gilbert & Gawith, merchants, 114, 155
Giles, Robert, 221
Gladdus, Dousbell, 10
Glebe Creek, 33, 117, 251
Goldsborough (Goldsboro), town, 230
Goldsborough, Anna Maria, 253
Goldsborough, Charles, 190
Goldsborough, Charles, Jr., 253
Goldsborough, Clarissa Tilghman, 275
Goldsborough, Elizabeth, 253
Goldsborough, Greenbury, 139
Goldsborough, Henry H., 214, 223-24
Goldsborough, Judge Robert, 140
Goldsborough, M. T., 251
Goldsborough, Nicholas, 128, 190
Goldsborough, Robert Henry, 172
Goldsborough, William, 150
Goldsborough family, 73, 77, 83, 91-92, 139-40
Goldsborough's drug store, 262
Goldsborough's wharf, 256
Goodwin, Frank, 302-3
Goose Creek (Dorchester County), 43
Gordon, Captain Thomas, 132
Gordon, Reverend Dr. John, 86, 95-97, 114; *illus.,* 95
Gorsuch, Loveless, 66
Gorsuch, Richard, 32
Gossage, James H., 221
Governor Emerson C. Harrington, ferry, *illus.,* 241
Grace, James H., 225
Grafton Mannour, 25
Graham, Alexander, 182
Graison, Robert, 73
Granger, Elmo, 323
Granite Lodge, Masonic Order, 266
Grant, President Ulysses S., 248
Grapevine House, Oxford, 240

Grason, Commodore Thomas, 134
Great Falls of the Potomac, 5
Greeley, Horace, 248
Green, Samuel, 204-5
Greene, Joseph, 50
Greensborough (Greensboro), 230, 296
Griffith, Corinne, 292-93
Groome, Samuel, 169, 170
Groome, William H., 225
Gross, Roger, 24
Gross Coat (Groce Coat), 24, 147
Grundy, Robert, miller, 78
Grymes, A. Johnson, Jr., 308, 309-10
Guilford Court House, 130

H

H. E. Clark Company, Easton, 274
Haddaway, Captain, 197-98
Haddaway, Thomas L., 155
Haddaway, W. W., 149-50
Haddaway's Wharf (Lowe's Wharf), 149-50
Hall, William P., 251
Hallings, Thomas, 30
Hambleton, 246-47, 285. See also Hole-in-the-Wall.
Hambleton, Dr. Alexander, 96
Hambleton, Edward N., 187, 190
Hambleton, Samuel, Navy purser, 168-69; *illus.*, 168
Hambleton, William, 25, 35, 115
Hammond, Dr. William T., 283
Hammond, Nicholas, 34, 169, 172, 179; *illus.*, 173
Hamner, J., 80
Hampden, estate, 32, 82; *illus.*, 108
Hampton, Virginia, 164
Hanson, Alexander Contee, 133
Hanson, John, 140
Hanson Street School, Easton, 338
Hardcastle, E. L. F., 230
Hardin, Reverend Durrie, 305
Harper, Dr. Samuel, 209
Harper, Fred, 236-37
Harper, John, 208
Harper family, 237, 291-92
Harper's Magazine, 249-50
Harrington, Norman, 317-19, 322,
325; *illus.*, 318
Harris, John, 25
Harris, Skinner, 156
Harris Creek, 25
Harrison, Dr. Samuel A., 56, 140, 153, 155, 166, 171-72, 174, 175, 189-90, 191, 205, 207-8, 209-10, 220-21, 223, 225, 228, 257-58
Harrison, George T., 245
Harrison, Ira, 244
Harrison, J. Camper, 245
Harrison, John B., 243
Harrison, John T., 243
Harrison, S. Taylor, 245
Harrison, Thomas, 115, 159
Harrison, William Henry, 177-78
Harrison & Jarboe Packing Company, 308
Harrison & Kemp, shipbuilders, 155
Hart, Albert Bushnell, 249
Hart, Mrs. Mitchell (Mary), 236, 257
Harwood, William, 37
Hathaway, A., 251
Hathaway, Malcolm, 300-1
Hathaway, Stephen, 300
Hathaway Airfield, *illus.*, 301
Hatton, Thomas, 23
Haukings (Hawkins), Robert, 30
Hawkins, Elizabeth, 11-12
Hawkins, Thomas, 11-12
Hayward, William, 190
Hayward family, 91-92
Head of Elk, 134
Head of Wye, 104
Hearts of Oak, militia, 129, 162-63, 166
Hemsley, Philemon, 58
Hemsley, William, 25, 30-31, 40, 129
Henderson, Charles E., 251
Henrietta Maria, Queen, 75
Henry, J. C. & Brother, store, 263
Henry, John, 140
Henry, Patrick, 119
Henry, Robert Goldsborough, 308
Henry, T. Hughlett, Jr., 315, 317-18
Henry VII, King, 6
Hepburn, Andrew, 329
Hermann, Augustine, 52-53
Hersloff, Sigurd N., 308

INDEX

Hesselius, John, *illus.*, 95, 105, 123
Hessian fly, 172
Hibernia, Queen Anne's County, 45, 64
Hicks, Governor Thomas H., 211-12
Higgins, Martin M., 275-77; *illus.*, 278-79
Highland Light, steamboat, 256
Hillsborough (Hillsboro), 231, 234, 256, 263
Hindman, Captain James, 120, 125-26
Hindman, William, 152
Historical Society of Talbot County, 301, 329, 332, 334, 335, 343; *illus.*, 110, 131, 335
Historic Easton, Inc., 331, 333
Hobkirk's Hill, battle of, 129
Hoffman, Lillian, 285
Hog Neck golf course and arena, 332, 345; *illus.*, 344
Hole-in-the-Wall, 80-81, 246-47, 285. See also Hambleton.
Hollyday, Anna Maria (Robins), *illus.*, 105
Hollyday, H. Robins, 140, 301
Hollyday, Henry I, 83, 118, 128; *illus.*, 105
Hollyday, Henry II, 172, 187, 190
Hollyday, James II, 128
Hollyday family, 25, 73, 77, 91-92, 251
Holt, R. J. (Jim), 335
Holy Trinity Episcopal Church, Oxford, 193
Home Guard, militia, 206
Hood, Zachariah, 109-11
Hookes, Jeremiah, 73
Hooper's Strait, 3, 5
Hooper's Strait Lighthouse, 335
Hopkins, Adeline, 248
Hopkins, Alexander, 248
Hopkins, Violet, storekeeper, 182
Hopkins Corner, 247
Hopkinson, Jonathan, 45, 46-48
Horney, John A., 173
Horse racing, 30-31, 70, 79, 86
Hotel Avon, 266, 293, 309; *illus.*, 232, 267

Hotel Norris. See Hotel Avon.
Hotel Queen Anne, *illus.*, 267
Hough, Robert, 252
Houghland, Stephen, 224
Houghton, Arthur A., Jr., 291
Howard, Benjamin C., 212
Howard, Governor John Eager, 140
Howard, Nina, 285
Howell's Point, 179, 205
Howeth, Harry R., 244
Howeth, Norman, 318
Hubbard, Sherwood M., *illus.*, 332
Hugh Jenkins, steamboat, 179
Hughlett, Thomas, 140
Hughlett, William, 140, 187
Hughlett, William R., Jr., 198, 199, 202, 238-39; *illus.*, 197
Hugh Orem, bugeye, *illus.*, 259
Hunter, Charles, 284
Hurlock, 295
Hurricanes, 13-14, 69
Hussey, Obed, 194-96
Hylliard, Ann, 29
Hynson, Thomas, Jr., 26, 29

I

Ida, steamboat, 256
Idlewild Baseball Club, 254-55
Idlewild Park, 247, 285
Independent Light Dragoons, 162
Independents, religious sect, 65
Indians, 7, 12, 14, 15, 17, 19, 21, 37, 45, 50-52, 74, 106; 1637 massacre by, 10; eventual fate, 39-45; smallpox and drinking problems, 41, 43, 44; legacy to whites, 44-45; last in Talbot, 177; *illus.*, 20. See also individual tribes.
Ingraham, Prentiss, 98, 185
Ingram, Major Thomas, 41
Internal improvements in Maryland, 186-88
In the Land of Legendary Lore, movie, 293
Iroquois Confederacy, 19, 42, 44, 117
Island Bird, log canoe, 243
Island Blossom, log canoe, 243
Island Creek, 32, 73, 105
Island Creek Neck, 107

Isle of Kent. See Kent Island.
Isthmus, The, estate, 116
Ivyville, 247
I Will Repay, movie, 292-93

J

Jackson, Andrew, 182
Jackson, Reverend Joseph, 150
Jackson, Thomas "Stonewall", 217
Jamaica Point, 198, 199, 256; *illus.*, 197
James I, King, 59
Jamestown, Virginia, 3, 5, 7, 8
Jefferson, Thomas, 43, 120, 151, 152-53
Jefferson Island Club, 293, 302
Jenkins, John, 39
Jenkins, Thomas, 132
Jesuit order, 16, 66, 107, 108
Jews, 67, 252
John Gilpin, brig, 173; *illus.*, 174
Johnson, Bridgett, 30
Johnson, Dr. Stephen T., 146
Johnson, Governor Thomas, 132, 133
Johnston, ship, 114
Jones, Captain, 114-15
Jones, David, 107
Jones, Mrs. W. Alton, 332-33; *illus.*, 332
Jones, W. Alton, 332
Jones, Wrightson, 173
Joppa, steamboat, 256, 295
Judkin, Obedia, 66
Jump, Captain Giles, 258-60

K

Kane-Miller, Inc., 299
Kappus, Adolf, 306
Keene, Reverend Samuel, 161
Kemp, Joseph, 173
Kemp, Mrs. Joseph, 242
Kemp, Robert, 33
Kemp, Thomas, 166-68, 242
Kemp, William H., 277
Kemp, William P., 278
Kemp family, 36
Kent, steamboat, 256
Kent County, 5, 11, 27, 78, 91, 117, 152, 159

Kent County, England, 9
Kent Island, 5-6, 9, 10, 11, 21, 24, 26, 28, 37, 39, 40, 44, 45, 60, 78, 106, 132, 234, 263, 310, 311, 317
Kent Narrows, 45
Kent News, 271-72
Kent Point, 134
Kerr, John Bozman, 215
Kerr, John Leeds, 187
Kerr, Rachel, 190
Kerr's Island, Oxford, 239
Key, Francis Scott, 87-88, 169
Kidd, Captain, 72
King George's War, 106
King William's War, 50
King's Creek, 53
Kingston, 53, 67, 73, 256
Kirby, Major William, 212-13
Kirby, William A., 248
Kirk, Thomas, 25
Kirkham, 25, 295
Knapp, Robert, 29
Knapp's Narrows, 29, 243; *illus.*, 245
Knightly, estate, 252
Know-Nothing movement, 198
Koch, Dr. Robert H. A., 176
Kuddle, log canoe, 243
Kuskarawaock Indians. See Nanticoke Indians.

L

LaFayette, General, 129, 134; *illus.*, 135
Lake Erie, Battle of, 168-69
Lambdin, Robert, 196, 257-60
Lamkin, Sergeant, 227
Lancaster, Pennsylvania, 163
Lancaster County, Virginia, 31
Land, Phillip, 23
Land of Legendary Lore, 98, 185
Landon, Alf, 302
Lane, W. Preston, Jr., 310, 316
Lane's Machine Shop, *illus.*, 272
Langsdale Houses, Easton, 331, 333; *illus.*, 334
Lawrence, War of 1812 raider, 168
Lawrie, Lee, 335-36; *illus.*, 338
Laws of Maryland, 102
Lay, Right Reverend Henry Cham-

INDEX

plain, 253
Layton, ship, 109
Lebanon Methodist Episcopal Church, Trappe, 159, 196
Leddra, William, 33
Lee, General Robert E., 218, 221, 226-27, 228
Leech, Joseph, 64
Leeds, John, 118
Leeds Creek, 245
Leonard, Nathaniel, 198, 238-39
Leonard, Thomas H., 208
Letters from a Farmer in Pennsylvania, 122
Lewes, Delaware, 234
Lewis, Father John, 107
Lexington, Massachusetts, 109, 115
Liancourt, Duke de la Rochefoucault, 93
Liberty Song, The, 123-24
Light Infantry Blues, militia, 162
Lillingston, Reverend John, 50, 65
Limbo, Isle of, 13
Lincoln, Abraham, 191, 207, 213, 215, 218-19, 220, 227, 228
Lincoln, General Benjamin, *illus.,* 135
Linton, estate, 24
Lippincott's Magazine, 249
Little Choptank Creek, 4
Liverpool Merchant, ship, 104
Livesley, Gilbert, merchant, 72
Lockhart, Anne N. B., 333; *illus.,* 333
Lockhart Building, 264
Lockwood, General Henry H., 211-12
Lockwood, J., 251
Locust Neck, Dorchester County, 43
Log canoes, 44, 70, 226, 243, 257-61; *illus.,* 258-59
Lloyd, Edward I, 24, 25, 26, 34-35, 46, 68
Lloyd, Edward II, 35, 57, 58, 73, 83
Lloyd, Edward III, 89-91, 100, 107
Lloyd, Edward IV, 86, 87, 118, 132, 134; *illus.,* 87
Lloyd, Edward V, 86, 91, 172, 190, 252; *illus.,* 56
Lloyd, Edward VI, 91, 189, 190-91
Lloyd, Edward VII, 91
Lloyd, Elizabeth Tayloe, 217

Lloyd, Henrietta Maria, 56, 73-76, 83, 92, 124
Lloyd, Henry, 252
Lloyd, Joanna Leigh, 118
Lloyd, Mary Tayloe, 87-88, 169
Lloyd, Philemon I, 35, 41, 51-52, 56, 68-69, 73
Lloyd, Philemon II, 73, 83
Lloyd, Richard Bennett, 118
Lloyd family, 35, 56, 77, 89-91, 92, 94, 217, 252
Lloyd graveyard, 76; *illus.,* 75
Lloyd's Creek, 231
Lloyd's Landing, 67
Long Island, Battle of, 125-26, 130
Longwoods, 263, 336
Lostock, estate, 325
Love Point, Kent Island, 234, 311
Lowe, Betty, 293
Lowe, Nicholas, 57-58, 70-71
Lowery, James, 243
Lowndes, Lloyd, 252
Lyons, Richard, 152

M

McCallum, Alexander, 139
McCallum, Archibald, 101
McClellan, General George, 226-27, 228
McDaniel, 243, 244, 245, 295, 308
McGovern, George, 293
McGrath and Godwin players, 147
McKean, Thomas, 136
McKeldin, Theodore R., 316
Macklin, Richard, 67
McManus, Rachel, 107
McMullen, pirate, 134
McPhail, John S., 214-15
Madbury, Elizabeth, 30
Madison, James, 163
Madison County, Mississippi, 190
Malkus, Frederick, 340
Man, Isle of, 85, 92, 99
Manila Times, 237
Maple Hall, 242
Marengo, estate, 153, 181-82, 251
Martin, Daniel, 252-53
Martin, Dr. Ennals, 145-46
Martin, Hannah, 32, 108

Martin, John N. F., 215
Martin, Thomas, 32
Martindale, Reverend T. E., 227
Martingham, estate, 25, 82, 168; *illus.*, 76
Mary, log canoe, 257
Mary Caroline Stevens, ship, 189
Maryland, Delaware & Virginia Railroad, 234, 294-95
Maryland, steamboat, 170, 179
Maryland Agricultural Society, 172
Maryland Airlines, 336-37
Maryland & Delaware Railroad, 193, 230-35, 294
Maryland Censor, newspaper, 182
Maryland Colonization Society, 189
Maryland Committee of Correspondence, 112, 119
Maryland Company of Players, 147
Maryland Convention, 119, 120-21, 132
Maryland Council of Safety, 42, 120, 127-28
Maryland-Delaware border dispute, 139
Maryland Gazette, 79-80, 89, 93, 98, 111, 113, 120
Maryland General Assembly, 11, 34, 43, 48, 54-58, 65, 102, 107, 133, 163, 198, 214, 252, 276; assigns court house to Dover, 138; grants Easton charter, 139; names Easton, 140; finances 1794 court house, 141; charters St. Michaels, 155; approves Eastern Shore railroad, 186
Maryland General Court, 141
Maryland Geological Survey, 272-74
Maryland Governor and Council, 52
Maryland Governor's Council, 22, 26, 27, 57-58, 73
Maryland Herald and Eastern Shore Intelligencer, 144, 146, 149, 150, 152-53
Maryland Highway Commission, 272-74
Maryland Historical Society, 76, 325
Maryland House of Delegates, 32, 119
Maryland in Liberia, 189
Maryland Junior, proposed steamboat, 179

Maryland Line, in Revolution, 125-26, 129
Maryland Oath of Allegiance (or Fidelity), 96, 118, 157
Maryland State House, St. Mary's, 48
Maryland State Police, 345
Maryland Steamboat Company, 179, 256
Mason-Dixon Line, 133
Masonic Lodge, 141, 146, 197, 266
Matapeake Ferry, 44, 306-7, 310, 311, 316-17
Matapeake Indians, 20, 43-44
Matapeake State Park, 44
Matthews, Captain Samuel, 104
Matthews, Samuel, 221
Matthewstown, 245
Maynadier, Hannah, 98
Maynadier, Reverend Daniel, 97-98
Medford's Wharf, 256
Medical and Chirurgical Faculty of Maryland, 146
Meersgate, 25
Melson, Washington R., 207
Memorial Hospital at Easton, 282-83, 284, 299, 306, 330, 332; *illus.*, 282, 343
Menéndez, Juan, 7
Merrimac, ship. See *Virginia*.
Methodist Episcopal Church South, 253-54
Methodist Protestant Church, 253-54
Methodists and Methodism, 38, 145, 159, 161-62, 204, 223, 254; origin and rise, 156-62; camp meetings, 160-61; in Trappe, 155; in St. Michaels, 175; post-Civil War split, 253-54; *illus.*, 160. See also Asbury, Francis; Methodist Episcopal Church South; Methodist Protestant Church; individual churches.
Mexican War, 197, 216
Michener, James A., 293, 342
Middletown, Delaware, 269
Mielke, Gus, 298
Miles Creek, 71
Miles River (St. Michaels River), 5, 6, 18, 24, 36, 37, 71, 73, 86, 153, 216, 241, 251, 256

INDEX

Miles River Bridge, 78, 235, 274-75; *illus.*, 276
Miles River Ferry, 45, 78, 134, 179, 180, 181; *illus.*, 235
Miles River Neck, 46, 80, 208, 252, 298
Miles River Yacht Club, 261, 287; *illus.*, 260
Mill Creek, 71
Mills and milling, 71
Milward, Mrs. William, 127
Minnesota, schooner, 226
Minnie Wheeler, steamboat, 256
Mitchell, Captain William, 22-24
Mitchell's Point, 24
Mitchum, Robert, 293
Mobile Bay, Battle of, 217
Mohican Indians, 42
Monitor, Union ironclad, 217
Monoponson Indians. See Matapeakes.
Monoponson Island. See Kent Island.
Moore, Ellianor, 28
Moore, L. W., 324
Moore, Sergeant P. M., 221
Moreland Block. See Stewart Building.
Morgan, Henry, 24, 25
Morgan, John, 26
Morgan St. Michael, 24
Morris, Andrew, 103
Morris, Captain Robert, 25, 53
Morris, Maudlin, 103
Morris, Robert, Jr., 102
Morris, Robert, Sr., 80, 84, 92, 96, 102-5, 240; *illus.*, 97
Mosco, Indian, 7
Mosley, Father Joseph, 107
Moton High School, 266
Mount Clare, estate, 86
Mulberry, Henry, 43
Mulberry, Molley, 43
Mulberry Hill, 185
Mullikin, Colonel James C., 218, 268
Mullikin, Patrick, 35
Mungummery, Ann, 29
Murray, Dr. William Vans, 43
Music Hall, Easton, 264, 294
My Lord's Gift, 25

Myrtle Grove, 83, 283; *illus.*, 90-91

N

Nansemond River, Virginia, 234
Nanticoke Indians, 10, 20, 21, 40, 41-42
Nanticoke River, 40
Nation, The, magazine, 249
National Baseball Hall of Fame, 255, 289, 290
Naval Academy, U. S., 34, 169, 216
Neale, Ann Gill, 75
Nealc, James, 75
Neale, James, cabinetmaker, 334
Neale, Joseph, *illus.*, 131
Nevius, Carl, 266
Nevius, Ronald, 266, 274
Nevius, Simon A., 266
Nevius hardware building, 223, 266, 274
New Brunswick, New Jersey, 115
New Castle, Delaware, 36, 115
New England, 14, 115-17, 173
New Orleans slave market, 189-90
New Theater (Avalon), 291
New York City, 111, 115, 187, 232, 263
New York Herald, 212
New York Tribune, 204-5
Newnam, William S. D., 336-37
Newtown. See Chestertown, Maryland.
Niagara Falls, New York, 200
Nichols, Colonel Charles, 234
Nichols (Nicols), Reverend Henry, 95
Nicholson, Governor Francis, 64, 66, 71
Nickerson, Charles C., 251
Nicols, Lizzie, 227
Nixon, Richard M., 340
Noble, John W., 279, 306, 323, 327, 328-29; *illus.*, 328
Noel, Dr. Perry E., 144, 146
Norfolk County, Virginia, 34
Norris Hotel, Easton, 283
Norris, James C., 265
Norris, Kate, 265
North Bend, estate, 36, 182
North East River, 5

O

Oakland Mills. See Tunis Mills.
Ocean City, 242, 249, 295, 301, 306, 317
Ocean City Flyer, illus., 236
Odber, Captain John, 39-40
Odd Fellows, St. Michaels, 196-97
Odd Fellows Building, 264, 283
Ogle, Governor Samuel, 42, 79, 106
Old Chester Church, 46, 149
Old Cordova Road, 78
Olds, George D., Jr., 321
Old Wye Church, 65, 149, 161, 291, 328; *illus.,* 151
Old Wye Mill, 46, 71, 129, 325; *illus.,* 47
Olive, steamboat, 256
O'Mealy (O'Mealia), Bryan, 33
Onandago Indians, 117
One Mill Place, 333
Original Floating Theatre. See Adams Floating Theatre.
Osiris, steamboat, 179
Otter, British sloop, 120
Ottwell (Otwell), 25, 46; *illus.,* 82
Oxenham brothers foundry, 193
Oxford, 14, 49, 65, 67, 71, 72, 77, 80, 84, 85, 92, 96, 126, 137, 219, 226, 256, 261, 294, 314; origins, 52-56; town laid out, 53-54; as county seat, 57-58; horse racing, 86; prosperous period, 102-6; Acadian incident, 106-7; 1765 rioting, 109-11; decline and fall, 105-6, 153-54; awakening, 1830s, 192-93; first rail service, 232; growth after 1870, 238-40; school desegregation, 338; fire and police service, 345; *illus.,* 53, 55, 154, 192, 193, 238, 239, 256
Oxford-Bellevue Ferry, 45, 154, 181; *illus.,* 347
Oxford Boatyard, 308, 310
Oxford Enterprise, 240, 268
Oxford High School, 239, 266
Oxford Military Academy (1847-1855), 192-93, 195, 212; *illus.,* 195
Oxford Military and Naval Academy (1885-1887), 240; *illus.,* 192
Oxford Museum, 240
Oxford Neck, 19, 25, 137, 177, 207
Oxford Savings Bank, 240
Oxford town cemetery, 137
Oyster harvesting, 196, 261
Ozinie Indians. See Wicomesses Indians.

P

Paca, Governor William, 137
Palmer, Dr. William N., 283
Palmer's Island, 9
Pan American Refining and Transport Company, 320-21, 324
Paris, Treaty of, 1783, 137
Parliament, British, 109, 112, 115
Parrott, Henry, 33
Parrott, John, 33
Parrott, Richard, 157
Parrott's Point, 157, 165
Pasadena Inn, 236-37, 291-92
Patapsco River, 4
Patrons of Husbandry (Grange), 235
Paul Jones, steamboat, 179
Peachblossom, estate, 29
Peachblossom Creek, 70
Peake (Indian money), 32
Peale, Charles Willson, 146-47; *illus.,* 116, 135, 148
Peale, Rembrandt, 146; *illus.,* 145, 216
Peck's Point shipyard, 156
Peggy Stewart, ship, 112
Pennsylvania Anti-Slavery Society, 200
Pennsylvania Indians, 44
Pennsylvania Railroad, 294-96, 311, 312-13
People's Monitor, 182
Perry, Bill, 341
Perry, Matthew C., 216
Perry, Oliver Hazard, 168-69
Perry, Shaw, Hepburn & Dean, architects, 328
Perry, William, 152
Perry Hall, ship, 173
Perry's Cabin, 169
Perry Spencer, ship, 173
Peters, Richard, 42
Philadelphia, 19, 92, 115, 117, 121-

INDEX

24, 145, 186, 200, 232
Philadelphia, steam ferry (Old Smokey Joe), 310-11
Philadelphia, Wilmington & Baltimore Railroad Company, 294
Philadelphia Athletics, 255, 288
Pioneer, steamboat, 209, 211
Pirates, in Delaware Bay, 72
Pitt (Pitte), John, 32, 53, 66
Pitt's Bridge, 57-58, 78
Plaindealing, estate, 127-28
Plaindealing Creek, 116, 325
Planning and zoning: in Easton, 311-13; in Talbot County, 315, 319-25
Playhouse (showboat), 284
Plimhimmon, estate, 25, 83, 137, 196, 211-12, 217; *illus.,* 211
Pocahontas, 61
Pocomoke River, 7
Poh Poh Caquis, trial, 50-52
Point Lookout prison camp, 217
Popeley, Richard, 9, 11
Poplar (Popeley's) Island, 5-6, 9, 10-12, 18, 28, 36, 78, 163, 184-86, 287, 293
Porridge Creek, 73
Port of Chesapeake Authority, Inc., 324-25
Potomac River, 4, 7, 8
Pott's Mill, 71
Powell, Howell, 32, 66
Powell, I. C. W., 214
Powell, Thomas, 32
Presbyterians, 65
Pressman, Hyman, 325
Preston, town, 283, 295
Pretzler, Adolph, 290
Price, Captain John, 41
Price, James E., 221
Price, William H., 221
Pride of Baltimore. See *Chasseur.*
Prince George's County, 36
Princess Anne, 281
Protestant Episcopal Church, 95-97, 161, 223, 253, 254. See also Church of England, individual churches.
Providence, Puritan colony, 34-35
Puritans, 25, 28-30, 33, 34-35

Q

Quakers, 31-34, 36, 63, 64, 66, 70, 84, 94, 107, 155, 161, 200, 223
Quaker schools, 85
Quaker shipbuilders, 73
Queen Anne, 234, 256, 294, 295, 345
Queen Anne's County, 5, 25, 26, 39, 44, 57, 65, 71, 88, 91, 105, 133, 140, 187, 266, 291, 295; separated from Talbot, 78; tories, in Revolution, 132; Wye Island proposal, 339-40
Queenstown, 58, 104, 133, 227, 263

R

Racial relations: before Civil War, 204; newly freed blacks, 247-48; segregation, 280-81; desegregation, 338-39; lack of job opportunities, 346-47. See also slaves and slavery.
Radcliffe, George L., 307
Railroad House, Claiborne, 242
Railroads, 186-87, 230-35, 262, 294-96; *illus.,* 233, 234, 236, 296
Raisin, Joseph, 224-25
Raleigh, Sir Walter, 8, 59
Rappahannock River, 5
Ratcliffe Manor, estate, 25, 53, 83, 118, 187, 251, 293, 300
Read, Reverend Edgar T., 291
Readbourne, 25
Reed, William T., 221
Reed (Read), George, 25
Rehoboth, Delaware, 234
Rend, Doris, 308
Republican Party, 220, 248, 340
Republican Star, 152-53, 182, 183, 288
Rest, The, estate, 216, 217, 251; *illus.,* 218
Revolution of 1689, 74
Riccards Cliftes (Calvert Cliffs), 4
Rice, Hugh, 80
Rice, Hugh, Jr., 115
Richmond, Virginia, 215, 218, 228
Rich Neck Manor, 22-24, 73, 119, 122, 217, 240-41, 325; *illus.,* 122
Ridgely, 231
Ridgeway, R. O., 185-86

Rignal and Reinagle opera troupe, 147
Ringgold, James, 26
Riverside, train stop, 295
Riverview House, Oxford, 240
Roanoke, Indian money, 32, 39-40
Robardet, Citizen, dance instructor, 149
Robin Hood Creek. See Barker Creek.
Robinson, Charles, 205
Robins (Robbins), George, 29, 70
Robson, Joseph, 173
Robson, Thomas K., 213, 214, 215, 223-24, 250-51
Rochambeau, Comte de, *illus.*, 135
Rolfe, John, 61
Roman Catholics, 25, 38, 56, 64, 66, 74, 94, 106-7, 253-54, 343. See also Jesuit Order, individual churches.
Romancoke, 311-17
Roosevelt, Franklin D., 293, 302
Roost, The, summer hotel, 242
Root, Irving C., 319
Ross, Benjamin, 199
Ross, Donald S., 294; *illus.*, 333
Ross, Sergeant Robert W., 221
Rouse, James W., 327, 339-40
Rouse, Willard G., *illus.*, 328
Route 50, 302, 317, 319
Royal Oak, 116, 163, 166, 224, 236-37, 254, 291, 295
Royer, Leroy M., 313-14
Rowen's stationery store, 274
Rule, George, schoolmaster, 85
Russell, Dr. Walter, 5
Russum, Dr. Sydenham T., 194
Ruth, George Herman (Babe), 288-90

S

Safety Beach, summer hotel, 242
St. Anne's Parish, Annapolis, 96
St. Catherine's, Ontario, 201-2
St. John's College, 24
St. Joseph's Catholic Church, 107, 254
St. Lawrence, British schooner, 166
St. Luke's Chapel, Wye Mills. See Old Wye Church.
St. Mark's United Methodist Church, 150, 330
St. Mark's Village, 288, 332
St. Mary's City, 11, 22-23, 24, 26, 28, 40, 45-46, 52, 53
St. Mary's County, 60
St. Mary's Square, St. Michaels, 155, 174, 197; *illus.*, 167
St. Michaels, town, 64, 67, 84, 157, 168, 185, 191, 198, 206, 207, 208-9, 210, 226, 266, 269, 271, 274, 286, 299-300, 314, 318, 322, 345; Ship *Johnston* incident, 114-15; town founding, 155-56; shipbuilding, 155-56; battle of St. Michaels, 129, 165-66; "blackout" legend, 164, 166; decline of shipbuilding, 172-74; comeback of 1840s, 196-97; pro-Union vote, 208; restrictions on blacks, 247; growth in 1880s, 252-54; oystering's peak, 257-61; 1928 movie, 291; opposes zoning, 321; *illus.*, 156, 167, 230, 268
St. Michaels Comet, 237, 268
St. Michaels Female Academy, 197
St. Michaels High School, 266
St. Michaels Osceolas, baseball team, 254-55
St. Michael's Parish, 54, 65, 84, 86, 88, 95-96, 132, 161
St. Michaels Patriotic Blues, 162, 164-65
St. Paul's Episcopal Church, Trappe, 196
St. Paul's Methodist Church, Oxford, 193, 253-54
St. Paul's Parish, 50, 64-65, 149
St. Paul's Parish Church, Hibernia, 67
St. Peter's Parish, 56, 65, 80, 84, 93, 97-102, 132, 150. See also Whitemarsh Church; Bacon, Reverend Thomas.
Saints Peter and Paul Catholic Church, 253
Saints Peter and Paul School, 343
Salisbury, 268, 274, 275, 282-83, 295
Salter, John, 49-50
San Domingo Creek, 164
Sandy Point ferry terminus, 310, 311, 316-17

INDEX

Sara and Louise, brigantine, 240
Sardis Chapel, St. Michaels, 157
Sassafras River, 4, 5, 21, 45
Satterfield, Andrew, 221
Saunders, John Monk, 291-92
Sayer, Mrs. Peter, 56
Scharf, J. Thomas, 124-25
Schiller, Morgan, 321-22
Schiller, Mrs. Morgan, 91, 321
Schmidt, Vincent A., 176
Schuyler, General Philip, 42, 117
Scott, James H., 221
Scott, John W., 230
Scott's United Methodist Church, Trappe, 36
Scribner's Magazine, 249
Secession movement, 187-88
Secretary Creek, 43, 256
Seemer, J. J., coach, *illus.*, 232
Seney, Joshua, 152
Sequoia, presidential yacht, 302
Servants, indentured, 62-63
Seth, James M., 225
Seth, Joseph B., 240-41, 282-83
Severn River, 34
Sewell's Mill, Trappe District, 235-36
Shannahan, E. McNeal, 286
Shannahan, J. H. K., Sr., 269
Shannahan & Wrightson store, 269, 271, 274
Sharp, Reverend Solomon, 160
Sharpe, Dr. Peter, 32, 33
Sharpe, Governor Horatio, 42, 79-80, 97, 100
Sharpe (Sharp), William, 32, 73
Sharp's Island, 5-6, 18, 28, 32, 134, 163-64, 242-43; *illus.*, 242
Sharp's Island, log canoe, 243
Shawnee Indians, 42
Sherman, B. Frank, 322
Sherwood, Daniel, 57-58
Sherwood, George W., 183
Sherwood, Hugh, 139
Sherwood, John, 58
Sherwood, village, 308
Shinplasters, as money, 180; *illus.*, 180
Shipbuilding and boatbuilding, 72-73, 155-56, 172-74, 239, 243, 257-61
Shippen, Peggy (Mrs., Benedict Arnold), 92
Shorgood, trade name, 299
Shorte, John, 30
Showboat, musical and film, 284-85
Sicatone town, 40
Silk worm mania, 184-85
Sinclair, Mrs. Margaret, 244
Sinclair House, Oxford, 240
Skillington, Thomas, shipyard, 72
Skinner, Richard, 115
Skipjacks, 260-61
Skipton, village, 263
Skipton Creek, 45, 46, 48, 256
Slaves and slavery, 35, 62, 92-94, 106, 161-62, 189-92, 199-206, 218-19, 225, 227; *illus.*, 94, 200-1. See also racial relations.
Smallpox, 41, 43, 44, 128
Smallwood Guard, militia, 206
Smith, Captain John, 3-9, 13, 14, 18, 21, 39, 41, 45; *illus.*, 4, 6
Smith, Francis, 29
Smith, Raymond D., 284
Smith, Reverend Dr. William, 96-97, 161
Smith, Thomas Perrin, 152, 162, 183, 288
Smith, William, 23
Society of Friends. See Quakers.
Solitude, estate, 155
Somerset County, 42, 71-72, 83, 132, 134, 140, 152
Sons of Liberty, 111, 123
Sot Weed Factor, The, 63
South, Thomas, 26, 30
Southbee, William, 33
Speck, J. J., 251
Spence, James A., 271
Spencer, Perry, 155, 173
Spencer, Richard, 155, 173, 191
Spencer Hall, estate, 155, 191
Spring Hill Cemetery, Easton, 177-78
Sprudance, Sarah, 29
Stagwell, Moses, 26
Stamp Act, 109-12
Standard Oil Company of Indiana, 320

Standard Oil Company of New York, 319
Star Spangled Banner, The, 87-88, 169
Steamboat Age, 169-70, 178-80, 256-57, 295. See also individual craft.
Steuben Glass Company, 291
Stevens, Dr. James E., 334
Stevens, Governor Samuel, Jr., 252
Stevens, John, 139, 165, 189
Stevens (Stephens), William, Jr., 32
Stewart, Glenn, 290
Stewart, Jacqueline, 290
Stewart, Mary, 240
Stewart, Maynard, 318
Stewart Building, Easton, 169, 266, 290, 333. See also Easton Hotel.
Stichberry, James L., 281
Stingray Point, Virginia, 5
Stoakes, James, 163
Strandberg, Captain H. I., 179, 193
Streets, E. E. (Eddie), 305
Stuart, Dr. Alexander, 152
Stuckey, Elizabeth, 29
Sudlersville, 159, 288
Summers, Solomon, 23
Supreme Court, U. S., 202, 325, 338
Surprise, steamboat, 169-70, 179
Surprise, War of 1812 raider, 168
Susquehanna River, 5, 9, 18, 21
Susquehannock Indians (various spellings), 5, 18, 21, 24, 44; *illus.,* 8
Swan Point, Kent County, 8
Sweatnam, Richard, 48-50, 74
Sweet Potatoe, log canoe, 243
Sybery, Jonathan, 53

T

Talbot, Lady Grace, 26-27
Talbot, locomotive, 232
Talbot, Sir Robert, 26-27
Talbot, steamboat, 257, 295; *illus.,* 296
Talbot Agricultural Center, 332
Talbot Committee of Observation, 96, 113-15
Talbot Council of Safety, 1861, 210
Talbot Country Club, 287
Talbot County, general: first record, 4; first sighting, 7; first planting, 10; flora and fauna, 14-17; geology and prehistory, 13, 18-19; Indians in, 19-20; county founding, 24-26; original borders, 28; Quaker influence, 31-34, 36-38; tobacco era, 59-76; first parishes, 65-66; prestige in 1700, 71-72; age of aristocracy, 77; break with England, 114-15, 120-21; rise of Methodism, 157-61; 1813 British attacks, 163-66; slave manumissions, 161-62; attitude toward slavery, 189-90, 202-4; pro-South strength, 206-9; benefits of railroads, 234-35; governors of Maryland, 252-53; craze for sports, 254-55; bootleggers and stills, 287; modern development, 329; racial desegregation, 338-39; fire and rescue service, 345; assets and liabilities, 342-47. See also Talbot County Court, Talbot County Court Houses, listings under specific headings.
Talbot County Alms House, 102
Talbot County Chamber of Commerce, 333
Talbot County Commissioners, 182, 323-24, 328-29. See also Talbot County Court, Talbot County Council.
Talbot County Council, 347; *illus.,* 27
Talbot County Court: first meetings, 26; powers of justices, 28; *illus.,* 27
Talbot County Court Houses: at York, 46-52, 65; at Oxford, 57-58; at "Pitt his Bridge" (1712), 18, 57-58, 157-59; at Easton (1792-4), 141, 181, 213-15, 221-22, 227, 263-64, 291, 315, 325, 327-29; *illus.,* 49, 142, 143, 249. See also York, Talbot Court House, Easton.
Talbot County Economic Development Commission, 322
Talbot County Fair, 247, 285; *illus.,* 286, 287
Talbot County Free Library, 264, 293-94, 344; *illus.,* 292
Talbot County Free School, 84-85, 96
Talbot County Garden Club, 325
Talbot County Medical Society, 194

INDEX

Talbot County Planning and Zoning Commission, 324
Talbot County Red Cross, 333
Talbot County sheriff's department, 345
Talbot County Telephone Company, 263
Talbot Court House, town, 58, 77, 79-80, 83, 84, 85, 93, 109, 112, 114, 120, 127, 133, 137, 138-40, 327. See also Easton, Talbot County Court House.
Talbot Humane Society, 333
Talbot Packing & Preserving Company, 235
Talbot Patriotic Troop, militia, 162
Talbot Times, 236, 268
Talbottown, 327
Talbot United Fund, 330
Talbot Volunteer Artillerists, militia, 162
Tangier Island, 133-34
Tanyard Branch, 265
Tavern of the Seven Stars, *illus.*, 110
Taylor, Hode, 244
Taylor, Thomas, 32
Taylor, William, 25, 46
Television, first in Easton, 313-14
Tequassino, Choptank king, 52
Teredo (shipworm), 80
Terry's Texas Rangers, 217
Thimbletown. See Cordova.
Third Haven Creek. See Tred Avon River.
Third Haven Heights, 332
Third Haven Meeting House, 18, 32, 36, 84, 212, 291, 325; *illus.*, 32
Thomas, Dr. Tristram, 145
Thomas, John Charles, 293
Thomas, Nicholas, 133
Thomas, Philip Francis, 253
Thompson, John, 155
Thompson, Mary, 33
Thompson, Richard, 10-11
Thornton, Reverend Thomas, 102
Thurston, Thomas, 31
Tidewater Inn, 266, 309-10, 340-41; *illus.*, 309
Tidewater Maryland Architecture and Gardens, 56
Tilghman, Anna Maria (Mrs. Tench Tilghman), 92, 134, 137
Tilghman, Anna (wife of Matthew), 92
Tilghman, Belle (Mrs. Oswald Tilghman), 238, 282
Tilghman, Brigadier General Lloyd, 217
Tilghman, Colonel Tench (1744-1786), 83, 92, 117, 135, 136-37; *illus.*, 118, 135, 136
Tilghman, General Tench (1810-1874), 172, 187, 192-93, 196, 208, 211-12, 217-18, 230; *illus.*, 210
Tilghman, Henrietta, 92
Tilghman, James, 117
Tilghman, John Leeds, 217
Tilghman, Lloyd, 92
Tilghman, locomotive, 262
Tilghman, Mary (Molly), 147; *illus.*, 148
Tilghman, Matthew, 86, 92, 112, 118, 119, 121, 129, 134, 137; *illus.*, 123
Tilghman, Molly, 96
Tilghman, Oswald, 217, 238, 240
Tilghman, Peregrine, 190
Tilghman, Philemon, 117
Tilghman, Richard, 25, 29, 67, 117
Tilghman, Samuel, 25
Tilghman, Tench Francis, 230
Tilghman, William H., 187
Tilghman Canning Company, 245
Tilghman family, 73, 77, 91-92, 117, 147
Tilghman High School, 266
Tilghman Island (Tilghman's Island, Great Choptank Island), 5, 6, 11, 46, 134, 163, 242, 243-45, 261, 308, 318, 321, 322, 345; *illus.*, 245
Tilghman Packing Company, 245, 308; *illus.*, 247
Tilghman Peninsula. See Bay Hundred.
Tilghman Point, 23
Tilghman's Creek, 241
Tilghman's Fortune, estate, 25
Tims, John, 133
Toast, Joan, 23

Tobacco era, 12, 59-64, 67, 69-70, 104-6; *illus.*, 61
Tockwhogh Indians, 5, 21, 45
Todd, Reverend Robert W., 254
Tonnard, Andrew, 73
Town Guard, militia, 162, 209
Townsend, Mrs. William, 206
Townside (Crumpton), 104, 105
Trail, L. W., 251
Transquakin Creek, 36
Trappe Blues, militia, 208
Trappe Creek, 46, 73
Trappe District, 36, 205, 248, 252, 287, 318, 319
Trappe Enterprise, 236
Trappe High School, 266
Trappe Index, 236
Trappe Landing, 256
Trappe (Trap), 150, 155, 221, 222-23, 228, 253-54, 255, 274, 275, 281; early Methodists, 159; town incorporation, 196; pro-Union vote, 208; prosperous era, 235-36; sewage system, 314; effect of Choptank bridge, 302; fire and rescue service, 345; *illus.*, 231
Travers, Dr. Phillip L., 283
Tred Avon, steamboat, 256
Tred Avon Flying Service, 300
Tred Avon River or Creek (also called Third Haven, Tread Haven, Trade Haven, etc.), 5, 6, 18, 24-25, 32, 37, 38, 53, 57-58, 70, 72, 73, 78, 84, 128, 154, 163, 170, 179, 194, 251; *illus.*, 222
Tred Avon Yacht Club, 238, 261, 287-88; *illus.*, 260
Tremont Military Band, 175
Tri-County High School, Queen Anne, 266
Trinity Cathedral, Easton, 253
Trinity Methodist Church South, *illus.*, 158
Trinity Methodist Episcopal Church South, Trappe, 254
Trinity Methodist Protestant Church, Easton, 305
Trippe, Morris, 248
Trippe, William, 128
Trippe Creek, 72, 234
Triumph, ship, 137
Troth, Mrs. William, 51
Troth, William, 50-52
Troth's Fortune, 50-51; *illus.*, 51
Troup, Dr. Charles, 145
Truman, Harry S., 293, 304
Tubman, Harriet, 199-204, 205; *illus.*, 202
Tuckahoe Creek, 5, 18, 36, 45, 78, 191, 256
Tuesday Club, 96
Tunis, W. W. and Brothers, Tunis Mills, 245
Tunis Mills, 159, 245
Tunney, Gene, 293
Turner, Frank, 240-41
Turner, J. Frank, 268
Turner, John, 152
Turner, Nat, rebellion, 204
Tweed, William M. (Boss), 251-52
Tydings, Millard, 307
Tylor, Wilson M., 268

U

Uncle Tom's Cabin, court case, 204-5
Underground Railroad, 199-204
Union Hotel, Easton, 175, 182, 223-24, 265-66
Unionville, 208, 247

V

Valliant, Jeremiah, *illus.*, 336
Valliant, W. H., 238
Valliant Packing Plant, *illus.*, 237
Vancouver Island. See Kerr's Island.
Varnum, William, 150
Veeck, Bill, 293, 346
Verrazano, Giovanni de, 6-7
Vespucci, Amerigo, 6
Veterans of Foreign Wars, 305
Vicksburg, Mississippi, 217, 227
Victoria, Queen, 191, 200
Vienna, Maryland, 42
Villa, The, estate, 249, 251-52; *illus.*, 250
Villa subdivision, 333
Vinyard, Lee C., 321
Violl, Virtue, accused witch, 28

INDEX

Virginia, 5, 9, 11, 19, 31-32, 33, 35, 86, 204
Virginia, Confederate ironclad, 216-17; *illus.*, 219
Virginia Company, 5, 8
Virginia Eastern Shore, 21, 187, 212, 221
Virginia Gazette, 99-100
Voshell, Bertram C., 318, 319

W

W. Alton Jones Foundation, 332
Wade, Zachary, 24
Wade's Point, estate, 24, 166, 168, 242, 320, 324-25
Walker, Aldace F., 321, 324-25
Walker, Caroline Burnite, 293-94
Walker, Mrs. Alonsita, 321, 324-25
Walker family, 325
Wall Street Journal, 307
Walsh, Dr. Harry, 341
Ward, Matthew Tilghman, 73
War Food Administration, 308
Warren, Admiral John B., 163
Warren, Susan, 23
Washington, D. C., Navy Yard, 216
Washington, George, 108, 116, 125-26, 129, 134, 135, 139, 147, 149, 150-51; *illus.*, 135
Washington, Martha, 149
Washington College, 85, 303
Waterfowl Festival, 341; *illus.*, 342
Watters, William, 157
Waverly Press, 312-13, 345
Way, Dr. Nicholas, 128
Wayman, Thomas, 155
Wayman's Landing, 256
Webb Field, airport, 300
Wedge, Mrs. John, 30
Wesley, John, 157
West, Cornelius, 141
West, George, 258-60
Westminster Parish, 97-98
West Point Military Academy, 193, 240
Wewohquap, Choptank Indian, 52
Whaples, Petter, 30
Wharton, Clifton, 251
Whig Party, 177-78

Whitaker, William, 73
Whitefield, George, 157
Whitemarsh Church, 46, 64, 65, 80, 100, 102, 104, 107, 161, 325; *illus.*, 66. See also St. Peter's Parish, Bacon, Reverend Thomas.
Whitmarsh, Samuel, 184
Whittaker, Reverend Nathanial, 97-98
Wicomesses Indians, 21, 39-41
Wicomico County, 71
Wilcox, Henry, 275
Wilderness, The, estate, 252
Wiley, Edward, boatbuilder, 196
Williams, Thomas P., 209
Williamsburg, village, 247
Williamsburg, Virginia, 325-28
Williamson, John, 249
Williamstadt. See Oxford.
William III, King, 14, 54, 65
Willis, J. McKenny, Jr., 298-99
Willis, J. McKenny & Son, 299, 324
Willis, John, 240
Wilkinson, Thomas, 29
Wilmington, Delaware, 128, 186, 199-200, 274
Wilson, Dr. and Mrs. S. K., 244-45
Winder, Brigadier General Charles S., 217
Winkles, Elizabeth, 48
Winstone Iles, 4, 5
Winters, Elisha, 127
Witches and witchcraft, 28
Wittman, village, 245, 254
Wolcott, W. K., photographer, 193-94
Wollaston, Thomas A., 223-25
Women's Christian Temperance Union, 254
Woodenhawks Bridge, 231-32
Woolfolk, Austin, 189-90
Woolman, Richard, 26, 29
Worcester County, 42, 71, 140
World War I, 283-84, 286; *illus.*, 300
World War II, 303, 304-8
Wray, Fay, 291
Wright, Elizabeth (Mrs. James Dixon), 282
Wrightson, John, 155
Wye Camp Grounds, 160-61

Wye East River, 56
Wye House, estate, 35, 39, 46, 57, 73, 76, 83, 91, 191, 217, 249, 252, 291, 321-22; first house, 35; orangerie and deer park, 91; Revolutionary War raid, 133-34; lavish entertainment, 190; *illus.*, 89. See also listings under Lloyd.
Wye Institute, 291
Wye Island, 124-25, 128, 134, 290, 339-40
Wye Landing, 67, 82-83, 256
Wye Mills, village, 25, 64, 157, 159, 160-61, 185, 194, 235, 263, 274, 291, 302. See also Old Wye Mill, Wye Oak.
Wye Oak, 194; *illus.*, 17
Wye River, 5, 6, 12, 16, 18, 20, 26, 38, 45, 46, 53, 73, 256
Wyetown. See Doncaster.

Y

Yeo, Reverend John, 64
Yeoungman, Samuel, 30
YMCA, 330, 332, 345; *illus.*, 343
York, first county seat, 18, 48-52, 57-58. See also Talbot County Court Houses.
Yorktown surrender, 134; *illus.*, 135
Young, Creighton & Diggs shoe company, 242-43